Understanding China

The series will provide you with in-depth information on China's social, cultural and economic aspects. It covers a broad variety of topics, from economics and history to law, philosophy, cultural geography and regional politics, and offers a wealth of materials for researchers, doctoral students, and experienced practitioners.

More information about this series at http://www.springer.com/series/11772

Shouwen Zhang

The New Horizon of China's Economic Law Theory

中国人民大学出版社
CHINA RENMIN UNIVERSITY PRESS

Springer

Shouwen Zhang
School of Law
Beijing Univeristy
Beijing, China

ISSN 2196-3134 ISSN 2196-3142 (electronic)
Understanding China
ISBN 978-981-15-8823-5 ISBN 978-981-15-8824-2 (eBook)
https://doi.org/10.1007/978-981-15-8824-2

This Springer imprint is published by the registered company Springer Nature Singapore Pte Ltd.
The registered company address is: 152 Beach Road, #21-01/04 Gateway East, Singapore 189721, Singapore

Foreword

The *Decision of the Central Committee of the Communist Party of China on Some Major Issues Concerning Comprehensively Deepening the Reform*, which was adopted at the Third Plenary Session of the 18th Central Committee of the Communist Party of China on November 12, 2013, underlines the construction of socialist rule of law theory with Chinese characteristics, and therefore explicitly states that "the socialist path, theoretical framework and system with Chinese characteristics are the fundamental course for the comprehensive promotion of law-based governance in all fields. We shall proceed from the basic national conditions of our country, adapt to the continuously deepened reform and opening up, summarize and utilize the successful experiences of the Party in leading the people to implement the rule of law, and concentrate on the major theoretical and practical issues concerning the construction of socialist rule of law, in an aim to constantly innovate the rule of law theory, develop a socialist rule of law theory that accords with China's reality, takes on Chinese characteristics and reflects the law of social development, which will become theoretical guidance and support for the law-based governance of the country".

Under such background, the China Law Society decides to produce a series of monographs on the theoretical framework of law with Chinese characteristics, in an attempt to comprehensively summarize and tease out the practices and theoretical research results in this regard. With these books as theoretical accumulation, it may extract a set of socialist law theory with Chinese characteristics and build a matched theoretical framework. Such endeavor is undoubtedly of great significance in the following four aspects, both theoretical and practical, for innovating the socialist rule of law theory with Chinese characteristics.

Firstly, it helps to develop and improve the study of the socialist theoretical framework with Chinese characteristics. Since the founding of New China in 1949, the Chinese people, under the leadership of the Communist Party of China (CPC), have started arduous explorations and practice in governing the country, especially in the new era since 1978 when the reform and opening-up policy was implemented, continuously promoted the Sinicization of Marxism, gradually built the socialist theoretical framework with Chinese characteristics that is connotatively rich and thought-provoking, successfully blazed a trail of socialism with Chinese characteristics, and scored world-renowned achievements. As proved by these past achievements, in order to advance and prosper the cause of socialism with Chinese characteristics, we shall always adhere to the path of socialism with Chinese characteristics and develop the matched theoretical framework.

The socialist theoretical framework with Chinese characteristics is composed of Deng Xiaoping Theory, the important thoughts of "Three Represents", the scientific outlook on development, and the Party Central Committee's new thoughts, new ideologies and new strategies of governing the country. This theoretical framework is inclusive, open and abreast with the times. It not only inherits and develops Marxism and Mao Zedong Thought, but condenses the wisdom and painstaking efforts of the Chinese people, which are led by generations of the communists, in making unremitting explorations in national renewal; it symbolizes the latest achievement of the Sinicization of Marxism, the most precious political and spiritual wealth of the CPC, and the common ideological foundation for the Chinese people of all ethnic groups to make concerted efforts. Moreover, its content includes the major thoughts and theories in the realms of history, economy, politics, culture, science of law, society, ecology, military matters, and party building. Among them, science of law is an important part of the socialist theoretical framework with Chinese characteristics. Given this, if we could summarize, refine and sublimate the practical achievements in the construction of socialist rule of law with Chinese characteristics since 1949, especially after 1978, coupled with the legal thoughts and theories developed in this period, and then have them systematized, it is sure to advance the study of the aforesaid theoretical framework.

Secondly, it helps to construct the socialist theoretical framework of law with Chinese characteristics. While we are advancing the construction of socialist rule of law in China, both the Party and the government have developed the policies and guidelines for the rule of law with distinctive Chinese characteristics and features of the times, the juristic and legal communities have come up with fruitful study results, and the general public remains diligent in the rule of law practice and innovation; all of them have become the fundamental and broad connotation of the socialist theoretical framework of law with Chinese characteristics. But these practical and theoretical achievements are scattered and fragmented at present, it is imperative to have them systematically summarized, teased out, integrated, and sublimated, so as to build a theoretical framework of law with an intact outer frame and a logical inner structure.

Thirdly, it helps to push forward the construction of socialist rule of law with Chinese characteristics. All theories originate from practice and in turn serve practice. The Chinese jurisprudential circle has all along been dedicated to legal studies and making contributions to the construction of rule of law. By keeping to the right direction and proceeding from China's realities, the jurisprudential circle has done fruitful research work, not only solved practical problems, but also achieved plentiful research results that could guide the rule of law practice.

Presently, the cause of building a moderately prosperous society in an all-round way has entered a decisive stage, and the reform is facing an uphill battle. To resolve the challenges and risks in sustaining reform, development and stability has become an unprecedentedly arduous task for the CPC and the government, no wonder they need feasible and effective theories to guide their action. Now that we have accumulated practical experiences and legal theories in the process of rule of law construction, we shall have them systematically summarized and teased out, integrated with some foreign theoretical achievements, and on this basis develop a set of socialist rule of law theories that conforms to China's reality, takes on Chinese characteristics, and reflects the law of social development to be our guiding theory.

Finally, it helps to show the world China's jurisprudential attainments and build up its discourse power in the international academic community. At a symposium on philosophy and social sciences, General Secretary of the CPC Xi Jinping pointed out that "although China has scored rich philosophical and social science achievements, with the size of research teams, quantity of papers, and government input ranking high in the world, its academic propositions, thoughts, viewpoints, standards and discourse power are no match for its comprehensive national strength and international status".

It is the same case for the realm of jurisprudence, which is a support to the development of philosophy and social sciences. The Chinese jurisprudence is neither prominent in national characteristics nor convincing enough on the international arena; it is unable to justify itself or disseminate its arguments after its justification. China's contribution to the world jurisprudential community is thereby restricted. In response to this awkward situation, the Chinese jurisprudential and legal circles shall further probe into the traditional legal resources, strengthen theoretical study on the practical experiences in the socialist rule of law construction, and work out a number of jurisprudential theories showing Chinese characteristics, Chinese style and Chinese manner, so that China will be able to make its own contributions to the world rule of law practice, and have a greater voice in the international academia.

Since the founding of New China, we have achieved fruitful results in building a socialist rule of law with Chinese characteristics. Chinese legal scholars have accumulated considerable experiences in interpreting and studying the socialist legal system, legal framework, and the practices of the rule of law with Chinese characteristics. The foremost task of producing the *Series on the Socialist Theoretical Framework of Law with Chinese Characteristics* is to summarize and refine the socialist legal theories that conform to China's reality, take on Chinese characteristics, and reflect the laws of social development. This legal framework should include the basic theories of the socialist rule of law with Chinese characteristics, theories of all sectoral laws, and special theories of the practice of socialist rule of law. Based on such considerations, this series of books mainly discusses the major topics in three aspects: some books explain the basic theories of the socialist rule of law with Chinese characteristics from a macroscopic perspective; some books talk about the development and innovation of legal science from the perspective of separate sectoral laws and systems; some books interpret the major theoretical and practical issues in the construction of socialist rule of law from a thematic perspective. All the writings not only contain rich theoretical conclusions, but also provide insightful responses to the practical problems. In short, theories and practices integrate with and complement each other to form a complete set of monographs on China's legal study.

While China is on the way to promote the socialist rule-of-law construction with Chinese characteristics, the Chinese legal workers have vast opportunities to display their talents and make contributions to China's legal study. The China Law Society initiated the compilation of the *Series on the Socialist Theoretical Framework of Law with Chinese Characteristics*, expecting to draw more and more Chinese legal workers to participate in the theoretical study of the socialist rule of law with Chinese characteristics, and thereby building an intact legal framework based on China's reality and in a Chinese style. Such a remarkable endeavor is sure to promote China's rule-of-law construction, advance the "Five-in-one Overall Layout", implement the Strategic Blueprint of "Four Comprehensives", achieve the "Two Centenary Goals" and realize the Chinese dream of the great rejuvenation of the Chinese nation.

Beijing, China Sujun Zhang

Preface

Since the United States, Germany, and some other countries initiated anti-monopoly and anti-unfair competition legislation in the late nineteenth and early twentieth centuries, they have experienced the baptism of two world wars and several economic crises. Economic law is therefore made as an important legal system in market economies, and even valued as the "economic constitution" in some countries. Since the 1920s, economic law has become a key subdiscipline of the science of law through systematic economic law theoretical research in Germany and other major civil law countries.

Although the development history of economic law in the world is only more than a hundred years, it is an important propellant to economic and social development and to the rule-of-law construction in relevant countries. Whether it was the Great Depression of the twentieth century, the global financial crisis in 2008, or the global pandemic of the COVID-19 viral disease in 2020, all countries have generally adopted macro-control and regulation measures, and their direct institutional support is all types of economic laws such as fiscal law, tax law, financial law, industry law, and competition law, which fully reflects the commonality of the functions of economic law systems in all countries.

Moreover, the formulation and implementation of economic law are directly related to the development stages of all countries and their problems that need to be resolved. Economic law is of outstanding modernity and ought to respond to the actual needs of economic and social development. Therefore, it is closely related to economic and social policies and prominently policy-related. It is a typical "distribution law" and "development promotion law". Since different countries are facing specific problems in resolving market failure or economic imbalance, and in coordinating the relationship between the government and the market and between the central and local governments, the economic law of each country has its particularity.

Considering the commonality and individuality of the economic law of various countries, comparison and reference are especially valuable for the theoretical research of economic law, which will help countries to learn from each other's strengths and continuously improve their own economic law system. More than that, it will also benefit the economic governance at the international level, form a sound international economic order, and jointly enhance the well-being of mankind.

Related to the above understanding, the Chinese jurisprudential circle has always attached great importance to learning from the economic law theories and economic rule-of-law practices in other countries, and at the same time, it has been integrating with the actual situation of China to deepen the economic law theoretical research and improve the economic rule of law. The substantial development of China's economic law theory was attributed to the reform and opening up initiated in 1978. Such reform endeavor stimulated the emergence and development of economic law, while China's economic law system has played an important role in promoting the reform and opening up. With the development of China's marketization, rule-of-law construction and internationalization, a lot of consensus has formed between the economic law theory of China and that of other countries. In addition, because of the staged economic and social developments and the particularity of relevant influencing factors, China's economic law research has its unique priorities and areas of concern.

Based on existing China's economic law theoretical results, and in a combination of the current national conditions and future development trend, this book brings forth some "new theories" in the realm of economic law that are worthy of attention, including system theory, development theory, distribution theory, risk theory, and rule-of-law theory. These theories are logically connected with each other. Their research not only helps to enrich and improve the entire economic law theory, but also helps explain many "complex problems" at the present times, guide the practice of economic law, and continuously improve economic rule of law. Besides, these theories have greater international commonality, meaning that their research will help scholars from different countries exchange opinions with each other, and jointly promote the development of theory and practice.

At the time when the English version of this book is to be published, I'd like to express my appreciation to the following individuals and organizations that have made painstaking efforts to its publication. I shall first thank Fang Ming, Guo Yanhong, and Cao Jianghong. As editors of Renmin University of China Press, they have done meticulous work for publishing the Chinese edition and organizing its translation into English. My gratitude also goes to the National Social Science Fund of China which has added this book into the "Translation Project of Chinese Humanities and Social Sciences" and sponsored its translation. The editors of Springer shall take credit for their careful proofreading of the English edition and its overseas distribution. Here, I must thank the translator who has made the English edition materialized. For those who have contributed to the publication of this book but are not named here, I'm grateful for everything you've done! Finally, I need to thank readers and experts who may point out any bias and inaccuracy in my book; your comments and suggestions are always welcome!

The theoretical and practical issues of economic law are extremely complicated. Each country has its own economic and legal systems, their issues of development, distribution, risks, and structure have different manifestations and solutions, and the public understanding of these issues is also varied. How to effectively solve these issues under the rule-of-law framework needs to be further discussed, especially extensive discussion among scholars from all countries.

September 2020

Shouwen Zhang
Peking University School of Law
Beijing, China

Contents

Chapter 1
Introduction: Theoretical Development and Extension of Horizon

1.1 Background and Problems

Since its implementation of the reform and opening-up policy in 1978, China has witnessed continuous development of economy, society and other undertakings, as well as constant improvement of its economic law system. Thanks to the joint efforts of academic circles, China's economic law theory has grown increasingly sophisticated out of nothing. And the academic attainments at different stages have been systematically summed up.[1] These summaries, while outlining the development course of economic law theory, are made to reveal the theoretical differences by country and by sector, so as to point out the way forward for China's economic law theory, and guide the ongoing "theoretical development research".

As for the differences by country, the economic law of each country is directly associated with the national economic policies since it was developed, which explains for its international commonality and national distinctiveness. The economic law grows in the soil of China is more peculiar than its foreign counterparts. Given this, the Chinese economic law scholars have made it their research approach and objective to solve China's problems from a global perspective, which constitute the distinctive content of China's economic law theory.[2]

As for the differences by sector, the modern economic law across the world has not gone a long way, if we take the rise of a separate market regulation law after entering the monopoly stage as its starting point. Being an emerging sectoral law, economic law not only coexists with traditional sectoral laws in modern society,

[1] There are abundant summaries of China's economic law theory, since the Chinese legal scholars tend to review and predict the development of China's economic law theory every ten years or so. For example, Wang et al. (1999), Issue 1; Yue (2008), Issue 5. Some scholars study China's economic law theory in historical terms, e.g., Xiao (2002a).

[2] China's economic law theory involves separate studies on the status and function of macro-control law, the problems about state-owned enterprises, system transition from planned economy to market economy, and administrative monopoly, which distinguish it from the economic law theories in the traditional market economies and other transitional countries.

S. Zhang, *The New Horizon of China's Economic Law Theory*, Understanding China,
https://doi.org/10.1007/978-981-15-8824-2_1

but transcends them or makes breakthroughs, which makes it difficult to extract economic law theories and convince people to approve them when they still hold onto their inherent knowledge or traditional views. That's why the economic law study goes through twists and turns in all countries; nevertheless, it is an inevitable course for developing new theories. We have to transform our traditional sense of law, only by this way can we gain a profound knowledge of economic law and the entire legal system, and comprehend the important contributions of economic law to the development of legal science on the whole.[3]

The development of China's economic law theory is, to a great extent, attributed to its continuous reform. By drawing lessons from both the past and the present times, we have fund that as long as the reform truly accords with the law, it will help to form a reasonable system architecture and promote ideological transformation. It is in the process where the legal system is improved day by day and the traditional ideas keep evolving[4] that China's economic law theory becomes mature and sophisticated. Presently, China is deepening the reform in an all-round manner and promoting the rule of law construction, the "tripartite relations" of reform, rule of law and development are of foremost importance, and the effective coordination of these relations is up to the proper adjustment by economic law. To be more specific, the relations between government and market, between reform and economic law, and between constitution and economic law are so important that they need theoretical explanations; and these relations—which are directly associated with the regime problems in economic law—are basis for the relevant studies in the domain of economic law.

As a concrete form of "economic constitution", economic law has been elevated to the point where it affects the overall governance of the country, i.e., it directly concerns the reform and development of various realms, and in the meantime affects the overall progress of the rule of law. Now that people are learning more about the positioning, functions and objectives of economic law, its realistic functions have become more prominent in the new era, the developmental stage and theoretical type of the present economic law are no longer the same as before, we shall observe and study the "new developments" of China's economic law theory, so as to create a "new horizon".

The "new developments" of China's economic law theory, i.e., the new explorations and new extensions of some theoretical fields, are fairly valuable for the development of science of economic law, overall legal science, and even social sciences. This book, based on the existing studies on the economic law theory and the recent developments of the economic law system, firstly discusses the important "tripartite relations" in the domain of economic law, and then dissects the new types of theories in economic law (including development theory, distribution theory, risk theory and

[3]Economic law scholars often talk about the contributions of China's economic law study to the overall legal science. According to Prof. Li Changqi, theoretical innovations should be counted as the biggest contribution of China's economic law study, since they have enriched and extended the basic theories of legal science. See Li (2009a), Issue 5.

[4]Just like J. M. Keynes had said "ideas shape the course of history". The ideological transformation is of tremendous impact on China's reform and opening up, and development of economic law theory, it is also important for further development of China's legal science on the whole.

crisis theory), and explores the approaches for strengthening the economic rule of law to promote development and equitable distribution, prevent and resolve crisis, for the purpose of better fulfilling the regulatory objectives of economic law.

1.2 Historical Basis for "New Developments" of Economic Law Theory

We're ought to examine the "new developments" of economic law theory in this new era, because the whole academic community has reaped rich fruits in their previous studies, which constitute a historical basis for these "new developments". Given this, it is necessary to briefly look back on the development course of China's economic law theory.

In the early 1980s, the once-interrupted China's legal study regained vitality. At that time, one of the research hotspots was to explore the approaches for strengthening the construction of economic law system and economic law studies that center on economic development. This widespread debate on economic law theory also drew participation of the scholars dedicated to other sectoral laws.[5] In 1986, the *General Principles of the Civil Law of the People's Republic of China* was promulgated, marking that the Chinese legislative body generally defined the respective objects regulated by civil law, economic law and administrative law. The *Civil Law* is therefore regarded as a crucial turning point for transition of China's economic law theory.

But the *Civil Law* of 1986 was no more than an institutional symbol, it was the *Reform Decision*[6] of 1984 that exerted a substantial impact on the development of economic law and civil law. This Decision integrated or embodied lots of important principles of economic law and civil law, laying an important foundation for the later reform of economic system and construction of economic law system. Along with deepening of economic system reform and constant improvement of economic law system, the problems once troubled the study of economic law theory are addressed one after another. Since the *Civil Law* was enacted in 1986, the economic law scholars have carried out more in-depth researches, and formed a great variety of economic law theories with a significant impact.[7]

From the autumn of 1992 to the spring of 1993, the state implemented the market economic system from political dimension to legal dimension, which provided relatively definite objects and basis for the economic law study, and thereby greatly increasing theoretical consensus. In order to adapt to and promote the development

[5]Quite a number of Chinese civil law scholars joined in this debate. See Jiang (1979), Issue 4; Xie (1984), Issue 2; Tong (1984), Issue 2; Wang (1984), Issue 3.

[6]It refers to the *Decision of the Central Committee of the CPC on Reform of the Economic System* adopted in October 1984, which is a prelude to the subsequent "reform decisions". See Zhang (2013), Issue 2.

[7]Zhang (2000), Vol. 1.

of the market economic system, the state spent three years in accomplishing the "economic law legislation", including market regulation legislation (1993), fiscal and taxation legislation (1994) and financial legislation (1995). By 1996, there had been an intact legislative framework for China's economic law, paving way for updating the overall economic law theory in the future. By around 1996, the theoretical system of economic law, which is in tandem with the market economy, had been improved day by day, and the "representative theories" had come out one after another.[8]

The Chinese economic law scholars on the whole had shown strong academic sharpness before 1996, since a number of "representative theories" compatible with the market economic system sprang up successively, and then gave rise to several influential economic law theories,[9] i.e., the "New Opinions" on economic law in the 1990s which were subject to constant summarization and refinement.[10] Unlike the "Old Opinions" in the 1980s, these "New Opinions" represent all kinds of theories "harmonized but not uniformed" in the discipline of economic law, all of them confirm the independent status and important functions of economic law, and their theoretical bases tend to be convergent.

In fact, the exploration of the economic law theory in line with the market economy could be traced back to 1992 or 1993.[11] Thanks to the efforts of some key scholars, China's economic law theory had not only grown out of nothing by 1996, but completed the transition from simplicity to sophistication.

Owing to the constant improvement of the economic law system in the 1990s, and other system reforms brought by China's entry into WTO in the early 21st century, the development of China's economic law theory has stepped onto a new stage: the academic community not only studies ontology, axiology and generation theory, but takes interest in normative theory, operational theory, category theory and methodology; their scope of study covers subject theory, behavioral theory, rights theory and responsibility theory, as well as multi-dimensional discussions on law enforcement, economic adjudication,[12] basic category and research technique, thus forming several "theoretical plates" and having greatly improved the theoretical system of economic law. By around 2006, the afore-said theoretical realms had scored achievements one after another, which further raised the systematic level and degree of consensus of economic law theory.[13]

---

[8]The Chinese academic community has reached consensus on the doctrines deriving from these "representative theories". Xiao (2002b), pp. 288–296.

[9]Most of the "representative theories" were established during this period. See Yang (1995), Issue 1; Yang (1994), Issue 2; Li (1995); Qi (1996); Liu (1995).

[10]Zhang et al. (1995), Issue 4.

[11]Wang (1993), Issue 2; Research Group of the Institute of Law at Chinese Academy of Social Sciences (1993), Issue 6; Zhang (1992), Issue 5; Zhang (1993), Issue 1.

[12]The *Organization Law of the People's Court of the People's Republic of China*, though revised in 2006, retains the provisions for setting an economic tribunal. How to give full play to the economic tribunal so as to better solve the problem of justiciability of economic law? It is still worth studying.

[13]Qiu (2005), Issue 6; Zhang (2006), Issue 3.

The afore-said "theoretical plates"[14] correspond to the various important problems in economic law theory and system that are ought to be resolved. Therefore, this period was of crucial meaning for building a theoretical mansion for economic law. Upon completion of the main works of this theoretical mansion, the academic community embarked on more elaborate and specific researches, leading the economic law study to enter into a stage of steady development on the whole.

In general, China's economic law theory changed notably in around 1986, 1996 and 2006, and each change brought about some "new developments" compared with the previous period. As such, the three time points are taken as symbols for the remarkable progress during the development of economic law theory.

All theories develop in a certain background, and they are subject to the spatial-temporal constraint, this is especially the case for economic law theory. In the context of worldwide economic downturn resulting from the 2007 financial tsunami, in order to overcome the economic woes and stimulate development of all realms, China made "three major decisions" of far-reaching impact in the dimensions of reform, rule of law and development from 2013 to 2015, in an attempt to deepen the reform, promote the law-based governance, build a moderately prosperous society in an all-round way, and address the economic, social, political, legal and cultural problems systematically. Since economic law is an especially important instrument for resolving these problems, we shall make new explorations and new extensions of economic law theory to lead its theoretical development into a "new period" or onto a "new stage".

1.3 New Changes on Theoretical Types

Since 2016, just after the "three major decisions" were made, the comprehensive correlation among reform, rule of law and development has become so important to the overall situation and the future. The economic law community is obliged to make a systemic response to the relations and overlaps among the "difficulties in reform", "priorities in rule of law" and "focus of development". To this end, shackles of old knowledge were discarded to pave for synthesizing new theories, which has not only elevated theoretical development onto a new stage, but brought new changes to theoretical types.

As mentioned above, since the reform and opening up, Chinese academic community has made argumentation of economic law's regulatory scope, internal structure, value pursuit, core ideas, target positioning, fundamental principles, formation basis and features of the times, which are associated with ontology, axiology and genetic theory. On this basis, the argumentation further extended to the subject theory, behavioral theory, right-obligation theory, responsibility theory, legislative theory, implementation theory and procedural theory in economic law, which gave rise to some relatively systematic theories like normative theory, operational theory and

[14]The formation of these "theoretical plates" helps to build a theoretical system of economic law; and timely update of their content is able to restructure the economic law theory. Zhang (2004).

category theory. In the meantime, the studies on theories and methodologies of the sectoral laws in economic law have made remarkable progress. Consequently, the above mentioned "theoretical plates" have constituted a relatively systematic theoretical system of economic law, and laid an important foundation for new theoretical developments.[15]

The so-called "new developments" is a relative term, since in each stage there is something new in contrast to the previous stage. Based on such understanding and taking account of the afore-mentioned time points, China's economic law theory had stepped onto a new stage by around 2016, meaning that some research topics were replaced by the new ones after the theoretical system of economic law was in the main established and theoretical consensus increased notably, although some basic problems left from the previous stage are still talked about. At this new stage, the urgent problems in front of the academic community are neither about ontology and axiology, nor establishment of normative and operational theories, but synthesis of corresponding theories in the realm of economic law based on existing studies and combining with the major and complicated problems in "reform, rule of law and development" both home and abroad.

The central thesis of economic law theory at the new stage is rooted in a given historical background. In the age of rapidly progressing globalization, informatization, industrialization and urbanization, there are so many urgent problems to be solved by economic law. For example, all of the problems of distribution, development, information and risks are related to market failure, they have been repeatedly discussed by the academic community, but no systematic theory is formed to date. In the wake of the global financial crisis, all countries have been trapped in economic doldrums, the downward pressure on their domestic economy makes it more pressing to solve the problems of distribution, development, information and risks, there shall be a comprehensive response to these problems from the economic law system, so that a corresponding and systematic economic law theory could be extracted. From the perspective of social sciences, there have been plenty of studies on the above problems in the realms of macro-economic control theory and market regulation theory, but it is still an important new topic to develop the theories about these problems in the realm of economic law from a "legal" point of view. If these theories could be systematically extracted, they may constitute "another theoretical system with different directions" that distinguish from the aforesaid ontological, axiological, normative and operational theories, thus making the entire theoretical system of economic law more sophisticated and systematic.

The above theories need to be systematically extracted at the new stage, with the problems of distribution, development, information and risks as the study objects, are directly related to the adjustment of specific economic law systems, and concerning the further refinement of the functions, goals, value and spirit of economic law. The systematic extraction of these new theories is both urgent and necessary, and the

[15]The innovations in China's economic law theory mainly refer to the non-traditional analysis of the ontology, axiology, normative theory, operational theory and methodology in economic law from a modern legal perspective. Li (2009b), Issue 5.

progress we have made in this regard demonstrates the new developments in China's economic law theory.

To date, the economic law theory could be divided into two major theoretical types: (1) The first type involves ontology, axiology, generative theory, normative theory and operational theory, which are collectively known as "established theories" since they have become sophisticated after going through intensive development in the 1990 s and accumulation in the first 15 years of the 21st century. (2) The second type involves the distribution, development, information and risk theories in the realm of economic law; they are labeled as "new theories" since they were born against the backdrop of financial crisis and economic downturn, and at the time that the problems of uneven distribution, imbalanced development, asymmetric information and mounting risks have drawn increasing attention.

Unlike the first type of theories which are mostly "theoretical plates", the second type of theories care more about the major practical problems that shall be resolved by multiple systems, they are on one hand "clues" or "meridians"[16] that traverse all kinds of systems, and on the other hand blend in and intertwine with those "plates", just like the invisible water pipelines and electricity wire laid inside buildings. In a word, these two types of theories, despite of different positioning and direction, are equally valuable.

1.4 Key Issues and Basic Framework of This Book

From the dimension of time, the development of China's economic law theory has stepped into a "new stage"; from the dimension of study objects, the "new types" of theories are on the way being formed. The achievements in these two dimensions constitute the "new developments" different from the past. The "plates" of the established China's economic law theory have preliminarily taken shape to form the basic theoretical framework involving ontology, axiology, normative theory, operational theory, generative theory, category theory and methodology. At this new stage, we shall keep improving these "theoretical plates", and in the meantime build a system for the new theories about distribution, development, information and risks based on the important "clues" or "meridians" that run through economic law theory and system.

The refinement and improvement of the new theories, which are indispensable for the development of macro-economic control law and market regulation law, will make the general economic law theory more like an integrated mass linked by the important "clues" or "meridians", which is favorable for forming close connection between pandect and sub-pandect, and between theory and system, and particularly significant for the development of China's economic law theory in the long run.

---

[16]Zhang (2009), Issue 6.

This book mainly expounds development theory, distribution theory, risk theory, and the relevant crisis theory based on the above analysis of the changes on theoretical types, and the established studies of the academic community. Effective development, equitable distribution, prevention and settlement of risks and crises are important functions and regulatory objectives of economic law. In order to fulfill these objectives, we shall firstly address the relevant regime issues, properly handle the relationship between government and market, between reform and rule of law, between constitution and economic law; and then vigorously promote the construction of economic rule of law, and resolve the problems about integrated legislation and pilot legislation in the realm of economic law.

In short, the content of this book is unfolded in the following six chapters:

This Chapter "Introduction: Theoretical Development and Extension of Horizon" introduces the "new developments" of China's economic law theory that differ from the past, analyzes the historical basis of these "new developments" and changes on the theoretical types, outlines the theme of this book, and then reveals the possible "new horizon" in studying China's economic law theory, so as to set the tone for the following discussions.

Chapter 2 "Tripartite Relations and Regime Theory", from the dimensions such as legal regulation of government-market relation, "reform decisions" and economic law consensus, as well as "economics" of constitution and economic law, interprets the "tripartite relations" between government and market, between reform and economic rule of law, and between constitution and economic law. There are discussions on government regime, market regime, economic system reform, decentralization regime in constitution, and the regime arrangement in the realm of economic law, as well as analysis of the regime theory. This chapter lays a basis for the content in the following chapters.

Chapter 3 "Development Ideas and Development Theories", starting from the idea and thought of coordinated development, mainly discusses the coordination thought in the realm of economic law; such thought is vital for promoting the coordinated development of economy and society. Moreover, it explores the coordinated development of constitution and economic law, which is important for giving full play to the function of the entire legal system and better promoting the all-round development of economy and society. In addition, economic restructuring is a key issue that concerns development, and the coordination between economic policies and economic law is also important, this chapter therefore stresses the need to examine the coordination between economic policies and economic law while studying the development theory of economic law.

Chapter 4 "Distribution as a Main Line and Distribution Theory" presents that distribution is a main line that runs through China's economic reform and construction of economic law system, and distribution theory is an important part in the realm of economic law. The distribution problems are directly related to the aforementioned development theory. If these problems fail to be properly solved, they will drag down the progress of development. Given this, this chapter discusses the "double pressure" in distribution that concerns the national economy and people's livelihood, explores the ways to solve the distribution problems through legal regulation of the distribution structure, and stresses that the problems arising from differential distribution shall be solved through macro-economic control and regulation based on economic law.

Chapter 5 “Risk Theory and Crisis Response” presents the risk theory in economic law, discusses the various crises that may arise when the afore-mentioned distribution and development problems fail to be properly solved, analyzes the causes for and response to the financial crisis from the dimension of economic law theory, explores ways to resolve the crises under the framework of economic rule of law and prevent the crisis in economic law itself. Moreover, it also stresses to refine the crisis theory through theoretical extension.

Chapter 6 “Economic Legislation and Theory of Rule of Law” stresses that legislation shall reflect in the afore-said theoretical realms (including the adjustment of the “tripartite relations”, settlement of regime issues, implementation of the idea of coordinated development, economic restructuring, settlement of distribution problems and improvement of distribution system, risk prevention and crisis response), and there shall be backup from economic rule of law. So it proposes to constantly improve legislative integration and quality, solve the problems in the pilot legislative work, protect the rights of tax payers and other concerned subjects, and keep building up the national governance ability by means of economic law.

Despite of this chapter, Chaps. 2–6 are respectively divided into three or four sections, and each section contains a conclusion, so there is no general conclusion at the end of the book. It should be noted that the conclusion of each section echoes with the “theoretical development” that is put forward in this chapter, in an attempt to extend the theoretical horizon of contemporary China’s economic law.

There is an internal logic in the above theoretical framework: the new developments of China’s economic law theory are directly related to the unbalanced and uncoordinated development of the national economy, society, law and other realms.

Based on the rudimentary principle of difference in economic law, we should face up to the differences in the realm of economic law, properly handle the “tripartite relations” between government and market, between reform and rule of law, between constitution and economic law, so as to lay a regime basis for the regulation of economic law, which helps to enrich the regime theory in economic law. In order to effectively handle the “tripartite relations”, we shall implement the ideas of coordinated development, express the thought of coordination in both the theory and system of economic law, and then have the ideas and thoughts of coordination manifested in the relation between economic law and constitution, and also in economic restructuring, which will enrich the development theory in economic law.

In the domain of distribution, which is closely related to development, the problems arising from differential distribution must be resolved, and the various interests are ought to be coordinated. Since the reform and opening up, distribution has been a main line running through China’s economic law theory and system, and the distribution structure has been subject to legal regulation. We shall continue the regulation of differential distribution, and extract a distribution theory on this basis, which are important tasks in the study of economic law theory. If the distribution problems are handled improperly, it will impede coordinated development, and then trigger all kinds of risks and crises. Even so, response to crisis is an important basis and motive for the economic law to come into being. We shall analyze the economic crisis with economic law theory, and explore ways for developing economic law while dealing with the crisis, which helps to refine the risk and crisis theories in the realm of economic law, and further enrich the economic law theory.

All of the above arguments may not remain on paper, but earnestly implemented. To this end, we shall strengthen legislation, discover the problems in legislative work and law enforcement, improve the level of economic rule of law, and ultimately enhance the governance ability and quality of the state.

The above discussion reveals that the various types of China's economic law theory are interconnected. There is close correlation, interconnection and mutual corroboration between established theoretical "plates", between new theories, or between established and new theories. Based on the established theories and their internal relations, we can integrate the theories in all realms, and constantly extract new theories from system practice, so as to promote the new developments of China's economic law theory in an all-round manner.

All in all, the theories and problems discussed in this book are closely related, and they are of particular concern to the economic law study in the new stage. The contemporary China's economic law theory, which is rooted in the land of China, of course has prominent "Chinese characteristics". In order to keep advancing the reform and developing economic law, China is in need of continuous theoretical breakthroughs. As such, when studying the theoretical problems about economic law, we'd better learn from both the domestic and foreign theories, so as to objectively analyze China's problems and facilitate their settlement. It is an important contribution of Chinese academic community to the world science of law.

References

Jiang, Ping. 1979. Demarcation between civil law and economic law. *Chinese Journal of Law*, Issue 4.

Li, Changqi. 1995. *Economic law: Basic legal means for government intervention into economy*. Chengdu: Sichuan People's Publishing House.

Li, Changqi. 2009. Contributions and shortcomings of China's economic law study in the past 30 years and its prospect. *The Jurist*, Issue 5.

Li, Changqi. 2009. The contributions, shortcomings and future of China's economic law study in the past 30 years. *The Jurist*, Issue 5.

Liu, Wenhua (ed.). 1995. *New economic law course*. Beijing: Higher Education Press.

Qi, Duojun. 1996. *Basic theories of economic law*, 2nd ed. Wuhan: Wuhan University Press.

Qiu, Ben. 2005. *Development and deepening of China's economic legal studies amid changes*, 6. Issue: Tribune of Political Science and Law.

Research Group of the Institute of Law at Chinese Academy of Social Sciences. 1993. Theoretical thinking, countermeasures & suggestions on building a legal system in the socialist market economy. *Chinese Journal of Law*, Issue 6.

Tong, Rou. 1984. Several theoretical issues about economic law. *Chinese Journal of Law*, Issue 2.

Wang, Baoshu. 1993. Development opportunities of market economy and science of economic law. *Chinese Journal of Law*, Issue 2.
Wang, Jiafu. 1984. Theoretical and practical issues about economic law. *Chinese Journal of Law*, Issue 3.
Wang, Yanlin et al. 1999. Review and outlook of China's economic law at the turn of the century. *Law Review*, Issue 1.
Xiao, Jiangping. 2002a. *Study on history of China's economic law theory*. Beijing: People's Court Press.
Xiao, Jiangping. 2002b. *Study on the history of China's economic law*, 288–96. Beijing: People's Court Press.
Xie, Huaishi. 1984. An interpretation of China's economic law by examining its formation. *Chinese Journal of Law*, Issue 2.
Yang, Zixuan. 1994. New explorations into the regulated objects of economic law. *Economic Legal System*, Issue 2.
Yang, Zixuan. 1995. On the new economic law system. *Peking University Law Journal*, Issue 1.
Yue, Caishen. 2008. Theoretical innovations and contributions of China's economic law in past 30 years. *Journal of Chongqing University (Philosophy and Social Science)*, Issue 5.
Zhang, Chuanbing et al. 1995. Review of the "New Opinions" on China's economic law theory. *Law Review*, Issue 4.
Zhang, Shouwen. 1992. Legal-economics analysis of science of economic law. *Chinese Journal of Law*, Issue 5.
Zhang, Shouwen. 1993. Summary of China's new economic law theory, *Peking University Law Journal*, Issue 1.
Zhang, Shouwen. 2000. *Retrospect and outlook for China's economic law study*. In Yang Zixuan (ed.), *Economic Law Review*, Beijing: Peking University Press, Vol. 1.
Zhang, Shouwen. 2004. *Restructuring of economic law theory (preface)*. Beijing: People's Publishing House.
Zhang, Shouwen. 2006. "Alikeness" and "commonality" in economic law study. *Tribune of Political Science and Law*, Issue 3.
Zhang, Shouwen. 2009. The veins running through the development of China's economic law—From the perspective of distribution. *Tribune of Political Science and Law*, Issue 6.
Zhang, Shouwen. 2013. "Reform Decision" and economic law consensus. *Chinese Journal of Law*, Issue 2.

Chapter 2
Tripartite Relations and Regime Theory

The realm of economic law involves quite a number of regime issues, while the regimes are tied to some important relations, such as the government-market relation: the regimes of macro-economic control and market regulation are associated with government decentralization, and government decentralization shall respect the requirements of the market economic regime. Moreover, while China is pressing ahead with the reform, it has to deal with the problem of carrying out the reform within the framework of rule of law, which manifests the relation between reform and rule of law, or between reform and regulation of economic law. In addition, all of the above regimes have something to do with the relation between constitution and economic law, since they are ought to be specified in both constitution and specific economic laws.

It can be seen that in order to solve the above regime issues, we shall properly handle the "tripartite relations": First, the relation between government and market, which is the basis for regulation of economic law, and also the fundamental relation concerning the reform of economic regime. Second, the relation between reform and economic law, now that economic development is closely related to reform, we need to play the important role of economic law in promoting reform and economic development within the framework of rule of law. Third, the relation between constitution and economic law shall be properly handled, since it affects the relation between economic law and other sectoral laws, and plays a part in addressing the problems in distribution, development, and risk control based on economic law.

The above-mentioned "tripartite relations" are the fundamental relations for studying the entire economic law theory; lots of theoretical and regime issues in the realm of economic law are associated with these relations. And the discussion of the "tripartite relations" is involved with the basic regime issues to be solved in the realm of economic law, including the decentralization between government and market subjects, reform of various regimes, the hierarchy and division of labor of both the constitution and laws.

The discussion of the "tripartite relations", which will help us to better understand the regime theory in economic law, involves the entire economic regime, the specific

S. Zhang, *The New Horizon of China's Economic Law Theory*, Understanding China,
https://doi.org/10.1007/978-981-15-8824-2_2

government regime and market regime, as well as the decentralization regime in constitution, legislative regime, regime reform, and guarantee of economic law; on this basis, it will be easier for us to extract the regime theory. The regime itself is a kind of "relation", implying that studying the "tripartite relations" is studying the regime issues, and also the fundamental issues in the realm of economic law that affect the overall situation.

In view of this, this book, firstly from the perspective of economic law, discusses the legal regulation of the relation between government and market, and the relation between the "reform decisions" and economic law consensus, and then analyzes the relation between the constitution and economic law from the perspective of "economics". In the above-mentioned "tripartite relations", many basic theories in the realm of economic law are involved, which are important basis for the following discussions of various theories.

2.1 Legal Regulation of Government-Market Relation

2.1.1 Background and Issues

Although the Chinese economy no longer develops swiftly as in the past, the tasks of enforcing the country and enriching the people, and strengthening the law-based governance ability remain arduous.[1] An important realistic subject in China's legal study is to explore ways for establishing a sound national governance system, improving the country's governance ability, properly handling the government-market relation, ensuring quality and efficiency of socio-economic development.

While China has been deepening the reform in an all-round manner, and making special efforts in the economic domain (streamlining administration and delegating power to the lower levels, and promoting marketization), "giving play to the decisive role of the market in resource allocation" has become a known and important proposition, and some scholars even argue that it is a major theoretical innovation.[2] Despite of so many people upholding this argument, disagreements remain in existence. In fact, the function or role of market and government has been a fundamental theoretical issue for hundreds of years, and there are a large number of research results in this regard, despite of differentiated viewpoints or conclusions, which have greatly

---

[1]In the wake of the global financial crisis, all countries were plunged into economic depression. Affected by multiple factors, China entered the "new normal" period that features mid-high-speed economic growth. In this important period, China is forced to deal with the challenges in economic restructuring, equitable distribution, and rule of law construction, as well as guaranteeing people's livelihood, making the state prosperous and people peaceful by overcoming the "Middle-income Trap".

[2]Zhang (2013), A03.

enriched the theories of social sciences, and formed an important theoretical basis for the present study.[3]

In reference to the past achievements, the roles of market and government are closely related, but also different from each other in direction, domain, scope and intensity. So they are usually examined together, and they even gave rise to "the government-market relation"—a fundamental issue of general concern in the realm of social sciences. In the current context where the political, economic and social reforms are in full swing, the traditional state control no longer prevails, a modern state governance system is to be established, and the rule of law has drawn increasing attention, it is especially necessary to delve into the roles of market and government and the guarantee of rule of law.

Since the comprehensive deepening of reform is a highly complicated and systematic endeavor, the construction of a modern state governance system is sure to be a large-scale systematic project, while the specific economic governance system (or the relevant economic system) is no more than a subsystem. Moreover, the "government-market relation", which is contained in the economic governance system, is at the same time embodied in the interactions of political, economic and social systems, so the state economic governance system shall be examined from the multi-system perspective. In addition, the state economic governance is inseparable from economic legislation and economic rule of law, while the resulting legal system or rule of law system directly affects the functions and roles of market and government. As such, we need to systematically analyze the state economic governance system from the perspective of structural functionalism.

Under the framework of constructing a modern national governance system, we shall, through multi-level systematic analysis and from a multi-disciplinary perspective, think of the "legal regulation of the government-market relation" in the new stage. In this process, we need to answer the important questions that concern economic reform and rule of law construction, e.g., how to properly position the functions and roles of market and government? How to implement the legal regulation of the government-market relation in the case of displacement or offside of government roles or market absence, so that build a good relation between them? How to effectively perform the functions and roles of market and government by strengthening economic legislation and promoting the economic rule of law?

This section stresses that the "two-way movement" (marketization in real economic life and government intervention to make up for market failure) shall be dialectical and combined with realistic problems. The market and the government, both are the subsystems of the overall resource allocation system, respectively play an important role in providing personal goods and public goods, and therefore

---

[3]The government-market relation is an important premise for the study of social sciences. It is also a basis for building the "public-private binary structure" hypothesis that runs through the social sciences, and benefiting the study of public law and private law in the realm of legal science. Zhang (2004b), pp. 34–36.

forming a "binary allocation" pattern. To ensure that the two allocation systems could do their best is an important mission of the contemporary rule of law construction.[4]

Considering the important role of market-based resource allocation, we shall define the government functions in accordance with law, streamline administration and delegate power to the lower levels, and safeguard the full freedom of the market in the domains irrelevant to public goods or interests. As for the outstanding problems in "two-way movement" and "binary allocation", we shall on the one hand strengthen the legal regulation (define the rights and powers of relevant subjects through legislative transformation), and on the other hand improve the governance ability and protect the interests of relevant subjects.

To this end, the subsequent analysis will be unfolded in three interrelated dimensions: First, introduce Karl Polanyi's "Two-way Movement" theory, and highlight the necessity for dialectical treatment. Second, in combination with the "binary allocation" pattern, emphasize the need to streamline administration and delegate power to the lower levels (pay attention to combine power limitation with power delegation), and fully protect the economic freedom of market subjects. Third, in combination with the preceding two dimensions, promote legislative transformation and build up governance ability.

In terms of the integrity problem in economic governance system or resource allocation system, it will be subject to systematic analysis and more specific structural and functional analysis in this section, and some relevant social science theories may be drawn as a reference, since this problem is so important for examining the theme of this book.

2.1.2 "Two-Way Movement" and Dialectical Approach

In the resource allocation system of a society, the market and the government are the most important subsystems. The positioning, scope, conflict and coordination of the two subsystems have become a long-lasting topic of the "government-market relation". The endless discussions and innumerable research results have given rise to different and even opposite understandings. But no matter how extreme the theorists are, they recognize the positive role of both the market and the government, even though to a varying degree.[5]

In recent years, the famous "Two-way Movement" theory put forward by Karl Polanyi has received more and more attention. Polanyi argues that in the market

[4]The market and the government are the substratum resource allocation systems, while the law shall stipulate the rights and powers associated with resource allocation, so that a large amount of legal provisions are about the roles or functions, rights or powers, duties or responsibilities of the market and the government, thus making resource allocation a core legal issue. And effective resource allocation is an important mission of the contemporary rule of law construction.

[5]The scholars who advocate laissez-faire, including Adam Smith and F.A. Hayek, do not deny the role of the government; likewise, the scholars who uphold state intervention, such as J.M. Keynes and Joseph Stiglitz, do not deny the role of the market.

economy where everything is commercialized, economic activities occupy a decisive position in social relations, and then constitute the movement of economic liberalism; in order to prevent the market mechanism from infringing on society, there exists a reversed social self-protection movement that calls for the government intervention in the market economy.[6]

In fact, in the "Two-way Movement" of marketization and reversed marketization, many people only see the efficiency of market-based resource allocation, while Polanyi and other scholars have noticed the shortcomings of the market and stress the need for moderate government intervention. Taking a full account of both the market and government-based resource allocation, we may reach the consensus on "using two hands together", i.e., under the real market economic condition, the "invisible hand" of the market and the "visible hand" of the government have their own functions (albeit their differences in domain, scope, and direction), and a separate impact on resource allocation. Because of this, all countries across the world actually implement a mixed economic system, rather than an absolutely pure market economy. Of course, for the sake of efficiency, where the market-based allocation is more effective, it is marketization that prevails; the government-based allocation, which is more rational, is only required in the case of market failure. In contrast to the government-based allocation, the market-based allocation boasts a broader scope, a larger scale, and a higher efficiency on the whole. So the resource allocation is usually subject to the market; in other words, the "invisible hand" of the market enjoys priority and occupies a decisive position.

The market-based allocation has limitations, even though it enjoys priority. The market-based allocation could be large-scale and applicable to an extensive scope, but it is not omnipotent. Where there is market failure resulting from the inherent defect of the market, particularly when the situation concerns public goods, external impact, fair competition and equitable distribution, the government-based allocation becomes more necessary, because the situation is not only about efficiency, but social fairness and justice. The reason why all countries implement macro-economic control and market supervision and promote equitable distribution is to compensate for the market limitation. Historically, as long as the market failure and government failure are effectively solved, the overall resource allocation system will be able to balance efficiency and equity in a better way.

Therefore, while China is actively promoting marketization, building a modern market system, and developing a unified market, it shall view the functions and roles of the market and the government objectively and dialectically, avoid overcorrection, and refrain from rigid interpretation of the "decisive role of the market". Only through a comprehension examination of the "Two-way Movement" and the overall resource allocation system can China understands the government-market relation dialectically.

Since the "Two-way Movement" exists in real economic and social life, we shall use "both hands" to deal with resource allocation, meaning that the market and the government shall do their best in economic governance by employing a "dialectical

[6]Karl (2007), p. 114, 136, 164.

approach", i.e., give full play to the important role of the market mechanism, make up for the market failure, and implement effective governance and dynamic adjustment in the case of market and government failures concurrently. In this process, we shall firstly detect the shortcomings of the market and government-based allocation (like doctors diagnosing patients), and then "dialectically" examine the circumstance and work out a solution, so as to distinguish the advantages of the two types of allocation, foster their strength and circumvent their weakness.

In fact, some important figures in economic liberalism and state interventionism have long ago elaborated on the roles of the market and the government in allocating resources. For example, A. Smith argues that the extent of the market affects the division of labor, which in turn affects productivity and "economic growth"; therefore, promoting marketization and expanding market size will help to fully leverage the role of the market in resource allocation and foster economic growth. This viewpoint is known as the "Smith's Theorem".[7] In contrast, J. M. Keynes holds that the spontaneous regulation of the market mechanism alone cannot guarantee the "steady economic growth"; when the effective market demand is inadequate, it is necessary to strengthen state intervention and use the "hand of the government" to create effective demand.[8] This viewpoint is worshiped by his followers as the "Keynesian Law". The doctrines of Smith and Keynes respectively reveal the important functions of the market and the government, and their combination will help to employ the "dialectical approach" in economic domain.

Regarding the "dialectical approach" in economic governance, the Chinese historian Sima Qian had long ago put it as "for spontaneous social activities, the state shall keep away from intervention. The best way is to let nature take its course, the second best way is to offer guidance according to the general law, the third best way is to persuade the people through education, and the fourth best way is to strengthen legal constraints, while the worst way is to compete for benefit with the people".[9] Among them, "let nature take its course" implies the best economic governance of a country, in today's view, is to give full play to the role of the market and let it do what it is capable of. "Offer guidance according to the general law" means that, as long as economic freedom is guaranteed, the state may exercise the means of motivation, guidance and regulation in light of the situation. "Strengthen legal constraints"

[7]According to A. Smith, "as it is the power of exchanging that gives occasion to the division of labor, so the extent of this division must always be limited by the extent of that power, or, in other words, by the extent of the market". Smith (2003), Vol. I, p. 16; Wang (2011), Issue 5; Yang (2008), Issue 1.

[8]After the 2008 global financial crisis, China was also struggling against the insufficient effective demand like other countries. In order to expand domestic demand, the Chinese Central Government came up with a 4 trillion yuan stimulus package, which is generally considered as the practice of the Keynesian Law in the contemporary era. Wang and Lu (2009), Issue 4.

[9]This idea put forward by Sima Qian in his *The Records of the Historian—The Biography of Huo Zhi* is also known as the "good cause theory". According to this theory, the governments in modern times shall be good at dealing with different situations and putting aside unnecessary regulation, so that the market can perform better in resource allocation. So to speak, "good causes have good results".

denotes that the state shall restrict private economic activities in accordance with the law, so as to keep them reasonable and well-organized.

In the governance system based on the "dialectical approach", Sima Qian puts "let nature take its course" at the first place, which could be interpreted as letting the private economy develop freely from government intervention.[10] Only when there is necessity for intervention, the government shall "offer guidance" and "strengthen legal constraints"—comparable to today's macro-economic control and market supervision which are important economic functions of modern states. In addition, "persuade the people through education" means that the government shall pay attention to the teaching of business ethics.[11] "Compete for benefit with the people" is the least desirable, implying that the government shall withdraw from the competitive sectors to concentrate on providing public goods.

Sima Qian's dialectical thought and its basic principles are collectively known as "Sima Qian's Theorem". It is not only containing the ideas of Smith and Keynes, but more aged and more comprehensive. In his systematic thinking about economic governance and value choices, Sima Qian made a ranking of economic freedom, state intervention and the intensity of state intervention, which is a valuable reference for today's "dialectical approach" in economic governance.[12] In the process of building an economic governance system, China shall "let nature take its course" to give full play to the role of the market; or "offer guidance" and "strengthen legal constraints" when there is need for government intervention.

The reason why the role of the market is put at the first place, which is the modern sense of "let nature take its course", is that the market is a complex system in which different subjects are taking part in numerous and complicated games. The government is also a complex system, and from an economic point of view, it is a form of economic organization that deals with fiscal and financial affairs. But the two systems have different functions and objectives in resource allocation: the market is for individuals to pursue their own interests, the accompanying public benefit is only on objective outcome; while the mission of the government is to, at least nominally, protect public interest and do good to the entire society, although not always satisfying.

In short, to define and distinguish government and market subjects, government and market-based allocation in the "Two-way Movement" is to emphasize that these two types of subjects and allocation mechanisms shall perform their duties and

---

[10]Some Chinese scholars hold that Sima Qian somewhat inherited the "cause" or laissez-faire teachings from Confucius and Mencius. See Shi (1989), Issue 6.

[11]The market economy is not only a rule-of-law economy, but a credit economy, meaning that moral elements are fairly important for the benign economic development, which is embodied in lots of economic legislations, e.g., China's civil and commercial laws and other laws in the realm of economic law have specified the good faith, public order and good customs or recognized business ethics.

[12]Sima Qian takes the three aspects as a whole or a system, which is consistent with the knowledge of the modern times. The measures adopted by the Chinese government, e.g., streamlining administration and delegating power to the lower levels, and micro-stimulation, is combination of "let nature take its course" and "offer guidance".

display their advantages, employ a "dialectical approach" in economic governance and solve the outstanding problems in resource allocation. To this end, China is ought to streamline administration and delegate powers, as well as promote marketization, so as to address the prominent problems of excessive government intervention and insufficient marketization.

2.1.3 "Binary Allocation", Streamlining Administration and Delegating Powers

Based on the "Two-way Movement" (marketization and government intervention to make up for market failure), the "binary resource allocation" based the market and the government is then formed. In this regard, we shall, by following the dialectical thought, specify the powers and rights of relevant subjects in law in light of their respective roles in resource allocation, and define the boundaries between the government and the market to avoid or resolve disputes; moreover, we shall reduce the excessive government imprisonment through streamlining administration and delegating powers, which need to be confirmed and guaranteed through legislation.

2.1.3.1 Two-Tier Allocation: Combination of Power Restriction and Delegation

The "binary allocation" of resources based on the market and the government manifests at two different levels, which is known as "two-tier allocation". Both the government and the market are a complex system composed of multiple subjects with different wills, goals and actions. Such circumstance is described by A. Smith as "in the great chess-board of human society, every single piece has a principle of motion of its own".[13] Similarly, in the big chess-board of the market, all subjects engaged in the game will, through their profit-making activities, raise the efficiency of resource allocation, increase the overall social welfare, and objectively improve the social benefit. Speaking of the government which is the subject that delivers public goods, it is due to put the public interest at the first place regardless of the game with market subjects or the game inside the government system; any deviation from the public interest will make its legitimacy questioned. Since the government is composed of ordinary people, they may, in the name of public interest, harm the rights and interests of private subjects while exercising the public power. It is for this reason that "restriction of public power" is prescribed by law, and government functions are limited to delivery of public goods or protection of public interest.

---

[13]Adam Smith stresses that when each member of society and the legislative body choose the same principle of motion, the chess game of human society will go on smoothly; otherwise, the game will become so bitter that the human society will be confined to a state of chaos at all times. Smith (2003), P302.

In fact, the government is highly capable of resource allocation; it may distort the market-based allocation if not legally restricted. For example, the large-scale fiscal revenue and expenditure of the state—especially the exercise of taxation power, bond issuance power, government procurement power, and transfer payment power—have a great impact on resource allocation. For another example, the exercise of the state financial control power– whether it is to regulate interest rate or adjust other financial instruments—vigorously affects the market-based allocation. More importantly, the government special subsidies, tax incentives and discount loans have a direct impact on market subjects. Although the government-based allocation is implemented to make up for the market failure or safeguard the public interest, it may sometimes yield positive additional benefits or distort the market-based allocation; such distortion behaviors shall be strictly limited and implemented according to law to safeguard proper resource allocation based on the market.

The scope of government-based resource allocation depends on government functions. If the government functions are unclearly defined or improperly expanded, it will greatly expand the scope and domain of resource allocation, thus squeezing the room for market-based allocation; so it is necessary to define government functions and restrict government powers by law. China has made it clearly that the government economic functions consist of macro-economic control and market supervision,[14] i.e., providing public goods in the economic domain to the market. It is a correct positioning. But in practice, indirect macro-economic control and specific market supervision are often equated with direct administrative intervention, which is a great misunderstanding. In addition, the control of market operations and the regulation of given markets shall be strictly enforced according to law, and those undue administrative approvals shall be abolished.[15] In the process of streamlining administration and delegating power, what should be curbed is the administrative behavior that distorts the market-based allocation and does no good to the public interest, rather than the necessary and legitimate macro-economic control and market regulation.

For the above reasons, in terms of the legal regulation of the two-tier allocation, its primary task is to transform government functions by abandoning undue functions and handing over the matters to the market that is capable of solving, thereby combining the restriction of public powers with the protection of private rights, and achieving the goal of "streamlining administration and delegating power". It is necessary to clarify and adhere to the "residue principle", i.e., in addition to the domains where resources are ought to be allocated by the government according to law, all the other domains shall be at the mercy of the market. The laws shall, with the focus

[14]As early as ten years ago, China defined the government functions as macro-regulation, market supervision, social management, and public services. The first two of them are important economic functions of modern states, and it is more appropriate to call them macro-economic control and market regulation.

[15]In the past two years, the State Council of China repeatedly made the "decisions" on cancellation, decentralization and adjustment of administrative examination and approval projects, and released the *Circular on Clearing up the Non-administrative Approval Projects of the Departments of the State Council* (GuoFa [2014] No. 16) on April 22, 2014.

placed on limiting government functions, specify and safeguard the functions of market in resource allocation.

The two-tier allocation shows that the two allocation systems (the market and the government) are not of the opposite relation at the same level. As Sima Qian once said, "the worst way is to compete for benefit with the people", the government should not compete with the market subjects at the same level, but retain its non-profit or commonweal nature. It is the basis for transformation of government functions. Moreover, any problem that can be solved at the market level shall be free from government invention. In other words, although some matters have all along been handled by the government, if they could be solved by the market more efficiently, then the government shall retreat from direct intervention,[16] it helps to improve government performance and the efficiency of the overall resource allocation system. Relevantly, we'd better seriously think about the scale of government procurement; the nature, hierarchy, size and number of state-owned enterprises (SOEs)[17]; promotion of mixed ownership; and the extent and depth of the government impact on economy, so as to make legal regulation accordingly.

The reason why the government and the market-based allocation is not of the "either-or" relation at the same level is also because the market is a resource allocation system pursuing private interest and efficiency, while the government-based allocation is for public welfare and equity (at least its starting point should be like this). If we are about to delimit the boundary of the government based on the aforesaid hierarchical classification, we shall create a "limited government" which keeps to its duties, never crosses over or improperly interferes with the market, so as to maintain the independency and integrity of the market system, and protect the constitution-conferred right to economic freedom of market subjects.[18]

The creation of a "limited government" calls for "streamlining administration" and "limiting on the power" of government, "delegating power" to market subjects and removing their restrictions, which will promote free trade and free competition, and improve economic efficiency. In the process of streamlining administration and delegating power, the matters about administrative examination and approval shall

[16]To fulfill its objectives, the government does not have to deal with all specific matters directly, but hand them over to the market based on specialized division of labor. Therefore, the government shall pay more attention to purchasing services, even the domain of special transfer payment that manifests the national policy may be moderately marketized.

[17]Whether SOEs shall be primarily competitive, profit-making or commonweal? Whether they are equated with ordinary enterprises or a carrier for providing public goods on behalf of the government? What is special about their size, quantity and positioning? All of these questions need to be resolved through the reform of SOEs.

[18]The right to economic freedom, which is a fundamental right granted to market subjects by constitution, is an important category of economic constitution. The right to economic freedom is also embodied in various sectoral laws, for example, the right to economic freedom in the realm of economic law is the market game right of market subjects, which is manifested in the enterprises' rights to free operation, fair competition, and legitimate competition. See Zhang (2004c), pp. 406–408.

be resolved. The "approval economy",[19] which features lengthy reviews, is "uneconomical" for both market subjects and the society as a whole. It has been criticized for being prejudicial to the economic freedom right of market subjects, and for the breeding rent-seeking and corruption, as well as inefficiency. Marketization needs market subjects to bear risks and shoulder responsibilities on their own, and the government neither takes on all things nor conducts antecedent supervision. And the functions of government and enterprises may not be mixed up; otherwise, it will be hard to establish a genuine market economy or an effective two-tier allocation.

2.1.3.2 Two-Way Allocation: Focus on Protection of the Right to Economic Freedom

The two allocation systems display their roles at different levels according to the above content on the two-tier allocation and "Two-way Movement". They also have different directions of resource allocation: the market subjects allocate resources in the direction of maximizing private interest, while the government allocates resources in the direction of maximizing public interest, thus forming the pattern of "two-way allocation". Owing to different levels and directions of resource allocation, the two allocation systems have different rights and powers that are in need of legal protection.

From the perspective of system economics, the market is not only an aggregation of commodity exchange venues or commodity exchange relations in the economic sense; the market itself is a kind of "system" that allocates resource.[20] Reasonable market arrangements will do better for protecting property rights, safeguarding transactions, and playing an active role in resource allocation; the core issues involved indicate the distribution of rights and the resource belonging therefrom. It is consistent with the requirements of the Coase Theorem.

In the market-oriented movement, the focus is on protecting the right to economic freedom of market subjects, specifying their various property rights and safeguarding their freedom in transaction and competition. Moreover, the laws of economy is ought to be respected, particularly the law of value and the law of competition; a modern market system and a unified market shall be established. In this process, we must truly "streamline administration and delegate power". We cannot effectively promote marketization unless we streamline administrative procedures, simplify and consolidate government functions, reduce administrative intervention, return relevant rights to market subjects and have them emancipated.

According to the afore-mentioned Smith's Theorem, promoting marketization and building a unified market will help to expand the market size, raise the efficiency of resource allocation, and stimulate economic growth. In order to fulfill the above

[19] Since the government may obtain economic benefits through countless administrative examination and approval, it is prone to be turned into an economic entity that seeks interests for department or work unit by employing administrative power. The resulting "approval economy" must be eradicated for fear of entailing endless trouble.

[20] Some scholars believe that "competing markets are taken as a system that maximizes welfare without any mutual care". Allan Schmid (1999), p. 35.

objectives, we need to define the rights of market subjects. No matter it is property right, creditor's right, intellectual property right or other rights, they shall be defined and protected according to law. So to speak, none of the property law, contract law, intellectual property law, tort law, and anti-unfair competition law is dispensable. In addition, along with the expansion of market size and continuous unification of the market, no restriction or segregation of the market is allowed any longer, which has made the anti-monopoly law become more important in backing up fair competition.

At the same time, we shall reduce all kinds of restrictions on market subjects, particularly the purchase limit, loan limit and price limit that restrict transactions, although they may benefit economic stability and fulfill the policy objectives in the short term, they will do no good to the resource allocation in the long run. Besides, the specialized division of labor, which is argued by Smith, demands for reducing market access restrictions, and removing market entry barriers and thresholds as much as possible,[21] so as to promote economic growth more effectively.[22]

In contrast to the above-mentioned direction of marketization, the government-based resource allocation, with the direct goal of making up for the market failure, is based on the definition and distribution of powers, which is a manifestation of public power or economic authority of the government in the domain of economy.

According to the Keynesian theory, although market-based allocation promotes the "growth" of economy, it cannot guarantee the "steady growth" of economy,[23] so that state intervention and government-based allocation is indispensable.[24] Both macro-economic control and market regulation are crucial means to solve market failings, and they are also important economic functions and economic authority of the government that must be prescribed by law.

From the perspective of system economics, the definition and clarity of the government authority is the core issue that directly concerns the economic structure, and influences the efficiency of long-term resource allocation. At the beginning of China's reform and opening up, the then Constitution stipulated that "the state practices planned economy", whereby the government-based allocation played a dominant role.[25] Until the 1993 amendment to the Constitution confirmed that "the state practices a socialist market economy" and that "the state shall strengthen economic

21 The *Reform Plan for Registered Capital Registration System*, which was ratified by China's State Council on February 7, 2014, states to reform the industrial and commercial registration system to make it more convenient, loose market access control and lower market entry thresholds, optimize the business environment, and accelerate the development of market subjects.

22 More measures can be adopted to promote the specialized and refined division of labor, e.g., tax incentives or reducing double taxation.

23 Since steady economic growth is the foremost goal of macro-economy of all countries, they have paid great attention to this issue in their legislation, and even promulgated special laws in this regard, Germany's *Act to Promote Economic Stability and Growth* (1967) is the best-known example.

24 The academic community has yet reached consensus on the Keynesian theory. Some scholars argue that this theory is more applicable to modern China. See Gong (2007), Issue 1.

25 According to Article 15 of China's Constitution at that time, "the state practices planned economy on the basis of socialist public ownership" and "it ensures the proportionate and coordinated growth of the national economy through overall balancing by economic planning and the supplementary role of regulation by the market", we can see that the national economic

legislation and improve macro-economic control", the market and government-based allocation systems were for the first time established in the Constitution, and then the macro-economic control and market regulation powers, which are important economic authority of the government, started to be specified in all types of legislations.

One of the important functions of law is to "identify the ownership of rights and settle the disputes". When examining the government-market relation, the first thing to do is to "identify the ownership of rights" by law, i.e., define their respective boundaries, functions and roles, as well as the rights and powers of relevant subjects. Everything beyond the government functions can be handed over to the market and the society. Accordingly, based on the legal definition of the state economic powers, the government exercises the powers of macro-economic control and market regulation, and "leaves the remaining powers to market subjects". The government functions and powers are so important for safeguarding the role of the market, so they shall be particularly specified—their definition had remained vague in the past. Only in this way can we "settle the disputes", i.e., halt the controversies about the government-market relation, prevent the government from competing for profit against the people, and guard against the government misbehaviors such as monopolizing and abusing administrative power.

When defining the government authority, it is important to prevent the expansion of government powers. To this end, the government administrative power shall be strictly restricted, but certain space shall be retained for the government economic authority. For example, in order to ensure the balanced, coordinated and sustainable development of the economy, and safeguard the economic stability in the long run, a system of macro-economic control shall be established, and the macro-economic power in this system differs from the general administrative power. When exercising the macro-economic power, the government has to examine the situation and make discretionary choices within a certain range of control, so as to fulfill the direct goal of benign economic operation and coordinated development. The macro-economic control is a kind of indirect approach at the macro-level,[26] it does not directly aim at a certain market subject, so it is neither equated with direct government intervention nor the micro-level market supervision. The market supervision power is similar to the administrative power (also following the principles for regulating administrative power), nevertheless, it has its independency and particularity.

The macro-economic control power and market supervision power are important economic authority of the government. Their exercise directly affects the protection of the economic freedom right of market subjects and effective market operations. So the resulting negative impact shall be avoided. In addition, the macro-economic control power and market supervision power are associated with multiple-level regime or decentralization, and they may affect the government performance or the

planning was the main form of resource allocation, and the government-based allocation played a dominant role at that time.

[26]In China's "Reform Decisions" (2013) there is an accurate description of the macro-economic control, which will help to clarify some misunderstandings.

provision of public goods. As such, when exercising the above economic authority, the government shall maintain the integrity of the resource allocation system, balance the relation between the two subsystems of allocation (market and government), promote their coordination and complementation, and give play to their respective positive roles.

In short, the "binary allocation" demonstrates the different levels and different directions of the two allocation systems (market and government). Both the promotion of marketization and restriction of the government macro-economic control and supervision powers shall be subject to legal regulation. The top priority of the "two-way allocation" is to achieve highly-efficient resource allocation by "streamlining administration and delegating power", relieving the government imprisonment to the market, releasing the market vitality, and safeguarding the economic freedom right of market subjects. Moreover, if we could specify the government economic authority in law and limit it to macro-economic control power and market regulation (supervision) power, it will help to safeguard the healthy and orderly operation of the market, and raise its resource allocation efficiency.

In the "binary allocation" pattern, "streamlining administration and delegating power" is the direction of China's reform and must be specified in laws, because the government has the impulse of administrative intervention. Although the successive major reforms aimed at streamlining administration and delegating power, the administrative intervention has fallen into a circle of "first reduction and then increase", which could be elucidated by "Huang Zongxi's Law".[27] If market-based allocation is not legally defined and strictly implemented according to law, it is prone to be intervened by the government from time to time. As a result, we need to further improve and refine the relevant legislations and build up the economic governance ability.

2.1.4 Legislative Transformation and Improvement of Economic Governance Ability

The above-mentioned "Two-way Movement" and "binary allocation" are in need of legal regulation. Only by incorporating them into the framework of rule of law can we better play the important roles of the two allocation systems. In the process of building a modern economic governance system, China shall ensure of the effective performance of the market and government functions. An urgent and pressing need is to promote legislative transformation in combination with the prominent problems

[27]Chinese historian and thinker Huang Zongxi (1610–1695), in his *Waiting for the Dawn*, pointed out that at the beginning of a tax and fee reform, the government tends to alleviate people's tax burden, but as time goes by, it will levy more and more "miscellaneous taxes", thereby imposing a heavier burden on the common tax payers. Chinese scholars describe this phenomenon with "Huang Zongxi's Law". In fact, the "government's streamlining administration and delegating power" shows the similar problem of "first simplification and then complication, or first reduction and then increase", which may also be elucidated by "Huang Zongxi's Law". Qin (2000).

in reality, and improve the level of rule of law and build up the economic governance ability by strengthening the legal regulation.

2.1.4.1 Legislative Transformation

In the preceding paragraphs about "binary allocation", we've discussed the importance and necessity in better safeguarding the economic freedom right of market subjects through streamlining administration and delegating power, and through combination of power restriction and decentralization. To this end, China shall accelerate the legislative transformation and stipulate important rights and powers in laws. The following three aspects are in need of special attention:

(1) Transform the legislative thinking, i.e., the legislation shall more and more reflect the spirit of streamlining administration and delegating power, and of protecting the economic freedom right of market subjects. Lots of the old legislations mainly embody the idea of administration and even regulation, overemphasizing government power, and not paying enough attention to the rights of market subjects. Consequently, a large number of "administrative laws" or "administrative regulations" have come out; more than that, the legislative purpose and specific system design are run through by the "administrative idea", thus forming an "administration-oriented" legislative system. How to transform from "administration-oriented" legislation to "governance-oriented" legislation? It is an important topic in promoting the rule of law construction.[28]

In order to establish a modern state economic governance system, the government and the market shall properly perform their duties and do their best. At the same time, full attention shall be paid to the rights and interests of various subjects (esp. market subjects) and the games between them, so that the legal system formed on this basis will be able to yield substantial results and a good outcome of "governance". Therefore, the legislative ideas that favor government "administration" or "regulation" must be changed, and the relevant legislative purposes, fundamental principles and specific rules shall be changed accordingly.

(2) Transform the legislative structure and legislative content. The transformation of legislative thinking or legislative spirit as mentioned above will affect the adjustment of the entire legislative system, and then affect the structure and content of legislation. The reform seems like dancing to another tune and replacing the old with the new, with the core of "revising the law"; and all of the important reforms shall be

---

[28]China has been vigorously simplifying administration and delegating power, reducing administrative examination and approval, and solving the problems of excessive pre-event administration. For example, according to the *Decision of the State Council on Cancellation and Decentralization of a Batch of Administrative Approval Projects*, released on January 28, 2014, China's State Council has cleared up the administrative regulations that were associated with the administrative examination and approval projects to be cancelled or decentralized. On July 29, 2014, the *Decision of the State Council on Amending Some Administrative Regulations* was promulgated, in aim to revise the 21 existing administrative regulations.

stipulated by law and implemented pursuant to law. Given this, the "Reform Decisions" of China to comprehensively deepen the reform, which are important political decisions, have a significant impact on the relevant legislations, meaning that the legislative structure and content shall be transformed to satisfy the requirements of the comprehensive reform.

Accordingly, in the state economic governance system, a modern economic legislative system shall be established. This system shall conform to the spirit of modern rule of law, and reflect the universal consensus and correct positioning of the government-market relation in modern countries; moreover, it shall abide by the afore-mentioned "Sima Qian's Theorem" to put in the first place of meeting the needs of market development, and fully protecting the economic freedom right or economic development right of market subjects,[29] because the development of private economy is the foundation of the overall national economy, and it directly affects the realization of the goal of prospering the country and enriching the people.

In order to reflect the above legislative ideas or objectives, the legislative structure of the modern economic legislative system may consist of civil and commercial law, economic law, administrative law and other sectoral laws, which helps to coordinate and regulate the government-market relation, and give full play to the respective functions and roles of the market and the government. In 2011, China's legislative body announced that the national legal system had already taken shape[30]; however, the quality, content, quantity and coordination of legislations are not yet able to fully meet the requirements of the modern governance system. Especially in the realms of economic law and administrative law, we shall continue streamlining administration and delegating power, adjusting the relevant legislative structure, transforming and simplifying government functions, and promoting institutional reform. Besides, more economic power shall be transferred from the government to the market and from the central government to the local governments, because the consensus of economics tells that the market is more efficient in providing personal goods, and local governments are doing better in delivering public goods in a given area. If the above knowledge could be embodied in the relevant legislations, there will be great changes to the legislative structure and legislative content, which will ultimately transform the overall legislative system.

(3) Pay attention to the legislative transformation amid the construction of specific systems. All legislative transformation shall be reflected in each specific system. In order to improve the modern economic legislative system by following the reform ideas and objectives, we shall establish and improve a variety of new specific systems.

---

[29]The right to economic development is particularly important for market subjects. See Shouwen (2012), The right to economic development: from the perspective of economic *law, Modern Law Science*, Issue 2.

[30]At the beginning of 2011, China's national legislative body announced that "a socialist legal system with Chinese characteristics has finally taken shape, with the Constitution as the core, the Constitution-related laws, the civil and commercial law and other sectoral laws as the trunk, the national laws and administrative regulations, and local laws and legal norms as components". However, considering the reality of China's rule of law construction and development of the market economy, such legal system needs to be further improved.

For example, by following the idea of streamlining administration and delegating power, the state has cancelled a large number of administrative approval procedures, which has led to revision of so many laws. In addition, in order to give full play to the role of the market, we shall safeguard fair and legitimate competition, and protect consumer rights. In terms of the market regulation law, the state has intensified the anti-monopoly law enforcement and constantly improved the supporting systems for the *Anti-monopoly Law*. Besides, China has completed the revision of the *Law on the Protection of Consumer Rights and Interests*, and started revising the *Anti-unfair Competition Law*.

While strengthening the construction of specific systems, we shall pay attention to some important legislations with fundamental status. For example, some basic laws for macro-economic control (e.g., the basic laws for stable economic growth and for finance) are still absent in China, which not only affects the restriction on the government economic power, but fails to fully meet the requirements of the "Reform Decisions" and the academic and industrial expectations. In addition, the construction of specific systems remains an arduous task beset by prominent problems. For example, the statutory taxation principle is yet implemented, even if the generally low-level taxation legislation is to be elevated in the future, it would remain hard to protect the property rights of market subjects unless the government taxation power is effectively limited. Therefore, it is so important for the construction of specific systems to reflect the transformation of the above legislative thinking.

2.1.4.2 Improvement of Economic Governance Ability

The above-mentioned legislative transformation will help to build up various abilities related to the state economic governance ability, such as the ability of rule of law, the game ability of market subjects, and the enterprise competitive ability. The enhancement of these abilities will further improve the overall governance ability, promote the market-oriented reform and deepen the comprehensive reforms, and benefit the development of economy, society and the rule of law construction.

An economic governance system is the foundation of the state economic governance ability. Correspondingly, the promotion of economic legal system construction through legislative transformation is fairly important for improving the economic governance ability. In the context where the rule of law thinking and approach is being advocated, we must pay attention to the rule of law in the economic domain. The ability of rule of law—a governance ability according to law—is so important that it directly affects the level of a country's law-based governance.

The market economy is a rule-of-law economy, and the market operation is inseparable from a good law-based governance environment. In order to govern the economy according to law, we shall firstly build up the legislative ability, and then improve law enforcement and judicial abilities. In the domain of economic governance, the foremost matter is to protect the economic freedom right or economic development right of market subjects, so that the statutory principle shall be strictly implemented to limit the government power and protect the basic rights of market subjects. However, for a number of reasons, the current legislative ability of China is not strong enough, some basic laws are either absent or imperfect, and unable to satisfy the requirements of the modern governance system. Therefore, we need to transform the legislative thinking, structure and content, and establish and improve specific legal systems, so that we can make relevant legislative adjustment to address the problems in economic governance, e.g., weak legislative and judicial influences, but excessive administrative intervention. In short, we shall vigorously reduce administrative intervention, and increase the influence of legislation and justice, which is an important manifestation of the dialectical approach and strengthened legal regulation.

In addition to the rule-of-law ability, the legislative transformation also helps to enhance the game ability of market subjects, as well as their competitive and tax-paying abilities. For example, the legislative transformation, which endorses streamlining administration and delegating power, is able to impose more restrictions on the government economic governance power, and release more economic freedom right of market subjects, thus enhancing their game ability. According to this, in their vertical game with the government, the market subjects can better protect its own interests based on their legal rights against the government administrative intervention or improper macro-economic control and market supervision. At the same time, in the horizontal game between themselves, the market subjects can trade and compete freely based on their legal rights, thereby increasing market freedom and economic efficiency.

The market freedom has multiple measurement indicators.[31] Among them, whether the market freedom (to enter or exit freely) or competition is restricted, which is closely related to the competitiveness of market subjects, is to measure the degree of marketization or market freedom. Generally, if the economic freedom right is better guaranteed, there will be a higher degree of market freedom, fuller competition, more efficient resource allocation, stronger competitiveness and better growth of enterprises. Some Chinese private enterprises have grown into world-renown companies by continuously improving their competitiveness while the government imposes less intervention and the market enjoys more freedom.[32] Therefore, the economic legislation shall fully guarantee the competitiveness of market subjects, which is fairly important for them to exercise their economic development right.

In addition, the above-mentioned legislative transformation not only helps to enhance the game ability or competitiveness of market subjects, but helps to raise the efficiency of market-based resource allocation, and improves the tax-paying ability

[31]Being influenced by many factors, market freedom has multiple measurement indicators. Some important ones include the degree of freedom in fiscal, finance, trade, investment, wage and price, as well as the impact of government regulation and property right protection. In the international community there has been a comprehensive judgment of economic freedom based on the above indicators. In this respect, the Hong Kong SAR has ranked first for more than a decade, while mainland China has been beyond the top 100 for years, which shows that there is still room for mainland China to further streamline administration and delegate power.

[32]For example, some Chinese Internet giants Baidu, Alibaba and Tencent (collectively known as "BAT), and the leading high-tech firms like Huawei and ZTE, have grown into world-renown companies with less government intervention.

of market subjects, thereby consolidating the material basis of government-based allocation.

Considering the tax burden of market subjects, China started paving way for the "structural tax cut"[33] since 2004, trying to reduce the tax burden and vitalize the market through multiple reforms such as VAT transformation and "replacing business tax with VAT". However, due to years' heavy burden, the enterprises have kept appealing for tax cut. To date, the proportion of direct tax-based revenue remains low, which is partially attributed to the level of economic development and the taxation system, and partially to excessive tax evasion or weak tax-paying ability. We have to advance the legislative transformation by following the ideas of "streamlining administration and delegating power" and "decentralization and profit-sharing" that were proposed at the beginning of the reform, so that we can truly reduce the tax burden on market subjects, thereby conserving tax sources, enhancing their competitiveness, and further building up their tax-paying ability.

Besides, giving market subjects more economic freedom right through legislative transformation also helps to enhance their ability to participate in co-governance or autonomy. The participation of market subjects in the creation of market governance rules will improve the compliance of rules and solve the problem of "governance failure".[34] In addition, the self-regulatory rules within certain enterprises or industries can provide lessons for national legislation. Therefore, a stronger ability in co-governance or autonomy has a positive significance for the construction of a state governance system.

In order to enhance the game ability and other specific abilities of market subjects, China has introduced a number of "promotional" systems to advance marketization, increase market freedom, and stimulate market vitality. Among them, "properly managing large enterprises while relaxing control over small ones" is an important legal regulation approach: on the one hand, "properly managing large enterprises" by cracking down on the monopolistic conducts and regulating the behaviors of large SOEs; on the other hand, reduce the burden on small and medium-sized enterprises or small and micro businesses through introduction of the systems involving economy, finance, industry and competition, and promote their development, so as to achieve the goal of "relaxing control over small ones". By employing such legal regulation approach we can do better in creating a level playing ground and promoting the healthy development of market economy.

[33]The "structural tax cut", which was officially put forward in 2008, has received widespread attention at the national level, particularly because of the global financial crisis. Before that, China started the pilot VAT transformation in 2004, and abolished or merged multiple taxes afterwards, which could be regarded as the preparations for the "structural tax cut" policy. See Zhang (2013a), Issue 5.

[34]Elinor Ostrom, Nobel Prize winner in economics, once put forward a "multi-center governance" theory which holds that the government is not the only center in governance, other entities like private institutions, non-governmental organizations and individual citizens are allowed to participate in governance, thus achieving "common governance". But in general, she is more interested in the "non-governmental non-market communications". See Zhu (2012), p. 6.

The above-mentioned "promotional" system arrangements are closely associated with the state control ability and supervision ability. Among them, the state fiscal control and financial control abilities directly affect the market operation and performance of market functions, if they could create a sound external environment for market operation, and ease the burden and pressure upon market subjects, there would be a virtuous circle.[35] At the same time, the improved market supervision ability will help to regulate unfair and illegal competition, establish a good market order, and encourage workable competition. An important approach to enhance the control and supervision abilities is to form a complete, coordinated, standardized and workable control and supervision system through legislative transformation.

For the special markets concerning the national economy and the people's livelihood, the government control and supervision are fairly necessary, but it should be reiterated that in the marketable domains, the administrative measures that distort resource allocation shall be avoided as much as possible. In view of this, the state has been learning to employ more market instruments. For example, in order to regulate the real estate market, the state insists on providing more affordable housing from a market-oriented perspective of increasing supply; it will not only meet the different levels of demand in the process of urbanization, but gradually eliminate the non-marketization means such as purchase limit and loan limit. In order to regulate the securities market, the state sticks to combine marketization with the rule of law approach, and has introduced several regulations to promote its healthy development.[36] These examples demonstrate that the state has transformed the ideas of control and supervision, which is helpful for constantly enhancing its control and supervision abilities in the process of system improvement.

In short, the "binary allocation" or "Two-way Movement" of the market and the government are in need of strengthened legal regulation. The transformation of legislative thinking, structure and content, and improvement of specific systems will help to build up China's law-based governance ability, control and supervision abilities, and help the market subjects to build up their game ability, and competitive, tax-paying and participation abilities, which will improve the state governance ability on the whole. Along with the advancement of economic legislation, the modern fiscal system, taxation system and financial system will become an important part of the economic governance system, so that the country will find the level of economic rule of law further improved.

---

[35] According to Polanyi, the introduction of free market is far from eliminating the need for government control, regulation and intervention, but greatly expands their scope of application. See Karl (2007), p. 120.

[36] The *Opinions of the State Council on Further Promoting the Sound Development of Capital Market*, which was issued on May 9, 2014, stress to adhere to the orientation of marketization and the rule of law, maintain an open, fair and impartial market order and safeguard the legitimate rights and interests of investors, particularly those of the small and medium-sized investors, enhance the competitiveness of enterprises, and better play the role of capital market in optimizing resource allocation.

2.1.5 Conclusion

As for the basic problems about the "government-market relation" in the realm of social sciences, there have been countless research results in the past, as a verse from a poem put it, "predecessors have left us vast intellectual legacies", especially in the realms of economics, political science and sociology; different people have different views. Nevertheless, at the time that China is deepening reforms in an all-round manner and building a modern state governance system, quite a number of problems on basis of China's special situations need be examined, e.g., how to correctly position the roles of the government and the market and safeguard their performance from a legal dimension? It concerns the achievement of effective legal regulation.

Considering the reality of resource allocation in different countries, this section states that both the government and the market are subsystems in the overall resource allocation system, operating at different levels and along different directions; they may have close contacts, interactions and even conflicts in the process of resource allocation. Therefore, it is especially necessary to define their respective functions and roles, and have them legally specified and guaranteed.

For this reason, the content in this section is unfolded in three interrelated dimensions: (1) Based on the "Two-way Movement" theory, this section examines the respective functions and roles of the market and the government and the "two failures" by employing a dialectical approach. It especially stresses to define the functions and positioning of the government and the market based on the "Sima Qian's Theorem", and limit the government economic functions and economic authority by law. (2) This section discusses the issue of "streamlining administration and delegating power" based on the "binary allocation", emphasizing that the government functions shall be transformed due to the "different levels" of the government and market-based allocation, the power restriction and decentralization shall be combined to protect the economic freedom right of market subjects, and promote marketization. (3) This section points out the specific path of legal regulation of the government-market relation, stressing the need for transforming the legislative thinking, structure and content, which will help to streamline administration and delegate power, and thereby enhancing the overall economic governance ability and build a sound government-market relation.

Presently, the comprehensive deepening of China's reform is still led by the reform of economic regime, the key is to properly handle the government-market relation, and the core issues include transformation of government functions, streamlining administration, decentralization and profit sharing. All of the past reforms have dealt with these core issues, but none of them is thoroughly resolved to date, demonstrating the difficulty of the government in "self-revolution". The "Huang Zongxi's Law"—"first simplification and then complication, first reduction and then increase"—exists in the government authority needs to be broken. If the "power restriction" on the government and the "full decentralization" to market subjects are not specified in law, and if there is no guarantee from the modern economic rule of law, the dilemma created by the "Huang Zongxi's Law" will be never shaken off, and the modern market system and the economic governance system will be out of the question.

Therefore, it is of great practical significance to probe into the legal regulation of the government-market relation from the perspectives of law and legal science. These discussions do not repeat or reaffirm some common sense or consensus, but emphasize the necessity and importance of correctly handling the government-market relation and strengthening the economic rule of law in the present era. Since China still has some domains that are inadequately marketized or excessively intervened, the vigorous promotion of marketization is no doubt important. Meanwhile, the government shall do a better job in macro-economic control and market supervision to create a good market environment and maintain market order, which helps to balance efficiency and equity.

In short, the government-market relation is not only a basic issue in law and in the entire realm of social sciences, but an enduring topic that needs to be examined in combination with the development of the times and from multiple dimensions such as politics, economy, society and law. With the advancement of China's comprehensive deepening of reform, specific legal issues related to this topic keep cropping up, only by employing the rule-of-law thinking and approach can we continuously improve the legal regulation of the government-market relation, promote the construction of economic rule of law, and completely build a state governance system.

2.2 "Reform Decisions" and Economic Law Consensus

2.2.1 Presenting Problems

The magnificent and comprehensive reform of China not only depends on the great practice of all Chinese people, but also on the planning and guidance of the government. All the "reform decisions"—important decisions made by the state ruling body to promote overall or partial reform—have stimulated the development of economic, political, social and other domains, and in the meantime contributed to the construction of China's legal system and the formation of consensus in the realm of legal science. An in-depth study into the internal relation between the "reform decisions" and the consensuses in law and legal science is so necessary, since it is of special significance for advancing legal science studies and system building.

The "reform decisions"—a major choice made by the state ruling body in restructuring system and adjusting policies, and embodied in a series of normative documents that have substantive binding force—have an important impact on the reform and improvement of many systems. Since China has made economic reform as the focus or driving force of the comprehensive reform, and stressed the economic rule of law construction, and the "reform decisions" are closely related to the legislation, law enforcement and justice in the realm of economic law, this section will, from the perspective of economic law, reveal the influence of the "reform decisions" on the economic law consensus and explore into their internal relation, as well as the "relation between reform and economic law".

The extraction of economic law consensus has drawn much attention from the academic community.[37] Generally speaking, the economic law consensus consists of theoretical consensus and system consensus, i.e., the basic and common understanding of the economic law theory,[38] and the common knowledge of the construction and operation of economic law system. The consensus in the two aspects is paramount for promoting both the theoretical and system development of economic law.

The formation of economic law consensus is attributed to multiple approaches and factors. This section attempts to demonstrate that all major "reform decisions" have an important impact on the formation of economic law consensus; their implementation have brought about the changes on ideas, theories and systems, they not only promote the overall development of legal science, but accumulate economic law consensus. The "reform decisions" affect the formulation of public policies in many domains and the adjustment of relevant systems; while these policies and systems are materials for economic law study, as well as sources and components of the economic law system. Therefore, the "reform decisions", which are an overall guideline for the theoretical innovation and system change, play an especially important role in the accumulation of economic law consensus. This is confirmed from the prosperity phase and leap-forward development of economic law theory and system.[39]

In fact, all the "reform decisions" have something in common or the same focal points. For example, some important "relations", including those between the government and the market, between the government and enterprises or individuals, or between the central and local governments, have always been the issues of concern. Closely related to these "relations" are a series of important "regimes", such as the overall economic regime and the specific economic, financial or planning regimes. Closely related to these "relations" and "regimes" is several important "mechanisms", like price mechanism, competition mechanism and execution mechanism. No matter it is the "relation", "regime" or "mechanism", they shall be reflected in the relevant "system", since the adjustment or reform of relations, regimes or mechanisms is implemented through the establishment and improvement of systems (particularly the economic law system that reflects the economic law consensus), which has a great effect on promoting reform. It can be seen that there is an internal link between the "reform decisions" and the economic law consensus.

---

[37]In recent years, the academic community has paid more and more attention to draw consensuses on economic law, which will help to solve the problems about theoretical accumulation. Xiao (2002a), pp. 175–81; Qiu (2013), Issue 4.

[38]In each important stage of the development of economic law, the academic community would review the economic law studies, most of which contain some economic law consensus. Wang and Cui (1989); Wang and Zhao (1999); Zeng and Xiao (2001).

[39]The "reform decisions" made in the mid-1980s and mid-1990s have brought forth the prosperity phase and leap-forward development in China's economic law theory and system, laying basis for the coexistence of economic law theories. Xiao (2002), pp. 162–168; Zhang et al. (1995), Issue 4.

Such clue as "relations-regimes/mechanisms-systems" is not only a logic main line running through the "reform decisions", but an important train of thought for understanding the economic law consensus. After it is simplified into "relations-regimes-system", this clue will help to discover the internal relation between the "reform decisions" at different stages, reveal the internal consistency between the "reform decisions" and the economic law consensus, become the important source for forming and developing the economic law consensus, and profoundly understand the relation between policies and laws (esp. the relation between the reform policy of the ruling body and economic law), thus promoting the theoretical and practical studies of the relations between reform and economic law, and between economic policy and economic law.[40]

Based on the above considerations, this section will examine, by interpreting the "reform decisions" with milestone significance, the main problems that are directly related to the economic law, and reveal their important influence on the development of economic law, especially on the formation of economic law consensus.[41] Moreover, it will explain why some economic law consensus could be incorporated into the recent "reform decisions", so as to demonstrate their respective independency and internal consistency, and the important influence of economic law consensus on the overall rule of law construction.

In reference to China's two important "reform decisions", this section firstly demonstrate their important impact on the formation of economic law consensus. On this basis, by placing focus on the 2013 "Reform Decision" and following the "relations-regimes-systems" clue, this section explores the internal link between "reform decisions" and economic law consensus. It is of great benefit for further condensing the economic law consensus and promoting the theoretical and system development of economic law.

2.2.2 *Important "Reform Decisions" Since 1978 and Their Impact on Economic Law Consensus*

Since China unveiled its grand reform strategy in 1978 and started comprehensive deepening of reform in 2013, a number of "reform decisions" had come out during this period, some focus on special domains, while some care about the overall situation, but all of them come down in one continuous line. From a historical perspective, the "reform decisions" adopted at the three third plenary sessions in 1984, 1993 and 2013 are of great importance on the formation and development of economic law

[40]Economic law has some traits of policies, which is an important consensus in the economic law community, and concerns the understanding of the relation between economic policy and economic law. Shi and Deng (1998), pp. 55–66; Wang (1999).

[41]Since the consensus is formed by history, we have to analyze the economic law consensus from a historical perspective. In fact, all of the researches on economic law consensus pay attention to the historical theoretical views or important systems.

consensus. Despite of separate focus, the three "reform decisions" are interrelated and containing some issues that draw continuous attention. To fully understand the 2013 "Reform Decision", we need to go over the previous two decisions, so that we can learn about their historical origins and clarify the future direction of the reform and its connection with economic law consensus.

2.2.2.1 A Review of the 1984 Reform Decision

The 1984 Reform Decision[42] has an important impact on the formation of the system consensus of China's new-born economic law. In the early days of the development of economic law, there had been short of theoretical consensus in this regard, so the formation of system consensus seemed more precious. It is based on the system consensus that the theoretical consensus on economic law could be further developed.

From the perspective of economic law and following the relation-system-institution clue, it is easy to find that the 1984 Reform Decision has made important breakthroughs in the following five aspects:

(1) In the aspect of relations between subjects: properly resolve the relations between the state and enterprises and between enterprises and employees by revolving round invigoration of enterprises—the center of the overall reform. The knowledge about the two relations lays an important basis for understanding the government-market relation, forming the binary architecture of the economic law subjects, and for raising the "binary structure" hypothesis in the realm of economic law.
(2) In the aspect of regime improvement: the traditional regime is characterized with some prominent problems, i.e., "the duties of government and enterprises are mixed; the roles of commodity production, value law and market are ignored; serious egalitarianism in distributions; and enterprises lack the autonomy they deserve". In view of this, the 1984 Reform Decision proposes to expand the enterprise autonomy to enable them to "become a legal person possessing certain rights and obligations", which has not only promoted the establishment of the legal person system in civil law, but cultivated the regulation receptors in economic law, and identified the subjects under macro-economic control and market regulation in the realm of economic law.
(3) In the aspect of system adjustment: the 1984 Reform Decision stresses to "consciously apply the law of value and implement a planned commodity economic system", further improve the taxation system, reform the fiscal and financial systems, and "pay attention to macro-economic regulation",[43] which is regarded as the prototype for the macro-economic control system, and has promoted the

---

[42]The 1984 "Reform Decision" is short for the *Decision of the Central Committee of the CPC on Reform of the Economic System*, which was adopted at the Third Plenary Session of the 12th CPC Central Committee on October 20, 1984.

[43]This "Reform Decision" stresses "to be good at comprehensively using economic leverages such as price, taxation and loan on the basis of keeping abreast of economic trends, so as to adjust the

formation of the consensus on macro-economic control law in the realm of economic law.

(4) In the aspect of government functions: the 1984 Reform Decision emphasizes that the main government functions include "developing strategies, plans, guidelines and policies for economic and social development; collecting and disseminating economic information; learning and utilizing economic regulation means; formulating economic laws and regulations and supervising their enforcement", thereby defining the important functions of the government which is the economic law subject.

(5) In the aspect of legal system construction: it attaches importance to economic legislation and economic justice,[44] which helps to raise people's awareness of the importance in formulation and enforcement of economic law.

Based on the above understanding on system construction (esp. the preceding third, fourth and fifth paragraphs), the state keeps making progress in system innovation, function transformation and legal system construction, and many important economic law systems have come out after the 1984 Reform Decision. For example, in 1984 China carried out an important tax reform and introduced several tax systems,[45] laying basis for establishing the macro-economic control system in the future. For another example, in order to accord with the economic restructuring at that time, the state introduced a number of important legal systems[46] about enterprises, price and other domains, and specially established the central bank system[47] before

---

proportional relations between total supply and total demand, between accumulation and consumption; regulate the flow of financial, material and human resources; optimize the layout of industrial structure and productivity; balance market supply and demand; and encourage foreign trade". It is fairly close to the currently prevailing concept of macro-economic control.

[44]According to this "Reform Decision", "as result of the economic regime reform and the development of the national economy, more and more economic relations and the norms for economic activities need to be specified by law". The national legislative body shall speed up economic legislation, the courts shall raise efficiency in the trial of economic cases, the procuratorates shall worker harder in dealing with economic crimes, and the judicial organs shall actively provide legal services for economic construction".

[45]On September 18, 1984, the *Decision of the Standing Committee of NPC on Authorizing the State Council to Reform the Industrial and Commercial Tax System and Issue Relevant Draft Tax Regulations for Trial Application* was adopted. According to the decision, the State Council came up with six draft tax regulations (product tax, VAT tax, salt tax, business tax, resource tax, and SOEs' income tax) for trial application. On April 10, 1985, the *Decision of the NPC on Authorizing the State Council to Formulate Provisional Provisions or Regulations on Economic Restructuring and Opening-up* was adopted, marking that the State Council's "legislative work" stepped onto on the fast track since then.

[46]In the domain of enterprises, there are *Enterprise Bankruptcy Law of the People's Republic of China* (Trial) (adopted at the 18th Session of the Sixth NPC Standing Committee on Dec 2, 1986), and the *Law of the People's Republic of China on Industrial Enterprises Owned by the Whole People* (adopted at the 1st Session of the Seventh NPC on Apr 13, 1988). In the domain of prices, there are the Regulations *of the People's Republic of China on Price Control* (released by the State Council on Sep 11, 1987).

[47]Refer to the *Decision of the State Council on the People's Bank of China to Specially Perform the Functions of the Central Bank* promulgated on Sep 17, 1983.

unveiling the "Reform Decision", thus constructing the basic framework for the later financial regulation system. The establishment of the above-mentioned systems is especially conducive to the formation of system consensus on economic law.

Revisiting the "reform decision" and system construction in the early stage of China's reform, we can find the connection between the system construction in the past and at the present, which helps to draw the economic law consensus that might be formed at that time. Since the economic law was a new thing at that time and there were many theoretical differences, the formation of system consensus is more conducive to accumulating theoretical consensus and promoting the overall development of economic law.

2.2.2.2 Interpretation of the 1993 Reform Decision

The 1993 Reform Decision[48] was of great significance for the economic law that remained at its infancy. In contrast to the 1984 Reform Decision that stresses to build consensus on the economic law system, the 1993 Reform Decision is beyond the scope of system consensus, and reaches out to theoretical consensus.[49] The 1993 Reform Decision elaborates on the theories and corresponding systems of the market economy, and introduces the internationally recognized theoretical basis and system basis of economic law, which is undoubtedly important for consensus-building in the realm of economic law.

If we stick to the economic law perspective and keep following the "relation-system-institution" clue, it will be easy for us to find that the 1993 Reform Decision has achieved some important breakthroughs in the following five aspects:

(1) In the aspect of inter-subject relation: the 1993 Reform Decision stresses to establish a modern enterprise system that suits well with the market economy, and also build an appropriate government-enterprise relation free from direct government intervention with the production and management activities of enterprises, which lays the basis for properly handling the government-market relation. Besides, this decision confirms that there is need to implement a tax-sharing system, i.e., establish a central tax system and a local tax system, for properly dealing with the relation between the central and local governments, which lays the foundation for mobilizing the central and local enthusiasm and ensuring the provision of public goods at the central and local levels.

(2) In the aspect of system improvement: the 1993 Reform Decision emphasizes to implement the market economic system and ensures that the market plays a

---

[48]The 1993 Reform Decision (*the Decision of the CPC Central Committee on Several Issues Concerning the Establishment of a Socialist Market Economic System*) was adopted at the Third Plenary Session of the 14th CPC Central Committee on Nov 14, 1993. The title of this document does not contain the word "Reform", but it is a reform decision in the "substantive sense", since the building of a new market economic system is counted as a great reform in China.

[49]Since the 1993 Reform Decision came out, the Chinese economic law community reached an unprecedentedly high degree of theoretical consensus, and began to think about the economic law issues based on the common market economy theory.

fundamental role in resource allocation under the state macro-economic control, thereby clarifying the government-market relation and their respective roles, and revealing the economic regime basis for the development of economic law, so that "economic law shall be based on the modern market economy" has become the basic consensus of the academic community.

(3) In the aspect of market rules: the 1993 Reform Decision emphasizes to regulate market behavior, break down regional and sectoral divisions and blockades, oppose unfair competition, create an environment of equal competition, and form a large, unified, open, competitive and orderly market, thus forming a market regime which is basis for economic law regulation.
(4) In the aspect of government functions: the 1993 Reform Decision requires to establish a sound macro-economic control system mainly based on indirect means, so as to ensure the healthy operation of the national economy, which has further clarified the macro-economic function of the government as the economic law subject.
(5) In the aspect of legal system construction: the 1993 Reform Decision confirms to establish a corresponding legal system around the above four aspects, so that "market economy is the rule-of-law economy" and "state strengthening economic legislation" have become a common consensus.

The preceding third, fourth and fifth paragraphs, based on the above-mentioned inter-subject relation and regime improvement, have discussed the construction of several systems; the improvement of these systems helps to establish the basic system of economic law, and form the "binary structure" consensus on macro-economic control law and market regulation law, and then promote the formation of other consensuses. Although such consensus was seldom mentioned before,[50] the macro-economic law and market regulation law as the main components of the economic law system since 1993 have gradually become the theoretical claims of many scholars, which are directly influenced by the "reform decision".

Take macro-economic control law for example, the 1993 Reform Decision states that the main tasks of macro-economic control are "maintaining the basic balance of economic aggregate and optimizing economic structure". In order to fulfill these tasks, China shall "establish the planning, financial and fiscal mechanisms that are mutually cooperative and restrictive, and strengthen comprehensive coordination of economic operations. The planning mechanism proposes the goals and tasks of national economic and social development, as well as the economic policies that need to be implemented. The financial mechanism (central bank) aims to stabilize the currency value, regulate the total currency supply, and maintain the balance of international payments. The fiscal mechanism employs the means of budget and tax to regulate economic structure and social distribution. By employing monetary and fiscal policies, we shall adjust the basic balance between total demand and total supply, and cooperate with industrial policies, so as to promote the coordinated development of the national economy and society". These ideas and corresponding system construction embody the basic rules of macro-economic control and the

[50]Zhang (1992), Issue 5; Zhang (1993), Issue 1.

common practices of all countries. It is important for the formation of a consensus on macro-economic control law.

For another example, with regard to market regulation law, the 1993 Reform Decision proposes to "improve and strengthen the management and supervision of the market. Establish normal market entry, market competition and a market transaction order, ensure fair trade, equal competition, protect the legitimate rights and interests of operators and consumers... establish an authoritative market law enforcement and supervision agencies". It is so important for the development of the theory and system of market regulation law.

Generally speaking, after the introduction of the 1993 Reform Decision, the theoretical and system consensus in the entire economic law community have increased notably.[51] The knowledge about the important relations between the government and the market, and between the central and local governments, as well as about the reform direction of the economic, financial and competitive regimes has become clear enough, so that the consensus on the economic law system and theory has increased greatly.

2.2.2.3 Brief Summary: A Brief Comparison Between the Two Sample "Decisions" and Their Impact

Through analysis of the above two examples, we can confirm that the two "reform decisions" have important influence on the formation and accumulation of economic law consensus. The 1984 Reform Decision came out at the time when China's economic law was just formed, the legal science community did not have rich theoretical accumulation or enough knowledge about the system in the realm of economic law, and the differences were more than consensus. The economic, financial and enterprise systems established by the 1984 Reform Decision are particularly helpful for the formation of an economic law consensus that had just sprouted. By the time when the 1993 Reform Decision was adopted, China's economic law had developed to a certain extent with system consensus increasing notably. But on the whole, in the first 15 years of the reform and opening up, the 1993 Reform Decision exerted a more significant impact on the economic law consensus, and the impact was mainly unidirectional, meaning that the poorly accumulated economic law consensus was yet able to have a great impact on the Reform Decision.

In terms of inter-subject relations, the 1984 Reform Decision cares about the relation between the state and enterprises, especially the enterprise autonomy, which is consistent with the later hot topics such as state-market relation and economic freedom right of market subjects (paying attention to economic freedom right is an important consensus in the economic law community, which is reflected in the 2013

[51] After the implementation of the market economic system, the basic views of the leading economic law scholars have gradually converged, thus forming lots of important economic law consensus. Some scholars believe that the formation of economic law consensus "should be firstly attributed to the transformation from planned economy to market economy". It also illustrates the importance of the 1993 Reform Decision on the formation of economic law consensus. Qiu (2005), Issue 6.

Reform Decision[52]). In contrast, the 1993 Reform Decision is more comprehensive and profound, since it not only stresses to establish a modern enterprise system, and cultivate reliable market subjects for forming a market system, but focuses on the relation between the central and local governments, which heralds in the tax sharing-based fiscal regime.

In terms of regime and system, unlike the 1984 Reform Decision that upholds a planned commodity economic system, the theme of the 1993 Reform Decision is to establish a market economic system. Since the two economic systems are substantially different, their corresponding legal systems (especially the economic law systems) differ greatly, which directly affects the formation of economic law consensus. It is because of the establishment of the market economic system that various types of economic law systems are built and improved, which have enhanced the system and theoretical consensuses of economic law, and laid an important foundation for the all-round and in-depth reform kicked off in 2013.

2.2.3 Relation Between the 2013 Reform Decision and Economic Law Consensus

Through 20 years' exploration since 1993, the 2013 Reform Decision[53] that advocates comprehensive deepening of the reform was finally unveiled, with the overall goal of "promoting the modernization of the state governance system and governance ability". In order to improve the state governance system, we shall ensure that the reform is "systematic, integrated and coordinated",[54] so that the system construction that reflects the spirit of reform is more "comprehensive" and "in-depth". From the perspective of economic system, the 2013 reform keeps revolving round the promotion of the market economic system, but it is more profound and extensive than the 1993 reform. If its goals could be achieved, the 2013 reform will vigorously improve the state governance system on the whole. From a legal point of view, although the law-based governance in economy is directly related to the regulation and system improvement in the realm of economic law, it also requires the integrated regulation by various sectoral laws such as civil and commercial law and administrative

[52]The 2013 Reform Decision highlights to "expedite the formation of a modern market system where enterprises operate business independently and compete on an equal footing, consumers make free choices and spend money on what they like, goods and factors are flowing freely"; the enterprise autonomy and consumer rights involved therein manifest the economic freedom right of market subjects. Zhang (2004a), pp. 406–408.

[53]The *Decision of the CCCPC on Some Major Issues Concerning Comprehensively Deepening the Reform* was adopted at the Third Plenary Session of the 18th Central Committee of the Communist Party of China on Nov 12, 2013.

[54]Paying attention to "systematic, integrated and coordinated" is an important economic law consensus. The realm of economic law always emphasizes systematic thought, integrated thought and coordinative thought, there are rich research findings in this regard, for example, Liu and Wang (2000), Vol. 2; Kong (2005); Liu (2006); Zhang (2001a), Vol. 2; Zhang (2011), Issue 1.

law, and even the means other than laws. Therefore, we shall gain a comprehensive understanding of the overall goals of the modernization of state governance ability, which will guide us to interpret the relation between economic law and other sectoral laws, and the value of legal norms and other norms.

The afore-mentioned "relation-system-institution" clue is also applicable to the interpretation of the 2013 Reform Decision, since it not only reflects the basic logic of the successive reform decisions and their interrelations, but demonstrates their connection with the economic law consensus. More than that, this clue reveals the inherent logic of the formation of the economic law system, i.e., "defining relations—improving regime—consummating system".

2.2.3.1 Relation: Between Government and Market

From mercantilists to physiocrats, from A. Smith to J. M. Keynes, and from westerners to the Chinese, the people around the world have never stopped exploring the government-market relation in the past centuries. Since the implementation of the reform and opening up in 1978, China has made this relation a key content of the successive "reform decisions". For example, the 1984 Reform Decision focuses on the relation between the state and enterprises, while the 1993 Reform Decision explicitly presents to build a government-enterprise relation based on the modern enterprise system and satisfying the requirements of the market economy. But the government-enterprise relation is in essence a kind of government-market relation with its foundational status underscored in the two decisions. The market is a domain for transactions and game between enterprises, between enterprises and consumers, and between enterprises and other subjects, it is able to fully reflect the autonomous right, option right and freedom right of the above-mentioned subjects, so the state-market relation is of constitutional significance; in other words, the state-market relation is the embodiment of the constitutional state-national relation in economic domain.

In reference to the *Constitution of the People's Republic of China*, the first paragraph of Article 15 provides that China implements a market economic system, while the second and third paragraphs respectively set out the state responsibilities in macro-economic control and market regulation, define the economic functions of the state under the market economic condition, which create an important constitutional framework and basis for understanding the government-market relation. Such provisions help to explain why the constitution and economic law make the government-market relation as an important and generalized "regulated object", and why there is internal consistency between the constitution and economic law,[55] and why the "reform decisions" are closely related to the economic law consensus.

The government-market relation or the state-national relation, and the resulting "binary structure" of subjects[56] have a direct impact on both public and private laws,

[55]Zhang (2013b), Issue 3; Zhang (2013c), Issue 4.

[56]The "binary structure" of subjects is also applicable to analyzing the government-business relation, government-enterprise relation, and government-society relation. Zhang (2004a), pp. 33–37.

since each legal territory makes legal regulation within the framework of the aforesaid relation. In the realm of economic law, the definitions of government-market boundary, government functions and market roles, and the thought on legalization of the government-market relation[57] not only concern the sphere, scope, intensity and direction of macro-economic control and market regulation, but directly affect the scoping and content arrangement of the applicable legal norms, which will in turn directly impact the consensus on economic law theory and system.

For the above reason, the 2013 Reform Decision underscores that "the economic system reform shall focus on the comprehensive deepening of reform, while the core issue is to properly handle the government-market relation so as to let the market play a decisive role in resource allocation and let the government better perform its functions". According to the 2013 Reform Decision, in order to comprehensively deepen the reform, we shall address the problems in the economic system reform, and the top priority is to properly handle the government-market relation. To this end, we need to define the respective functions and roles of the government and the market, delimit their boundaries, give full play to the decisive role of the market in resource allocation, and better perform the government functions. We should not overemphasize the roles of the market or disregard or abandon the roles of the government, nor should we weaken or even deny the important effect of economic law. Based on an understanding of the roles of the market and the government, the following paragraphs will reveal their correlation with the economic law consensus.

(1) Analysis based on the market decisive role

In terms of the government-market relation, how to look at the roles of the market? How to transform the government functions? They are required questions for the reform and development. The answers to these questions, which represent the understanding of the law of market economy and the law of legal system construction, are essential to reaching concensus on the economic law theory and system construction.

The 2013 Reform Decision underscores "the decisive role of the market in resource allocation". Such argument once invoked heated discussions, and quite a number of people took it as a "major theoretical innovation". Before that, China acknowledged the "basic role" of the market in resource allocation, which is corresponding to the government-based macro-economic control. Now that we admit the coexistence of private economy and public economy, and take macro-economic control as strong backing, we should not deny the fundamentality of market-based resource allocation. The reason why we stress the "decisive role" of the market is to highlight its prominent efficiency in resource allocation. i.e., the resource allocation shall be at the mercy of the market which is more efficient than other mechanisms.

In fact, a genuine and narrowly-defined market economy is a domain where the subjects with private interests are making deals with each other; it is mainly embodied in the form of private economy. The decisive role of the market means that the market subjects with private interests make choices and decisions on their own, and affect the supply-demand pattern and resource allocation. But in the domain of

[57] Yue and Li (2010), Vol. 7, pp. 16–17.

public economy, resources may be allocated by the state through macro-economic control or resource redistribution.[58] Of course, the market is usually more efficient in resource allocation, so that we should "substantially reduce the direct government-based allocation" and implement "indirect macro-economic control". But the means of macro-economic control and market regulation shall be legalized[59] and constrained by the law. Based on the above understanding, "economic law is the law for the market economy" and "economic law is the modern law based on the modern market economy" have become a basic consensus in the economic law community. There is internal consistency between this consensus and the significant role of the market in resource allocation.

Each country may have different understandings of the importance of market economy in different periods. In China, the continuous development of market economy has enabled both authorities and private sectors to deepen their understanding of the market, but it does not mean that the real role of the market is given full play. Similarly, even if the "reform decisions" put forward the "decisive role of the market", it does not mean that the market "determines everything", but stresses that under the conditions of market economy, the resource allocation conforms to the common principles of market economy, and there shall be market rules, price mechanism and competition mechanism that freely play their roles, so that the market transactions are determined by market factors, rather than the government will. Such economy is a "market-based" economy; otherwise, it is no different from a planned economy where resources are allocated by the government. The argument that market plays a decisive role helps to clarify the government positioning, on this basis the government and the market, the public and private domains will respectively provide public and private goods to the society according to separate principles and rules. The resulting "binary structure" in theory and system is fairly important for the formation and development of economic law consensus.

In line with the above understanding of the market role, the 2013 Reform Decision also proposes that "letting the market determine resource allocation is the general law of market economy", which makes the role of the market as predominant as the "law". But the "dialectical approach" may not be overlooked, i.e., the decisive role of the market is limited to the resource allocation under the market economy condition, instead of universally valid. We may not give up the government-based macro-economic control and market regulation, or weaken the economic law system that regulates the control and regulatory behaviors. In all countries that implement the market economy, there will be market failures, which call for the macro-economic control and market regulation, as well as the corresponding legal restrictions. It is a common practice in all countries and an economic law consensus. "Historical experiences are worth noting"—the bumpy course of market economy development, especially the 2008 global economic crisis, is directly related to market failures,

---

[58]Musgrave and other scholars highlight the importance of the state-based resource allocation in the domain of public economy. There are also rich studies on the redistribution function of economic law. Qi (2008), Issue 4; Feng and Li (2012), Vol. 10.

[59]Zhou (1995), Issue 10; Wang (1995), Issue 3.

economic imbalances, and inadequate macro-economic control and market regulation of concerned countries.[60] If we ignore the effective economic law regulation, the economic imbalances and crises caused by a large number of market failures may occur frequently or aggravate.

In order to play the decisive role of the market, "we must actively and steadily promote the market-oriented reform in both breadth and depth, and substantially reduce the direct resource allocation by the government". Accordingly, the specific reforms are implemented to improve the basic economic system, modern market system, macro-economic control system and open economic system, which are directly and closely related to the scope of economic law regulation. For example, the modern market system and the open economic system are economic foundations for economic law regulation; the basic economic system lays the system basis for the implementation of economic law systems; the macro-economic control system is a major component of economic law.

In the final analysis, to underscore the decisive role of the market is for better promotion of development. To this end, we shall "uphold the major strategic judgment that development is the key to solve all problems in our country". In fact, all the goals and measures set out in the "reform decisions" intend for better development. Related to this, economic law is not only a law for market economy, but a law for promoting development, which is an important consensus in the economic law community.[61] Economic law distinguishes from the traditional law that simply solves disputes, because it stresses to promote the overall economic and social development from a larger time-space dimension. Among all kinds of system reforms, the traction of economic system reform is fairly important. Accordingly, in terms of the adjustment of legal systems, the economic law that is closely related to economic system reform also plays an important role. Economic law shall play a crucial part in guaranteeing the rationality and legitimacy of macro-economic control and market regulation, or in safeguarding the legitimate rights and interests of market subjects and maintaining market order. It can be said that without the effective and thorough implementation of economic law, we would have no legal means to guarantee the macro-economic control and market regulation which are necessary for the development of market economy, or safeguard the legal interests of market subjects and the market order for fair competition. Therefore, no matter it is relevant system reform or economic law regulation, they shall take the promotion of development as an important goal, thereby improving economic law in an all-round manner.

(2) Analysis based on the government functions

In order to properly deal with the government-market relation, we shall not only to play the decisive role of the market, but define and perform the government functions. From the perspective of economic law, among lots of government functions,

---

[60] Wu (2008), Issue 12; Yang (2009), Issue 1; Zhang (2009), Issue 3; Gu (2010).

[61] There have been rich studies on the development category, development ideas and development rights in the realm of economic law. Cheng (1999), Issue 1; Shan, et al. (2000), Issue 5; Zhang (2012), Issue 2.

the economic function is so important that it affects the dominant position of the government in economic law, directly concerns the regulatory means and regulatory sectors of economic law, as well as the formation of economic law consensus.

Through years' exploration, the economic law community mainly divides the government economic functions into macro-economic control and market regulation, which is a basic economic law consensus. The macro-economic control function is performed to maintain a benign operation of the macro-economy, promote stable economic growth, prevent and mitigate the risks in economic cycles or resolve economic crises. The market regulation function is performed to strengthen market supervision, maintain market order and promote fair competition. According to the 2013 Reform Decision, "the responsibilities and roles of the government are performed to maintain macro-economic stability, strengthen and optimize public services, guarantee fair competition, improve market supervision, safeguard market order, promote sustainable development and common prosperity, and make up for market failures". It accords with the existing theoretical consensus of economic law, or it embodies such theoretical consensus to a considerable extent.

The economic functions of modern government are directly related to the solution of market failures, while the existence of market failures and the need to solve them are the premise and motivation for economic law to come into being. The above-mentioned theoretical consensus of economic law, which summarizes the law of emergence and development of economic law in all countries, is attributed to the influences of the 1993 and 2013 "reform decisions". Generally speaking, the market failures and the resulting economic imbalance are the basic problems under economic law regulation.[62] The widely concerned issues, such as the impediment to competition, provision of public goods, external effect, information bias and unfair distribution, are blamed for market failures. They cannot be solved or effectively solved by market mechanism and traditional sectoral laws, thus requiring the government to perform its economic functions. According to the 2013 Reform Decision, the government economic functions are mainly performed to deal with market failures. For example, to resolve the problems of impediment to competition and information bias, the government shall intensify market supervision, maintain market order, and guarantee fair competition; to stabilize the macro-economic operation, the government shall perform the typical function of macro-economic control; to maintain sustainable development, the government shall properly deal with the external effect and provide public services; to achieve the goal of common prosperity, the government shall effectively solve the problem of unfair distribution. It can be seen that all government economic functions are directly related to the resolution of market failures, and the economic law regulation is an important legal approach for solving market failures.

With regard to performance of government economic functions, the 2013 Reform Decision emphasizes that the most prominent problem at present is "too much government intervention and inadequate regulation", which is indeed a long-standing reality. In response to excessive government intervention that affects the role of the market,

---

[62] Xi (2011), Vol. 8.

we should reduce government intervention, give the market more freedom to effectively realize its resource allocation function; meanwhile, in response to the negative effect of the market mechanism, we should put the right supervision in place and strengthen market regulation. Since direct government intervention is different from indirect macro-economic control, we cannot simply equate government intervention with state intervention.[63] Given this, in the realm of economic law, it is the improper government intervention that needs to be restricted.

In addition, in order to effectively perform the government economic functions, we shall pay attention to the division of labor between the central government and local governments, which is directly related to the hierarchy of public goods. To this end, the 2013 Reform Decision proposes that the central government shall strengthen its responsibilities and abilities in macro-economic control, while local governments shall conscientiously perform their duties in public services and market supervision. It is an economic law consensus. For example, the economic law community generally holds that the macro-economic control power is owned by the central government[64] instead of local governments. In view of this, we underscore the macro-economic responsibilities and abilities of the central government and distinguish them from the functions of local governments, which is consistent with the established consensus in the economic law community.

The above understanding of the government responsibilities in macro-economic control corresponds to the functions or tasks of the macro-economic control itself. According to the 2013 Reform Decision, the main task of macro-economic control is to "maintain the balance of economic aggregate, coordinate the major economic structures and optimize the layout of productive forces, mitigate the fluctuations brought by economic cycles, guard against regional and systematic risks, stabilize market expectations, and achieve healthy and sustainable economic development", so that the goal of macro-economic control will return to prevention of risks, delay of economic cycles, structural optimization, and balance of economic aggregate. This is particularly helpful for avoiding the generalized understanding of macro-economic control as before and preventing certain administrative interventions from being equated with macro-economic control. The responsibilities and tasks in macro-economic control, as defined above, should not only be followed by government departments, but taken as an important economic law consensus.

The main means of macro-economic control include fiscal policy, monetary policy and other relevant policies. In this regard, the 2013 Reform Decision emphasizes to "improve the macro-economic system that is guided by the national development strategy and planning, and mainly relying on the means of fiscal policy and monetary policy". The macro-economic control system herein accords with the understanding of economic law community. Based on the basic proposition that "economic law is legalized economic policies", the legalization of a large number of macro-economic control policies and means has constituted the basic system of macro-economic

[63]Many scholars hold that it is inappropriate to equate macro-economic control with government intervention. Yang (2009), p270.

[64]Li and Hu (2002), Issue 2; Zhang (2001b), Issue 3.

control law, which covers the laws respectively for economic control, financial control and planning control. It is an important consensus in the realm of economic law. This consensus is of great significance for solving the problems of generalizing macro-economic control, and equating it with government intervention.

2.2.3.2 Regime: Framework for Operation of Relevant Mechanisms

The above positioning of the government-market relation lays an important foundation for the overall economic system reform. The comprehensive reform of the economic system is to be achieved by means of improving a large number of economic mechanisms, and the reform itself provides an important framework and guarantee for the effective operation of various mechanisms. No matter it is the economic system or the corresponding economic mechanism, it is of significant impact on the emergence and development of economic law.[65] It is an important dimension for understanding the close relation between the reform decisions and the economic law consensus.

Based on the previous understanding of the government-market relation, the state shall improve the corresponding macro-economic control and market regulation system, and establish a modern market system, so as to build a framework for decentralization of economic power between the state and the national. As mentioned earlier, as long as a country implements the market economy system, it needs to have a modern market system. However, the degree of marketization in some domains of China is yet enough, with improper government intervention remaining in existence, which directly affects the free choice of market subjects and the effective resource allocation. Given this, the government economic functions shall be limited to macro-economic control and market regulation to ensure stable economic growth, maintain market order and promote fair competition. It can be seen that what the government should do is to strengthen necessary control and regulation, and avoid improper administrative intervention, so as to create conditions for maintaining benign economic operation and good market order. At the same time, it is necessary to intensify the economic law constraint for the control and regulation behaviors, which has been an important economic law consensus for a long time.

No matter it is control or regulation, neither of them is inseparable from the relevant economic systems and specific mechanisms. All types of economic systems shall be legalized in order to provide an effective legal framework for the operation of relevant mechanisms. The legalization of economic systems may be embodied in the "economic constitution" of certain countries,[66] and prevalent in the realm of economic law to become a major content of economic law, thus making the "system

[65]Zhang et al. (1993), pp. 4–7.

[66]Chapter 10 of the *Basic Law of the Federal Republic of Germany* has specific provisions for the fiscal system of Germany. The second chapter in Part VI of the *Constitution of the Bolivarian Republic of Venezuela* sets out specific provisions for the systems of budget, taxation, monetary system and macro-economic control and regulation.

law" an important factor that affects the structure of economic law system, and an operational basis for the specific control system and regulation system.

Therefore, there are multiple regulations for the specific fiscal system, tax system, financial system, investment system, price system and competition system. These regulations contain the content about the distribution of macro-economic control power and market regulation power, as well as a coordinative mechanism for government departments, so as to ensure the effective functioning of relevant systems and provide a legal framework for the benign operation of relevant mechanisms.

In fact, within the framework of the statutory economic system, it is increasingly important to strengthen the coordination of relevant policies and systems, so as to ensure the benign operation of relevant mechanisms. To this end, the 2013 Reform Decision emphasizes to "promote the establishment of macro-economic control goals and the institutionalization of policy instruments, strengthen the coordination of fiscal policies, monetary policies, and industry and price policies... to form a mechanism for coordinating the international macro-economic policies". Correspondingly, in the realm of macro-economic control law, we shall firstly emphasize the coordination between the fiscal control system and the financial control system, and make them consistent with the goals and the means of control that are decided by the planning control system. Besides, we also need to coordinate the cooperation of fiscal control and financial control systems with industry control and price control systems, which is very important for economic restructuring, regulation of general price level, balance of economic aggregate, and stabilization of economic growth. In addition, while stressing the coordination and cooperation of the above-mentioned systems, we shall also pay attention to their consistency with the macro-economic control system at the international level, and promote the establishment and improvement of the mechanisms for coordinating the institutions that implement all systems.

The coordination mechanism is equally important in the realms of macro-economic control and market regulation. In order to solve the problems of power division and discordance in market regulation, the 2013 Reform Decision emphasizes "unification" in many aspects, e.g., implement a unified market access system, establish fair, open and transparent market rules, "reform the market supervision system and implement unified market supervision", "clean up and abolish the regulations and practices that hinder the national unified market and fair competition", which has laid an important system basis for the "unified market" and "unified supervision" required by the market economy. Moreover, it is necessary to prohibit the behaviors of destroying the unified market and hampering market competition, i.e., "forbid and punish all kinds of behaviors that illegally implement favorable policies, oppose local protection, monopoly and unfair competition", and ensure the implementation and improvement of the anti-monopoly law and the anti-unfair competition law in the realm of market regulation.[67]

[67]The goal of the above reform is to form a "unified" and "orderly" market. Since the "establishment of a unified, open, competitive and orderly market system is the basis for the market to play a decisive role in resource allocation", it is very important to promote the improvement of the market regulation law.

In addition to the problems in the systems and mechanisms on the whole, we shall also care about the improvement of specific systems. For example, the improvement of the economic system is of great significance for the overall reform. To this end, the 2013 Reform Decision emphasizes that "a scientific fiscal and tax system is the system guarantee to optimize resource allocation, maintain market unity, promote social equity, and achieve long-term stability in the country". In order to better improve the fiscal and tax system, we need to establish several important "mechanisms". For example, in order to improve the budget system, it is necessary to "establish a multi-year budget balancing mechanism", "establish standardized and reasonable debt management and risk early-warning mechanisms for both the central and local governments", and "improve the general transfer payment growth mechanism". Related to this, we shall also "establish a transparent and standardized investment and financing mechanism for urban construction". It can be seen that the systems provide an effective operational framework for the mechanisms, while the latter plays an important role in the improvement of the former.

2.2.3.3 System: Observation from the Perspective of Economic Law

No matter it is the above-mentioned government-market relation, or the various regimes and specific operational mechanisms established on basis of this relation, they must be embodied and implemented in the form of systems. Many of these systems are in the realm of economic law, so they need to be examined from the perspective of economic law. It is able to further reveal the internal correlation both in the "relation-system-institution" chain and between the reform decisions and the economic law consensus.

(1) Important "relations" requiring adjustment of the economic law system

Among the many factors affecting the formation and development of economic law systems, the government-market relation is no doubt of paramount significance.[68] Besides, the relation between the central and local governments, the competitive relations between enterprises, and the relation between enterprises and consumers are closely associated with the relevant economic regimes and economic law systems[69]; they on the one hand affect the generation of relevant economic law systems, and on the other hand need effective adjustment of economic law systems.

Simply from the perspective of the government-market relation, in order to play the decisive role of the market, the macro-economic control and market regulation

[68]The government-market relation is so important that "government" and "market" have become the keywords for studying the general principles of economic law. Guan (2009), Issue 4.

[69]The relation between the central government and local governments concerns multiple laws such as the fiscal law; the competitive relation concerns the anti-monopoly law and the anti-unfair competition law; and the relation between enterprises and consumers concern the consumer protection law. Generally speaking, properly handling these important relations is inseparable from the adjustment of economic law, which makes economic law occupy an important position in the legal system.

behaviors of the government shall be regulated to ensure the rationality and legitimacy of those behaviors, and protect the economic freedom right of market subjects. For this purpose, there is need to establish an effective economic law system, which exactly manifests the value of economic law and the reason for its existence. In fact, as a branch of law, economic law also has the function of regulating the subject behaviors: on the one hand, it regulates the government regulation behaviors in the economic domain (different from the government administrative behavior in the administrative domain, or the government guarantee behavior in the social domain); on the other hand, it regulates the coping behaviors of market subjects, including their horizontal coping behavior (e.g., the competitive behaviors of enterprises) and vertical coping behavior (e.g., the behaviors to avoid regulation). The economic law system thereby established will be more capable of solving market failures and government failures.

While paying great attention to the decisive role of the market, we shall give a "better" play to the economic function of the government. Even if we are comprehensively deepening the reform, we may not go from one extreme to the other, but learn the historical lessons brought about by the market defects and shortcomings, admit the importance of the government-based macro-economic control and market regulation, and recognize the necessity to regulate the control and regulation behaviors. Therefore, the government shall be bound by economic law when performing its control and regulation functions, and earnestly abide by the law of the market, instead of exercising any improper administrative intervention in the name of "control and regulation", or infringing on the rights and interests of market subjects and harming the market vitality. Besides, the market regulation of the government shall be a genuine regulation behavior that follows the law of the market, so that the government will effectively regulate the market activities through positive incentives and negative restrictions, for the sake of safeguarding the market order and fair competition, and playing the role of the market in a better way.

In a certain sense, the government economic function determines the scope and objects under the economic law regulation, and also determines the system of economic law. The macro-economic control function and its related planning control, fiscal control and financial control, which are underscored in the 2013 Reform Decision, constitute the basic framework of the macro-economic control law. The provisions for the market supervision function of the government—mainly involve anti-monopoly, anti-unfair competition, and consumer protection—are in the realm of market regulation law. The composition of the system of economic law is able to fully exhibit the internal consistency between the "reform decisions" and the economic law consensus.

(2) System adjustment triggered by changes on regimes and mechanisms

The modernization of the national governance system requires, inter alia, strengthening economic governance and improving various economic regimes. The improvement of the economic regimes and mechanisms will bring about corresponding adjustments to the economic law system. The system adjustment triggered by the changes in regimes and mechanisms is an important path for forming the economic law system.

The "reform decisions" made by China at different stages—a ruling blueprint of the ruling subject—are actually the plans for continuously improving the decisions or reform programs of the relevant systems. As transformed or implemented by competent state organs, these decisions or plans will bring about changes in many aspects such as legislation, law enforcement and justice, and will directly affect the system changes in the realm of economic law. For example, the 2013 Reform Decision proposes to "establish a modern fiscal system", "improve the tax system", "implement a comprehensively standardized, open and transparent budget system", and "establish a system where the powers are compatible with expending responsibilities", "implement a unified market access system", "gradually replace the paid-in registered capital registration system with the subscription registration system", "reform the stock issuance registration system", "improve the national and local tax collection and management system"; all of them will lead to the changes on the economic system and economic mechanism which are under the economic law regulation; given this, there is need for the establishment, revision, innovation or improvement of many economic law systems.

Many of the above institutional reforms are triggered by the changes in systems and mechanisms. For example, the next-step reform of China is to reform the economic system, so the relevant budget system, tax system, national debt system, and transfer payment system shall be adjusted accordingly. For another example, due to the changes in the financial supervision system and mechanism, China has to adjust the stock issuance system accordingly. Relatively speaking, the 2013 Reform Decision pays more attention to the reform of the economic system, and cares less about the financial system and investment system.[70] In view of this, the institutions which are associated with the changes in the economic system and mechanism will become the focus of reform.

In contrast to other sectoral laws, the legislation of China's economic law remains an arduous task. The changes in systems and mechanisms initiated by the state are usually accompanied by the establishment, revision and abolition of economic law systems. However, some existing systems and mechanisms are yet complete enough, and the relevant economic law consensus is not cohesive and influential enough, so there is still a long way to go for China to fulfill the system construction of economic law.

---

[70] After introducing the 1993 Reform Decision, China unveiled some specific "reform decisions" on its fiscal, financial and investment systems, including the *Decision of the State Council on Implementing the Tax Sharing Fiscal Administration System* (GuoFa [1993] No. 85) on December 15, 1993, the *Decision of the State Council on the Reform of the Financial System* (GuoFa [1993] No. 91) on December 25, 1993, and the *Decision of the State Council on the Reform of the Investment System* (GuoFa [2004] No. 20) on July 16, 2004, which have a great impact on the formation of economic law consensus.

(3) Impact of economic law consensus on system reform

The preceding paragraphs have discussed the important consensuses on the regulatory scope, basic framework, economic basis, essential issues, basic assumptions and regulated objects of economic law. Thanks to the implementation of several "reform decisions", all kinds of economic law consensuses have been strengthened; and some of them are included into or manifested by certain "reform decisions". In fact, where there is more developed economic law, the theories will be more elaborate, and the resulting consensuses will have a greater impact on the "reform decisions" and a higher value of guidance on the institutional reform.

After more than 30 years of development, China's economic law system that came out with the reform and opening-up keeps perfecting, and the theoretical consensus of economic law has increased notably.[71] However, many people's understanding of the economic law theory still lingers in the 1980 s, which is adverse for the overall rule-of-law construction and the development of legal science. Economic law and science of economic law have always been closely linked to reform and development. If the reform is more comprehensive and more profound, it will be able to better reflect the spirit and ought-to-be requirements of economic law. Moreover, market economy is inseparable from the regulation of economic law; if we intend to develop the market economy more vigorously, we shall pay more attention to the guarantee of economic law, and build up the theoretical and system consensuses of economic law.

The economic law consensus has a great impact on system reform. With the consensus on solving market failures and government failures, the state specially built a set of systems to solve the "two failures". For example, in order to solve market failures, it is necessary to break from the old practices and establish a new economic law system, no matter it is for anti-monopoly or anti-unfair competition, no matter it is for the special protection of economic subjects' information right or the provision of public goods in economic domain, no matter it is for the reduction of transaction costs in economic domain or the solution to the problems concerning distribution equity. For another example, although solving market failures is an important government function, the resulting government failures shall be highly valued in the meantime. Given this, regulating the government regulation behaviors has always been an important task of economic law, so that the economic law system is bound to regulate the government regulation behaviors. If the administrative law is to set a normative framework for the government administrative behaviors, then the economic law is to delimit legal boundaries for the government macro-economic control and market regulation behaviors.

The reason why the economic law consensus is able to influence the system reform is mainly because it contains people's understanding of the regularity of economic law theory and system. Both economic law theory and principle shall accord with the relevant laws to form stable consensus, better guide the construction of economic law system, and enable the corresponding economic law system to abide by the same

[71] While China's economic law system keeps developing, the theoretical consensus of economic law has been increasing, and the rule-of-law level has been improving. Guo (2008).

laws. The economic law system that follows the general laws has certain international commonality, which explains why the economic law systems in different countries have similar material meanings.

Like the economic law consensus, a good "reform decision" also needs to follow the relevant laws and manifest people's consensuses. The "consistency" between the "reform decisions" and the economic law consensus shows people's understanding of the relevant principles or laws of the market and the rule of law. For years "the market economy is the rule-of-law economy" has been a slogan familiar to the public and an important consensus on economic law. As long as the market economy is implemented under the rule-of-law premise, the relation between efficiency and equity shall be balanced. From the perspective of economic law, between a good reform and economic law regulation, or between a good "reform decision" and economic law consensus, there shall be multi-faceted internal "consistency": on the one hand, they shall have "economics" (i.e., help to reduce transaction costs, and improve economic efficiency, administrative efficiency or overall governance efficiency); on the other hand, they shall help to achieve equity and justice, so that market subjects can get their place in fair trade and fair competition, and the government can promote social justice by creating a fair external environment, and insisting on impartial law enforcement and administration of justice.

Owing to their internal "consistency", the "reform decisions" and the economic law consensus are inevitably interactive and then jointly influencing the system reform. In the early days of China's reform, the "reform decisions" had a greater impact on the economic law consensus which was inadequate at that time. However, with the accumulation of economic law consensus, its influence on the "reform decisions" has been gradually increasing. Take the 2013 Reform Decision for example, its definition of government functions and emphasis of the statutory taxation principle are embodiments of the economic law consensus. It should be noted that it was the economic law community that firstly put forward the "statutory taxation principle", which has become the consensus of all intellectual circles.[72] This principle, which embodies the universal law of the law-based taxation, is applicable in all countries that implement the rule of law, and therefore included into China's "reform decisions".

According to the rule-of-law spirit and the statutory principles, the reform (i.e., system change) shall abide by the statutory principles, which is another important economic law consensus. On this basis, all types of system changes shall stress rationality, particularly legitimacy, i.e., to ensure the "law-based reform". It not only directly relates to the implementation of the "reform decisions", but concerns the compliance of relevant system changes and tends to cause various problems. Whether we can promote the system changes based on the economic law consensus that embodies the rule-of-law spirit, and safeguard the systematization and coordination of the system changes, it directly concerns the outcome of various reforms.

---

[72]The statutory taxation principle has become an economic law consensus. Zhang (1996), Issue 6; Wang (2004), Issue 3.

2.2.4 Conclusion

In the course of its reform, China has introduced several "reform decisions", which are in fact the "master plans" developed by the ruling body for the national reform and development in a certain period in the future, involving the economic, political, social, cultural and other domains, and even concerning the construction of the political party and the army,[73] therefore far more extensive than the pure "national economic and social development plan". More than that, the "reform decisions" have a strong guiding force, through the corresponding legislative procedures and law enforcement actions, they will bring about large-scale system changes, and directly affect the related rule-of-law construction and system civilization. For the above reasons, the "reform decisions" shall be studied from the perspectives of policy, law and also science of law.

From the perspective of influence, the 1984, 1993, and 2013 "reform decisions" are so far regarded as the most influential reform programs. The latter one follows the former one in the same vein, and the reform initiated by each reform decision is more comprehensive and more profound than the preceding one. The "reform decisions"—the ruling plan developed by the ruling body—are the basis for the state to lay down various plans, so their basic spirit shall be conveyed by or embodied in the state legislative planning and development planning. Given this, the "reform decisions" are closely related to all kinds of legal systems that reflect the reform results, and especially related to the concomitant economic law.

In fact, all the "reform decisions" are associated with a large number of economic law issues. An in-depth exploration into these "reform decisions" will help to deepen the understanding of economic law issues, and increase the theoretical and system consensuses on economic law. The proceeding paragraphs have, on multiple levels, described the significant impact of the "reform decisions" on the formation of economic law consensus, and at the same time stressed that with the development of economic law, some economic law consensus will be included into the "reform decisions" and somewhat affect their implementation.[74] This subsection illustrates the correlation and interaction between the "reform decisions" and economic law consensus, which are of great significance for advancing the rule-of-law construction, deepening the reform, and improving relevant theories.

With a view to the specific situation, the correlation and interaction between the "reform decisions" and economic law consensus in different periods are different. This subsection firstly selects the 1984 and 1993 reform decisions as samples to analyze their impact on the formation of economic law consensus. We can find that the

[73]The scope of the 2013 Reform Decision is much wider than the previous reform decisions. In the 2013 Reform Decision, ecological civilization is an important content, but whether it should be juxtaposed with the domains such as economy and politics is worth discussion.

[74]For example, the 2013 Reform Decision emphasizes to "implement the statutory taxation principle", which has become a theoretical and system consensus of economic law. Based on such consensus, it will be easier to promote the formulation of relevant tax laws and win strong support, which is sure to facilitate the implementation of the "reform decisions".

1984 Reform Decision has a greater influence on the formation of system consensus on economic law, while the 1993 Reform Decision has not only enhanced such system consensus, but exerted a significant impact on the formation of theoretical consensus on economic law. It can be said that the 1993 Reform Decision has greatly increased the economic law consensus, while the 2013 Reform Decision has further consolidated and strengthened all of the consensus, and formed the tight connection between the "reform decisions" and economic law consensus: on the one hand, the "reform decisions" promote the formation of economic law consensus; on the other hand, such consensus is integrated into the "reform decisions" to guarantee their implementation.

The analysis in this subsection follows the "relation-system-institution" clue, which is a logical main line running through three "reform decisions", so that they can come down in one continuous line. If we follow this clue to explore the key content of each "reform decision", we can find out the internal relations between the "reform decisions" in different periods, and between the "reform decisions" and the economic law consensus, as well as the formation mechanism for the economic law system. In fact, economic law cares about such relations between the government and the market, and between the central and local governments; these relations directly affect the fiscal, financial and competition systems, and the corresponding mechanisms. All the relations, systems or mechanisms need to be embodied and confirmed by relevant institutions. Among so many institutions, the guarantee of the economic law system is especially important. It is the adjustment of these important relations and the reform of the relevant systems and mechanisms that promote the system development and theoretical innovation in the realm of economic law.

By following the above clue, this subsection unfolds the analysis from the perspective of economic law, and in combination of the government-market relation, reform of the economic system and its supporting mechanisms, and corresponding institutional changes that are involved in the 2013 Reform Decision. This subsection covers lots of important consensuses in the economic law community. These consensuses are consistent with the "reform decisions", while such consistency is more sustainable since it is based on the understanding of the basic principles and basic laws of the market economy, government functions, and economic rule of law.

In addition to teasing the key content on the close relation between economic law and the "reform decisions", this subsection also refines some important theoretical and system consensuses on economic law. Although these consensuses are holistic and general, and far from being able to represent all consensuses that are reached in the academic community, they are still crucial for developing economic law theory and improving economic law system, since they are associated with the foremost and the most basic relations, systems and mechanisms. As long as the academic community keeps working on the basis of existing consensus, it is sure to better promote the theoretical research and system construction of economic law.

2.3 Interpretation of the Relation Between the Constitution and Economic Law from the Perspective of "Economics"

2.3.1 Presenting Problems

The development of the market economy benefits from the optimization of economic system, while the latter is subject to the system arrangements for the decentralization of economic power that is prescribed in both the constitution and economic law. Whether the constitution and economic law of a country can effectively promote and guarantee the economic system reform and then facilitate economic growth, it depends on, to a large extent, the coordination between the constitution and economic law. Because of this, the relation between the constitution and economic law is not only an important theoretical issue, but a major practical issue that requires special attention and in-depth study.

Regarding the relation between the constitution and economic law, the previous studies mainly reveal their connection and differences based on their hierarchy and attribute; this is undoubtedly an important way of thinking. But this subsection attempts to analyze their relation from the dimension of "economics". Although the academic community has separately discussed the economics of the constitution and the economics of economic law, there are yet in-depth study on the internal relation between the two types of economics, and the resulting correlation and consistency between the constitution and economic law, so it is necessary to explore their commonality in economics, and based on this, probe into their relation, promote the interdisciplinary study, and let constitutional adjustment and economic law adjustment jointly advance China's rule-of-law construction.

In terms of the existing studies that focus on the "economics of the constitution" and "the constitution of economics", the academic community highlights the study of the "constitutional norms of economics" while strengthening the "economics analysis of the constitution".[75] In countries implementing different genealogies of law, such study has differentiated into the research realms such as "constitutional economics"[76] and "science of economic constitution".[77] Their research results have positive significance for exploring the "economics" of the constitution and the constitutional issues in the realm of economic law, promoting the interaction between the constitution and economic law, and advancing the construction of specific systems.

---

[75]Zou (1995), Issue 12.

[76]G. Brennan, J. M. Buchanan, *Constitutional economics*, Feng Keli et al. (trans.); Feng (2004), p. 2.

[77]Some scholars hold that the focus of constitutional economics is the impact of different systems on economic growth, while the science of economic constitution not only concerns the system guarantee of stable economic growth, but also the position of human rights and individual basic freedoms in the economic system. Wu (2007), p. 4.

However, no matter they are "constitutional economics" or "science of economic constitution", no matter they are based on economic or legal perspective, the constitution has remained their research object or realm,[78] and they have yet consciously and fully revealed the internal relation between the constitution and economic law, or revealed their propellant role in economic and social development. To this end, we need to find the "intersection" between the constitution and economic law, and identify an appropriate entry point to carry out the analysis.

Through an initial examination of the economic law theory or system, we can find that there are lots of constitutional issues worthy of attention. The close relation between economic law and the constitution manifests in many aspects, their compatibility and interaction during their development since they emerged are especially worthy of great attention. If we take their compatibility and interaction as a perspective and entry point, it will undoubtedly help to promote the study of the relation between the constitution and economic law.

This section argues that the important "intersection" between the constitution and economic law is attributed to their economics, which is the basis for the compatibility and interaction of the two laws. If we conduct an "economics" analysis of the relation between the constitution and economic law from the perspective of economics, it will not only help us to learn about the time features of the modern constitution and the fundamental characteristics of economic law, but to better understand why the constitution and economic law are closely correlated, and why modern states focus on the economic realm of constitutional revision. It will also help us to discover the system absence in the constitution and economic law, so that we can better coordinate their relation and fully realize the goal of legal regulation.

In addition, since economics is of great significance in the emergence and development of the constitution and economic law, and also in maintenance of their close relation, an "economics" analysis not only helps to promote the study on the generation theory and change theory of the constitution and economic law, but to explore and improve the specific path for achieving the coordination and interaction between the constitution and economic law.

Based on the above consideration, the following content will further account for that the economics shared by the constitution and economic law, and their economics is internally consistent. Economics constitutes the basis for the close relation and effective interaction between the two laws. Only by promoting the system interaction and mutual consistency between the constitution and economic law can we construct a benign interaction between the two laws, which is of great benefit for the development of economy, society and the rule-of-law construction.

[78] Although the concept of economic constitution was thought to have originated from the study of German economic law, the German scholars Rinck et al. hold that the economic constitution is a constitutional norm or a fundamental law. Zhao (2001), Issue 4.

2.3.2 *Economics Shared by the Constitution and Economic Law*

Scholars often discuss the relation between the constitution and economic law, but fail to pay enough attention to the basis of or cause for their close relation. An economics analysis reveals that the close relation between the constitution and economic law is attributed to their outstanding attribute of economics. It is the economics that constitutes the basis of their close relation and manifests their commonality. It is also the common economics that enables the constitution and economic law to interact and integrate with each other.

In the realm of economic law study, most scholars agree that economic law has outstanding attribute of economics. It is an undoubted conclusion. But they have yet reached consensus on whether the constitution has economics or whether "the constitution of economics" really exists. Among the existing studies, the public choice theory, which was initiated by the US scholars Buchanan and Tullock, represents an in-depth research on the economics of the constitution. They prefer studying the economic functions of the constitution, the impact of the constitution on economic changes, and the impact of economy on the constitution from the perspective of economics. Besides, based on an analysis of the constitution through an economic approach, they have pushed the study of "constitutional economics"[79] to a new depth.

In addition, the Freyburg School, led by the German scholars Eucken and Böhm, was forerunner in taking an interest in "economic constitution" or "the constitution of economics" and caring about the constitutional norms related to the economic domain. They pay particular attention to the study of the state restrictions on economic freedom and the definition of state intervention from a legal perspective, thus forming the research realm of "economic constitution", and promoting the study on the constitution and economic law.[80]

Whether a study focuses on science of economics or science of law, and whether it highlights ideas or rules, it is premised on the recognition that the constitution has "economics" or that there exists "the constitution of economics". Therefore, the economics of the constitution is widely recognized by these studies.

Among the Chinese scholars that study the constitution, a majority of them are interested in the "politics", "legality" or "normality"[81] of the constitution, instead of caring about its economics. Now that law is of responsiveness, in different eras there are laws and constitutions of different contents, particularly in modern times

---

[79] Tullock (2000); Buchanan (2004).

[80] Some well-known economic jurists such as Böhm and Rinck attach great importance to studying the relation between the constitution and economic law. Like the economist Eucken, they focus on the close relation between the economic constitution and "order", and stress that the economic constitution is the overall choice for the maintaining the order of the national economic life.

[81] Some scholars take "politics" and "legality" as the two attributes of the constitution, while some scholars have respectively extended the research scope of political constitution and normative constitution by taking account of "politics" and "normality" of the constitution. Gao and Tian (2011), Issue 3.

where there is a great need for economic development, thus making a large scale of economic legislation a necessity, and the norms of economic systems are ought to be included into the constitution, so that the economics of constitution has become more prominent.

The economics of the modern constitution has become increasingly prominent—a response to the important needs of the times and a manifestation of the state economic functions in the constitution, which not only exerts a significant impact on the formation of economic law system, but highlights the economics of economic law. In fact, there is not only close relation, but rich commonalities between the economics of the constitution and that of economic law. Their "common economics" is embodied in the following aspects:

(1) No matter it is the property rights or the boundary between the state power and civil rights as defined by the constitution, no matter it is the constitutional provisions or the "right-duty structure" of relevant subjects as specified by economic law, all of them are designed to lower the overall economic operation cost, mitigate frictions and raise efficiency by defining the attribution of right and preventing disputes. In short, both the constitution and economic law shall, in an all-round manner, guarantee and promote the economic development of the country to be more "economic".

(2) In order to achieve the above goals, both the constitution and economic law shall observe the "laws of economy". For example, the constitution provides for economic systems and exerts impact on the specific systems of economic law, which are directly associated with legislators' knowledge and comprehension of the "laws of economy". In fact, which economic system a country chooses is not only a political choice,[82] but relying on its knowledge of the "laws of economy". Given this, Article 15 (1) in the *Constitution of the People's Republic of China* stipulates that "China implements the socialist market economy", which manifests China's comprehension of the "laws of economy". Moreover, when a country implements the market economy system, it shall execute macro-economic control and market regulation, while macro-economic control and market regulation are important realms where which economic law plays a role.

Article 15 (2) of the *Constitution of China* stipulates that "the state shall strengthen economic legislation and improve macro-economic control", which reflects the requirements of "laws of economy" under the conditions of market economy. In China—a fast-growing big country and an emerging market economy—it is especially important to continuously improve and strengthen macro-economic control. Moreover, the market economy needs a level playing field where monopoly and unfair competition are under control, and a good market order is maintained. To this end, Article 15 (3) of the *Constitution of China* stipulates that "the state prohibits any organization or individual from disrupting the social economic order. There are other examples, in the *Constitution of the United States* there are "interstate trade

---

[82]In the foreword to the journal of *Order of Economy* (1937), Böhm and Eucken stress to take the economic constitution as an overall choice for the order of the national economic life. This choice is certainly a political choice, but it is also directly related to the understanding of the "laws of economy".

provisions",[83] and in the *Constitution of the Russian Federation* there are provisions on anti-unfair competition,[84] all of which manifest the understanding of "laws of economy" in market regulation, and they are reflected in the specific legislation of economic law.

(3) The above-mentioned macro-economic control and market regulation shall be firstly subject to separation of powers in the constitution. No matter it is the macro-economic control power or the market regulation power, they are different from the traditional "political power", but each has its new characteristics, and they are even described as the "fourth power".[85] Since they are important powers that affect the fundamental rights of citizens, they shall be firstly separated in the constitution. To this end, the constitutions of many countries have specified the powers of fiscal, taxation, finance and industrial adjustment, as well as the powers of market regulation for anti-monopoly and anti-unfair competition, thus forming the constitutional norms for the economic system, and these norms constitute the basis of "system law" in the realm of economic law. This is an important internal connection between the constitution and economic law.

(4) Both the constitution and economic law specify the basic macro-economic control power and market regulation power, making the relevant norms manifest "economics". Moreover, since the above-mentioned provisions are legalized "economic policies" (esp. legalized "economic policy tools"), they also have "economics". No matter it is for macro-economic control or for market regulation, the legalized means such as budget, tax, national debt, monetary means and anti-monopoly regulation are indispensable, and they important components of the economic law system. Besides, the legalized economic means are employed to safeguard the overall benefits of macro-economic operations. All of the above aspects make the "economics" of economic law more prominent, and thus will further promote the development of the constitutional norms of economics.

In short, both the constitution and economic law shall respond to the economic requirements of the times and have the outstanding economics that manifests as follows: they shall demonstrate the state economic functions and regulate the state economic behaviors; follow the laws of the economy and limit the economic powers such as macro-economic control and market regulation; embody the legalized economic means, promote the benign economic operation, and pursue the overall economic benefits. The above-mentioned common economics of the constitution and economic law are the basis and link of the close relation between the two laws.

---

[83] Article 1 (8) of the *US Constitution* sets out the "interstate trade provisions", highlighting the legislative power of the Congress to control and regulate interstate trade. On this basis, the United States came up with the *Interstate Commercial Act*, the *Sherman Anti-trust Act* and other important economic legislations.

[84] Article 34 (2) of the *Russian Constitution* stipulates that "no economic activity seeking monopoly and unfair competition is allowed", which lays the constitutional basis for the anti-monopoly act and the anti-unfair competition act.

[85] Some scholars like to name these powers as the state regulatory power and take them as the fourth form of power. Chen (2007), Issue 6.

In addition, in view of the economics requirements of the constitution, the constitutions of all countries shall contribute to the promotion of economic development. Any system and institution, though stipulated by the constitution, failing to promote or even hinder economic development should be reformed. It is very important for solving the development problems of all countries. With regard to the revision of the constitution of China and other countries, the continuous improvement of the economics norms of the constitution points out the important direction for realizing the "Pareto Improvement".

2.3.3 Interaction Between the Constitution and Economic Law from the Perspective of Economics

The relation between the constitution and economic law is not only reflected in their outstanding economics, but also in their interaction based on economics, including the important impact of the constitution on economic law, and the implementation of the constitution driven by economic law. These two aspects will be separately discussed in the following paragraphs from the perspective of economics.

2.3.3.1 Impact of the Constitution on Economic Law

In the constitutions of all countries, the norms with prominent economics (or the constitutional norms of economics) mainly include the basic economic systems such as the economic structure and ownership, and the provisions on the distribution of economic powers. As a typical "economic constitution" or the "constitution of economics", the above norms have a direct and important impact on economic law. The examples are as follows:

(1) From the perspective of separation of economic powers, the constitution—"general charter" of a country—not only represents the political existence of a country, but its economic existence. From an economic point of view, the operation of any organization requires financial support, and the state needs strong financial security to perform numerous functions. To this end, the constitution shall contain a large amount of economic content, clearly distinguish public economy from private economy, and correspondingly, it shall clarify the property rights and economic interests of different subjects. Therefore, a "binary structure" is formed between the "state fiscal power" and the "national property rights" at the constitutional level. It is not only the basic framework for the separation of economic powers between the state and the nationals in the constitution, but the foundation for the implementation of

economic law systems, and has an important impact on the formation of economic law systems.[86]

(2) Related to the above-mentioned binary structure in property rights, the constitution of a country shall directly or indirectly reflect its basic economic system. Although the specific provisions in this regard may be different and the legislative system is not uniform, most of them include the basic ownership, distribution system and economic structure. For example, in terms of ownership, does a country implement public ownership or private ownership? Correspondingly, in terms of land system, is the land publicly owned or privately owned?[87] In terms of economic system, does a country implement market economy or planned economy? In terms of distribution system, is the distribution based on work load or other factors? In terms of protection of property rights, how to protect private property rights and public property rights? In the above aspects, the *Constitution of China* has set out clear provisions. The above-mentioned provisions on economic system and the provisions on protection of citizens' economic freedom constitute the basic content of the "constitution of economics". The formation and development of the entire economic law system is also based on the economic structure specified in the constitution. More than that, the system implementation shall fully protect citizens' economic freedom.

(3) The constitution also stipulates the "economic powers" of state organs, including the important economic powers for fiscal, budget, tax, bond issuance, note issuance, and anti-monopoly. Some countries even provide for the revenue distribution of all levels of government in their constitutions.[88] From an empirical point of view, the constitutional provisions not only provide a political perspective, but an economic perspective; the constitution is not only a "political literature" or a "legal document", but an "economic literature". For example, the spirit of "no taxation without representation" embodied in the *British Magna Carta* directly affects the division of taxation power, and is essentially related to the division of economic functions and economic powers. In fact, although the constitution is the result of political struggle or multi-party game, it is also a "centralized manifestation of the economy" and is directly related to the economic interests of various subjects. It is precisely because the *US Constitution* is also a law formulated by interest groups for interest distribution, it underlies countless economic issues. The famous scholar Charles A.

---

[86] Some scholars hold that the property rights system is the core of the fundamental economic system (such as the market economy system or the planned economy system) specified in the constitution. Yushi (2005), p20 ~ 21.

[87] For example, Article 8 of the *Constitution of Russia* states that "in the Russian Federation, private property, state property, local property and other forms of ownership are equally recognized and protected"; while Article 9 states that "land and other resources may be taken as the private property, state property, local property and other forms of ownership".

[88] For example, Articles 157 and 158 of the existing *Constitution of the Federative Republic of Brazil* (promulgated on Oct 5, 1988) specify the tax revenue distribution for the governments at all levels.

Beard pointed out that "the constitution is in the main an economic document".[89] The above-mentioned economic powers stipulated in constitution, e.g., fiscal and financial powers, are also the control power or regulation power needs to be specified by economic law. It can be said that the constitutional provisions for the economic powers have laid an important foundation for the system construction of economic law.

(4) The main structure and the corresponding rights structure established by the constitution have a significant impact on economic law. Based on the "binary structure between subjects" of the state and the nationals established by the constitution, the provisions on the state governance structure and the civil rights structure are the core content of the constitution. From the perspective of power decentralization, the decentralization between the state and the nationals forms the basic rights of nationals or citizens, and they constitute the content of the so-called civil rights bill (or "rights constitution"). At the same time, the power decentralization between the state organs, whether it is horizontal or vertical, is of paramount importance to the state governance, which involves the relevant content of "economic constitution".

The above-mentioned structure of subjects and the corresponding rights structure established by the constitution directly influence the theoretical and system structure of economic law, which not only help to understand the "binary structures" in economic law theory, such as state intervention and economic freedom, state regulatory behavior and market coping behavior, but provide an important analytical framework for studying various issues in economic law.

In short, if we examine the significant impact of the constitution on economic law from the perspective of economics, it is easy to find that the constitution-based definition of state fiscal power and national property rights has established an important framework for the "economic property rights". Based on this framework, a country needs fiscal and tax systems to influence public economy and private economy, and a financial system to safeguard the effective operation of economy, as well as a national debt system, an industrial policy-making system and an industrial organization system that play their respective roles.

The above-mentioned framework serves as the constitutional basis for the fiscal system, tax system, financial system, industrial system and competition system, and the basis for the overall economic law, since all of these systems are an important component of economic law.

In addition, the economic system established by the constitution directly affects a country's choices of public ownership and private ownership, state ownership and private ownership. These choices are fundamental and important constraints that directly affect stable economic growth—a goal of economic law regulation. Moreover, the economic structure established by the constitution is of paramount importance to the system construction of economic law. Without the constitution-based market economic structure, there would be no need for the state macro-economic

[89]This is the conclusion drawn by the famous American historian Beard when interpreting the *US Constitution* with an economic history perspective and an economic approach based on the "economic determinism". Beard (2011), p. 243.

control and market regulation, or the need for economic law-based macro-economic control and market regulation. In fact, China included the market economy into the constitution as early as in 1993, becoming a strong impetus to the overall development of economic law.

When discussing the important impact of the constitution on economic law, it is necessary to distinguish the "constitutional norms of economics" from the "economic law norms related to the constitution". It not only helps to reveal the connection and difference between the constitution and economic law, but helps to emphasize that the study of economic constitution cannot substitute the study of economic law norms, and the independent existence of economic law cannot be negated simply by dividing the economic law norms into economic constitution and economic administrative law. This important theoretical and practical issue shall be clarified; otherwise, the study of economic constitution may be unhelpful for economic law research, and even cause new confusions.

2.3.3.2 Implementation of the Constitution as Promoted by Economic Law

Since both the constitution and economic law have economics, their interaction is not only reflected in the impact of the constitution on economic law, but also in the implementation of economic law required by the constitution and the development of the constitution as promoted by economic law.

The constitution is the fundamental law of the highest rank, and its full implementation depends on the implementation of ordinary laws. Without formulation and effective implementation of economic law, the constitutional norms of economics may be shelved. It is in this sense that the economic rule of law directly affects the vitality of the constitution. Without implementation of economic law, the economic constitution may be in vain.

Related to this, economic law and the constitution may complement each other through interaction and mutual promotion. While implementing the constitutional norms, economic law at the same time promotes the development of the constitution. In fact, although economic law and the constitution are key components of the entire legal system, the former is more directly and closely related to economic life in contrast to the latter. Some practical needs, which are generated from economic and social development, may sometimes manifest in economic law in the first place to form important economic law systems, and then either directly or indirectly transmit to and reappear in the constitution, which is interpreted as a propellant effect of economic law on the constitution.

Economic law is able to promote the development of the constitution, such effect mainly manifest in the impact of the developing contemporary economy and economic law on the constitutional changes. In spite of this, when economic law was yet systemized, the economic law norms, which directly concern the protection of basic national property rights, has greatly promoted the stipulation and development of the constitution. For example, the *British Magna Carta* and its subsequent constitutional or legislative activities involve the realms such as budget and tax that should be specified by today's economic law. It is the realistic need to solve the problems of distribution of budgetary power and taxation power that has constantly enriched and developed the constitutions of all countries.

In addition, during its reform and opening-up, China often makes some explorations and system changes in the realm of economic law. When the time is ripe, it will add the relevant provisions into the Constitution. The amendments to the *Constitution of China* demonstrate the impact of system changes of economic law on constitutional changes. With the continuous development of China's economic law, there will be pressing need for incorporating the statuary taxation principle and statuary monetary principle into the Constitution. If so, it will be another important example showing how economic law promotes the development of the constitution.

In conclusion, based on their shared economics, the constitution interacts with economic law: on the one hand, the fundamental legal status enables the constitution to exert an important impact on economic law; on the other hand, the strengthened state economic functions and the realistic needs of economic life make the constitution norms of economics increase constantly, and need to be implemented by economic law. Meanwhile, the development of economic law has vigorously promoted the development of the constitution. Only when the constitution and economic law interact positively and harmoniously can we better promote the development of economy, society and the rule-of-law construction. To achieve a benign interaction between the constitution and economic law, we shall pay attention to the "consistency" between them.

2.3.4 "Consistency" Between the Constitution and Economic Law from the Perspective of Economics

Considering the economics shared by the constitution and economic law, and the resulting interaction between the two laws, they have inherent "consistency" from the ought-to-be perspective. First, in terms of their common economics, both the constitution and economic law are consistent in safeguarding benign and coordinated economic operation, as well as in observing the laws of economy, so as to make economic operation "more economical". And they are also consistent in emphasizing the legitimacy and constitutionality of macro-economic control and market regulation. Second, in terms of their interaction, the constitution has a direct and important impact on economic law, and economic law may not conflict with the constitution, so economic law shall be consistent with the constitution in the sense of constitutionality. Moreover, economic law is able to promote constitutional changes in the process of implementing the constitution, and make it more accord with the realist needs, so that the two laws could maintain consistent.

In addition, from the perspective of general legal principle, the constitution is a fundamental law and a basic law, so the constitutional provisions have "groundwork" implications. In order to implement the constitutional provisions, economic law shall, by means of concrete system arrangements, make the "groundwork norms" of the constitution more operable, so as to ensure effective implementation of the constitutional norms. And economic law shall be consistent with the constitution, since the "norms of economics" in the constitution—basis for laying down the economic law norms—have a fundamental significance for the system construction of economic law.

The consistency between the constitution and economic law shall be stressed, which is fairly important for strengthening their interaction and sustainable development. Since the constitutional norms of economics are implemented by economic law, while the basic systems of economic law need a constitutional basis, the two laws may respectively lay down principle-oriented and more concrete provisions for the same issue. For example, in the realms such as anti-monopoly, note issuance, budget, taxation and bond issuance, many countries not only have principle-oriented provisions in the constitution, but concrete provisions in economic law, and the two levels of provisions are highly consistent. The United States, Germany or Russia, despite of their different regimes, provide for the above realms in both the constitution and economic law,[90] so as to maintain the consistency between the two laws. Of course, it is related to the status of the constitution and its impact on economic law.

More than that, the constitution separates powers by means of coordination or compromise, and the regulation by economic law is based on the constitutional decentralization, which also reflects coordination, compromise, competition and cooperation, and multiple-level game. In the above-mentioned decentralization and game, economic law concerns the division and distribution of control and regulation powers at the national level, as well as the effective control of these regulation powers, so economic law is more closely related to the constitution. Only by better maintaining the consistency with the constitution can economic law more accord with the constitutional provisions, and more likely to reflect the rule-of-law spirit.

Emphasizing the consistency between the constitution and economic law is not an ought-to-be matter, but for solving the realistic problems that violate the requirements for "consistency". In practice, any inconsistency between the constitution and economic law will generate so many problems. To address these problems, there shall be timely "dynamic coordination" of the constitution and economic law, so as to maintain the "dynamic consistency" between the two laws.

In a historical view, the economic law of China is directly close to the reality of the reform and opening-up, and able to demonstrate the results of system reform in a timely manner. But the amendment to the constitution lags behind. Therefore, in

[90]For example, Article 71 of the *Constitution of the Russia* sets out the domains under the jurisdiction of the Russian Federation: "7. The legal basis for defining a unified market; the basis for fiscal, foreign exchange, credit, customs adjustment, note issuance and price policy; federal economic institutions (including the federal bank). 8. Federal budget; federal taxation and fund-raising; development funds in the federal districts". These domains also need to be specified by economic law.

the process of economic system reform, the "consistency" between the constitution and economic law was sometimes broken, causing certain specific economic legislation to violate the constitutional provisions. For example, China has done a lot in economic legislation to cope with the market-oriented reform, but contradicted with the hysteretic constitutional provisions at that time, and then triggered discussions and debates on "benign unconstitutionality" in the academic community.[91] In order to satisfy the rule-of-law requirements, the consistency between the constitution and economic law shall be emphasized, and the constitution shall be subject to scientific design and timely modification, only by this way can the unconstitutional issues be prevented more effectively.

At present, China is on the way to advance the reform and opening-up, some important systems are yet finalized, which has directly affected the formation of relevant system laws. For example, the provisions for the "system laws" are not developed in China, the functions and responsibilities of some state organs are not defined by the basic legal provisions, but through alternative means (e.g., "three defines" program[92]). At the same time, some important economic system reforms are still promoted by the State Council. For example, the tax-sharing fiscal administration system, the financial system, and the investment system are decided by the State Council.[93] In China, the system legislation is in serious undersupply, partially because the system reform is not fully in place, and mainly for the deep influence of selfish departmentalism, departmental interests, and group interests.

Since the implementation of the *Constitution* (1982), China has increasingly emphasized the promotion of the reform and opening-up, and the development of market economy within the framework of the rule of law. Based on the rule-of-law requirements, all of the above-mentioned systems should be relatively stable and established by law as much as possible. At the same time, we should pay more attention to the stability and predictability of laws, and avoid the contradiction between the constitution and economic law. To this end, we should pay more attention to the issue of unconstitutionality in the realm of economic law from the perspective of "consistency", and care about whether the constitution deviates from the realistic economic life, and maintain the consistency between the constitution and economic life through the system interaction between the two laws, so as to comprehensively build a benign interaction between the constitution and economic law, and better promote the development of economy, society and the rule-of-law construction.

---

[91] Generally speaking, with the improvement of the rule of law, it is necessary to avoid the occurrence of various unconstitutional issues, no matter it is "benign unconstitutionality" or not. Hao (1996), Issue 4; Tong (1996), Issue 6.

[92] It is a programmatic document to define functions, define institutions and define staffing for the party and government agencies, mass organizations and public institutions.

[93] The *Decision of the State Council on Implementing the Tax Sharing Fiscal Administration System* (GuoFa [1993] No. 85) issued on Dec 15, 1993; the *Notice of the State Council on the Reform Plan for Income Tax Revenue Sharing* (GuoFa [2001] No. 37) issued on Dec 31, 2001; the *Decision of the State Council on the Reform of the Financial System* (GuoFa [1993] No. 91) issued on Dec 25, 1993; and the *Decision of the State Council on the Reform of the Investment System* (GuoFa [2004] No. 20) issued on Jul 25, 2004.

2.3.5 Conclusion

The relation between the constitution and economic law is an important theoretical and practical issue. In reference to the existing studies and from the perspective of economics, this subsection discusses the "common economics" of the constitution and economic law to reveal the basis of their close relation; and analyzes the important impact of the constitution on economic law, and the implementation of the constitution as promoted by economic law, so as to testify to their interaction. On this basis, this subsection puts forward the issue of "consistency" between the constitution and economic law, stressing to solve the "inconsistent" problems in practice based on their common economics and due consistency, and constitute positive interaction between the two laws under the rule-of-law framework, which is quite important for the development of economy, society and the rule-of-law construction.

The relation between the constitution and economic law shall be clarified, since it has an important theoretical value for both the study of "economic constitution" (or "constitution of economics") and the study of the "constitutional issues in economic law"; more than that, it helps to address the unconstitutional problems in the realm of economic law or the disconnection between the constitution and economic law, both of them may occur in the rule-of-law practice. This subsection unfolds the analysis from the perspective of economics, taking account of the basic objectives of the constitutional and economic law adjustment, and covering the fundamental contradictions and problems that all modern countries have to deal with. The analysis is instructive and meaningful to the development of the rule of law in the future.

As human consensus on economy and rule-of-law civilization increases, more and more constitutional issues that concern the economic domain need to be specially resolved by economic law; in the meantime, lots of economic law issues, which are in essence constitutional issues, need to be resolved through the improvement of the constitution. Being directly associated with economic life and the constitution, economic law may become a bond that links the constitution with real economic life. The economics shared by the constitution and economic law, and the resulting interaction and integration between the two laws help to continuously build up their consistency and self-improvement, which is of paramount significance for China to advance the rule-of-law construction in an all-round way.

References

Buchanan, Brennan. 2004. *Constitutional economics*. Feng Keli et al. (trans.), Beijing: China Social Sciences Press.

Beard, Charles A. 2011. *An economic interpretation of the constitution of the United States*.He Xiqi (trans.), Beijing: The Commercial Press, p 243.

Cheng, Xinhe. 1999. The trinity of development, equity and security: An analysis of the basic category of economic law. *ECUPL Journal*, Issue 1.

Chen, Yunliang. 2007. The state regulatory power: The fourth form of power. *Modern Law Science*, Issue 6.

Feng, Guo. 2008. The great transformation from a power economy to a law-based economy: Review of China's economic law system construction in past 30 years and look forward to its future. Wu Zhipan (ed.), *Economic Jurists*, Beijing: Peking University Press.

Feng, Guo, and An'an Li. 2012. Financial equity from the perspective of income distribution reform. Zhang Shouwen (ed.), *Economic Law Review*, Vol. 10, Beijing: Peking University Press.

Feng, Xingyuan. 2004. *Constitutional economics*, 2. Beijing: China Social Sciences Press.

Gao, Quanxi, and Feilong Tian. 2011. Problems, positioning and methods of the political constitutional study. *Journal of Soochow University (Philosophy & Social Science)*, Issue 3.

Gong, Gang. 2007. Keynes and modern macroeconomics: On the 70th anniversary of the publication of the General Theory of Employment, Interest and Money. *China Economic Quarterly*, Issue 1.

Gu, Gongyun. 2010. *The latest developments in the financial crisis and economic law*. Beijing: Peking University Press.

Guan, Bin. 2009. Research on general principles of China's economic law in thirty years: A perspective of keywords. *Northern Legal Science*, Issue 4.

Gui, Yushi. 2005. *China's constitutional economic system*, 20–21. Wuhan: Wuhan University Press.

Hao, Tiechuan. 1996. On benign unconstitutionality. *Chinese Journal of Law*, Issue 4.

Karl, Polany. 2007. *The great transformation: The political and economic origins of our time*, Feng Gang and Liu Yang (trans), Hangzhou: Zhejiang People's Publishing House, 114, 136, 164.

Karl, Polany. 2007. *The great transformation: The political and economic origins of our time*. Feng Gang & Liu Yang (trans.), Hangzhou: Zhejiang People's Publishing House, 120.

Kong, Dezhou. 2005. *Systematic economic law*. Beijing: China Legal Publishing House.

Li, Changqi, and Guangzhi Hu. 2002. Legal interpretation of some basic categories of macroeconomic control law. *China Legal Science*, Issue 2.

Liu, Shuilin. 2006. *The holistic interpretation of the basic category of economic law*. Xiamen: Xiamen University Press.

Liu, Wenhua, and Changhe Wang. 2000. The essence of economic law: Coordination and its foundation of economics. *Economic Law Review* 2.

Qi, Duojun. 2008. The redistribution function of economic law and the reform of China's income distribution system. *Journal of the Party School of the Central Committee of the CTC*, Issue 4.

Qiu, Ben. 2005. Development and deepening of China's science of economic law amid changes. *Tribune of Political Science and Law*, Issue 6.

Qiu, Ben. 2013. On the consensus of economic law, *Modern Law Science*, Issue 4.

Qin, Hui. Nov 03, 2000. Tax merge reform and "Huang Zongxi's Law", *China Economic Times*.

Schmid, Alfred A. 1999. *Property, power and public choice: An inquiry into law and economics*. Huang Zuhui et al. (trans.), Shanghai: Shanghai Joint Publishing Press, Shanghai People's Publishing House, 35.

Shan, Feiyue et al. 2000. Discussion on the development ideas in economic law. *Journal of Xiangtan University (Philosophy & Social Sciences)*, Issue 5.

Shi, Jichun, and Feng Deng. 1998. *General theories of economic law*, 55–66. Beijing: Law Press·China

Shi, Shiqi. 1989. Sima Qian's "good cause theory" and its contribution to the tactics of making a living. *Journal of Peking University (Philosophy & Social Sciences)*, Issue 6.

Smith, Adam. 2003. *The theory of moral sentiments*, Jiang Ziqiang et al (trans.), Beijing: The Commercial Press, P302.

Smith, Adam. 2003. *An inquiry into the nature and causes of the wealth of nations*, Vol. I, Guo Dali and Wang Yanan (trans.). Beijing: The Commercial Press, 16.

Tong, Zhiwei. 1996. "Benign unconstitutionality" should not be affirmed. *Chinese Journal of Law*, Issue 6.

Tullock, Buchanan. 2000. *The calculus of consent: Logical foundations of constitutional democracy*. Chen Guangjin (trans.). Beijing: China Social Sciences Press.

Wang, Baoshu, and Qinzhi Cui. 1989. *A summary of the studies on science of economic law*. Tianjin: Tianjin Education Press.

Wang, Baoshu. 1999. *Principles of economic law*. Beijing: Social Sciences Academic Press.

Wang, Hongmao. 2004. Restudy on the statutory taxation principle. *Law Review*, Issue 3.
Wang, Xi and Rong Lu. 2009. Short and long-term effects of China's 4 trillion yuan stimulus package amid the crisis. *Journal of Sun Yatsen University (Social Science Edition)*, Issue 4.
Wang, Xianlin. 1995. On Macro-economic control and the rule of law. *Law Science*, Issue 3.
Wang, Yanlin and Xiong Zhao. 1999. *China's science of economic law: Review and outlook of the 21st century.*
Wang, Yao. 2011. The Smith's Theorem and economies of scale: Marshall's dilemma is a false proposition, *Economics Information*, Issue 5.
Wu, Yue. 2007. *Introduction to economic constitutional science: The game between economic rights and powers in transitional China*, Beijing: Law Press China, p 4.
Wu, Zhipan. 2008. Legal issues in the Wall Street financial crisis. *Law Science*, Issue 12.
Xi, Yuemin. 2011. Transformation and innovation of the basic theories of China's economic law. *Tribune of Economic Law* 8.
Xiao, Jiangping. 2002a. *Study on History of China's economic law theory*, 175–81. Beijing: People's Court Press.
Xiao, Jiangping. 2002b. *Study on the history of China's economic law*, 162–68. Beijing: People's Court Press.
Yang, Song. 2009. Legal reflections on the US financial crisis. *Journal of Liaoning University (Philosophy & Social Sciences Edition)*, Issue 1.
Yang, Yonghua. 2008. Comparing the studies of Zhuo Jiong, Yang Xiaokai and Schultz on the Smith's Theorem, Academic Research, Issue 1.
Yang, Zixuan. 2009. *The theory of state coordinating*, 270. Beijing: Peking University Press.
Yue, Caishen, and Yongcheng Li. 2010. Report on China's economic law development in the past thirty years. *Tribune of Economic Law* 7: 16–17.
Zeng, Donghong, and Jiangping Xiao. 2001. *A review on the introduction to economic law.*
Zhang, Chuanbing et al. 1995. Review of the "New Opinions" on China's economic law theory. *Law Review*, Issue 4.
Zhang, Shouwen. 1992. Analysis of science of economic law from the perspective of economics of law. *Chinese Journal of Law*, Issue 5.
Zhang, Shouwen. 1993. An Outline of China's "new economic law theory". *Peking University Law Journal*, Issue 1.
Zhang, Shouwen. 1996. On the statutory taxation principle. *Chinese Journal of Law*, Issue 6.
Zhang, Shouwen. 2001a. Systematic analysis of economic law system. Yang Zixuan (ed.), *Economic Law Review*, Vol. 2, Beijing: Peking University Press.
Zhang, Shouwen. 2001b. Legal interpretation of macro-economic control power. *Journal of Peking University (Philosophy & Social Sciences)*, Issue 3.
Zhang, Shouwen. 2004a. *Reconstruction of economic law theory*, 33–37. Beijing: People's Publishing House.
Zhang, Shouwen. 2004b. *Reconstruction of economic law theory*, 34–36. Beijing: People's Publishing House.
Zhang, Shouwen. 2004c. *Reconstruction of economic law theory*, 406–08. Beijing: People's Publishing House.
Zhang, Shouwen. 2009. Interpretation of world financial crisis from an economic law perspective. *Legal Forum*, Issue 3.
Zhang, Shouwen. 2011. On coordination thought in economic law: From the theory of the state coordinating. *Social Science*, Issue 1.
Zhang, Shouwen. 2012. The right to economic development: From the perspective of economic law, *Modern Law Science*, Issue 2.
Zhang, Shouwen. 2013a. The issue of tax-cut right in "structural tax reduction". *China Legal Science*, Issue 5.
Zhang, Shouwen. 2013b. Analysis of the "economics" in the constitution and economic law. *Legal Forum*, Issue 3.

Zhang, Shouwen. 2013c. Coordinated development of economic law and the constitution. *Modern Law Science*, Issue 4.
Zhang, Shouwen. et al. 1993. *Market economy and new economic law*, 4–7. Beijing: Peking University Press.
Zhang, Zhuoyuan. Nov. 13, 2013. Let the market play a decisive role in resource allocation: A major theoretical innovation and spotlight, *Shenzhen Special Zone Daily*, A03.
Zhao, Shiyi. 2001. Basic issues in science of economic constitution. *Chinese Journal of Law*, Issue 4.
Zhou, Yongkun. 1995. Outline of legalization of macro-economic control. *Law Science*, Issue 10.
ZhuZhu, Xianchen (ed.). 2012. *Self-governance and expansion order: A dialogue with Elinor Ostrom*, 6. Zhejiang University Press: Hangzhou.
Zou, Pingxue. 1995. *Stress the study on the economics of the constitution. Law Science*, Issue 12.

Chapter 3
Development Ideas and Development Theories

"Economic law is the law that promotes development"—basic consensus in the academic circle of economic law. In order to promote the comprehensive development of economy and society, economic law shall fully absorb all kinds of development ideas, and then form its own development theory.[1] Any development theory is influenced by certain development ideas; in all kinds of development ideas, the idea of coordinated development has special significance for the theoretical development and system construction of economic law, as well as for the development theory of economic law.

Based on the principle of difference in economic law, and considering the uneven development in all aspects, coordination is so important that needs to be strengthened. For this reason, in the realm of economic law, the idea and thought of "coordination" have been in existence for a long time; and coordination is also important for handling the relation between economic law and other sectoral laws, especially between economic law and the constitution. In addition, the coordination advocated in the realm of economic law involves the coordination between economy and society, between economic structure and other structures, between all types of economic instruments, and between economic law and economic policies. The coordination in these aspects is a manifestation of the coordinated development idea in different domains, and also an important content of the development theory in the science of economic law.

For the above considerations, the layout of this chapter is as follows: Firstly, discuss the coordination thought that is directly associated with the idea of coordinated development, and underscore its important value in economic law theory and system construction. Secondly, analyze the coordination between sectoral laws within the legal system, with focus placed on the coordinated development of the constitution and economic law, which is of foremost importance for the development of the overall legal system and for the realization of rule-of-law functions. Finally, discuss how to better coordinate economic policies and economic law in

[1]Zhang (2016), Issue 4.

S. Zhang, *The New Horizon of China's Economic Law Theory*, Understanding China,
https://doi.org/10.1007/978-981-15-8824-2_3

specific economic domains so that they can jointly promote the "double adjustment" of economic structure, and benefit the coordinated development of economy and society.

The above discussions involve the ideas, relations and norms of coordination at different levels, all of them affect the coordinated development of relevant domains. Therefore, the corresponding studies will help to promote the formation and improvement of the development theory of economic law. In addition to paying attention to the coordination of development, the systematic development theory of economic law also cares about the issues such as development concepts, development subjects, development ability and development right.[2] These specific issues may be left for elaboration in other monographs.

3.1 Coordination Thought in Economic Law

The development of China's economic law theory is inseparable from the academic thought infiltrating it. Among them, the coordination thought—an important academic thought that runs through the various theories of economic law—has a great effect on enhancing the theoretical consensus of the academic circle. At present, among the most influential economic law theories,[3] a majority of them do not bear the term "coordination", but they still contain the coordination thought in varying degrees.[4] In the "Theory of the State Coordinating", the coordination thought could be no more obvious. In fact, the coordination thought is closely related to the characteristics of economic law, and directly concerns the theory and system construction of economic law. To highlight the theme, this section will focus on the "Theory of the State Coordinating" and other influential economic law theories to analyze the "coordination" thought in economic law and its inspiration to the economic law study.

[2]Zhang (2005), Issue 3; Zhang (2016), Issue 4; Zhang (2012), Issue 2.

[3]The scholars have reached consensus on certain important types of theories in the realm of economic law, although they still hold their own understandings. Xiao (2002), pp. 288–96; Yang (2009a), pp. 71–80.

[4]For example, Prof. Liu Wenhua argues that the essence of economic law is coordination, and economic law should be based on the coordination of social interests and the overall interests of individuals. Liu and Wang (2000), Vol. 2; Li and Huang (2002), Issue 5.

3.1.1 Basic Knowledge of Coordination Thought

The coordination thought in the general sense has existed since ancient times.[5] As long as there are different systems, different subjects and different subject behaviors, there will be discord or conflict, which creates the need for coordination. Generally speaking, the coordination thought is closely associated with the "regime thought" or "system thought", i.e., it involves the internal or external coordination of a regime or system, emphasizing non-conflict, non-intersection and non-overlapping so as to play the integral effect of a regime or system. Therefore, coordination concerns the integrity, integral functions and efficiency, as well as the issues such as operation of the integral system and realization of the integral goals. Given this, coordination is both a means and a goal, it is needed for achieving the goal of harmony and appropriateness or such kind of a state, or facilitating the achievement of such goal or state.

Coordination thought may be explored from the semantic perspective in addition to the usual philosophical perspective. For example, according to the Theory of State Coordinating, the term "coordination" has two implications: one is "appropriately coordinated" (used as an adjective), while the other is "to make it appropriately coordinated" (used as a verb). The term "coordinating" in the Theory of State Coordinating is a verb,[6] i.e., the state is the subject, and "coordinating" is the behavior of the subject. From the perspective of economic law, no matter it is for economic and social development, distribution of power and rights, or system construction of economic law, state coordinating is inseparable. When economic and social development is out of synch and thereby causing problems, state coordinating is needed; when the distribution of power and rights is seriously imbalanced and thereby infringing on the protection of legal interests, state coordinating is needed; when the time, space or sphere of economic law legislation is imbalanced or conflicted, state coordinating is needed. As such, the coordination behavior and thought exist extensively in the realm of economic law. In a broad sense, coordination denotes an "appropriately coordinated" state or "to make it appropriately coordinated", covering both goals and means, both state and behavior. And these two dimensions of coordination are incorporated into the Theory of State Coordinating.[7]

The above-mentioned "coordination thought in the general sense" is helpful for understanding the "coordination thought in economic law". Broadly speaking, the coordination thought in economic law also includes the general coordination thought; but in a narrow sense, it refers in particular to the coordination thought

---

[5]For example, Confucianism advocates the coordinative effect of ethics on interpersonal relations; and the ancient Chinese thought of "harmony between man and nature" endorses the coordination between human behaviors and nature.

[6]The basic connotation of "coordination" is "an appropriately coordinated, harmonious or concerted state". Where a coordinated state is unattainable, it should be adjusted to become "appropriately coordinated". It is important for a comprehensive understanding of the two dimensions of "coordination".

[7]The term "coordinated" in "coordinated development" indicates an "appropriately coordinated" state according to the Theory of State Coordinating. Yang (2009b), p. 348.

containing specific economic law implications and embodied the theory and system of economic law. To probe into economic law, the coordination thought in both broad and narrow senses is a required course. The Theory of State Coordinating comprises the coordination thought of the two dimensions.

According to the Theory of State Coordinating, the so-called "state coordinating" is a situation where the state employs legal and non-legal means to make the economic operation accord with the objective law and to promote the national economic growth.[8] Given this, in the realm of economic law, "coordination" shall be interpreted from the most basic aspects as follows:

(1) The state is the subject of coordination. Presently, the mainstream viewpoints in the realm of economic law uphold that the state is an important subject of economic law and playing a leading role. It is true and will remain so for a long time in the foreseeable future.

(2) The object of coordination is economy, or "economic operation" to be precise. So the coordination in the domain of economy is "economic coordination".

(3) The coordination is exercised through legal and non-legal means, but mostly legal means. Among the legal means, the economic means in a legal form, i.e., legalized economic means (or legalized economic policies), occupy an important position in the state coordinating.

The Theory of State Coordinating involves three basic dimensions of coordination, i.e., state coordination, economic coordination and legal coordination, which focus on the subject, object and means of coordination, respectively. The three dimensions are interrelated. An understanding of the three dimensions of coordination will make it easier to comprehend, analyze and solve the important theoretical issues about economic law, and enlighten the economic law study, which are elaborated as follows:

(1) Exÿamine the relevant theoretical issues from the perspective of "state coordination"

The Theory of State Coordinating argues that the state is the subject of coordination, which directly affects the study of the nature of economic law, and the determination of the legal territory of economic law; both of them have been important issues when studying the economic law theory. Whether economic law is a public law or a social law that blends public and private laws, there are still disagreements in the academic community. From the perspective of subject (esp. with a view to the dominant position of the state), and considering the imbalanced right-interest structure (an outcome of dominance of state power in the norms of economic law), economic law should be a public law of which the subject is also the state. Therefore, in the Theory of State Coordinating, the legal territory of economic law is definite, i.e., it is classified into the public law.[9] Now that the Theory of State Coordinating

[8] Yang (2009c), p. 127.

[9] Yang (2009d), pp. 192–193.

determines the economic law has state subjectivity and public law attribute, it sets the tone for the viewpoints on many theoretical issues of economic law.

In fact, the state subjectivity and public law attribute have solidified the mandatory attribute of economic law. In other words, "coordination" is also mandatory, but its mandatory intensity may be adjusted according to the object, sphere, time and space. The state subjectivity of economic law prominently manifests in the realm of macro-economic control law (involving fiscal, financial or planning matters), and also in the realm of market regulation law (involving anti-monopoly and anti-unfair competition). The public law attribute of economic law is especially evident because of great attention paid to national interest and social public benefit.

The national subjectivity, public law attribute and mandatory attribute of economic law directly affect our understanding of the subject structure, behavioral structure, right-interest structure, and responsibility structure of economic law, the specific system structure of economic law, as well as the relation between economic law and other laws, e.g., civil and commercial law, social law, and administrative law.[10]

(2) Examine the relevant theoretical issues from the perspective of "economic coordination"

According to the Theory of State Coordinating, what the state coordinates is economic operation. So it defines the "sphere" of state coordination: "economic" coordination, rather than political or social coordination. Moreover, this theory identifies macro-economic control and market supervision as economic coordination. Related to this, the science of economic law studies the coordination in the domain of economy, not the problems about administrative or social management. The specific sphere of economic law regulation is therefore determined.

The specific regulatory sphere is so important that it distinguishes economic law from other sectoral laws.[11] In view of the development course of economic law theory, the definition of the regulatory sphere, to a great extent, affects the system construction of economic law. Since the academic community has made the relation between macro-economic control and market regulation as the core relation under economic law regulation, such specific regulatory sphere of economic law is now widely acknowledged, which has vigorously built consensus on economic law theory.

The specific regulatory sphere is closely related to the market failure theory, legal system development theory, and functional theory of economic law. The existence of multiple market failures has made macro-economic control and market regulation especially necessary; and new legal sectors need to be created in the existing legal

---

[10]It is very important to determine the state subjectivity and public law attribute of economic law, which helps to increase the theoretical consensus on economic law. To this end, in the book *The Theory of State Coordinating*, the author repeats the public law attribute of economic law for several times, and demonstrates the public law attribute of various sectoral laws in the realm of economic law, e.g., fiscal law, financial law, and planning law, which will guide readers to distinguish some vague knowledge in the academic community.

[11]The specific regulatory sphere somewhat represents the specific regulated objects. The regulatory sphere and regulated objects are closely correlated. The regulated objects were used to be overlooked or belittled, such practice is ought to be rectified.

system to regulate macro-economic control and market regulation, and make up for the flawed regulatory functions of traditional laws. The basic problems to be solved by economic law and its due functions, as well as the response of legal system, have determined the specific regulatory sphere of economic law, which helps to explain the problems about occurrence theory and value theory in the realm of economic law.

(3) Examine the relevant theoretical issues from the perspective of "legal coordination"

According to the Theory of State Coordinating, the state mainly employs legal means to exercise economic coordination, implying that the means of coordination shall be the laws on macro-economic control and market regulation, instead of simple policies or administrative orders, which determines the legality of economic law, and the statutoriness of the goals and means of economic law regulation.

Despite of a prominent "policy attribute", the legality of economic law requires the important economic policies to be legalized. Owing to its legality, the statutory principle holds an important position in economic law, and gives rise to separate statutory principles for each sectoral law, e.g., there is a respective statutory principle for budgeting, taxation, currency, and planning. The statutory principle in economic law is generally recognized,[12] because it is inherently consistent with the following aspects: the exercise of public power based on state subjectivity and power restriction, the significant impact from the sphere of economic coordination on the national rights and interests, and the legality requirements of economic law itself. While the development of economic law theory is going deeper, people not only examine the theoretical issues of economic law from a non-legal perspective, but from the perspective of legality, and give thought to everything from entities to procedures.

It can be seen that the development of economic law theory is under direct impact from its state subjectivity, specificity of legal territory, and statutoriness of rights and duties. As such, we shall examine the core issues of the Theory of State Coordinating, which will help us to analyze the multi-faceted theoretical issues of economic law, and deepen the relevant studies.

3.1.2 Goals of Coordination and Interest Coordination

After defining the subject, object and means of state coordination—the major issues in the Theory of State Coordinating, we shall go on exploring the goals of state coordination, which represent the theme of the coordination thought. According to the Theory of State Coordinating, "the aim of coordination is to make economic operation accord with the objective laws and promote the development of the national economy".[13]

[12]Yang (2009e), p. 362; Wang (1999), p. 38.
[13]Yang (2009c), p. 127.

In short, following laws and promoting development is the core purpose of coordination. The laws are more advanced than the "rules and regulations" developed by human beings; they cannot be created, altered or eliminated. We shall follow the laws of economy that are recognizable and employ the laws embodied in the legal form, so that we can ensure the economic operation to be more in line with the objective laws and more coordinated, and ultimately promote economic development.

According to the goals and ideas of coordination, the state may not arbitrarily interfere with the economic operation regardless of the objective laws, but size up the situation and "offer judicious guidance in light of the circumstances"—a conduct in line with the objective laws. Such conduct itself is an effective way of coordination. In order to promote economic development in a better way, the state must abide by the objective laws, and exercise coordination pursuant to the legal provisions that embody the objective laws.

As is well-known, development is the theme of the contemporary era, and promoting development is the core goal of state coordination. Is coordination bound to be exercised by the state? How to exercise the coordination? There are yet definite answers to these questions in the academic community. Some scholars, especially those from the schools of liberalism, interventionism, evolutionism and constructivism, are at odds on the role of the state, as well as the cost and benefit of state coordination. Nevertheless, from a realistic perspective, especially from a countercyclical perspective, strengthening state coordination is a universal choice made by all countries. The outbreak of the 2008 financial tsunami enabled people to learn about the importance role of the state more clearly.[14]

The state coordination is indispensable from the perspective of system economics. In the case of exorbitant transaction costs, the interest conflicts among individuals are hard to be resolved on their own, so the state—provider of public goods—shall play the role of "coordinator"; and the state coordination itself is for providing public goods. Since the provision of public goods is selfless and non-profit, and the provider shall have a superior status and powerful strength, the task of "coordination" can only be undertaken by the state that meets the above conditions.

In fact, the state coordination resolves the interest conflicts between individuals, between the state and individuals, and between the state interest and social welfare. All of the state interest, social welfare and private interest fall into the regulatory sphere of economic law, although they care about different interests of different subjects. In the final analysis, the goals of state coordination, which are underscored in economic law, are achieved through the coordination of interests.

The interest coordination directly concerns the legal interest protection. There are diverse interests to be protected by economic law. All the interests that are specified and protected by economic law are legal interests in the realm of economic law. According to the Theory of State Coordinating, the interests protected by economic

[14]After the global financial crisis broke out in 2008, all countries adopted various measures to strengthen macro-economic control and market supervision, showing that they are aware of the significant role of the state or government, and highlighting the importance of economic law. Zhang (2009a), Issue 3.

law are not limited to social welfare, but also include private, collective and state interests.[15] For example, in terms of the state interest, all of the fiscal, taxation and financial interests need to be protected by economic law. Only when the various legal interests are protected in a balanced manner, the economic law will have a more coordinated legal-interest-protection structure. If the economic law only protects social welfare, and ignores the basic private interest or the crucial state interest, the protection of social welfare will be in vain. In a word, the purpose of economic law is to protect the interests of various subjects and coordinate the interests of different economic law subjects".

The interest coordination directly concerns the "quantification" of interests. In this regard, the Theory of State Coordinating argues that "coordination of interests" differs from "balance of interests"; the interests of economic law subjects shall be "appropriately matched", it does not mean that their interests need to be equal, egalitarian or roughly egalitarian[16]; instead, it means that "everything is in its right place", so as to protect the legal interests of various subjects, exercise control and regulation at different stages or in different periods, balance efficiency and equity by preventing one-sided emphasis on subject interests or equalization, which will help to maintain the order of market economy, promote the benign operation and coordinated development of both economy and society.

3.1.3 The Coordination Thought Directly Related to Systematic Thought

The above two subsections mainly discuss the state coordination in the realm of economic law, which is an important content of the Theory of State Coordinating. But this theory also pays attention to the coordination thought in the general sense, since it is in the same vein with the systematic thought. So to speak, we can make sure of better "coordination" by following the systematic thought and employing the systematic approach.

In fact, the emphasis on and attention to the coordination in the realm of economic law is a manifestation of the systematic thought. Since the systematic thought requires the coordination inside and outside of a system, the economic law, which is a form of system, shall maintain coordinated both internally and externally. To this end, the coordinative relation within and beyond the realm of economic law shall be properly handled.

In terms of internal coordination, the academic community has been discussing "how the system of economic law is constituted"—a fundamental issue in the ontology of economic law. In recent years, the scholars like to make macro-economic control law and market regulation law (or market supervision law) as the core of economic law, which is endorsed by the Theory of State Coordinating and other

[15] Yang (2009f), pp. 342–343.

[16] Yang (2009g), pp. 361–362.

economic law theories since they are more beneficial to the internal coordination in the realm of economic law.

In terms of external coordination, the coordination between economic law and civil law, and between economic law and administrative, commercial and social laws has become increasingly distinct through years' discussion. The knowledge of the difference and connection between economic law and relevant sectoral laws, as well as the independent status and value of economic law has been converging.

Relevant to the internal and external coordination of the system of economic law, the "coordination" at each link of economic law (legislation, law enforcement and judicial decision) also needs to be underscored. According to the coordination thought, the coordination of the systems such as legislation, law enforcement and judicial decision is an important yardstick for measuring the rule-of-law level in the realm of economic law. The coordination of relevant systems, which directly concerns the functions and goals of economic law, is a noteworthy issue in economic law study.

In addition, according to the systematic thought and systematic approach, we shall pay special attention to the coordination in the aspects of entirety, level, structure and function.[17] It helps to solve the theoretical and practical problems in economic law. The details are expounded as follows:

(1) Whole coordination

Emphasizing the whole coordination is consistent with the holism thought. In fact, the entire economic law community cares about the "holistic" problems, since the holism thought is an important guiding ideology for economic law study. In addition to individuals, economic law also pays attention to the whole, including the holistic interest, holistic development and holistic benefit, which distinguish it from traditional laws. In view of the important holism thought in economic law, we shall pay special attention to the whole coordination.

The whole coordination is so important because individual interests and behaviors are bound to have conflicts and contradictions. Unremitting efforts shall be made to resolve the contradiction between individuals' profit pursuit and social welfare (a basic contradiction in the realm of economic law), and the problems arising from valuing individuals but ignoring the whole, so that we can better realize the whole interests, efficiency and benefit, and ensure the whole economic operation to be more "economical", more coordinated, more profitable.

Being directly related to the goal of legal interest protection, ideas and values of economic law, the whole coordination is focus of various types of economic law theory. For example, the Theory of State Coordinating points out that economic law, economic legal system, and science of economic law are separate systems, while the

[17] Yang Zixuan, Liu Ruifu and other economic law scholars have elaborated on the systematic analysis approach in their works; such approach is fairly important for achieving the internal and external coordination of various systems in the realm of economic law, and for building consensus on economic law theory. Yang (2009h), pp. 12–13; Liu (2000), pp. 21, 24–25.

holistic approach is able to analyze these systems as a whole,[18] which is of great significance for the internal and external coordination of economic law, economic legal system, and science of economic law, as well as for the coordination of multiple interest subjects.

(2) Levels of coordination

The economic law regulation involves a broad sphere of time and space, meaning that the levels of coordination are accordingly different. For example, there is interest coordination between the central and local governments, and between the governments at different levels.

In addition, the economic law study encompasses the coordination at domestic and international levels. In other words, the coordination thought is universally applicable in the realms of domestic economic law and international economic law. Because of this, after the 2008 global financial crisis, the international community agreed on the necessity to strengthen policy coordination and system coordination; otherwise, if policies and systems are not coordinated enough or even contradicted with each other, it will cause a negative impact on the world economic operation. In short, the Theory of State Coordinating is applicable in the realm of international economic law.[19]

The coordination at domestic and international levels is an important revelation for the current legal study: the coordination in the realm of international economic law is a kind of compromise between countries, but it is still based on the national laws of each country. As such, the domestic law theory will, to a great extent, affect the international law theory. If it could be applicable to the study of international economic law, the domestic economic law is sure to stimulate the development of international economic law. Of course, the development of the theory and system of international economic law will affect that of domestic economic law. Such interaction also exists in the sectoral laws in the realm of economic law, e.g., domestic tax law and international tax law, domestic financial law and international financial law, domestic competition law and international competition law.

(3) Coordination between structure and functions

Generally speaking, a specific structure has specific functions, so the coordination between the structure and functions within a system is quite important. To ensure that economic law has certain functions for accomplishing specific tasks, the structure of economic law shall be adjusted when it fails to perform certain functions, so that the structure would be coordinated with the functions and consistent with the goals of economic law.

[18] Yang (2009h), pp. 12–13.

[19] Many years ago, Prof. Yang Zixuan had applied the coordination thought in the Theory of State Coordinating to the realm of international economic law, and came up with the Theory of International Coordinating. This new theory is more important for further developing the theory of international economic law as a whole, and it is also in line with the practice of international economic law. Yang (2000); Yang (2009i), pp. 175–187.

In terms of the structural adjustment, it involves the structure of sectoral laws in the realm of economic law and the internal structures of specific systems, i.e., subject structure, behavioral structure, right-duty structure, and responsibility structure. These structures shall be more coordinated to better perform the integral functions of all economic law systems. It is of great practical significance for the system construction of economic law.

The coordination between structure and functions is a fundamental and important issue that directly affects the development of the normative theory and system construction of economic law. It is in need of further exploration. At present, various types of economic law theory and doctrines have a lot in common; if we could keep promoting the study on the coordination between structure and functions, the theoretical consensus will be greatly increased.

3.1.4 Coordination Though and Category Refinement

Based on the general coordination thought and the coordination thought in the Theory of State Coordinating, we shall pay attention to the refinement of some important categories in the realm of economic law, e.g., the subject, object, means, goal and ability of coordination. These categories are already mentioned in the previous sections, but in need of in-depth exploration, which will help to promote the development of the entire economic law theory.

Only some important categories closely related to the coordination thought are selected and analyzed as follows:

For the coordination subject, the Theory of State Coordinating holds that the state is the subject of coordination. In the subject system of the entire economic law, the Theory of State Coordinating proposes a "binary structure" of state coordination (covering the subject and receptor of state coordination), which is a systematic refinement of the subject category. It is of great significance for perfecting the subject system and promoting the study of the subject theory in the realm of economic law.

For the coordination object, the Theory of State Coordinating holds that the object of state coordination is economic operation, rather than enterprises or individuals; and the coordination is not "direct intervention", but adjustment of interests by following the objective laws and legal provisions, which conforms to the constitutional spirit of modern countries. "The object of state coordination is economic operation", such argument is internally consistent with the idea of "let the state guide the market, and let the market guide enterprises", which was put forward by China years ago. Since all enterprises are participants in economic operation (i.e., market subjects), the state shall employ macro-economic control, particularly the means of regulating economic operations, to exert influence on the market subjects.

For the means of coordination, the Theory of State Coordinating stresses to employ legal means and certain non-legal means. According to the traditional rule-of-law thought, legal means remain our first choice are present. Despite of varied understandings of specific legal origins, the basic legal origins shall be the crucial means of coordination and focus of economic law study. Of course, it does not rule out the study of "soft law".[20]

For the goal of coordination, the Theory of State Coordinating holds that the state coordination aims at "promoting economic development". It can be said that economic development is the direct goal of state coordination. But in the process of fulfilling this goal, the state also promotes social development for the sake of coordinating the development of economy and society. Therefore, both the theoretical research and system construction of economic law reflect some social policy requirements, and also the requirements for coordinating economic and social policies, so that economic law demonstrates certain "sociality" in some aspects. For this reason, in the Theory of State Coordinating, "promoting economic development and social progress, so as to coordinate the interests of economic law subjects" is made as the purpose of economic law,[21] and the category of "coordinated development" is hereby proposed.

For the coordination ability, although it is not a focus in the Theory of State Coordinating, it is connected with the coordination subject and coordination behaviors, and directly related to the achievement of coordination goal. Because of this, while studying the categories of coordination subject and coordination behaviors, we'd better pay some attention to the category of "coordination ability", which is closely associated with the subject theory, behavioral theory and responsibility theory in the realm of economic law.

Besides, the important goal of coordination is to build up the "coordinativeness" of a system, including the coordinativeness of economic development, social development or between economic and social development, as well as the coordinativeness of the system of economic law and of economic legislation. Now that coordinativeness concerns all sectors of economic law, the category of "coordinativeness" is also worth studying.

Closely related to the above categories and from the perspective of legal science, the issues such as coordination power, coordination duty and coordination responsibility in the realm of economic law are also worth studying. According to the Theory of State Coordinating, the coordination power belongs to the state; only the subject ascribed with coordination power is an eligible subject of state coordination. So it is impossible for an industrial intermediary organization to be the subject of state coordination, but it may become the receptor of state coordination under certain conditions.[22] More than that, the coordination subject enjoying coordination power also assumes coordination duty, and both coordination power and duty are statutory. As such, in case of violating its statutory duty, the coordination subject shall bear

[20]Cheng (2007), Issue 4.

[21]Yang (2009j), p. 340.

[22]This judgment is important for denying the middle-level social stratum or industrial intermediary organizations as the subject of state coordination. On this basis, we need to confirm if it is necessary to identify industrial intermediary organizations as a subject of macro-economic control or market supervision, or a subject holding an important position. Yang (2009k), p. 325.

statutory responsibility. The coordination responsibility shall be clearly defined to guarantee the justiciability of economic law.

In addition, the Theory of State Coordinating divides the state coordination behaviors into two types: macro-economic control behavior and market supervision behavior, which are consistent with the government functions of "macro-economic control and market supervision". Owing to the widespread game behaviors in the market, the state has to pay a high "coordination cost" in exercising the two coordination behaviors. This coordination cost is a part of the transaction cost in a broad sense. Accordingly, the state shall confirm the necessity of coordination, the conditions for coordination, the need to provide public goods and the cost of coordination. It directly affects the state coordination ability or financial capacity, and the choice of specific coordination behaviors, and makes the system arrangements for economic law.

The above important categories in the realm of economic law are formed on basis of coordination thought. All of these categories involve the coordination issues, and they are of particular concern in the Theory of State Coordinating. At the same time, they have brought revelations to the entire economic law study. For example, we should pay special attention to the coordination issues such as subject, ability and cost; since the important function of economic law is to make the overall economic operation more "economical", it is necessary to reduce transaction or coordination cost. For another example, in order to achieve "effective coordination", we shall build up the coordination ability of the state, and fully take account of the game of coordination receptors. The interests of various subjects shall be coordinated to promote the benign operation and coordinated development of economy and society, which is the goal of economic law regulation.

3.1.5 Conclusion

While the development of economic law study is going deeper, the academic community shall pay attention to the study of academic thoughts. As an important thought of economic law, the coordination thought is embodied in several economic law doctrines, running through the entire realm of economic law, and especially evident in the Theory of State Coordinating. Even if there are rich academic thoughts contained in the Theory of State Coordinating, the prominent position of coordination thought is irreplaceable. A comprehensive understanding of the coordination thought will help to solve many theoretical and practical problems in the realm of economic law, and enlighten the academic community to futher promote the economic law study.

This section discusses two types of coordination thought: one is the general coordination thought in the broad sense, and the other is the specific coordination thought in the Theory of State Coordinating; and the latter is a concrete manifestation of the general coordination thought in economic law theory. In the study of economic law, the two types of coordination thought are equally valued; and the Theory of State Coordinating also underscores the general coordination thought.

Emphasizing the coordination thought helps to better comprehend the "superiority" of economic law, discover the "relatedness" between the regulation of economic law and other laws, and further demonstrate the "modernity" of economic law. In addition, the expression of coordination thought in several economic law doctrines has greatly increased the consensus on economic law theory, and resolved many important theoretical issues in this regard. For this reason, a comprehensive understanding and earnest implementation of the coordination thought is of great significance for the entire of realm of economic law, not only for deepening the knowledge of ontology and axiology, and but for resolving the problems about normative theory and operational theory.

The revelations brought by the coordination thought to the economic law study help to solve the major theoretical problems that are still pending, and explore the important academic thoughts contained in the economic law theory. They are of great significance for advancing academic progress and promoting theoretical integration; moreover, they facilitate the formation of China's economic law schools and continuous development of economic law theory.

3.2 Coordinated Development of Economic Law and the Constitution

3.2.1 Presenting Problems

No matter how the world changes, development has remained theme of the times. The overall development of a country, including economic growth, social progress, political justness and cultural prosperity, is closely related to its law-based governance. As a law for promoting development, economic law is closely connected to the overall situation of the national economy and people's livelihood; its development not only concerns the development of economy and society, but has a profound impact on the development of all sectoral laws and the rule-of-law construction. Therefore, the economic law scholars shall care about both the "creation" and "development" of economic law, and conduct explorations in an all-round way.[23]

Since the development of economic law concerns the structural adjustment and system changes of the legal system,[24] it is necessary for us to, through structural function analysis, examine the specific functions of all sectoral laws in the legal

[23]The academic community has been more interested in the development of science of economic law, they'd better care more about the study on the development of economic law itself. Cheng (2008), p. 104–08; Zhu and Li (2008), Issue 3, pp. 65–73.

[24]The emergence and development of economic law has altered the basic structure of all countries' legal systems. At the same time, the system changes in the domains of fiscal, taxation, finance and competition have a substantial impact on the protection of property right, and thereby promoting economic development. It is in fact consistent with the "Institution Change Theory" presented by Douglass C. North. He holds that the basic services provided by the state constitute the basic rules

system, so as to promote the "coordinated development" of the entire legal system. Different sectoral laws have varied regulatory scope and means, but no one should be ignored, since each of them has its own strengths. Related to this, while advancing the rule-of-law construction in China, we should have both rule-of-law thinking and systemic thinking, so as to coordinate the development of various components of the legal system.

There are multiple dimensions for studying the development of economic law. Among them, an evidently important path is to examine the relations between economic law and other sectoral laws and promote their coordinated development. In the past, when the academic community was studying the "adjacent relation" or "external relation" between economic law and other sectoral laws, they cared more about the "bipartite relation" between economic law and a certain sectoral law. It is of course important, but if taking account of political, economic, social, cultural and other factors for consideration, we'd better examine the "tripartite relation" in an extended system. For example, based on the predominant government-market relation in the realm of economic law, we need to explore the "tripartite relation" among economic law, civil and commercial law, and administrative law; in case of any extension, we shall also think about the "tripartite relation" among economic law, constitution and social law.

No matter the research object is "bipartite relation" or "tripartite relation", we shall think about how to better coordinate the development of economic law and relevant sectoral laws. The sectoral laws have distinct "historical backgrounds" and "multiple bases", as well as diverse tasks, missions and functions, and all of them will keep developing under the "contemporary background." More than that, the sectoral laws usually encounter lots of common or closely correlated problems, which have made their relations more complicated. We shall further study and carefully sort out these relations so as to better promote their coordinated development.

In present times, both economic law and constitution play an important role in the economic and social development of all countries and also concern their political and legal development. From the perspective of economic analysis, the economic law and constitution of modern countries have outstanding "economics". All major demand in economic and social development shall be reflected in economic law and even in constitution, and the constitutional spirit shall be materialized through the implementation of economic law. As such, the "coordinated development" of economic law and constitution is of paramount importance.

Every sectoral law shall moderately develop and maintain "coordinated development" with other sectoral laws. Moreover, the development of both constitution and economic law is a serious matter, so their coordinative relation is of crucial significance. As such, this section mainly discusses the "coordinated development of economic law and constitution" from the perspective of their relation, analyzes the constitutional basis of economic law development, and the promotion of the development of constitution by economic law, so as to demonstrate the necessity for

of the game, and the purpose of which is to define property right and increase taxes; while the constitution and economic law are important for achieving this purpose. North (1994), p. 24.

developing economic law, and explain the reasons why all countries need to vigorously develop economic law; on this basis, this section examines the consistency between economic law and constitution in development, and explores the ways to achieve coordinated development of the two laws.

3.2.2 Constitutional Basis for Economic Law Development

The development of economic law has a solid constitutional basis. In the contemporary era, all countries are vigorously developing economic law and promoting the stipulation and implementation of substantive economic law, it is not because "economic preference" is their common legislative focus, but because economic law plays a crucial part in promoting economic and social development, and aims at better reflecting the requirements of the constitutional norms and fully realizing the overall function of the legal system.

The vigorous development of economic law reflects the requirements of the constitutional norms. In the context where all countries include more and more economic norms into their constitutions and thus forming "economic constitutions",[25] if they fail to vigorously promote the stipulation and implementation of economic law, a large number of constitutional provisions will be unenforceable, resulting in "failed constitution". It does not conform to the provisions and spirit of constitution, and in the meantime seriously affects the overall effect of the legal system, and may give rise to other problems.

According to the Rank Theory of Law, the constitution is ranked as a fundamental law or basic law, i.e., it is groundwork of other laws. The development of economic law shall satisfy the requirements of the constitution.[26] In all countries, most of the constitutional provisions that concern economy are directly associated with economic law. These constitutional norms of economics involve the fundamentals of an economy such as the economic structure, ownership, and distribution system, which constitute the "economic constitution" of each country and lay an important constitutional basis for economic law development.

For example, Article 15 of the *Constitution of China* is of great significance for the development of economic law.[27] This article included important provisions for

---

[25]The economic constitution is an important basis of economic law. The German economic jurist Böhm was one of the pioneer scholars that started studying the "economic constitution", and advanced this study together with Eucken and other scholars. The study of constitutional economics, which was initiated by Buchanan, also involves a large number of issues about economic law system. Therefore, when studying the economic law development, we need to pay attention to the close relation between the above-mentioned relevant systems and theories.

[26]The rank theory highlights the hierarchical relation between the constitution and other laws, and states that economic law shall obey the requirements of the higher-leveled constitution. Grimm and Liu (2010), p. 14.

[27]This provision should be focus of the constitutional interpretation, since it fairly important for providing constitutional support for the system construction and theoretical study of economic law.

the planned economy before the *Constitution* was amended in 1993. The currently prevailing three paragraphs of this article are directly related to economic law; they not only determine the economic structural basis of economic law, but reveal the necessity of stipulation and development of economic law. These paragraphs also define the scope, basic architecture or system of economic law regulation. Each of them is introduced as follows:

Paragraph 1 stipulates that "the state implements a socialist market economy".[28] This was the first time that China established the market economy system in the Constitution, which is of great significance for the development of economic law, because the modern market economy is an important premise and foundation for the emergence and development of economic law. In fact, as long as the market economy system is implemented, macro-economic control and market regulation need to be strengthened, and there shall be macro-economic control law and market regulation law in the realm of economic law. If the market economy system is not implemented, there will be no need for control and regulation of the market economy, let alone the existence of modern economic law. It can be seen that the above-mentioned provisions for the market economy system are directly related to the emergence and development of economic law, and they are also basis or necessity for the existence of economic law. Although not every country explicitly provides for the market economy system in its constitution,[29] as long as the market economy is implemented, economic law shall be vigorously developed.

Paragraph 2 stipulates that "the state shall strengthen economic legislation and improve macro-economic control and regulation",[30] which is directly related to Paragraph 1. As long as the market economy system is implemented, the state shall strengthen economic legislation, especially the legislation for economic law, which is the premise for improving macro-economic control and regulation. In China's economic law legislation, macro-economic control and regulation accounts for a large proportion, because China is a "big country" and also because the market economy system was just established. While China is advancing the rule-of-law construction, if it intends to "improve macro-economic control and regulation" by "strengthening economic legislation", it shall intensify the enactment and implementation of the laws for macro-economic control and regulation. In some countries, macro-economic control and regulation is not directly specified in the constitution, but contained in the constitutional interpretations. For example, the "Commerce Clause" in the *US*

[28]The original provision was "the state implements a planned economy on the basis of socialist public ownership". This great change in the economic structure involves many important theoretical and system issues of the Constitution and economic law, thus directly affecting the development of economic law.

[29]For example, Germany does not provide for the economic structure in its constitution, so it triggers some disputes on application of theories and laws, and gives rise to diverse understandings of the scope of the "economic constitution". Huang (2009), Issue 4, p. 559–573.

[30]The original provision was "the state guarantees the coordinated development of the national economy proportionately through the comprehensive balance of economic plans and the auxiliary role of market regulation". The "comprehensive balance" and "coordinated development" herein are somewhat consistent with the "macro-economic control and regulation" in the revised Constitution.

Constitution is believed to prescribe the federal macro-economic control power. Since the Marshall's times to date, the US Supreme Court has delivered lots of important judgments that have made the federal trade control power recognized and expanded in the derivative interpretations.[31]

Paragraph 3 stipulates that "the state prohibits any organization or individual from disrupting the social and economic order in accordance with law". It is an important guarantee for the healthy development of the market economy. Under the market economy system, the market order shall be effectively regulated pursuant to law for maintaining the overall social and economic order. To this end, it is necessary to strengthen the enactment and implementation of market regulation law. According to the German scholar Böhm, economic constitution could be viewed as a public choice or overall choice for maintaining the order of national economic life, proving that economic order or market order is valued universally in the constitution of all countries. In fact, it is for the purpose of protecting the social and economic order underscored by the constitution, there is the need for strengthening market regulation or market supervision, implementing market regulation power and market regulation law.

In short, the above three paragraphs in Article 15 of the Constitution of China emphasize the institutional foundation and the two regulatory spheres of economic law (the spheres of macro-economic control and market regulation), clarify the binary system and application scope of economic law, reveal the constitutional basis for promoting the economic law development, thereby laying an important constitutional foundation for the system construction of economic law and for the development of science of economic law.

The above content revolves round the constitutional provisions of China to illustrate the constitutional basis for the development of economic law, and the requirements of the constitution for the development of economic law. In fact, with the development of the constitution of each country, the norms of economics have been increasing, especially in the domains of fiscal, tax, finance and competition, which have formed a framework constituted by the binary structures of state and national, government and market, central and local, and provided a fairly important constitutional basis for the development of economic law.[32]

Of course, the constitutional basis of economic law includes the direct provisions in the constitution, and the ideas and values of equality, freedom, equity, efficiency, justice and security that are embodied in the constitution.[33] Therefore, even if some

---

[31]Zhang (2001), Issue 2, pp. 141–150.

[32]Chapter 10 of the *Basic Law of the Federal Republic of Germany* has specific provisions for the fiscal system of Germany. Part VI of the *Constitution of the Bolivarian Republic of Venezuela* (effective as of Dec 30, 1999) specially provides for the social and economic system, and the second chapter in Part VI sets out specific provisions for the systems of budget, taxation, monetary system and macro-economic control and regulation; in which Article 311 contains the principle of budget balance and the principle of fiscal balance, and Article 316 specifies the statutory taxation principle.

[33]Article 151 of the *Constitution of the Republic of Germany* (*Weimar Constitution*) stipulates that the order of economic life shall conform to the basic principles of justice and serve the purpose of guaranteeing the survival of all people with dignity. Individual economic freedom is protected in

countries do not directly define or only roughly define the economic law in their constitutions, the ideas, values and overall design of the constitution can also lay an important foundation for the development of economic law.

To achieve great development of economic law, we shall pay full attention to its constitutional foundation, and draw nutrition and support from the constitution. At the same time, while promoting the all-round implementation of the constitution, we shall also stress the development of economic law, because lots constitutional principles and rules are implemented through economic law; if the development of economic law is not fully enough, it will affect the realization of the constitutional goals. In fact, the development of economic law is not only a requirement of the constitutional provisions, but a requirement for developing the constitution itself, i.e., it is able to promote the development of the constitution.

3.2.3 Development of Economic Law to Promote Development of Constitution

The development of economic law helps to enrich and improve the content of constitution, and then promote its development. A large number of "system laws" in the realm of economic law are related to the constitution; given this, in the process of resolving the problems concerning the constitution-related systems, the development of economic law will naturally promote the development of constitution. The system arrangements and the rule-of-law construction concerning fiscal, tax, finance, industry, competition and foreign trade in the realm of economic law have a greater impact on the development of constitution.

In the early days of economic law, in order to strengthen market regulation, the US Congress successively adopted the *Interstate Commerce Act of 1887* and the *Sherman Antitrust Act 1890*, and also established some independent regulatory agencies such as the Interstate Commerce Commission and the Federal Trade Commission, thereby forming a set of special regulatory systems.[34] They are as important as the milestones for the subsequent development of economic law. The emergence and development of economic law system not only triggers the changes in the relevant control and regulatory systems, but also promote the development of constitution.

For example, according to the trade provisions in the afore-mentioned *US Constitution*, the stipulation of the *Interstate Commerce Act of 1887* is a manifestation of

this context. Article 217 of the *Constitution of the Dominican Republic* (adopted on Jan 26, 2010) prescribes that the economic system is established in the framework of free competition, equal opportunity, social responsibility, and participation in solidarity, and based on economic growth, wealth redistribution, social fairness and justice, social and territorial cohesion and environmental sustainability. All of the above provisions reflect the value and spirit of the constitution.

[34]In the realm of administrative law, the studies on the regulatory bodies are inspiring for understanding the market regulation in the realm of economic law. Song (2010), Issue 6, pp. 53–71.

the trade control power of the Congress,[35] but after the implementation of this Act, with the development of trade and the emergence of many disputes, the trade control at the federal level and the exercise of trade control power became an important issue, forcing the US Supreme Court to make complex interpretations for years.[36] In the process when these interpretations were made, the trade control and regulation power has expanded, the development of economic law had made headways, and the constitution itself has also been enriched and improved.[37]

The contemporary economic law of China emerged and developed during the transitional period from a planned economy to a market economy. While China's reform and opening-up was promoting the emergence and development of economic law, it has also brought about the development and prosperity of the commodity economy, and gradually realized a consensus on the implementation of the market economic system and the strengthening of macro-economic control. In fact, at the beginning of reform and opening-up, China recognized many shortcomings of the government's direct management of the micro-economy, and begun to emphasize "macro-regulation", which is in essence "macro-control".[38] In the 1980s, China's regime reforms and economic law system practices in the fields of fiscal, taxation, finance, and prices, especially the "decentralization and profit-sharing" and "deregulation"

[35]According to Article 1 (8) of the US Constitution, the Congress has several important powers, including taxation power, loaning power, coinage power, and the power for controlling and regulating international trade and interstate trade. These powers are directly related to the macro-economic control power and market regulation power in economic law.

[36]The different cases in different periods have given rise to a rich variety of theories and principles, such as the "production-trade" distinction theory, the "trade flow" theory, the "direct correlation" principle, the Cooley Doctrine. In the process of constitutional changes, the federal regulatory power has kept increasing, and the scope of state intervention has expanded. The above-mentioned constitutional interpretation process is the process of continuously developing the constitution by integrating the practice of economic control and regulation. It can be seen that the constitutional interpretation is fairly important. "It is the core issue of the contemporary constitution and judicial review theory". Whittington (2006), p. 2.

[37]Marshall, Chief Justice of the United States Federal Court, believes that the constitutional provisions can only outline the grandeur and point out important objectives. The good interpretation of the constitution should allow the national legislature to have the discretion of choice, thus fulfilling its highest responsibilities in the most beneficial way for the people. As long as all the appropriate means are consistent with the letter and spirit of the constitution, it is constitutional. Marshall's ideas help to understand the relationship between economic law and the constitution, as well as the constitutionality of economic law. Zhang (2011), p. 98–100.

[38]On October 20, 1984, at the Third Plenary Session of the 12th CPC Central Committee, the *Decision of the Central Committee of the CPC on Reform of the Economic System* proposed "macro adjustment", emphasizing "using prices, taxes, and comprehensively on the basis of timely grasp of economic dynamics". Economic leverage such as credit, in order to regulate the major proportional relationship between total social supply and total demand, accumulation and consumption, adjust the flow of financial, material and human resources, adjust the layout of industrial structure and productivity, regulate market supply and demand, and regulate foreign economic exchanges. "This is roughly equivalent to the later understanding of "macro-control." By September 30, 1988, the concept of "macro-economic control" had begun to be used in the report of the Third Plenary Session of the 13th CPC Central Committee.

of the state, have deepened the system construction of market-oriented reforms[39]; it was in fact a process where the state kept improving macro-economic control and regulation mainly through the legalized economic means. The above-mentioned regime reforms have greatly promoted the emergence and development of economic law, while the development of economic law and related economic system reforms have played an important role in promoting the final establishment of the market economic system and macro-economic control in Constitution, and for promoting the overall revision of Article 15 of the Constitution.

"Macro-economic control and regulation" was included into the *Constitution of China* and became an important legal concept, it is especially important issue for the development of macro-economic regulation and control law in economic law. With the deepening, improvement and stabilization of the economic system reform, the important achievements of various system reforms and regime changes, which were achieved after China's constitutional amendment in 1993, are not only defined in economic law, but contained in the further constitutional amendments in the future, which will be another important impetus of economic law for the development of constitution.

In the process of reform and opening-up in China, the National People's Congress has a lot of delegated legislation in the field of economic law, the "pilot legislative model" is popular, many regime changes are often "going and trying beforehand" in the field of economic law, and sometimes there may even be "benign unconstitutionality" (it concerns the issue of the consistency between economic law and constitution, which will be discussed later). At the same time, because the unconstitutionality is "benign" and economically rational, it will also promote the revision and improvement of constitution. This is also the promotion of economic law development to the development of constitution.

The promotion of economic law to the development of constitution has different manifestations in different periods and in different countries. Because China's constitutional provisions are relatively simple and principled, so the changes on the constitutional form that are slightly affected by the development of sectoral law. In the countries where the constitutions contain more detailed and complicated textual content, the development of economic law and other sectoral laws is able to promote the development of constitution more prominently.

The above paragraphs, by taking the US market regulation act and China's macro-economic regulation and control law as examples, explain how the development of economic law promotes the development of constitution, from which we can learn the different characteristics of the development of economic law and constitution in different countries and in different periods. However, even if the system construction of a country is unique, it should pay attention to the coordination of economic law and constitution in the development process.

[39]Zhang (2009b), Issue 6, pp. 122–35.

3.2.4 Coordination of Economic Law and the Constitution Amid Development

Based on the above understanding, the interaction between economic law and constitution in development is worthy of attention: on the one hand, the development of economic law needs to be based on constitution, and vigorously developing economic law is both a requirement of the constitutional provisions and a need to implement the constitution; on the other hand, the development of economic law contributes to the enrichment and perfection of constitution, and thus promotes the development of constitution. Therefore, while studying the development of constitution and economic law and exploring their relationship, we must consider the two-way interaction between these two laws, and especially pay attention to their respective economics and normativity, so as to enhance their consistency and coordination, and ensure of their "coordinated development".

The "economics" shared by constitution and economic law[40] is an important prerequisite for the coordinated development of the two laws. With the increasing economic norms in constitution, the "economics" of constitution has become increasingly prominent. The continuous enrichment of economic constitution reflects the needs of the times and the requirements for development; and from the perspective of development trends, the economic constitution may increase with each passing day. To implement and embody economic constitution, we must vigorously promote the development of economic law. Otherwise, if a country's economic law cannot be materially developed, then its constitutional provisions cannot be implemented, the economic development may be substantially impaired. In fact, major countries have been or are working hard to build a relatively complete and developed economic law system, which is very important for promoting their economic and social development.

The "normativity" shared by the constitution and economic law constitutes the basis for the coordinated development of the two laws. As an important part of the legal system, both the constitution and economic law have regulatory functions and similarities in terms of normativity.[41] In addition, as mentioned earlier, constitutional norms and economic law norms correspond to two different types of order, and the two types of norms have different levels or ranks. Therefore, economic law norms are not allowed to collide or conflict with higher-level constitutional norms, but based on the economic norms in constitution and consistent with the economic constitution. It should be said that clarifying the levels of various norms is very important for the coordinated development of the two laws.

Considering their common economics and normativity, we shall pay attention to the consistency between the constitution and economic law. On the one hand,

---

[40]Zhang (2009c), pp. 48–59.

[41]The regulatory nature and regulatory functions of economic law, which have been frequently discussed in the academic community, are different from the regulatory function of the constitution which might be understood as the function of norm or restriction. van Maarseveen et al. (2007), p. 315.

from the perspective of legal effect, economic law norms shall be consistent with constitutional norms, otherwise there may be danger of unconstitutionality; on the other hand, from the perspective of legal development, the constitution shall incorporate the development results of economic law and make appropriate adjustments in a timely manner, so as to maintain consistency between the two laws. Only by achieving consistency on the basis of economics and normativity can the coordinated development of the two laws be achieved.

In order to improve the consistency or coordination between economic law and the constitution, judicial or non-judicial judgment is needed to determine whether there is any inconsistency or incoordination between economic law and the constitution. Among them, the "judicial judgment" made by the court through judicial review has legal effect and is therefore very important. The constitutional review of the judiciary based on the constitution is unidirectional. In a certain period of time, the legislation involving economic law norms may be declared as "unconstitutional".[42] However, with the deepening of the court's understanding of the state control and regulatory functions, the interpretation of the constitution is also changing. For example, in the United States, some individual economic law systems (e.g., income tax system) that were once considered to be inconsistent with the Constitution are no longer considered "unconstitutional"; and some countries even provide the income tax system directly in their constitutions.[43] The changes in the afore-mentioned judicial judgments or constitutional interpretations, and the development of related specific systems, reflect the mutual influence and adaptation of the constitution and economic law in the process of development.

In addition, scholars and non-judicial subjects such as the public and related organizations can make their "non-judicial judgments" on the consistency or coordination of economic law and the constitution based on their own observations. With the improvement of people's legal awareness, especially constitutional awareness, people are paying more and more attention to legality and constitutionality, which will promote the coordination between the constitution and economic law in the development. On the one hand, based on the important influence of macro-economic control and market regulation on national property right, economic freedom, and other basic rights, the constitutionality of the formulation and implementation of economic law systems is becoming increasingly important; therefore, economic law must conform to and coordinate with the constitutional provisions. On the other hand, based on the requirements of the economic constitution, we must vigorously strengthen the formulation and implementation of macro-economic control law and market regulation law, limit the power of the state in accordance with the law, and protect the

[42]For example, the United States declared the *US Federal Income Tax Law* unconstitutional in 1895 (the income tax was not resumed until 1913), the declared the *National Industrial Recovery Act* unconstitutional in in 1935.

[43]For example, the United States no longer considers the income tax system unconstitutional. In the German basic law or the constitutions of Brazil and other countries, the income tax system is specified, and there are multiple provisions for the macro-economic control system and market regulation system that involve fiscal, tax, and financial functions.

right to economic development of market entities,[44] instead of being captured by interest groups or arbitrarily obstruct the development of economic law. At present, the ice that hinders China's development needs to be broken through reform, and many regime bottlenecks, such as the economic system and the financial system, need to be broken through; and the barriers to fair competition need to be broken. In order to solve the above-mentioned problems one by one, the coordinated reforms of economic, political and social systems are especially needed, and the coordinated development and common guarantee of economic law and the constitution is also needed.

The constitution is developing, so is the economic law. Whether at the normative level or at the value level, it is necessary to maintain coordination between the two laws in dynamic adjustment; otherwise, if the two laws are not coordinated or inconsistent, many negative effects may occur. Both the lagging development of the constitution and the lagging development of economic law will bring adverse effects on the overall construction of the rule of law.

3.2.5 Conclusion

Economic law is a law that promotes development, but its own development issues are also extremely important and in need of intensive study. Whether economic law and other sectoral laws could develop in a coordinated manner involves both the "adjacent relation" in the legal system and the quality and benefit of economic law development. Most of all, the coordinated development of economic law and the constitution shall be thoroughly inquired, since it has broad implications and concerns the long-term development of economic law and the constitution.

This section mainly discusses the constitutional basis for the development of economic law, and the promoting effect of the economic law development on the development of the constitution. It is evident that the economic law development is out of the question without the support and guarantee of the constitutional basis, and promoting the economic law development is not only a requirement of the constitutional norms, but also a need to implement the constitution. On the other hand, the development of economic law itself enriches and improves the constitution to some extent, and then promotes the development of the constitution. The above discussion helps explain why all countries should promote the development of economic law, and promote the coordinated development of economic law and the constitution.

All in all, this section focuses on the interaction and coordination between economic law and the constitution in the development process, and attempts to discover and solve the inconsistency between the two laws based on their common economics and normativity, and in reference to judicial and non-judicial judgments, in an aim to improve their consistency and coordination, and coordinate their development in an all-round manner.

[44] Zhang (2012), Issue 2, pp. 3–9.

Maintaining the dynamic and coordinated development of economic law and the constitution helps achieve good law-based governance, and address the unconstitutional problems (or "benign unconstitutionality") of economic law. Moreover, if we can combine the dynamic development of economy and society, pay attention to the dynamic regime changes and system adaptation, and strengthen the substantial judicial review, it will greatly benefit the benign development of economic law.

We need to probe into the large number of constitutional issues involved in economic law and the large number of economic law issues involved in economic constitution. It is increasingly important to pay attention to the relationship between economic law and the constitution, and promote their coordinated development. Given this, the economic law research in the future should not only stress the cross-research results such as "constitutional economics", but the cross researches on science of economic law, science of constitutional law, and other legal disciplines. This is very important and greatly beneficial to the promotion of overall legal science prosperity and the development of the rule of law.

3.3 Thinking of "Double Adjustment" in Economic Law

3.3.1 Presenting Problems

Structural adjustment is closely associated with economic growth, and directly affects the quality and quantity of economic development. One-sided emphasis on economic growth will inevitably lead to breeding of shortcomings, fail to overstep the "limits of growth", and make economic development unsustainable.[45] For this reason, while paying attention to economic growth, it is still necessary to appropriately adjust the structure of the economic system, and make the economic structure more optimized. Since the structure of the economic system determines its function, economic structural adjustment is a basic problem that a country needs to constantly solve.[46] It is long-term and sustainable problem, not any temporary bail-out measure. Therefore, regardless of occurrence of a financial crisis or implementation of a "low-carbon" economy, the economic structure needs to be adjusted in a timely manner.

Economic restructuring is carried out with effective economic means and legal means. The academic circle has made plenty of discussions about the economic means, including economic policies and policy tools, but not put energies into the

[45] In the 1970 s, the economists with the Club of Rome raised the issue of "limits to growth", which did not receive widespread attention at that time, it is the numerous problems occurring nowadays make people aware of the importance of this theoretical foresight. Meadows (2006).

[46] Many economists have done in-depth research on the basic issues of economic restructuring. Among them, Fischer, Clark, Leontief, Kuznets, Rostow, Channery, Lewis and Tinbergen have all made great contributions, and their research provides important basis of economics for exploring the legal issues of economic structural adjustment.

study of the legal means, including the legal system and its adjustment approaches.[47] In fact, the adjustment of the economic structure directly affects the rights and interests of the relevant subjects, so legal means are indispensable; the economic behaviors of various subjects, in particular, need to be regulated by economic law.

It can be seen that in real economic life, in many industries and fields, in order to achieve effective economic development, it is necessary to continuously adjust the economic structure at the economic level and strengthen the adjustment of economic law at the legal level, so as to form "coexistence of economic structural adjustment and economic law adjustment" and "coexistence of policy adjustment and legal adjustment", thus raises the issue of "double adjustment" worthy of attention.[48]

The above-mentioned "double adjustment" is directly related to many complex issues in the economic, social, political, and legal fields; it is a cross-cutting issue that involves macro, meso and micro levels, and related to development economics, development sociology, development politics and development science of law.[49] This issue runs through the economic development of a country and directly determines whether a country's economy can grow steadily and healthily. However, due to many reasons, the systematic and comprehensive exploration of the "double adjustment" issue still needs to be deepened. It should be especially thought about and explored from the perspective of economic law.

This section presents an opinion that economic structural adjustment depends on the effective adjustment of economic law, the relationship between policy adjustment and legal adjustment shall be properly handled, and the problem of "emphasizing policies and neglecting laws" commonly existing in the process of "double adjustment" shall be addressed. To this end, it is necessary to strengthen the adjustment of the regulatory structure and legislative structure of economic law, solve the important economic law issue of "double adjustment", and thereby improving the level of rule of law in economic structural adjustment.

Following the above line of thought, this section attempts to show that improving the level of rule of law in economic restructuring is a new important proposition in the science of economic law and the science of law. As a kind of macro-economic control behavior, the economic structural adjustment at the national level involves many rights and responsibilities of the subject and the recipient of the regulation; only by introducing and emphasizing the adjustment of economic law, can we ensure the standardization of the structural adjustment behavior, and better protect the legitimate rights and interests of relevant subjects, protect social welfare and basic human

---

[47] At present, the monographs on the issue of structural adjustment from the legal perspective of law are hard to come by, the academic circle is more interested in studying certain types of economic structures such as regions and industries; moreover, in the construction of legal system, few attention was paid to the macroscopic issues such as economic structural adjustment.

[48] Chinese economist Xie Guozhong proposed that China's economic structural adjustment has entered a "double adjustment" stage combining cyclical adjustment and structural adjustment, but this still focuses on economic adjustment without considering legal adjustment. This chapter pays more attention to the "double adjustment" at the economic and legal levels, as well as the policy adjustment and legal adjustment of the corresponding means.

[49] Zhang (2005), Issue 3.

rights, and achieve the adjustment goals of economic law while promoting the stable development of the economy.

3.3.2 *Economic Structural Adjustment Depends on Effective Adjustment of Economic Law*

Economic structural adjustment and economic law adjustment fall into different types and levels. Generally speaking, the adjustment of economic structure depends on the effective adjustment of economic law, and the latter has important value for ensuring the legality and effectiveness of the former. Through many measures taken in the process of adjusting the economic structure, we can see their internal relationship more clearly.

Generally speaking, the economic structure includes industrial structure, investment structure, consumption structure, distribution structure, regional structure, etc. There are complex relationships between these multi-level and multi-type structures, concerning lots of realms such as society, politics, and law, and directing affecting the stable development of economy and society and the long-term stability of the country. Since the outbreak of the economic crisis in 2008, China has attached great importance to the adjustment of the above structures and tried to solve the problems of structural imbalances or uncoordinated development. In terms of industrial structure, China developed plans for the adjustment and revitalization of the "ten industries".[50] In terms of consumption structure, China stresses to improve the consumption power of the people, continuously expand domestic demand, and implemented a number of measures such as "home appliances to the countryside".[51] In terms of distribution structure, various measures such as adjusting economic policies are adopted based on the imbalance in the distribution ratio of the state, enterprises and individuals, and the problem of unequal distribution in the realm of personal distribution.[52] In terms of regional structure, in order to solve the imbalances in regional development

[50]The state intensively introduced the plans for the adjustment and revitalization of ten major industries, including automobiles, steel, textiles, equipment manufacturing, shipping, electronic information, petrochemicals, light industry, non-ferrous metals and logistics, covering all important industrial industries in China. The core of the multiple implementation rules and related policies that support the above-mentioned "Ten Major Plans" is to adjust the structure and change the development pattern.

[51]Some policy measures have drawn wide concern, e.g., the "down to the countryside" policy (to enable rural residents to access to home appliances, agricultural machinery, automobiles and motorcycles), the polity for halving the purchase tax of small-displacement passenger cars, and the policy for replacing old appliances with new ones.

[52]The *Notice on Further Strengthening the Management of Collection of Personal Income Tax for High-income Individuals* (GuoShuiFa [2010] No. 54) issued by the State Administration of Taxation (SAT); and the *Notice on Adjusting the Business Tax Policy for Individual Housing Transfer* (CaiShui [2009] No. 157) issued by the Ministry of Finance and SAT.

and the dual structure of urban and rural areas, some regulations to promote regional development are promulgated.[53]

Many of the above-mentioned measures for adjusting the economic structure have been implemented in the form of policies and legal provisions, which directly correspond to the right-obligation structure and right-interest structure in the realm of law. In view of this, the economic structural adjustment cannot be understood simply from an economic perspective, but from a legal perspective. To ensure that the economic structural adjustment could comply with the rules governing subjects and procedures, and the legitimate rights and interests of relevant subjects are protected, economic law should be adjusted properly.

The economic structural adjustment depends on the effective adjustment of economic law, because the economic law adjustment has a significant impact or adverse effect on the economic structural adjustment, and provides an important legal guarantee for the economic structural adjustment, and thereby helpful for fulfilling the goals of economic structural adjustment. Considering the actual situation, the economic structural adjustment has prominent policy nature, while the adjustment of economic law shows prominent legality. Since economic structural adjustment involves the rights and interests of various subjects, the relationship between policies and laws needs to be properly resolved, so economic structural adjustment cannot be separated from the comprehensive regulation and effective adjustment of economic law.

Effective "adjustment" of economic law involves two aspects of content: on the one hand, relevant economic relations need to be adjusted. on the other hand, the economic law system also needs to be changed accordingly in the process of economic structural adjustment, so as to provide legal prerequisites and system basis for the economic structural adjustment, it is also an important reason why all countries are strengthening the legislation for economic structural adjustment. At the same time, the "effectiveness" of economic law adjustment shall be emphasized. Since the purpose of economic structural adjustment is to improve the efficiency and effectiveness of economic operation, the adjustment of economic law must also conform to the "performance principle", i.e., optimize the economic structure to achieve the goals of structural adjustment, and finally realize the healthy operation and coordinated development of economy.[54]

In addition, the effective adjustment of economic law also has a prominent "regulatory nature", i.e., it has the attribute of combining positive promotion with negative restriction and prohibition. This is inherently consistent with the policy nature of the economic restructuring. For example, the industrial restructuring is compulsory and arbitrary, restrictive and introductory. Fully grasping the regulatory nature of economic law adjustment will help to better understand and solve the problem of rule of law in economic restructuring.

---

[53]The *Opinions of the State Council on Further Implementing the Revitalization Strategy for the Old Industrial Bases in Northeast China* (GuoFa [2009] No. 33).

[54]Zhang (2009), p. 21.

3.3.3 *Prominent Problems in "Double Adjustment"*

The economic structural adjustment relies on the economic law adjustment, but this "double adjustment" process in China is characterized with a prominent problem of "putting policies before laws", i.e., great attention is paid to working out or amending the fiscal, financial, industrial and foreign trade policies for economic structural adjustment, yet giving little care to the corresponding legislation and law enforcement, which results in a relatively low-level rule of law in economic structural adjustment.

The economic structural adjustment is an economic problem, yet it is associated with the changes on the property right and interests of the relevant subjects, making it a necessity to define the rights, obligations and responsibilities of the relevant subjects according to law, and in particular, the state macro-economic control right shall be specified by law. However, the legislation in many realms remains absent or low-level at present, so that the dominant role of policy is even more prominent.

For example, in terms of industrial structure, the current legislation mainly includes the industrial restructuring provisions and guiding catalogues issued by the State Council,[55] but such legislation hierarchy is too low for such an important realm. In terms of investment structure, the direct legislation of the highest hierarchy is administrative regulations, the regulations on entities and procedures are quite inadequate; because of this, the "4-trillion-yuan stimulus package", which was a provisional means to deal with the financial crisis, triggered people to worry about the inadequate legislation or non-compliance in the realms of budget law, national debt law, and investment law.[56] In terms of distribution structure, China still lacks a comprehensive arrangement, and the policies and legal norms on distribution are scattered and without unified goals, leading to chaotic distribution order and unfair distribution. In terms of consumption structure, consumption power, consumption level and CPI are directly related to the adjustment of consumption structure, and are also closely linked to the micro-level subject rights and the macro-level economic operation, but the lack of overall consumption legislation directly causes inadequate domestic demand.

In addition, in terms of regional structure, there are similar prominent problems. For example, in order to solve the problem of unbalanced regional development, based on the differences of different regions in the east, west, central, and north-east, and based on the special characteristics of different economic zones such as the Yangtze River Delta, the Pearl River Delta, and the Bohai Rim, combined with

---

[55]Such as the *Interim Provisions for Promotion of Industry Structure Adjustment* issued by the State Council in 2005, and the years' multiple versions of the *Catalogue for Guiding Industrial Restructuring* ratified by the State Council in several years.

[56]Any huge budget expenditure requires adjustment of the original budget arrangement, which is already specified in the *Budget Law of the People's Republic of China*. But the State Council did not implement the budget adjustment procedure, and the National People's Congress did not exercise its budget oversight power, which triggered people to doubt about non-compliance.

economic geography and legal geography, China has introduced a series of opinions and related systems were introduced,[57] but the regional structural adjustments that have far-reaching effects on the national economic map were more affected by policies and the level of rule of law was relatively low.

To sum up, the adjustment of economic structure calls for paying attention to economic level and policy level, as well as to the legal level, especially the level of economic law (to stress the role of economic law in the adjustment of economic structure). To improve the level of rule of law in economic restructuring, it is necessary to view the role of policies and laws objectively, strengthen legislation, improve the hierarchy and quality of legislation, and at the same time strengthen law enforcement, so as to ensure that the laws are strictly observed. Both legislation and law enforcement are directly related to the structural adjustment of economic law itself.

3.3.4 "Double Adjustment" and Structural Adjustment of Economic Law

To solve the prominent problems in the "double adjustment", it is necessary to make moderate adjustment to the structure of economic law; in particular, the normative and legislative structures of economic law shall be optimized. The normative structure of economic law mainly indicates the internal constitution of economic law norms, including the subject structure, right-duty structure, and responsibility structure of economic law. The legislative structure of economic law denotes the internal constitution of the economic law legislative system, including the laws, regulations, and rules of the nature of economic law. These two structures of economic law are closely related: the adjustment of the normative structure is reflected through legislation and affects the changes in the legislative structure; the adjustment of the legislative structure affects the adjustment of subject structure and right-duty structure. To this end, we should pay attention to the "dual structure" formed by the normative structure and legislative structure of economic law, and make appropriate adjustment to these structures. The following paragraphs will unfold analysis by taking the normative structure of economic law as an example.

From the perspective of the normative structure of economic law, the adjustment of economic structure concerns two types of subjects: one is the subject that adjusts the economic structure, mainly including the government and its functional departments; the other is a subject that exists in a certain type of economic structure and needs structural adjustment, mainly including the diverse types of main market players. In different economic structures, the specific combinations of subjects may roughly fall into the above two types, and then form the "dual structure" of subjects.

[57] The *Opinions of the State Council on Further Implementing the Revitalization Strategy for the Old Industrial Bases in Northeast China* (GuoFa [2009] No. 33); the *Guiding Opinions of the State Council on Further Promoting the Reform and Opening-up and Economic and Social Development in the Yangtze River Delta Region* (GuoFa [2008] No. 30).

The above-mentioned subject structure corresponds to the complex right-duty structure of economic law, and involves the complicated power/right allocation issues. For example, at the national level, the power of the central government to adjust the economic structure is an important macro-economic control power, which directly affects the overall economic operation and the improvement of the economic system. In terms of the economic subjects in a certain economic structure, it involves many specific rights, such as investment right, distribution right and consumption right (the above rights are summarized from the perspective of economic structural adjustment), and each right is related to multiple economic structures. Among them, the investment right involves the amount of investment, investment area and investment scope, and is related to the investment structure, industrial structure and regional structure. The distribution right is the right to enjoy the return on investment, and other rights to participate in wealth sharing; it is related to the distribution structure and consumption structure. The consumption right includes corporate consumption right and personal consumption right, production consumption right and living consumption right, and they are related to the consumption structure and investment structure. It can be seen that the structural adjustment or institutional arrangement in economic law is related to the allocation of the above rights or the formation of a specific right-duty structure, which has a direct impact on the economic structural adjustment.

In fact, in various types of specific economic structures such as industrial structure, investment structure, consumption structure, and distribution structure, they respectively contain or correspond to a specific "normative structure". Generally, the adjustment of the normative structure directly affects the adjustment of economic structure, and the adjustment of economic structure necessarily involves a given normative structure.

For example, the adjustment of industrial structure, which is an important type of economic structure, involves institutional arrangement (e.g., industry entry and exit), qualifications of relevant subjects, investment right or property right of market entities. From the perspective of the correlation between economy and law, the adjustment of industrial structure is also the adjustment of the property right structure, all the problems about the allocation of rights and powers shall be properly resolved. In fact, in the process of industrial structure adjustment, the entry or exit of different subjects in different industries is directly related to the exercise of industry control power. Sometimes, the industry control power may conflict with the property right of relevant market subjects. To this end, it is necessary to identify which subjects enjoy investment right, and the limits and boundaries of the state's exercise of industry control power, in order to effectively allocate rights and powers, and thereby form a specific right-duty structure in the realm of industry law.

By an extension of this logic, the regime of both constitution and economic law may concern the protection of property right of market subjects, the exercise of power by governments at different levels and their functional departments.[58] We

---

[58]According to Douglass C. North, there shall be a certain mechanism that brings social returns and private returns closer to each other. Once ownership is not determined or not implemented,

shall properly solve the various structural problems in economic law and constantly improve its normative structure, so that we can better adjust economic law and achieve the goal of economic structural adjustment.

In the process of adjusting and improving the normative structure of economic law, attention must be paid to the inherent correlation between various types of economic structures. For example, the consumption structure is associated with consumption power and consumption right, while consumption power (including the consumption ability in production and livelihood) is related to the distribution structure.[59] In the entire distribution system, the respective proportions of governments, enterprises, individuals and other subjects are related to the consumption capacity of various subjects and affect the consumption structure. In addition, a country chooses to focus on government consumption, corporate consumption or household consumption, it will affect the adjustment of relevant investment structure and industrial structure. In short, if the distribution structure could be effectively adjusted, it will affect the consumption structure and investment structure, and in turn affect the industrial structure; while the adjustment of the industrial structure will affect the regional structure and then affect the overall economic structure.

The internal connection between the above-mentioned various economic structures is the basis for exercising macro-economic control power and protecting investment power, consumption power, and distribution power in economic law. All kinds of powers and rights shall be effectively allocated according to the above-mentioned relations and conflicts between powers and rights, so as to achieve the coordination of various structures and improve the internal structure of economic law.

The adjustment and improvement of the normative structure of economic law will help to bring into play the function of the economic law system, improve the level of rule of law in economic structure adjustment, and provide a solid legal basis and guarantee for the optimization of economic structure. The adjustment of the above-mentioned structures also requires the optimization of the legislative structure, including the improvement of the legislation hierarchy, the improvement of the origin system, the appropriate relationship between the number of legal norms, so that we can better solve the important economic law issues in the "double adjustment".

---

there will be inconsistencies between the two, and then affect a country's economic growth. This conclusion is inspiring for examining the correlation between economic structural adjustment and legal structural adjustment, and for emphasizing the protection of the rights and interests of relevant subjects in the process of structural adjustment. North (2017), p. 7.

[59]To improve residents' consumption power, we need to adjust the national income distribution structure, increase the income level of low-and middle-income residents, pay attention to the role of employment and labor remuneration in primary distribution, and pay attention to the role of social security and public services in secondary distribution. They are important issues that must be addressed when adjusting the national income distribution structure.

3.3.5 *Important Economic Law Issues in "Double Adjustment"*

Whether it is the "double adjustment" of economic structure and economic law, or the "double adjustment" of the structure of economic law itself, a series of important economic law issues must be resolved. These issues include regimes, macro-economic control power, allocation of rights of market subjects, protection of the rights and interests of various subjects, the implementation of the structural adjustment, the coordination of various sectoral laws of economic law, and the coordination of the legislative structure of economic law. Studying these issues will help to better solve the problem of "putting policies before laws" that is common in the process of economic structural adjustment.

From the perspective of regime, all economic structural adjustments are related to a specific system. For example, the industrial structure involves the planning system or the specific industrial management system, the investment structure involves the investment system and financial system, and the distribution structure involves the overall distribution system, especially the fiscal system and the taxation system. The formation of the above regimes is directly related to the current legal system, especially the regime law in the realm of economic law. The adjustment of various economic structures is subject to a certain management system. Whether a regime is optimized is often directly related to whether the economic structure is optimized. Therefore, it is necessary to make adjustments and reforms to certain management systems and readjust the authority of the relevant economic law subjects. However, in recent years, while China is adjusting its economic structure, it fails to pay enough attention to the regime adjustment; it is an important issue that needs special attention during the adjustment of economic law.

Directly related to the afore-mentioned regime issues is the issue of the right to adjust the economic structure. In the entire regime system, which organ or institution has the right to adjust the type of specific economic structure, and which aspects of adjustment power (such as the right to adjust the industrial structure, and the right to adjust the investment structure) must be legally defined.

At the national level, the above-mentioned adjustment powers are usually embodied in certain types of macro-economic control power, such as industry control power and investment control power. These types of control power, if compared with economic control or financial control power, seem to be less "macroscopic", but they are more "integrated" than the two macro-control powers; and they are as integrated as the planning control power (so they can fall into the category of the generalized planning control power), but they are slightly "microscopic" and "concrete" than the narrowly-defined planning control power. In-depth study is needed to probe into the above-mentioned control powers, in particular, when exercising the right to adjust the distribution structure and regional structure, multiple types of macro-control powers shall be employed at the same time so as to achieve the corresponding goals.

Closely related to the above-mentioned structural adjustment power are the many specific rights of various subjects such as market entities, including investment right, consumption right, and distribution right. In the process of structural adjustment, how to fairly protect the specific rights of various subjects is an important issue that needs special attention and should not be ignored.

In order to solve the above-mentioned regime issues, effectively limit the power to adjust the structure, and fully protect the specific rights and legitimate rights and interests of various subjects, we shall give full play to the specific economic law systems to optimize various economic structures. In terms of the adjustment of consumption structure, in order to expand household consumption, the government shall allocate subsidies and adopt other measures, and at the same time strengthen the protection of the consumer rights and interests pursuant to law, rectify and standardize market order, safeguard food and drug safety, and develop consumer credit, etc. The above-mentioned multiple measures involve various realms of economic law, e.g., finance, consumer rights protection, product quality, competition, and banking. We shall employ the above-mentioned various economic law systems in a coordinated manner, so as to achieve the goal of adjusting the consumption structure.

In terms of the adjustment of the adjustment of distribution structure, in order to increase the proportion of resident income in the distribution of national income and the proportion of labor remuneration in the primary distribution, coordinate the growth of urban-rural resident income and labor remuneration with economic development, we must expand the size of the middle-income group to form an "olive-shaped" income distribution structure.[60] This not only affects the income-earning capacity and consumption capacity of the economic law subjects, but also involves the overall income distribution issue; it requires the integrated adjustment of economic law systems (fiscal, taxation and securities law systems), and social law systems (e.g. labor and social security laws).

The coordination of the above-mentioned various types of economic law systems should be particularly reflected in the coordination of specific economic law measures. For example, the adjustment and revitalization plan of the "Ten Major Industries" issued by China in response to the financial crisis and economic restructuring, stipulated a series of important measures that needed to be coordinated, including fiscal subsidies, export tax rebates, preferential loans, and so on. The coordination of these specific measures is directly related to the aforementioned system, structural adjustment rights, and the specific rights of various subjects, and is the core content of coordinating various economic law systems.

The above discussion of important economic law issues helps to further explain: Why does economic structural adjustment depend on the effective adjustment of economic law? Why do we need to continuously improve the level of rule of law in economic structural adjustment? In fact, prominent real-life problems in the process of economic structural adjustment, such as illegal budget adjustment in economic law that the public is concerned about, and poor transparency in fiscal revenue and expenditure, will have a negative impact on economic structural adjustment. The reason why the above problems exist is related to the long-term "policy advancement, administrative advancement" thinking, weak legal awareness, and insufficient

[60] Li (2010), Issue 11.

attention to relevant legal procedures. Therefore, to solve the long-standing problem of "putting policy before law", there is still "a long way to go".

3.3.6 Conclusion

The benign operation and coordinated development of the economy and society require both adjustments to the economic structure and adjustments to the economic law, thus forming a "double adjustment" at different levels and with different natures. The adjustment of economic structure depends on the effective adjustment of economic law. However, in the process of "double adjustment" in China, the problem of "putting policy before law" is very prominent, which has many negative effects on the adjustment of various specific economic structures Therefore, continuously improving the level of rule of law in economic structural adjustment is a long-term and important task. To ensure the effectiveness and legitimacy of economic structural adjustment, it is necessary to make appropriate adjustments to the structure of economic law. Regardless of whether it is the adjustment of the regulatory structure of economic law or the adjustment of the legislative structure of economic law, it is very important to solve important economic law issues in the process of economic structure adjustment. Only by effectively carrying out the "double adjustment" on the structure of economic law and improving the internal structure of the "double adjustment" of policy adjustment and legal adjustment can we improve the effectiveness of economic law adjustment and better achieve the goal of economic structure adjustment. Only by promoting effective economic development can we improve the level of rule of law in economic structural adjustment and ensure the fairness and legality of structural adjustment.

The "double adjustment" discussed in this section contains three levels of implications: The first level of "double adjustment" indicates the economic structural adjustment and economic law, which is the most basic and throughout the realm of economic law. The second level of "double adjustment" indicates that in the process of "double adjustment", it is common to common across the problems of valuing policy adjustment but debasing legality adjustment. In order to solve the problem of "putting policy before law", the structure of economic law needs to be improved, both the content and form of the normative structure and legislative structure of economic law shall adjusted, this is the third level of "double adjustment". The "double adjustment" at the above three levels are closely related and involve a wide range of issues, which require more in-depth discussions in the academic community.

In the economic system and the legal system, the adjustment of economic structure and the adjustment of legal structure has always been a basic and continuous problem. Regardless of the type of structure to be adjusted, we need to stress the rationality of the internal structure from a systemic and global perspective; in order to determine whether a certain type of structure is reasonable, a structural analysis is required. Being an important systematic analysis method or holistic approach, structural analysis is of great value to the study of economic law.[61] In fact, in the process of "double adjustment", only by grasping the structure in the system and grasping the direction and intensity of adjustment on the basis of the structure, the overall adjustment can be successful.

In addition, the reason why structural analysis is so important is directly due to the principle of difference in economic law. The actual situation shows that there are differences in the capability of subjects (such as their consumption, distribution, industrial competition and regional development capabilities), the rights and duties of subjects, and scale of subjects, and it will directly affect the balance and optimization of the economic structure. The structural imbalance is an important prerequisite and basis for structural adjustment or optimization. If we could carry out effective structural analysis on basis of the universal differences in real economic life, and the resulting structural imbalances and deterioration, it would be more efficient to comprehensively solve all kinds of specific structural problems.

Directly related to the above-mentioned differences, the regulatory nature shown in the adjustment of economic law is of particular concern. In fact, the differences in reality and the necessity for structural optimization require the regulation of economic law, so as to give full play to its "promotion law" function.[62] According to economic law theory, the principle of difference and the principle of regulation are important for studying the "double adjustment" problems. Mastering these principles helps to better guide the implementation of economic law, achieve the goals of economic structural adjustment, promote further development of economic law theory, and improve the level of rule of law in economic structural adjustment in an all-round way.

References

Cheng, Xinhe. 2007. Hard law, soft law and economic law. *Gansu Social Sciences* (4).

Cheng, Xinhe. 2008. Study on China's economic law development in the past 30 years. *Journal of Chongqing University (Social Science Edition)*, p 104–108.

Grimm, Dieter, Gang Liu. trans. 2010. *Emergence and effectiveness of modern constitutionalism: past, present, and future*, 14. Beijing: Law Press China.

Huang, Hui. 2009. Application of the constitutional provisions for economic structure: on the disputes about German economic constitution. *Peking University Law Journal* (4), 559–573.

Li, Changqi, and Maoqin Huang. 2002. On the spatio-temporality of economic law. *Modern Law Science* (5).

Li, Keqiang. 2010. Several issues on adjusting economic structure and promoting sustainable development. *Qiushi* (11).

Liu, Ruifu. 2000. *Principles of economic law*, 21, 24–25. Beijing: Peking University Press.

Liu, Wenhua, Changhe Wang. 2000. The essence of economic law: coordination and its foundation of economics. *Economic Law Review* 2.

Meadows. 2006. *Limits to growth*, trans. Li, Tao et al. Beijing: China Machine Press.

[61] Wang and He (2008), Issue 5.

[62] Zhang (2008), Issue 5.

North, Douglass C. 1994. *Structure and change in economic history,* 24. Shanghai: Shanghai Joint Publishing Press, Shanghai People's Publishing House.
North, Douglass C. 2017. *The rise of the western world: a new economic history*, trans. Robert Paul, Thomas, and Li, Yiping et al., 7. Beijing: Huaxia Publishing House.
Song, Hualin. 2010. The independent regulatory bodies specified in the US administrative law. *Tsinghua University Law Journal* (6), 53–71.
van Maarseveen, Henc, et al. 2007. *Written constitution: a computerized comparative study*, trans. Chen Yunsheng, 315. Beijing: Peking University Press.
Wang, Baoshu, ed. 1999. *Principles of economic law*, 38. Beijing: Social Sciences Academic Press.
Wang, Quanxing, He Ping. 2008. On structural study in science of economic law research. *Journal of Chongqing University (Social Science Edition)* (5).
Whittington, and Keith E., Du Qiangqiang et al., trans. 2006. *Constitutional interpretation – textual meaning, original intent, and judicial review*, 2. Beijing: China Renmin University Press.
Xiao, Jiangping. 2002. *Study on History of China's economic law theory*, 288–296. Beijing: People's Court Press.
Yang, Zixuan. 2009a. *The theory of state coordinating*, 71–80. Beijing: Peking University Press.
Yang, Zixuan. 2009b. *The theory of state coordinating*, 348. Beijing: Peking University Press.
Yang, Zixuan. 2009c. *The theory of state coordinating*, 127. Beijing: Peking University Press.
Yang, Zixuan. 2009d. *The theory of state coordinating*, 192–193. Beijing: Peking University Press.
Yang, Zixuan. 2009e. *The theory of state coordinating*, 362. Beijing: Peking University Press.
Yang, Zixuan. 2009f. *The theory of state coordinating*, 342–343. Beijing: Peking University Press.
Yang, Zixuan. 2009g. *The theory of state coordinating*, 361–362. Beijing: Peking University Press.
Yang, Zixuan. 2009h. *The theory of state coordinating*, 12–13. Beijing: Peking University Press.
Yang, Zixuan. 2009i. *The theory of state coordinating*, 175–187. Beijing: Peking University Press.
Yang, Zixuan. 2009j. *The theory of state coordinating*, 340. Beijing: Peking University Press.
Yang, Zixuan. 2009k. *The theory of state coordinating*, 325. Beijing: Peking University Press.
Yang, Zixuan. ed. 2000. *New theory on international economic law: theory of international coordinating*. Beijing: Peking University Press.
Zhang, Qianfan. 2001. The regulation of US Federal Government over interstate trade. *Journal of Nanjing University (Philosophy, Humanities & Social Sciences)* (2), 141–150.
Zhang, Qianfan. 2011. *The United States federal constitution,*98–100. Beijing: Law Press China.
Zhang, Shouwen. 2009. *Pandect of economic law,* 21. Beijing: China Renmin University Press.
Zhang, Shouwen. 2005. "Science of development law" and development of legal science – on the development concept in economic law theory. *Law Science* (3).
Zhang, Shouwen. 2008. On the promoted economic law. *Journal of Chongqing University (Social Science Edition)* (5).
Zhang, Shouwen. 2009a. Interpretation of the world financial crisis from an economic law perspective. *Legal Forum* (3).
Zhang, Shouwen. 2009b. The transcendence of China's economic law development: from the perspective of distribution. *Tribune of Political Science and Law* (6), 122–135.
Zhang, Shouwen. 2009c. *Pandect of economic law*, 48–59. Beijing: China Renmin University Press.
Zhang, Shouwen. 2012. The right to economic development: from the perspective of economic law. *Modern Law Science* (2) p 3–9.
Zhang, Shouwen. 2016. A preliminary study of the development theory of economic law. *Law and Economy* (4).
Zhu, Chongshi, Xiaohui Li. 2008. Openness: the approach and enlightenment of China's economic law development. *Journal of Xiamen University (Arts & Social Sciences)* (3), 65–73.

Chapter 4
Distribution as a Main Line and Distribution Theory

Distribution has always been an important issue that affects economic and social development. No wonder it is an important research topic in the realms of development economics, development sociology and development politics. As a typical "distribution law", economic law shall pay more attention to the legal regulation of distribution, which is the system basis for extracting the distribution theory.

Historically, China's economic law came out along with the reform and opening up in 1978, since then distribution has become a main line running through both the theory and system of the economic law; even the economic rule of law is distribution oriented on the whole. It is because the distribution of China is obliged to resolve the "double pressure" on national economy and people's livelihood. To dissolve such pressure, we shall keep optimizing the distribution structure through regulation of economic law, so as to mitigate the imbalances caused by differential distribution. The distribution theory, which is formed while solving all distribution problems, is another important component of the economic law theory.

For the above considerations, this chapter mainly discusses the following issues:

(1) It firstly introduces the main line or "meridian" of distribution that runs through the theory and system of China's economic law, in this process we can find the distribution-oriented economic rule of law has Chinese characteristics;
(2) It analyzes the "double pressure" upon the state and nationals, and upon the government and market subjects, explains the reason why distribution has become a main line running through the theory and system of economic law, and reveals the necessity and feasibility of employing economic law to mitigate the "double pressure";
(3) It explores the ways to adjust and optimize the distribution structure according to economic law, so as to help resolve the distribution problems;
(4) Based on the principle of difference in economic law, it sets out the idea of differential distribution—an important category of the distribution theory, and then goes on interpreting the basic structure and specific content of this theory.

S. Zhang, *The New Horizon of China's Economic Law Theory*, Understanding China,
https://doi.org/10.1007/978-981-15-8824-2_4

4.1 The Main Line of Distribution Running Through the Theory and System of Economic Law

No matter it is the economic law theory and system or the economic rule of law, their development course is run through by the main line of distribution, which gave rise to the important "distribution-oriented economic rule of law". A thorough understanding of distribution provides another viewpoint for examining the development course and problems of economic law theory and system, and also provides theoretical support for extracting the distribution theory, advancing the construction of economic rule of law, and solving the distribution problems more effectively.

Given the above, this section reviews the development course of the economic law theory and system from the perspective of distribution, and explains why economic law could come out and keep developing, why it aims at solving the distribution problems, and why it has the function of regulating distribution behavior. In addition, while elaborating on the prominent problems in distribution, this section points out the development direction for the economic law theory and system.

4.1.1 Main Line of Distribution and "Two Types of Distribution"

4.1.1.1 Reasons for Paying Attention to the Main Line of Distribution

The modern economic law has not existed for more than a century since its inception. Compared with other branches of law, the history of China's economic law is particularly short.[1] Almost every ten years, the academic community likes to review their past achievements in the realm of economic law to promote academic accumulation, increase theoretical consensus, and motivate the development of the economic law system.[2] Through several rounds of summarization, many perplexities are clarified, but the understanding needs to be further deepened. Given this, we shall learn more

---

[1]The academic community has different views on the beginning of China's economic law. Some scholars argue that the translation and comment on the foreign economic law theories in the 1930s symbolize the emergence of China's economic law. But most scholars prefer to take the year 1978 as the starting point of China's economic law.

[2]Ma Hong, 1989, Review of the debates on the basic theoretical issues of economic law in the past decade, *Journal of Finance and Economics*, Issue 12, p. 55; Xie Cichang, 1989, Development of economic law in the past decade and urgent problems to be solved, *China Legal Science*, Issue 3, p. 36; Young and Middle-aged Scholars' Conversation by Writing, 1998, Discussion on several theoretical issues of economic law, *Peking University Law Journal*, Issue 3, p. 90; Young and Middle-aged Scholars' Conversation by Writing, 1998, China's science of economic law facing the 21st century, *Studies in Law and Business*, Issue 6, p. 3; Li Changqi, 2009, Contributions and shortcomings of China's economic law study in the past 30 years and its prospect, *The Jurist*, Issue 5, p. 25.

about distribution – the main line or "meridian" that runs through the development of China's economic rule of law.

As a medical term, "meridians" seem like the pathways throughout the human body. The system of economic law or science of economic law also has meridians.[3] The "meridians" running through the development course of economic law and science of economic law are interlinked or even unified. Pinpointing the "meridians" of economic law helps to study economic law and science of economic law as a whole; comprehending the "meridians" of economic law helps to probe into the underlying problems in economic law system construction or legal study, thereby seeking appropriate remedy to solve the problems and promoting the healthy development of economic law. To this end, it is really necessary to explore into the "meridians" that run through China's economic law.

What are the important "meridians" that run through economic law? There are different opinions in this regard. From an "ought-to-be" perspective, the "meridians" shall run through all dimensions of economic law, i.e., spanning all stages of development and covering all essential content. Therefore, we can interpret the economic law theory or system by going along its "meridians" of development, and identify the key content of research.

Throughout the development course of economic law, there are at least three main lines or paths worthy of attention: (1) The path of distribution (adjustment of the distribution relations) which directly concerns the ownership of interests and affects the goals of economic law regulation. We can identify the original motivation of the reform, the focus of system arrangements, and the impetus for the changes on economic law system. (2) The path of the policies related to interest distribution. The changes on these policies demonstrate how politics-oriented policies are replaced by economics-oriented policies, and reveal the value of economic policies for the reform and opening-up, economic law system construction, and legal research. (3) The path of legalization, i.e., to convert the economic policies into legal provisions. In short, along with the development of reform, adjustment of distribution relations, and changes on economic policies, both laws and legal systems are undergoing changes accordingly, it is in this process that economic law came into being and keeps developing.

The above three paths ("distribution-policy-legalization") are interconnected, dealing with both surface problems and underlying problems. In fact, they are main lines or "meridians" running through the process where economic law and science of economic law came out and keep developing, and they are also an indispensable content in economic law system construction and legal research. These "meridians" will lead us to find better solutions to the problems in economic law system and legal research.

---

[3]According to China's earliest medical classics *Yellow Emperor's Canon of Internal Medicine*, "the meridian is where the disease arises and cured". The "meridians" that pervade in the realm of economic law are as important as those one throughout the human body. Any problem in the meridians may paralyze the normal operation of entire system, so they shall maintain healthy and unobstructed.

Each of the three paths involves multi-faceted problems. In order to make the topics of discussion concentrated, the following paragraphs will mainly follow the path of distribution to review the evolution of China's economic law system or economic regulation which came out with the reform and opening up, probe into the state functions, economic policies and legal system construction that are related to distribution, and reveal their internal relations, and finally highlight the great value of distribution—an important "meridian" throughout economic law and science of economic law – to the development of economic rule of law in China.

4.1.1.2 "Two Types of Distribution" Affecting the Reform and Opening up and Development of Economic Law

Economic law is often taken as a typical "distribution law". Both the ancient sages and great thinkers thought highly of distribution.[4] Whether it is the fiscal distribution of the state or the national income distribution; whether it is the distribution of fiscal powers between state organs or the distribution of property rights between market subjects, all of them are important issues of concern in the studies of economic law system and legal science. Therefore, the perspective of distribution is very important for the economic law study.

In fact, there are diverse distribution issues in the realm of economic law, and all sectoral laws are directly associated with distribution. For example, the income and expenditure in economic law, the monetary supply in financial law, and the competition rights and interests in competition law; all of them are about the distribution of powers, rights, and interests among relevant subjects. With a view to the development history of China's economic law, the national interest distribution (including individuals and enterprises) and the state fiscal distribution are predominant types of distribution. The need to adjust the relation between the two types of distribution is a vigorous motivator that promotes China's reform and opening up and drives the emergence and development of economic law.

(1) Basic motivation: to adjust the interest distribution among individuals

The contemporary China's economic law was born in the wake of the reform and opening up. In the era of planned economy, the economic law was unable to solve the "two failures"; it was the reform and opening up that gradually created the micro-foundation and macro-framework for the regulation of economic law. Therefore, the

[4]As early as the 18th century, Morelly raised the issue of "distribution law or economic law" in his writing *Code de La Nature*, the latecomer Dezamy did so in his *Code de La Communauté* in the 19th century. In addition, Germany enforced the "act on wartime controlled economy" during the World War I, and the United States put into effect of the "crisis response act" in the 1930s, both of them were directly related to distribution. Chinese economic law scholars are also aware of the importance of distribution. In the early days of the market economy, some of them even took the legal norms on distribution as an independent law in parallel with the macro-economic control law. Li Changqi, 1995, *Economic law: the basic legal form of state intervention*, Chengdu: Sichuan People's Publishing House, pp. 403–405.

emergence and development of China's economic law is attributed to the reform and opening up, and it is the most prominent legal construction result brought by the reform and opening up.

Historically, the adjustment of the interest distribution concerning individuals and enterprises was the basic motivation for the reform and opening up. The reform is usually required when the productive relations no longer promote the development of productivity, while distribution relation is of cardinal significance in the productive relations. So many "order-chaos cycles" in history were closely related to the adjustment of distribution relation. Prior to China's reform and opening up in 1978, there had been demand for improving the interest distribution between individuals in both urban and rural areas. Driven by this demand, the farmers in some poverty-stricken areas, particularly those in Xiaogang Village in Fengyang County, Anhui Province, took the lead in implementing the household contract responsibility system. Through the reforms, with "farm output quotas fixed by household" as a basic principle, the notably improved distribution relation aroused the enthusiasm of farmers for production, marking the rural reform had achieved initial success, which built up the confidence of the decision-makers to launch an urban reform. With focus placed on enterprises, the urban reform since 1984 deals with the interest distribution among the state, enterprises and individuals. Each stage and each sphere of the reform is associated with interest distribution, e.g., "decentralization of power and transfer of profits", "separation of two powers", establishment of a modern enterprise system[5]; property right reform, price reform or other reforms, because the reform itself is to adjust the existing interest distribution pattern and create a new distribution relation.

The need to adjust the individual interest distribution is the primal motivation for the reform and opening up, and it is also the direct driving force for the emergence, change and development of China's economic law. The redistribution of individual interests not only needs the support from traditional rules and systems, but also needs new rules and new norms to solve the problems that traditional rules are incapable or less capable of solving. The practical need to adjust the individual interest distribution gave rise to the economic law.

In addition, the adjustment of the individual interest distribution reflects the profit-seeking nature of individuals, but economic law is ought to coordinate and balance the relation between individual interests and social welfare; whereas the protection of social welfare relies on the state fiscal distribution.

(2) Immediate motivation: state fiscal distribution

The need to adjust the individual interest distribution is the basic motivation for the reform and opening up, and also an important driving force for the emergence

[5]"Decentralization of power and transfer of profits", "separation of two powers" (separation of ownership from control), and the establishment of a modern enterprise system are generally recognized as the milestones in China's SOE reform. They are directly related to the reform of the distribution system, especially the adjustment of the distribution relation between the state and enterprises.

of economic law. Relatedly, the need for the state fiscal distribution is the immediate motivation for the reform and opening up, it has promoted the development of "constructive" economic legislation.

According to the researches of J. A. Schumpeter and other famous economists, and the resulting "Schumpeter-Hicks-North Proposition",[6] we can conclude that fiscal pressure is a direct motivation of reform. This proposition is also applicable to China. Before the reform and opening-up, the national economy of China was "on the verge of collapse",[7] and it's not difficult to imagine the heavy fiscal pressure at that time. Due to inadequate vitality and poor economic benefit, the domestic enterprises found it increasingly hard to transfer their profits to the state, thus making the state fiscal system, which mainly relies on business profit, become more precarious, and forcing China to embark on the reform. In today's view, the quick resolution of the fiscal crisis was the direct and important driving force for China to launch the enterprise reform in cities. From the perspective of development, the state was thinking about how to properly deal with the distribution relation between enterprises and the state, and clearly define their positioning in the primary distribution. Because of this, in the process of adjusting the interest distribution among the state, enterprises and individuals, the adjustment of the interest distribution between the state and enterprises was placed at a prominent position, which was of significance not only in fiscal or economic terms, but also in legal terms. From the perspective of economic law, we were ought to properly handle the basic distribution relation, let enterprises have independent interests and become a genuine legal person, which is the premise for laying the main foundation of the market economy; on this basis, we will be able to conduct macro-economic control and market regulation by employing economic law. Otherwise, the development of the commodity economy and economic law will be unimaginable.

The state fiscal distribution is closely related to its economic and social functions, with the core of providing public goods. Therefore, the state fiscal distribution differs from the individual interest distribution, since it represents the public benefit. Now that the state fiscal distribution depends on the benefits of private subjects such as enterprises and individuals, there may be the conflicts among individual interest, national interest, and public benefit, which may give rise to the contradictions between individual profitability and public benefit; these contradictions may evolve into those between efficiency and equity[8] that need to be resolved by relevant legal norms. In the traditional legal system, the functional positioning of each sectoral law is definite, implying that they are not suitable for extended application. Therefore, economic law as a new sectoral law is required to resolve these contradictions.

---

[6]Fan (1998).

[7]Hua Guofeng, the then Acting Premier of China's State Council, was among the first Chinese leaders that put forward such argument. Hua Guofeng, Feb 26, 1978, *Let's Unite Together and Strive for Building China into a Socialist Modern Power—The Report on the Work of the Government Delivered at the 1st Session of the Fifth National People's Congress*.

[8]These contradictions are the basic contradictions in the realm of economic law; each sectoral law in the realm of economic law shall keep coordinating and resolving these contradictions.

In short, the individual interest distribution and the state fiscal distribution, respectively as basic and direct motives, will further advance the reform and opening-up and the in-depth development of economic law. In the realm of economic law, we shall pay attention to the relation between the individual interest distribution and the state fiscal distribution, properly solve the basic contradiction between individual profitability and public benefit, and balance efficiency and equity; they are important goals and functions of economic law regulation, so they shall run through the relevant systems of economic law and serve as an important path for the development of economic law. The adjustment of the above-mentioned distribution relations is a "complexity matter", and it will become more complicated along with the development of economy and society, as well as the deepening of reform and opening-up. In order to properly solve this matter, the economic law system shall be constantly improved, and the economic law study shall be further deepened.

4.1.2 Shift of Focus of Distribution and "U-Shaped Curve"

4.1.2.1 Focus of Distribution: "Shift from Product Distribution to Right Distribution"

The above discussion on the individual interest distribution and the state fiscal distribution mainly explains the motivation and cause for China's reform and opening-up from an economic perspective. In the context where the binary structures exist everywhere, e.g., private desires and public desires, private goods and public goods, private interests and public interests, the above two types of distribution will continue advancing the reform and opening up, and promoting the development of the economic law system that reflects and guarantees the reform and opening up achievements. Besides, in the development process of the two types of distribution, various subjects have been "shifting the focus of distribution from product to right", which is directly related to the changes in economic structure, economic system and legal system.

During the planned economy period where products were in short supply (which was described as "shortage economy"[9] by János Kornai), there had been system arrangements such as unified purchase and marketing, and coupon-based supply. In addition to the State Planning Commission, the Ministry of Finance and other ministries and commissions, China also set up some functional departments such as the Ministry of Materials and the Ministry of Commerce to solve the problems in the distribution of materials and products. At that time, what the people cared most was the distribution of materials and products. In contrast, in the era of the

[9]The Hungarian economist János Kornai is known for his in-depth study on the problem of shortage, the study results were contained in his writings in the early 1980 s. Kornai, *Economics of Shortage*, Zhang Xiaoguang et al. (trans.), 1986, Beijing: Economic Science Press; Kornai, *Growth, Shortage and Efficiency: A Macro-dynamic Model of the Socialist Economy*, Cui Zhiyuan et al. (trans.), 1986, Chengdu: Sichuan People's Publishing House.

commodity economy, both materials and products have become tradable commodities, they are no longer allocated or rationed according to the national plan, the government cannot exercise flat regulation arbitrarily, but respect the legitimate rights and interests of various subjects. From a micro-level perspective, under the conditions of the commodity economy, property rights and debt rights have become important, and the relevant rights in other forms have become increasingly abundant. Both the rights of transaction subjects and the rights of management subjects have become scarce resources. How to define and protect the property rights? How to guarantee various subjects to perform their rights effectively? These issues have gradually become the focus of attention. In fact, the dentition of rights, which is also a process of allocating rights and interests, is still a matter of distribution in the final analysis.

The reason why the entire society attaches more importance to the distribution of rights is that under the conditions of a commodity economy or a market economy, transactions are more complex and in a larger volume, it is important for both individuals and the entire society to ensure the security and efficiency of transactions, reduce the costs and risks in transactions. According to the Coase Theorem, in the presence of transaction costs, the primary distribution of rights is of great significant. Therefore, the laws such as civil and commercial law, and economic law, which deal with the primary distribution of rights, have an important impact on the distribution of various rights, and directly concern the size of transaction costs at the micro-level and the overall social cost at the macro-level. In short, paying great attention to economic law and other relevant laws is fairly important, at both the micro and macro levels, for the distribution of rights and for the constant improvement of the relevant economic law systems.

The above distribution of rights is in a broad sense. The legal system practices usually include the division of power and the distribution of rights. The development process of the reform and opening up and of economic law is accompanied by the wane and wax of power and rights: the various types of economic power of the state are decentralized or decomposed, while the rights of market subjects have increased accordingly; the state has been gradually shifting from centralized administration to hierarchical decentralization, and striving to give play to the subjective initiative of market subjects as free economic subjects. Economic law has played a positive role in the above process. The decentralization and adjustment of a large amount of state power, especially the distribution of economic power (e.g., macro-economic control and market regulation), was mainly established in the form of economic law. The civil and commercial law remained underdeveloped at that time, it was neither able to solve the problem of decentralization directly, nor able to prescribe the "system law". Generally speaking, the process of highlighting the division of power and the distribution of rights is the process where the system law and regulation law in the realm of economic law came into being and started continuous development.

In the process where China's planned economy was replaced by the commodity economy and then by the market economy, the reform and opening-up policy was initiated and implemented to date, the economic law came out and keeps developing, the Chinese people have "shifted the focus of distribution from products to rights". In a word, a perspective of distribution is suitable for a better analysis of the development of economic law.

4.1.2.2 Empirical Analysis: "U-Shaped Curve" in Distribution and Its Inspiration

(1) Proposition of "U-shaped curve"

No matter it is the individual interest distribution and the state fiscal distribution—important drivers of the reform and opening-up, or the shift of distribution focus from products to rights, it will benefit a qualitative study on the basic path of the reform and opening-up from the perspective of distribution. Meanwhile, it will help to reveal the internal contradictions and basic problems in the process of the emergence and development of economic law. Besides, distribution directly concerns the amount of income or wealth, while the flow or increment of income or wealth directly reflects the direction of income or wealth distribution, as well as the adjustment of relevant powers and rights, therefore, if one of the above types of distribution is selected for empirical analysis, it will be helpful to reveal the development trajectory of the reform and opening-up and economic law from the perspective of "quantity", and further demonstrate the changes in state functions and power distribution. Considering that the perspective of the state fiscal distribution is more direct in explaining relevant issues, the following paragraphs will take fiscal revenue as an example to put forward a "U-shaped curve"[10] in distribution, reveal the reform path from the planned economy system to the market economy system through the U-shaped trajectory of fiscal revenue, and examine the changes in economic functions and related legal systems, as well as the problems about economic law development.

In each country, the fiscal revenue and expenditure directly reflects the state participation in the distribution of national income. Given this, analyzing the fiscal revenue and expenditure helps to account for the country's allocation of fiscal power and administrative power, and the provision of public goods, as well as the tightening or expansion of specific state functions. Since the data of the state fiscal revenue are relatively accurate and able to directly reveal the relation between the state and its citizens, the changes in the state functions could be examined from the perspective of fiscal revenue. The data of China's fiscal revenue and GDP from 1978 to 2013 are listed in Table 4.1:

[10]In a paper titled *Economic Growth and Income Inequality* published in 1955, the famous American economist and statistician S.S. Kuznets put forward the "inverted-U hypothesis" of income gap, i.e., in the long period where developing countries are transiting to developed countries, the gap in income distribution of residents shows a trend of "firstly deteriorated and then improved", which could be depicted by an "inverted-U curve". The Nobel Laureate Prof. Lewis also drew similar conclusions in his research on the binary economic structure. According to Kuznets, laws, political decisions and technological progress are of great importance for mitigating the income gap; such argument is enlightening for studying the "U-shaped curve" of fiscal revenue.

Table 4.1 China's GDP and fiscal revenue over 1978–2013 (Unit: billion yuan)

Year	GDP	Fiscal revenue	Year	GDP	Fiscal revenue
1978	365	113	1996	7,118	741
1979	406	115	1997	7,897	865
1980	455	116	1998	8,440	988
1981	489	118	1999	8,968	1,144
1982	532	121	2000	9,921	1,340
1983	596	137	2001	10,966	1,639
1984	721	164	2002	12,033	1,890
1985	902	201	2003	13,582	2,172
1986	1,028	212	2004	15,988	2,640
1987	1,206	220	2005	18,494	3,165
1988	1,504	236	2006	21,631	3,876
1989	1,699	267	2007	26,581	5,132
1990	1,867	294	2008	31,405	6,133
1991	2,178	315	2009	34,090	6,852
1992	2,692	348	2010	40,151	8,310
1993	3,533	435	2011	47,310	10,387
1994	4,820	522	2012	51,947	11,725
1995	6,079	624	2013	56,885	12,914

Source National Bureau of Statistics (all the figures are rounded)

The above data can be analyzed from the perspectives of absolute number and relative number. (1) From the perspective of absolute number: from 1978 to 1984, China had seen its annual fiscal revenue remain above 100 billion yuan, which exceeded 200 billion yuan over 1985—1990 with slight growth year by year. Since the establishment of the market economy system in 1992, the fiscal revenue of China started increasing by about 100 billion yuan every year, such annual growth went beyond 200 billion yuan in 2000 and had maintained a rapid growth momentum since then. (2) From the perspective of relative number, i.e., the proportion of fiscal revenue in GDP. It is a new research perspective in recent years. From the late 1970s to the early 1990s, the absolute number of fiscal revenue had been growing slowly with a small growth rate, but the value of GDP in the same period rose notably year by year, showing a robust upward trend. Consequently, the proportion of fiscal revenue in GDP presented a relatively downward trend year by year, and even hit the bottom around 1995.[11] Such proportion was as low as 10.3% in 1995 but went up to 10.4%

[11]According to the statistics in the *Finance Yearbook of China*, the fiscal revenue accounted for 12.9% of China's GDP in 1993, marking the lowest point since the reform and opening-up. In 1993, the amendment to the *Constitution of China* declared that "the state implements a socialist market economy system", after the market economy system was established a year ago. It was also in 1993 that China started strengthening economic legislation and improving the macro-economic control.

in 1996, since then the relative number of fiscal revenue has been on the rise, thus forming a curve of "falling before rising" on the trajectory of fiscal revenue. This curve is named "U-shaped curve" (see the figure below), of which the upper opening is so large due to the low proportion of fiscal revenue in GDP and a long time span for this study).

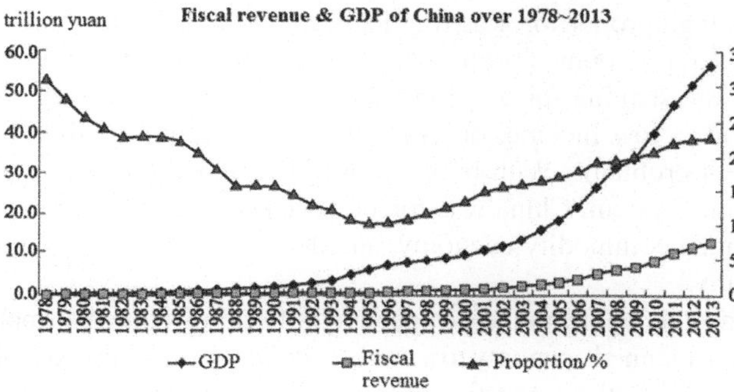

(2) Enlightenment of "U-shaped curve"

The "U-shaped curve" helps to analyze many important problems amid the reform and opening-up and the development of economic law. For example, the "U-shaped curve" roughly reveals the changes in the state economic functions, and the changes in the relevant functions and regulatory goals of economic law. Moreover, it is also helpful for revealing the system changes about the distribution of rights and powers, and able to extend the "Wagner's Law". We can confirm that the interest distribution is an important path for studying the reform and opening-up and the development of economic law. The enlightening role of the "U-shaped curve" is introduced in the following aspects:

(a) The relations between the "U-shaped curve" and the economic functions and right distribution of the state, as well as the economic law functions:

As fiscal revenue is directly related to fiscal expenditure, while fiscal expenditure is directly associated with the state public functions, especially the economic and social functions, we shall pay attention to the following interaction between fiscal revenue and the state economic functions: on the one hand, the changes in fiscal revenue affect the performance of the state functions. In case of high fiscal revenue, the state will have favorable conditions to better perform its economic functions; in case of low fiscal revenue, the performance of state functions will be restricted. On the other hand, in order to better realize its relevant functions and even expand these functions, the state will inevitably have the urge to increase fiscal revenue, and strive to expand fiscal revenue through system arrangements. The above-mentioned

A low proportion of fiscal revenue in GDP and the resulting negative impact on the state forced China to launch a large-scale tax reform since 1994.

interaction between fiscal revenue and state functions is of great concern in the study of economic law.

Through analyzing the "U-shaped curve", we find that as early as 1978 the proportion of China's fiscal revenue in GDP[12] could reach 31.1%, proving that the government exerted a strong impact on the economy in the period of all-encompassing planned economy. But in combination of the nation conditions at the time, the foundation of such high proportion was fragile, because the fiscal revenue mainly originated from the large amount of profits paid by SOEs; this distribution system deprived enterprises of the stamina for development, dampened the working enthusiasm of individuals with a low income, dragged down the economic efficiency, and bred numerous latent problems. With both a flawed distribution system and a defective overall economic system, China was forced to dance to another tune, i.e., it implemented a planned commodity economy, and decided to gradually replace it with a market economy.

As mentioned above, from the perspective of fiscal revenue distribution, China's transition from a planned economy to a market economy seems could be depicted by a "U-shaped curve", i.e., the proportion of fiscal revenue in the total GDP was relatively high at the beginning, then gradually dropped in the reform process of "decentralization of power and transfer of profits", and finally hit the bottom after China established the market economy system. With the increasing knowledge about the market economy and the state economic functions, the Chinese people came to realize that the market economy also needs government-based control and regulation, and such functions shall be further enhanced; at the same time, the relevant social functions also need to be strengthened. From the legal perspective, the process of transforming and legalizing government functions is the process where there is wane and wax of powers and rights, and also a conversion from quantitative change to qualitative change: on the one hand, the state control over the economy has gradually loosened in both scope and quantity; on the other hand, both enterprises and individuals have seen their rights gradually expanded, and obtained more and more benefits. In the process of the "decentralization of power and transfer of profits" in the early days of the reform and opening-up, individual rights had kept increasing and all individuals became more aware of their rights. This process not only affects the development of the Constitution, administrative law, civil and commercial law, but directly affects the emergence and development of economic law.

With a view to the development course of economic law, the original functions and goals of economic law were associated with the functions and goals of the state at that time. While the state economic functions remain uncertain, it is hard to determine the functions and regulatory goals of economic law. In the era of great changes, the continuous changes in the state economic functions directly affect the construction of relevant systems, thereby altering the content of the goals of specific

[12]Many economic scholars attach great importance to the proportion of fiscal revenue in GDP. Lots of them believe that such proportion shall be at least 25% in developing countries and at least 35% in developed countries. But some Chinese scholars still have different views on the statistical caliber of the data.

economic law systems. It is an important reason why the academic community found it difficult to reach consensus on the functions and goals of economic law before the establishment of a market economy system. After the market economy system was established, the state economic functions have become increasingly definite, mainly because the functions of economic regulation and market supervision were defined[13]; the macro-economic control and market regulation functions of economic law, as well as the corresponding goals of regulation, have been increasingly valued. It not only benefits the legislative integration of economic law, but helps to increase the theoretical consensus on economic law.

(b) Extended discussion on the "U-shaped curve"

Firstly, the "U-shaped curve" is an indirect expression of the Wagner's Law and also its extension. According to Wagner's Law, along with the expansion of government functions, the fiscal expenditure will also demonstrate a growth trend[14]; while the amount and distribution of fiscal revenue will affect the realization of government functions. Historically, with the deepening of the "decentralization of power and transfer of profits", and with the planned economy transiting to the commodity economy, the proportion of the state revenue in the GDP has been declining, and the government has been retreating from direct management of economic activities. In this sense, it is possible to extend the Wagner's Law: the relative decrease in fiscal revenue, or the smaller proportion of fiscal revenue in GDP, has a substantial "shrinking effect" on government functions; at the same time, the reduction of government functions will further reduce the scale of fiscal revenue or fiscal expenditure. Of course, the above extension is only a theoretical hypothesis, and it needs to be verified by the practices of many countries in different periods and in a larger spatio-temporal range.

Secondly, the "U-shaped curve" may be applicable to multiple scenarios in a larger spatio-temporal range: (i) It can be applied to other transitional countries. While they are transitioning to a market economy, their government functions are firstly reduced and then expanded, and the economic legislation will turn from inadequate to abundant, such transitional process can be depicted by the "U-shaped curve". (ii) With a "big history" perspective,[15] from the period of free competition to the period of monopoly, from the state non-intervention to intervention, and then to moderate intervention, this kind of historical trajectory looks like the "U-shaped curve". (iii)

---

[13]China once divided the government functions into four categories: economic regulation, market supervision, social management and public services. Among them, the functions of economic regulation and market supervision generally correspond to the macro-economic control and market regulation in the realm of economic law.

[14]According to Musgrave, the predictions made by Wagner in 1893 proved to be correct, and the growth of public sectors has become a decisive feature of the Western world in the 20th century. Buchanan, Musgrave, *Public finance and public choice: two contrasting visions of the state*, Lei Chengyao (trans.), 2000, Beijing: China Financial Publishing House, p. 48.

[15]The "big history" approach, presented by Prof. Huang Renyu (Ray Huang), features the induction and synthesis of the historical issues in different periods. It is more suitable for the overall study of the issues with a larger spatio-temporal range. Huang Renyu, 1997, *China: a macro history* (preface to the Chinese edition), Beijing: SDX Joint Publishing Company.

Along with the development of human history, changes will happen to the state functions, so the quantity or the economic impact of economic legislation will change accordingly, showing certain periodicity that may lead to the periodic variation,[16] which may be reflected as a continuous "U-shaped curve". (iv) The cycle of economic development will bring about a cycle of economic law adjustment (e.g., the adjustment cycle and counter-cycle of the macro-economic control law have consistent requirements), these cyclic changes seem like a "U-shaped curve". The U-shaped changes in the economic cycle will bring the U-shaped changes in the adjustment of economic law; therefore, an intercepted section of the curve is enough to reveal many of these problems, thereby helping to improve the predictability of economic and legal development and prevent drastic fluctuations, postpone the occurrence of relevant cycles, so as to mitigate economic and social shocks, and better achieve the goal of stable development.

Finally, the "U-shaped curve" helps to reveal the trajectory of economic law system construction and legal studies. As mentioned earlier, the state fiscal distribution affects the government functions, while the government functions are able to affect the fiscal distribution under the legal framework; moreover, the government functions will also affect the system law in the realm of economic law, which in turn affects the specific economic control and regulatory laws. Therefore, the changes in the government functions not only have an impact on the Constitution and administrative law, but also have a greater impact on economic law. The system construction of economic law generally has the same direction and trajectory with the fiscal distribution and the government functions. Similarly, the trajectory of economic law study is consistent with that of the above aspects. This may be an important law for the development of economic law and science of economic law in China.

4.1.3 Changes in Distribution Policy and Development of Economic Law

4.1.3.1 The Spiral Return of Economic Policies: "Tight-Loose-Tight"

The above-mentioned distribution relation directly concerns the vital interests of relevant subjects. Therefore, in the early days of the reform and opening-up, the adjustment of distribution relation became focus of many economic policies. In addition, along with the reform and opening-up, the property right relation and price relation that are directly related to distribution have gradually become an important content of economic policies, which gave rise to the reform ideas that center on property right reform or price reform. Since the reform is a progressive process, which seems like "wading across the river by feeling stones along the way", making it difficult to directly specify the reform by law; but people's behaviors need to

[16] Zhang (2002), The periodic variation of macro-economic control law, *Peking University Law Journal*, Issue 5, pp. 695–705.

follow some guidelines. For the above reasons, the role of various economic policies or distribution policies has become increasingly prominent.

In the early stage of the reform, economic policies or distribution policies were far from mature, and sometimes they would show traces of the planned economy, but they were in essence the important means and basis for the state to guide and manage the reforms in relevant domains. At the beginning, most of the important economic policies were in the form of documents released by the CPC Central Committee or the State Council. For example, there are "No. 1 Document" on rural reform released by the CPC Central Committee for years in a row, and the *Decision of the Central Committee of the CPC on Reform of the Economic System* (1984)[17]; a great part of their content is about distribution policies. During this period, the economic policies were characterized with the close integration between party policies and public policies, and between political policies and economic policies, as well as prominent government functions in direct management. With the continuous deepening of the reform and opening-up, especially the continuous improvement of the state governance ability and the ruling ability, China started attaching importance to the implementation of the legal system, advocating the law-based reform, and safeguarding the reform pursuant to law. At the same time, China became more skilled in employing the economic policies, and gradually taken them as a kind of public policies for regulating economic activities indirectly, so that the application scope and implementation of economic policies has attracted worldwide attention.

Economic policy is an important means of regulating the economic performance in all countries, but its role varies greatly in different periods and in different economic systems. During the period of planned economy or controlled economy, China implemented centralized economic control and market control, making some economic policies compatible with the market economy unable to play their role; in contrast, in the period of commodity economy or market economy, the state implements macroeconomic control and market regulation, so the economic policies that cater to the market economy can play a significant role. These two different periods are part of the process of China's reform and opening-up; an examination of the characteristics of these two periods helps to deepen the understanding of the development course of China's economic law.

In the period of planned economy, the state was exercising "unified regulation" (i.e., control[18]) in many domains; multiple types of individual freedom such as free operation might be restricted, some economic activities were banned, and many

[17]The CPC Central Committee issued the "No. 1 Document" on agriculture, rural areas and farmers for five consecutive years from 1982 to 1986, making specific arrangements for rural reform and agricultural development. Moreover, the Central Government made public the five copies of "No. 1 Document" on "three rural issues" from 2004 to 2008. Back in October 1984, the 3rd Plenary Session of the Twelfth CPC Central Committee adopted the *Decision of the Central Committee of the CPC on Reform of the Economic System*, which systematically presents and expounds a series of major theoretical and practical issues about the reform of the economic system, abandons the traditional perception of antagonizing the planned economy with the commodity economy, confirms that the socialist economy of China is a planned commodity economy based on public ownership.

[18]The "control" here is not identical with the pure controlled economy or economics of control. In the 1930 s, China was influenced by various factors such as the Keynesian theory, the Japanese

restrictions might be imposed upon the distribution policies. Given this, the period of control was also a period of "restriction", with the economy-related policies implemented for the purpose of control and restriction. As people were gradually aware of the drawbacks of control and restriction, the state started "deregulating" the economic policies or specific distribution policies. The so-called "deregulation" includes emancipation of thought, devolution of power, and release of bondage. Therefore, it is also likened to "untying", which is reform in essence, requiring opening up to the world, opening the market and opening the barriers to ensure freedom of trading. Such kind of "deregulation" helps to emancipate people's mind and reform the systems that unreasonably restrict economic freedom, including the "deregulation" in the domain of distribution. Of course, "deregulation" shall be carried out gradually and moderately; otherwise, it may bring about lots of negative effects. In fact, after going through more extensive and more profound "deregulation", the increasingly prominent market failure has made people fully aware of the necessity for moderate government regulation, so that China departed from the period of "deregulation" and entered the period of moderate government regulation. It can be seen that China's economic policies or distribution policies had gone through three different periods of "restriction-deregulation-moderate regulation".

From the perspective of the state, the economic policies or distribution policies in the above three periods reflect the process from initial restriction to deregulation to moderate regulation, so they can also be simply referred to as a "tight-loose-tight" process. But the second "tight", which represents moderate concentration, is not at the same level as the first "tight", which is highly concentrated; so this chain in fact describes a spiral regression. This "regression" is consistent with the "U-shaped curve" of the aforesaid fiscal allocation. This also shows that there is a positive correlation between China's fiscal distribution and its economic policies, economic functions and economic legal system.

In this "tight-loose-tight" process, the period from "restriction" to "deregulation" is the period from "tight" to "loose". In this process, the state mandatory plan and unified administration have been are diminishing. In the period of deregulation, the centralized control and market regulation have become increasingly loosened. "Simplified administration and decentralization" or "decentralization and profit-sharing" are the mainstream economic policy content in this period. It is in this period of implementing these policies that the micro-foundation for the regulation based on civil and commercial law and economic law has formed.

With the planning economic policies gradually waning and increasingly developed commercialization and marketization of the economic domain, the main forms of Chinese economic policies have gradually become clearer, transforming from the relatively comprehensive rural policies and corporate policies into those closely

doctrine, and the state of wartime. Ma Yinchu and other Chinese scholars were devoted themselves into the study of controlled economy. In recent years, some scholars emphasize that although the controlled economy is close to the planned economy—both of them reflect the state unified control over many domains such as price and trade, it is somewhat different from the latter since it takes the mixed economic system as the premise. Zhong Xiangcai, 2008, Thoughts on controlled economy in China in the 1930 s and 1940 s, *Historical Review*, Issue 2, p33.

related to market economy, such as economic policies, monetary policies, industrial policies, competition policies, and foreign trade policies. The government has gradually learned to use economic policies for macro-economic control and market regulation. Especially after the goal of implementing the market economy system was established in 1992, China has become more and more skilled in employing the relevant economic policies. For example, in 1993, China followed monetary policies and financial laws to carry out the macro-economic control and regulation in the financial domain, succeeding in solving the problem of overheated economy at that time, and dissolving the later financial crisis (1997 Asian financial crisis) that hit so many countries in advance; after the 1998 disastrous flood, China kept implementing the proactive fiscal policies and successfully solved the problems of inadequate domestic demand, deflation, and the resulting cold economic development.[19] For years China has been exercising macro-economic regulation and control to cope with the ups and downs in the domestic economy, and implements strong regulations on the economic order during the transitional period.

The above-mentioned important e economic policies are relatively mature and stable, and they are often reflected in the relevant economic legislation. In this sense, "economic law is legalized economic policies", and at the same time, "economic law plays an important role in ensuring the effective implementation of economic policies". The goals and tools of economic policies and the regulatory goals and means of economic law are inherently related. Because of this, economic policies are closely linked to economic law and makes economic law prominently policy-oriented.[20] Following the path of economic policy, it is also possible to grasp the economic law and science of economic law on the whole.

4.1.3.2 Specific Impact of Economic Policies on Economic Law—Taking Economic Distribution as an Example

As we all know, China's economic system reform has been carried out along the thought of progressive "decentralization and profit sharing". On the one hand, through the continuous decentralization of power to enterprises and sharing profits with the private economy, China is cultivating market subjects gradually, and trying to make enterprises become independent market subjects. On the other hand, by continuously transforming government functions and the fiscal system, China attempts to adjust the distribution relation between different levels of governments, so as to establish a more

[19]To cope with the 2008 global financial crisis, China also introduced a proactive fiscal policy, which was directly related to the successful experience of ten years ago in dealing with the Asian financial crisis.

[20]Many scholars take the policy nature has an important feature of economic law. In fact, the policy nature is directly related to economics and regulative nature (basic characteristics) of economic law; it is a direct reflection of the modernity of economic law. Some scholars have investigated this issue from a judicial perspective, see Liu Sixuan, 2011, Empirical investigation of the policy nature of economic law: based on the 31 years' work reports of China's Supreme People's Court, *Journal of Nanjing University (Philosophy, Humanities and Social Sciences)*, Issue 1, pp. 58–72.

standardized and stable tax-sharing fiscal system among governments. These two aspects are related to the afore-mentioned two types of distribution, i.e., individual interest distribution and state fiscal distribution. Both types of distribution involve economic policies. Therefore, the following content takes economic policies as an example to analyze the path of the reform and opening-up and the development path of economic law.

As mentioned earlier, fiscal pressure is the direct motive for China to implement the reform and opening-up, while individual interest distribution is the basic driver of the reform and opening-up. In the late 1970s, China was facing two conflicting issues: on the one hand, in order to fund the survival and development of enterprises and individuals, the state was forced to reduce burdens, decentralize power and transfer profits; on the other hand, in order to alleviate fiscal pressure, the state was forced to sustain the growth in fiscal revenue. In fact, as the "North Paradox" reveals: the state is both the source of economic growth and the cause of economic decline. If the "Northern Paradox" is expanded in an opposite direction, then it will express that the individual interest distribution may become both a source of economic growth and a cause of economic decline.[21] Therefore, the economic policies concerning distribution shall properly deal with the above two issues.

At the outset of the reform and opening-up, China was thinking out how to promote the development of enterprises and increase economic benefit of individuals. In terms of economic policies, the economic conditions were relatively poor at that time, making economic instruments unlikely to become important regulatory tools. While China keeps pressing ahead with the reform and opening-up, its GDP has been increasing year by year, showing a growth pace even faster than that of fiscal revenue (see the afore-mentioned "U-shaped curve"), the role of fiscal policy in adjusting interest distribution has become increasingly apparent. Especially after the implementation of the market economy system, economic policies have become an extremely important tool for China to arrange income distribution and exercise macro-economic control.

It is worth noting that in the reform process of "decentralization of power and transfer of profits", although the state has delegated certain powers to lower levels, it firmly holds the fiscal power, which partially explains for the heavy burden on some enterprises, it deviates from the requirements of fair taxation. For example, after China started "replacing profit delivery by taxes", the income tax rate of large and medium-sized SOEs was as high as 55%; moreover, the enterprise income adjustment tax might be collected, which exacerbated the tax burden upon SOEs. In addition, collective enterprises implemented the eight-grade progressive rates (levied on the income in excess of specific amounts) which might be up to 55%. The tax burden of

[21] The "North Paradox" focuses on the state fiscal distribution, while the reversed expansion here pays more attention to the individual interest distribution; they can be regarded as two aspects of a problem. Historically, Britain and the Netherlands had been developing at a faster pace than France and Spain in 200 years, which was attributed to the differences in the institutional arrangements for the individual interest distribution. R. H. Coase, D. North et al., Liu Shouying et al. (trans.), 1994, *Property rights and institutional changes*, Shanghai: Shanghai Joint Publishing Press, Shanghai People's Publishing House, p331.

foreign-invested enterprises without such historical "burdens" was the lightest, with a nominal tax rate of only 33%, and many companies actually implement a tax rate of only 15% or even lower. Since SOEs make the greatest contribution to fiscal revenue, the harder they work, the heavier the tax burden they would bear. Therefore, the above-mentioned economic police is also known as the "whipping cow" policy, and its "ratchet effect" is very prominent[22] and brings many problems (e.g., the problems of state-owned enterprises) that have long plagued China's economic development. In addition, the slant distribution of foreign-invested enterprises, although conducive to the implementation of open-up policies such as attracting foreign investment, has resulted in internal and external inequities and created discrimination issues. There were two other sets of taxation systems, both internal and external, and the "1994 tax reform" could not be resolved, it was not until the implementation of the unified *Law of the People's Republic of China on Enterprise Income Tax* on January 1, 2008 that the internal and external injustices were greatly relieved in form.[23]

The major adjustments to the enterprise tax policies include the two major tax reforms in the early 1980s and early 1990s. The two-step "replacement of profit delivery by taxes" implemented from 1983 to 1984 (the relevant reform of "replacing fiscal allocation with loans"[24] also concerns distribution), which enabled enterprises to convert from the profit delivery to tax-paying, it has an important role in cultivating market subjects. The outstanding problems of the tax policy and tax system formulated through the 1984 Tax Reform are inconsistent tax laws, unfair tax burdens, and unclear tax systems. These problems and the requirements for fair tax burden and fair competition under the market economy have promoted the larger-scale tax reform in

[22]The term "ratchet effects" was originally used to study the Soviet-style planned economy system. Under the planning system, a company's annual production indicators were continuously adjusted according to its actual production of the previous year, implying that good performance would bring adverse consequences. That's way some smart managers concealed the actual production capacity of their companies to deal with planning authorities. This trend of rising standards with performance is called the "ratcheting effects". This term was developed by economist James S. Duesenberry for emphasizing that consumers are apt to spend more money after earning a higher income, but hard to cut their consumption in case of declining income, i.e., such pattern is irreversible, just like the ancient Chinese politician Sima Guang had said "it is easier to go from frugality to extravagance than from extravagance to frugality".

[23]There are many issues of substantial inequity, e.g., there are still differentiated provisions for different enterprises in the newly implemented *Law on Enterprise Income Tax*. Zhang Shouwen, 2008, The integration and limitations of the *Law on Enterprise Income Tax*, Taxation Research, Issue 2, pp. 50–53.

[24]"Replacing fiscal allocation with loans" has a huge impact on enterprises. During the planned economy period, the supplementary capital of SOEs was directly from the state finance, and all corporate profits were turned over to the fiscal departments. In the early 1980 s, in order to raise the use efficiency of the state-owned funds, the state no longer directly allocated funds to enterprises, but supported the enterprises through an indirect approach as bank loans. Later, during the SOE reform, the state successively introduced a number of policies to transfer the funds from loans to the capital of SOEs. "Replacing fiscal allocation with loans" involves both the adjustment of the distribution relation between the state and enterprises and the reform of the financial system. Through these reforms, the state no longer assumes unlimited responsibilities; it is the enterprises themselves that bear the responsibilities.

the early 1990s, and stimulated China to take account of the market orientation and fair taxation when introducing tax policies.

Historically, the changes in China's economic policies are reflected in the "tight-loose-tight" process. At first, during the period when the enterprise form was relatively single, the state taxation policies were described as "tight" since they were characterized with centralized management of public-owned enterprises. With the increasing number of enterprises, especially foreign-invested enterprises and private enterprises, the state has begun to formulate different tax policies for various types of enterprises. Correspondingly, the legislative power of the SOE income tax was generally delegated to the State Council, and the tax rate was continuously lowered to achieve "decentralization of power and transfer of profits", which is a "loose" process. However, the problems of decentralized legislation and unfair tax burden have kept cropping up, the state shifted focus to tight income tax policies and other economic policies, so as to solve many problems during the period of "legislative laissez-faire" or "extensive legislation". Accordingly, the objective of the 1994 tax system reform was determined to be "unified tax law, fair tax burden, simplified tax system, and reasonable decentralization of power", with a view to further realizing the goal of securing income and macro-economic control. It is for the achievement of these goals that the fiscal and tax powers began relatively concentrated. At the same time, based on the requirements of statutory fiscal principles, the state has posed higher requirements for the standardization and legalization of various economic policies.

As mentioned earlier, economic law is the legalization of economic policies. The legalization of the above-mentioned economic policies related to distribution constitutes an important content of economic law. Therefore, the development of the economic law system is inherently consistent with the changes in the afore-mentioned economic policies. With a view to the change of economic policies directly related to distribution, we can discover and comprehend the development laws of economic law.

4.1.4 The System and Theory Running Through the Main Line of Distribution

The development of economic law legislation and theories can be divided into two major stages based on the development course of the market economy, and divided by the 1993 Constitution Amendment[25] which included "market economy" into

[25] According to the *Amendment to the Constitution of the People's Republic of China* adopted at the 1st Session of the Eighth National People's Congress on Mar 29, 1993, Article 15 of the Constitution, which originally states that "the state implements a planned economy on the basis of socialist public ownership. The state ensures the coordinated development of the national economy through the comprehensive balance of economic plans and the auxiliary role of market regulation", was to be revised like this "the state implements a socialist market economy"; "the state shall strengthen economic legislation and improve macro-economic control". These revisions are very

the *Constitution of China*. The first stage (1978–1993) was a period in which the economic law theory developed along with the economic system reform and with the preliminary development of China's legal system. Various theories came out and kept changing, thus making this period characterized by the start-up and volatility of economic law and science of economic law. The second stage (1993 to date) is a period of steady development of economic law and science of economic law. During this period, due to the common economic foundation, the basic theoretical understanding of the market economy and related legal system construction was relatively consistent, so the goals of legal system construction became more explicit and more certain, and the commonality and consensus of economic law theory gradually increased. This is very important for the steady development of economic law.

4.1.4.1 Construction of Economic Law System Running Through the Main Line of Distribution

Ever since the 3rd Plenary Session of the Eleventh Central Committee of the CP China in 1978 put forward the idea of "focusing on economic construction", the landscape of China has changed dramatically. The construction of the legal system, especially the economic legal system, has achieved outstanding achievements. In order to better develop the economy and improve people's livelihood, China has been dedicated to adjusting the "take-grant relation" between enterprises and individuals for years, and trying to solve the problem of distribution, which has become an important clue in the construction of the economic legal system.

Regarding the legislation of economic law, although there are various levels and types of legislation, it always runs through the main line of distribution. From rural reforms to urban reforms, from corporate benefits to personal benefits, from individual benefits to fiscal benefits, there are many laws and regulations in the field of economic law, and only representative laws and regulations in different stages as follows: At the beginning of reform and opening up, the State Council issued on July 3, 1979, the *Provisions on Several Issues in the Development of Social Team Enterprises* (Trial Draft),[26] this involves not only the development and industrialization of rural enterprises, but also the adjustment of important distribution relationships. In addition, on July 1, 1980, the State Council issued the *Interim Provisions on Promoting Economic Union*[27] (it was soon replaced by the *Provisions on Further Promoting Horizontal Economic Cooperation* issued by the State Council on March

important for advancing the construction of the rule of law and legal research in the realm of economic law.

[26]It has been replaced by the *Law of the People's Republic of China on Township and Village Enterprises* passed and promulgated by the Standing Committee of the NPC on October 29, 1996, and the *Regulations of the People's Republic of China on Village Collective Ownership Enterprises* issued by the State Council on June 3, 1990.

[27]The regulation emphasizes that economic union helps attract local and corporate material and financial resources to the areas that are urgently needed for national construction; it helps to communicate horizontal links in accordance with economic laws, breaks regional blockades, and

23, 1986), this involves not only the competition relationship to be adjusted by economic law, but also the distribution relationship. It can be seen that due to various reasons, the initial reform and opening up legislation tends to be more comprehensive, and adjusting distribution relations is always its important content.

At the beginning of the reform and opening up, the distribution of individual benefits was closely linked to the distribution of financial benefits. Both types of distribution are difficult problems that need to be effectively addressed in economic legislation. To this end, the 1980 "Interim Provisions on the Implementation of" Dividing Revenue, Expenditure, Hierarchical Contracting "Financial Management System" emphasized that the state implements a "Dividing Revenue, Expenditure, Hierarchical Contracting" financial management system to all provinces, "in consolidating the central leadership and unification of the central government. Under the premise of ensuring the central government's indispensable expenditures, the financial rights and responsibilities of all levels of finance should be clarified, a combination of powers and responsibilities should be performed, and each one should perform their own duties and responsibilities, and give full play to the central and local enthusiasm". On September 10 of the same year, the 3rd Session of the Fifth National People's Congress passed the *Law on Individual Income Tax*, which is intended to better resolve the distribution of intergovernmental financial benefits while better addressing issues between the state and individuals (especially foreign individuals allocation problem). Based on the same considerations, in January 1981, the State Council issued the Decision on Balance of Fiscal Revenue and Expenditure and Strict Fiscal Management and the People's Republic of China Regulations on Treasury Bills, which have used unused government bonds for many years to balance fiscal revenue and solve the difficulty of the country's fiscal distribution. In addition, on December 13 of the same year, the 4th Session of the Fifth National People's Congress passed the *Foreign Enterprise Income Tax Law of the People's Republic of China*, which is intended to further resolve the relationship of interest distribution between the state and foreign enterprises. Opening up to the outside world, safeguarding the national financial interests, and fairing the tax burden of various types of enterprises have positive significance.

With the deepening of reform and opening up, especially the start of urban reform, the relationship of state-owned enterprise and state interest distribution has been placed in a prominent and important position. As compared with the above-mentioned foreign enterprises and individuals, state-owned enterprises (SOEs) are the most important providers of state financial revenue. For this reason, in the early 1980s, the country began to implement "profit-for-tax reform" with important economic and legal significance. From the perspective of the legal system, the "profit-for-tax reform" puts the distribution relationship between the state and state-owned enterprises on the track of legal adjustment, which has gradually brought the state-owned

---

separates sectors; it helps to follow the principle of professional cooperation for industrial reorganization, avoid overcrowding by small, repeated factory building, and blind production. In the two "provisions" on promoting economic union, both fiscal and taxation issues are directly related to distribution.

enterprises economically on the path of autonomous operation and self-financing, while legally State-owned enterprises have gradually become truly independent legal persons. In accordance with the Provisional Measures for the Second-stage Profit-to-Tax Reform of State-owned Enterprises approved and promulgated by the State Council on September 18, 1984, and a series of *Tentative Regulations on Taxation* (draft) that were subsequently formulated, China has levied product taxes, value-added taxes, and salt taxes, business tax, resource tax, urban maintenance and construction tax, real estate tax, land use tax, vehicle and vessel use tax, SOE income tax, and SOE adjustment tax, etc., thereby making the tax law a distribution of income or division of wealth between the state and the national "important tool".

The above tax law system, as an important part of the economic law system, played an important role in promoting reform and opening up in the mid-to-late 1980s. However, after China established the market economy system in 1992, its many deficiencies have become increasingly apparent, which has already been mentioned before. To this end, China has implemented the "1994 Tax Reform", which has a far-reaching effect in parallel with the tax sharing system, and established the basic tax law system after China's implementation of the market economy system. Since the reform and opening up, although the tax system has been reformed almost every ten years, after 2004, no large-scale tax reform as in 1984 or 1994 has occurred.[28] This also shows that "after the establishment of the basic market system, although the relevant system is in the process of being perfected, there will generally not be any significant changes". This may also be a basic law.

The basic laws such as the impact of the above-mentioned economic system on relevant legal systems, and the more fundamental economic foundation's decisive role in economic law, have long been recognized. In general, China has gone through several stages such as a planned economy system, a planned commodity economy system, and a market economy system. Therefore, in terms of the country's economic management, it is also necessary to shift from a "controlled economy" to a "regulated economy" (i.e., from "uniform regulation" to "control and regulation" of the economy), the construction of the economic law system must reflect these characteristics accordingly, i.e., from the initial comprehensive legislation to more specific legislation. At the same time, the content of the entire legislation must be closely related to the results of reform and opening up, and the main economic policies must be legalized. In this process, the content of distribution is always an important content of legislation, or in other words, distribution is always an important main line that runs through the entire construction of the economic law system. Because of this, distribution is not only an important issue in the process of reform and opening up, but also an important meridian throughout the construction of the economic law system.

---

[28]The 2004 tax reform was marked by the transformation of the VAT in the Northeast, far less vigorous than the previous two tax reforms. If a new tax reform was launched in 2004, it can be considered as the beginning of a new "structural tax cut". This is because the structural tax reductions that have been carried out since then have continued and promoted the further optimization of the overall tax law structure.

4.1.4.2 Legal Study Running Through the Main Line of Distribution

Since the distribution of individual interests and the distribution of national finance have always been important contents of institutional construction of economic law and legal research, therefore, the distribution of clues has naturally become an important way to connect economic law system construction and legal research, and penetrates into relevant legal theory.

As mentioned earlier, at the beginning of reform and opening up, the overall economic planning was still strong, the concept of the legal system was weak, and the laws of the country were generally few.The laws enacted were mainly concentrated in traditional legal areas such as criminal law and criminal lawsuits, and economic aspects. Legislation is mainly reflected in tax laws and other areas that concern national sovereignty. Since the country's initial positioning of reform goals was not clear, and the legislative capacity of the National People's Congress was relatively weak, the State Council was an important subject of economic legislation; the regulations and documents formulated by the State Council are, in essence, important legal sources, which are closely related to the authorization legislation of the National People's Congress.[29] During this period, there was a lot of disagreement about the creation of economic law theories and the adjustment of economic law. At that time, the academic circles were difficult to distinguish the boundaries between departmental laws such as civil and commercial law and economic law, and they lacked a clear understanding of the functions, goals, and adjustment targets of the law, as a result, many people advocate adjusting both vertical and horizontal economic relations, thus forming the theory of vertical and horizontal unified economic law, or "the theory of vertical and horizontal unification," which had a great influence during this period. Although this theory was influenced by the Soviet Union, it was also directly related to China's economic system at that time and its overall concept. Whether it is the "universal and unified theory" or other doctrines directly related to it, as far as the economic, political, social, and legal development stages of the time are concerned, they all have certain rationality.

With the increase of market factors and the implementation of a planned commodity economic system, especially the promulgation of the General Principles of the Civil Law in 1986, the state began to clarify that vertical economic relations should be adjusted by economic and administrative laws,[30] economic law norms adjusting the vertical relationships that were considered at the time (the subsequent tax laws and regulations related to "profit-for-tax reform" were also introduced during

[29]The Standing Committee of the NPC and the National People's Congress made the decision to authorize legislation in 1984 and 1985, respectively, which greatly expanded the legislative authority of the State Council. If there is no deadline, it will have a negative impact. At present, its negative effects are increasingly apparent.

[30]Wang Hanbin once pointed out that the government's economic management, vertical economic relations or administrative management relations between the state and enterprises and within enterprises are not economic relations between equal subjects, and are mainly adjusted by relevant economic and administrative laws and regulations. Wang Hanbin, *Explanation on the General Principles of the Civil Law of the People's Republic of China (Draft).*

this period). The deepening of reform and opening up, and changes in the economic system, have caused the contents of the economic law system to change drastically, and directly affected the study of economic law theory. Since it has been clearly defined in legislation that civil law mainly adjusts horizontal economic relations, many views of the economic law academic community have been adjusted accordingly. The most influential one is the "management-collaboration theory". This theory is a high-level summary of the actual development of the economy and the law at the time. It reflects both the "planned" side and the "commodity economy" side. The economic law systems associated with this system are all internally consistent.

As we all know, it was not until 1992 when China clearly implemented the goals of the market economy system that economic law systems compatible with the market economy system were promulgated. In particular, the promulgation of laws on market regulation in 1993 (such as the Anti-unfair Competition Law, the Consumer Rights Protection Law), the introduction of the economic and legal system in 1994 (especially a large number of temporary tax regulations), the introduction of the financial legal system in 1995 (such as the *People's Bank of China Law*, the *Commercial Bank Law*), the major laws of the most important departmental laws of economic law have come out one after another, and basic legalization has been realized. The establishment of economic system reform goals and the improvement of the economic law system have not only promoted the rise of related sector laws such as economic law, financial law, and competition law,[31] but also promoted the great development of economic law theory. In fact, from the end of 1992 to the beginning of 1993, in combination with the new market economic system, there have been some theoretical discussions on economic law. By 1994, theoretical research on economic law had once again entered a booming period. Compared with the past, not only was the theoretical study of economic law more mature at this time, but the establishment of a market economic system also led to a higher degree of consensus, thereby forming a new "economic law theory".[32] Because the new theories generally reflect common economic and legal principles under the conditions of a market economy, people's understanding of many issues has also become more convergent. From today's perspective, many scholars of economic law have no fundamental differences in their understanding of the basic assumptions, adjustment objects, characteristics, systems of economic law, and specific theories of subjects, behaviors, and responsibilities. It can be seen that a stable economic system plays an important role in

---

[31]These three sectoral laws have developed the fastest in recent years, and the related research results are also the most. This has something to do with the needs of the development of a market economy and the relatively complete legal system in these areas.

[32]In the early 1980s, there was a lively discussion on the theory of economic law. Many well-known scholars in the field of departmental law joined the big discussion and formed the then Chinese economic law theories. Editing Group, 1987, Essays on Chinese Economic Law, Beijing: Law Press China. After 1994, some representative viewpoints in the field of economic law have appeared one after another, and the academic circles call these viewpoints the "new theory" of Chinese economic law. Xiao Jiangping, 2002, *Study on History of China's economic law theory*, Beijing: People's Court Press.

forming a more stable economic law system and the basic consensus of economic law theory.

Generally speaking, China's economic system, economic policy, economic law system, and economic law theory will be affected by regulatory thoughts-liberalism-moderate regulation and other ideas at different times. The specific development process is in legislation, it is also reflected in legal studies. In the system of economic law, the above-mentioned ideas are reflected in many aspects such as the purpose, principles, and regulations of adjustment methods of economic law; in economic law theory, it is reflected in the understanding of the functions, objects, characteristics, and systems of economic law in different historical periods. For example, it is not difficult to find the functions of ensuring macro-control and market regulation based on economic law: economic law is "modern law", which has outstanding modernity and is a law that can effectively solve the modern problems outstanding in modern society; economic law is "the law for development", and it helps to solve development problems that are of common concern to modern nations; economic law is the "policy law", which has prominent policy nature and is therefore modulating; and so on.[33]

The practice of China's reform and opening up has shown that: changes in production relations, especially distribution relations, have promoted changes in the economic system, which has also brought about changes in laws, and economic laws have emerged and developed continuously; at the same time, the ideas, concepts, viewpoints, and theories of economic law have also changed rapidly or slowly. In this process, both the economic, social, and political developments, as well as the development of the legal system and legal theory, have profoundly affected the institutional construction and legal research of economic law. It can be seen that institutional changes, ideological changes, and theoretical changes in the field of economic law have been comprehensively affected by various factors, but distribution is undoubtedly one of the important influencing factors. It is an important meridian that penetrates the system construction and legal research of economic law.

4.1.5 Conclusion

Based on the discussion in this section, we can find that China's reform and opening up began with distribution and deepened with the adjustment of the distribution relationship. The distribution of individual interests is the basic motivation that affects reform and opening up, and the distribution of national finance is the direct motivation that affects reform and opening up. It is these motivations in the distribution that

---

[33]Zhang Shouwen, 2004, Reconstruction of economic law theory, Beijing: People's Publishing House, pp. 227–237. In addition, economic law plays a particularly important role in promoting development, so economic jurisprudence and social jurisprudence belongs to the emerging branch of jurisprudence-an important part of the development of jurisprudence. Zhang Shouwen, 2005, "Science of development law" and development of legal science—on the development concept in economic law theory, *Law Science*, Issue 3.

promote the initiation and deepening of reform and opening up, and also promote the emergence and development of China's economic law.

From the perspective of distribution, China's reform and opening up has undergone the process of "from heavy product distribution to heavy power distribution". In this process, how to divide and allocate power and rights in distribution has always been the focus of attention of various subjects; therefore, it is also a key issue or even a core issue that the institution of economic law and law research should pay attention to. This makes distribution an important "meridian" that runs through the development of China's economic law and economic law.

The process of China's reform and opening up is a process of "decentralizing power and giving profits" to cultivate market players, then centralize power appropriately, and conduct macroeconomic regulation and market regulation. In this process, the state's power control has undergone the process of "tight-loose- tight". It has gone through the process from control to decentralization to moderate regulation, which is positively related to the performance of state functions and the exercise of powers. Changes can be reflected by changes in national fiscal allocations. The change in the data on fiscal revenue since China's reform and opening up is exactly reflected in a "U-shaped curve", which is consistent with the "tight-loose-tight" path of the aforementioned power control. With the help of the "U-shaped curve", a lot of research can be carried out, and it is especially helpful to reveal the inherent relationship between the distribution and the state's economic functions, economic system, economic policy, economic law system, and economic law theory.

The above-mentioned various types of distribution will be reflected in various economic policies, especially in economic policies that directly affect distribution. China's economic policy is directly related to the country's economic functions and economic system reform, so its development path is also reflected in a "U-shaped curve". At the same time, since economic law is the legalization of economic policy, the development of economic law system construction and legal research is also reflected in the "U-shaped curve". There is inherent consistency in changes in economic functions and adjustments in economic policies. Based on this consistency, it can be argued that the previous discussions of "two types of distribution" and economic policies related to distribution are actually revealing the issues of institutional construction and legal research of economic law from different aspects.

There is a close and internal relationship between the economic law system and the theory of economic law. Distribution is an important link connecting the economic law system and theory. Grasping the course of economic law system development and its existing problems will help to better grasp the key points, difficulties and problems of economic law theoretical research, thereby helping to better promote the theoretical development and system construction of economic law, and enable the economy Law has become a modern law that effectively promotes economic and social development.

In short, as an important way to study economic law, distribution is an important "meridian" that runs through China's economic law system and economic law theory. It is closely related to national interests and individual interests, and is of great value for reform and opening up, for the transformation of national economic functions, for the formulation of economic policies and the formation of economic law systems. Constantly solving the problem of distribution is not only an enduring task of economic law system construction, but also a new field in economic law theoretical research and a direction that needs to be worked on in the future.

4.2 Economic Law Pathway to Mitigate "Double Pressure"

4.2.1 Presenting Problems

National planning and people's livelihood are the main points of governing the country. If the national economy and people's livelihood are worry-free, the country will be governed. Therefore, a country can only effectively protect the national economy and the people's livelihood, and effectively solve the problem of distribution.

However, throughout China and abroad, in both ancient and present times, it is not uncommon for the national economy and people's livelihood being suffered. Regardless of the decline of national strength, the deficit of the national treasury, or the widespread starvation, a country will face tremendous pressure on the national economy and people's livelihood. Constantly alleviating and releasing the pressure on the national economy and people's livelihood, and avoiding the resulting economic imbalances, social imbalances, or political turmoil, are always the highlights of the development of each country.

In order to alleviate and release the tremendous pressure on the national economy and people's livelihood, various countries in the history have adopted various means such as launching wars, reforming laws, and developing the economy in order to achieve long-term security and sustainable development. In modern countries ruled by law, legal adjustment has become an important means of "regulating pressure", "decompression", and "stabilization". Among them, the adjustment of economic law is of great significance in resolving the imbalance between the public and private economy and mitigating the pressure on the national economy and the people's livelihood. Therefore, it has been more widely recognized and used.

The pressure from the national economy and people's livelihood may be "existing" or "coexisting" in a certain period of time. This section believes that the pressures currently existing in China from the two aspects of national planning and people's livelihood have constituted a "double pressure" in the field of distribution,[34] effectively alleviating and releasing the "double pressure" is a major practical issue that

[34] At present, the "double pressures" that the country is more concerned about are "inflation pressures" and "growth pressures", i.e., "stagnation" pressures that coexist with stagnation and inflation. These are the two types of economies that have prevailed in emerging economies in recent years' pressure. But from a more fundamental and long-term perspective, from the perspective of political, economic, social, and legal impact, more attention should be paid to the "dual pressure" of national planning and people's livelihood.

the country should draw great attention. The mitigation of "dual pressure" requires both economic and social efforts, and cannot be separated from the framework and path of the rule of law. Among them, the effective adjustment of economic law helps to improve the profitability of relevant subjects and protect their legitimate rights and interests, which is an important way to alleviate the "double pressure". Solving the problems of national economy and people's livelihood requires especially effective regulation of economic law. Because of this, the state should effectively use and continuously improve economic law, give full play to the institutional functions of economic law, and comprehensively promote the rule of law and good governance.

Relatively insufficient research on the path of economic law to mitigate the "dual pressure",[35] however, if we can conduct in-depth discussions on this, it will not only help to reveal the function, purpose, and institutional structure of economic law, but also answer the questions about the basis of economic law and its development momentum; at the same time, it will not only help to promote the theoretical research and institutional improvement of economic law, but also to analyze and resolve the frequently occurring "double pressure" problems from the perspective of economic law.

To this end, this section will analyze the inherent relationship between economic pressure and the adjustment of economic law based on its actual existence and its manifestation, and reveal its impact on the formation and development of economic law, and how economic law can ease the dual pressure. On this basis, it is intended to analyze the relationship between "dual pressure" and the rights, powers, and related obligations of the subjects of economic law from the perspective of the structure of rights and interests. It is important to study the specific ways to use economic law to alleviate "double pressure", stress the need to strengthen the comprehensive adjustment of various sector laws of economic law and even relevant sector laws other than economic law.

4.2.2 The Reality of "Dual Pressure"

Is there pressure in China's national economy or people's livelihood, and does it coexist with "double pressure"? This is the question that needs to be answered first. From the perspective of people's livelihood, as long as there are problems such as high unemployment, high inflation, high prices, high taxes, etc., the people's livelihood will remain high, resulting in huge pressure on people's livelihood. At present, our country has entered the "high-cost era", and people's livelihood issues are very prominent. At the same time, the path to the realization of the right to survival and development of the people is not yet clear, which further increases the

[35]There have been some research results on fiscal pressure, but no special research results on the "double pressure" of the national economy and people's livelihood have been found. With the increasing pressure on people's livelihood and the "double pressure" problem, research results in the field of law will continue to increase.

pressure on people's livelihood and directly affects the quality of life and well-being of the people and the realization of basic human rights. In addition, the haze of the international economic crisis persists, and the impetus for economic growth and social development has also increased the pressure on people's livelihood.

In fact, not only the pressure on the people's livelihood, but also the country or the government is also facing tremendous pressure on survival and development. This is reflected in the economic level as the pressure of the public economy, that is, the public "national pressure" or financial pressure.[36] It has many differences with people's livelihood pressures (such as "residents' family pressure" and "competition pressure" of enterprises, etc.). The above two types of pressures mainly correspond to the public economy and the private economy, but there are interactive effects: on the one hand, the private economy or people's livelihood issues have a fundamental status and have an important impact on the resolution of public economic or financial issues; on the other hand, the solution of public economic or financial problems will also strongly promote the development of the private economy and the solution of people's livelihood problems.

There is outstanding pressure on people's livelihood in China, for which people have no doubt about it; but whether there are financial pressures at the moment, we have different opinions or doubts. Many people may think that since the growth rate of fiscal revenue in recent years has greatly exceeded the growth rate of GDP, the absolute fiscal revenue of the country has increased in successive years, so there should be no fiscal pressure. But in fact, the fiscal system of China's tax-sharing system has outstanding "asymmetry", the distribution structure of fiscal revenue is not reasonable, so that fiscal revenue is mainly concentrated in the central government,[37] although local governments assume a large number of functions, their financial resources are relatively inadequate, thus creating a financial pressure of "the lower the level of the political power, the heavier the burden". In particular, it should be noted that the fiscal pressures of local governments as a whole have not changed due to fiscal surpluses in some places, because the fiscal revenue of many places mainly comes from "land finance", and the revenue model of "land finance" is unsustainable, which has become more prominent after the real estate market has been tightened. As the functions of local governments have not been reduced, or even continuously expanded, their financial pressure can be imagined. It is based on this financial pressure that many localities have borrowed on a large scale, and the scale of borrowing has exceeded the total fiscal revenue of the country.[38] If we consider the

[36]Before the term "fiscal" was introduced from abroad, in ancient China, "fiscal" was referred to as "national plan", "national use", "degree support" and "year-old plan". Among them, "national plan" refers to national finance. Therefore, "national pressure" is often called "fiscal pressure".

[37]The asymmetry of China's financial system is reflected in the multiple functions of local governments, and the corresponding financial support is sometimes insufficient. Kong Shanguang, 2007, Symmetry of local governments' financial rights after implementing the tax sharing system, *Comparative Economic & Social Systems*, Issue 1.

[38]The local government debt approval limit approved by the NPC was approximately 17.18 trillion yuan in 2016 and 18.82 trillion yuan in 2017. If "contingent debt" is added, the debt burden of local governments would be even heavier, and strengthening legal regulations necessary. Huang

government "contingent liabilities", slowing economic growth, increasing people's livelihood input, and "structural tax cuts", the fiscal pressure across the country is not significant.

It can be seen that, whether it is the state and the national, or the national plan and family budget, survival and development, there is a huge pressure, which constitutes a series of objective "double pressure", and it is prominently reflected in the "double pressure" of finance and people's livelihood, and the "double pressure" of public and private economy. This is a phenomenon that deserves special attention in contemporary economic and social development. For the subject who is under pressure, they must constantly "mitigate" their pressure so that they can survive and develop. For the overall economic system and social system, the pressure must be constantly "relieved" to ensure the overall safety of the system. Therefore, "sustained release" of "dual pressure" is a major realistic problem that the country must resolve.

The aforementioned "double pressure" also exists to varying degrees in other countries. For example, whether it is Greece, Spain, or Italy, Portugal or other European countries that have been hit by the sovereign debt crisis, their fiscal pressures are very great. In order to reduce fiscal deficits, the above-mentioned countries have adopted measures such as tightening spending and reducing national welfare, which have directly affected the provision of public goods and increased pressure on people's livelihood. Similar to the above-mentioned countries, in recent years, the financial pressure and livelihood pressure of many countries have become increasingly prominent and overlap with each other, forming a universal "double pressure".

The existence of "double pressure" is an important manifestation of the "imbalance" of the economy or the "imbalance" of development. It is inherently related to the imbalance between the public and private economy and will directly affect the stable growth of the economy and society Harmonious and stable. Considering that "double pressure" will exacerbate economic imbalance, and economic imbalance will further affect the mitigation of "double pressure", In addition, economic imbalance and "double pressure" are directly related to the adjustment of the law to a certain extent. Therefore, it is necessary to find a legal way to relieve the "double pressure". In view of the fact that countries generally use economic law to solve the problem of "economic imbalance" in order to relieve "double pressure", therefore, the internal relationship between "dual pressure" and the adjustment of economic law should be further explored to reveal the internal mechanism that the adjustment of economic law can mitigate the "dual pressure".

Tao, 2015, The legalization of China's local debt from the perspective of central-local relations, *Law Science*, Issue 4; Zhang Shouwen, 2016, Legal risks and legal constraints of borrowing rights, Journal of Soochow University (Philosophy & Social Science), Issue 3.

4.2.3 The Internal Relation Between "Double Pressure" and Economic Law Regulation

Why can the adjustment of economic law be an important way to mitigate the "double pressure", and what is the internal mechanism? To answer these questions, we need to reveal the relation between "double pressure" and the adjustment of economic law. On the whole, "double pressure", as an important manifestation of the imbalance in economic development, is inherently related to the adjustment of economic law: On the one hand, mitigating the "double pressure" requires the adjustment of economic law, and this actual demand has promoted the emergence and development of economic law; On the other hand, the effective adjustment of economic law and the development and progress of economic law will further promote the relief and release of "double pressure", so as to promote the effective resolution of related economic and social problems.

In fact, the existing financial pressures and people's livelihood pressures urgently require countries to adopt corresponding policy measures in the economic, social and other fields, and further make legal responses, this is of great significance for promoting economic reform and institutional change. It is in the process of solving many problems brought about by "double pressure" that important sector laws such as economic law have been formed and developed. This perspective is extremely important to promote the study of the theory of economic law.

From the perspective of financial pressure, as mentioned earlier, the research of the famous economists Schumpeter, Hicks, North, etc. has proposed an important proposition: "fiscal pressure is a direct driver of reform".[39] If this proposition is extended, it can be argued that "fiscal pressure is also a direct driver of legal development", this is because reforms are accompanied by changes and directly affect the development of law. In addition, if we extend the above proposition, we can also think that: As well as financial pressure, people's livelihood pressure is also an important cause of reform, but also a more fundamental cause. The demand generated under the pressure of people's livelihood is a lasting motive and an inexhaustible source of economic law and other legal developments.

For example, before China's reform and opening up, fiscal pressure and people's livelihood pressure were very prominent. It is precisely because of the pressure of people's livelihood that the country has implemented the reform of the responsibility system for joint production in rural areas; it was under the pressure of financial pressure and people's livelihood that the country initiated urban reform that focused on "enterprise reform".[40] Among them, "profit-for-tax", "allocation to loans" and other reforms related to finance, taxation, finance, and planning, as well as the corresponding economic law system, have played a role in improving economic efficiency,

---

[39]Fan (1998).

[40]Some scholars believe that the main reason for the reform of state-owned enterprises and the reform of profit and taxation is to increase government fiscal revenue and ease fiscal pressure. Gu Zhihui, Cai Fang, 2005, China's fiscal pressure and economic transition from 1978 to 2002: theory and evidence, *Management World*, Issue 7.

alleviating fiscal pressure and people's livelihood, and implementing and improving macroeconomic control very huge, it has directly promoted the establishment and development of legal systems such as economic law that are compatible with the commodity economy.

In the process of institutional reform with "delegating power and transferring profits" as the main line in the early stages of reform and opening up, a large number of economic law norms were generated, which not only promoted the development of the commodity economy, but also solved the problem of people's livelihood to a certain extent. After 15 years of reform and opening up, China began to implement a market economy system. At that time, fiscal pressure was huge, which was reflected in the proportion of fiscal revenue in GDP and the proportion of central fiscal revenue in the total fiscal revenue. The "two proportions" were seriously low. The realization of national capacity is seriously affected.[41] In order to improve the "two proportions", China carried out a large-scale economic and legal system reform in 1994 in an attempt to alleviate the problem of excessive fiscal pressure. After nearly 20 years of hard work, China's economic and legal system has played a huge role, and the country's total fiscal revenue and the above-mentioned "two proportions" have increased considerably, thereby effectively alleviating fiscal pressure at the national level. Practice has shown that fiscal pressure has promoted the emergence and development of the economic law system, and effective reform of the economic law system can greatly alleviate fiscal pressure.

The changes in the economic law system mentioned above only reflect one aspect of the changes in the economic law system. In fact, various economic law systems, including the financial law system, industrial law system, competition law system, and foreign trade law system, have also been continuously generated and developed in the process of reform and opening up to alleviate financial pressure and people's livelihood pressure. Together with the traditional civil and commercial legal systems, they all play a comprehensive role and provide an important institutional platform for alleviating the "double pressure". It is in this process that economic law has been effectively developed.

In recent years, with the development of the market economy, fiscal pressures have eased, but people's livelihood pressures have continued to increase. Since many important issues in the field of people's livelihood need to be solved by expanding fiscal expenditures, it will further constitute new financial pressures, and the financial pressure of local governments is particularly prominent, thus creating a situation where people's livelihood pressures and financial pressures coexist.

Looking at the above development process, it is not difficult to find: China faced "double pressure" at the beginning of reform and opening up. With the deepening of reform and opening up and the development of the commodity economy, the pressure on people's livelihood has relatively eased, but financial pressure has continued to increase; After the implementation of the market economy system, with the development of the economy and the improvement of the legal system, China's fiscal revenue has increased year by year, and fiscal pressure has eased slightly. However,

[41] Wang and Hu (2018).

the people's livelihood problem has become increasingly prominent, forming a very prominent pressure on people's livelihood and relatively hidden financial pressure. In fact, it is still "dual pressure" coexisting and showing a spiraling upward trend. Solving the practical needs of the above-mentioned "double pressure" not only promotes the emergence and development of economic law, but also the effective adjustment of economic law has indeed played an important role in solving the problem of "double pressure", thus forming an important mitigation of "double pressure" and "economic law path".

In short, there is an internal connection between "double pressure" and the adjustment of economic law: "double pressure" has not only strongly stimulated economic and social changes, but also an important driving force for the development of the rule of law and institutional changes. It is precisely to solve the financial pressure and people's livelihood pressure that the state needs to promote the development of the economy and the rule of law, and thus promote the emergence and development of economic law; once economic law is formed, its purpose and mission, its value and function, determine that it plays an important role in alleviating the "double pressure". Economic law, as a "development promotion law", is particularly helpful for ensuring the stable development of the economy and society, stimulating the potential of economic development, enhancing the momentum of development, and preventing "weak development". Economic law, as a "crisis countermeasure law", is particularly helpful in preventing and defusing all kinds of risks, alleviating and releasing all kinds of pressure, so as to avoid economic and social crises as much as possible.[42]

A prominent livelihood problem in a country will directly affect fiscal sustainability, which will increase fiscal pressure; and the increase in fiscal pressure may also make the government work hard to increase fiscal revenue, thereby further increasing the livelihood pressure. Therefore, there is also an internal relationship between people's livelihood pressures and financial pressures, and it is almost unavoidable that "double pressure" often appear in modern society. The existence of "double pressure" implies multiple risks, which need to be resolved through "effective development", and in particular, the economic law's vigorous promotion of economic and social development is required; at the same time, the risks caused by the above pressures need to be prevented and resolved through institutional arrangements and effective adjustments in economic law. In view of this, not only should we pay attention to the positive advancement of "double pressure" on the production and development of economic law, but also see the important role of economic law adjustment in mitigating the "double pressure", and we should further reveal the "double pressure" and economic law. The inherent relation between the subjects' right structure and the protection of their rights and interests, so as to better solve the "double pressure" problem through the distribution and adjustment of economic law's powers, rights and duties, and responsibilities of relevant subjects.

[42]Zhang (2011).

4.2.4 "Double Pressure" and the Right-Duty Distribution of Economic Law Subjects

From the above-mentioned internal relationship between the "double pressure" and the adjustment of economic law, the important way or mechanism for economic law to mitigate the "double pressure" is to influence the rights and interests of economic law subjects through the distribution of the rights and meanings of the relevant economic law subjects. From a legal perspective, the reason for the existence of "double pressure" is directly related to the unreasonable distribution of the rights and meanings of the subjects of economic law and the unfair distribution of rights and duties.

In fact, in different historical periods, in response to the pressure of people's livelihood or financial pressure, the provisions of economic law on the distribution of subject rights and interests have different effects on the rights and interests of related subjects. For example, at the beginning of the reform and opening up, China was still in a period of low income and low cost. In terms of quantity and quality requirements, it was relatively difficult to solve the "double pressure". The efforts to alleviate the pressure on people's livelihood were also mainly reflected in the solution of food and clothing. And eliminate poverty. The "double pressure" currently facing China is formed in the "high-cost era" after entering the "middle-income countries". The high costs in all aspects have not only promoted the increase in GDP, but also brought about changes in the distribution structure and formed the country. The distribution pattern of high taxes and high fiscal revenue has led to problems such as excessive distribution gaps and unfair distribution.[43] In this situation, the pressure on people's livelihood is different from that in the past, because many changes have taken place in both the living pressure and the pressure on the country to improve people's livelihood. At the same time, because the solution of people's livelihood is closely related to the government's financial support, although the total fiscal revenue of governments at all levels has increased year after year, the huge investment required to solve a large number of people's livelihood problems still makes the government feel great financial pressure. In fact, the increasing scale of local government debt is directly related to fiscal pressure.

To mitigate the "double pressure" in the new period, it is necessary to comprehensively use various systems of economic law and other relevant sector laws; among the various specific legal means of "decompression", it is particularly effective to adjust the distribution of the rights and interests of economic law subjects, allocate the powers, rights, duties and responsibilities of various subjects, so that they have their own advantages in the process of mitigating pressure.

From the perspective of rights, "double pressure" relates to the realization of the right to survival and development of the subject of economic law, and involves many

---

[43]Problems such as excessive distribution gaps that cause imbalance in the distribution structure need to be effectively resolved through legal adjustments. Zhang Shouwen, 2011, Finance and tax law adjustment of distribution structure, *China Legal Science*, Issue 5.

specific powers and rights of the subject of economic law.[44] For example, to achieve the relief of fiscal pressure, we need to pay attention to the distribution and exercise of fiscal power, reasonably allocate fiscal revenue rights and fiscal expenditure rights in fiscal law, and establish a more effective tax-sharing fiscal system to better maintain the survival and development of the state and other subjects. For another example, to realize the relief of people's livelihood pressure, we should pay attention to the distribution and exercise of the rights of citizens such as the right to employment, competition, management, and income distribution.

From the perspective of obligations, fiscal pressure is directly related to the state fiscal expenditure obligations (or expenditure responsibilities). Generally, the greater the fiscal expenditure obligation, or the larger the scope and amount of fiscal expenditure, the greater the fiscal pressure on the country. Based on the fiscal principle of balance of payments, the state fiscal expenditure is largely constrained by fiscal revenue. Under the situation of relatively limited income and expanding spending obligations, the country will face greater fiscal pressure. Generally, the more "rigid expenditure" a country has, the greater the pressure on expenditure.[45]

People's livelihood pressure is directly related to national expenditure obligations. If national expenditure obligations are heavy, people's livelihood pressure will be greater. Judging from the actual situation, it is the high tax burden, high prices, high fees, etc. that make the national tax obligations, payment obligations, and payment obligations heavier, increase the overall national expenditure obligations, and thus create greater pressure on people's livelihood. In addition, even if prices are high, if national employment is sufficient and income growth is much higher than expenditure growth, the pressure will be relatively reduced. Therefore, the lack of national income is also an important reason for the pressure on people's livelihood. The reason why China's livelihood pressure is relatively large is directly related to the slow growth of national income and the relative decline in ability to pay.

It can be seen that financial pressure and people's livelihood pressure are directly related to the distribution of rights and interests in law, especially to the allocation of rights and interests in economic law. To alleviate or release the above pressures, it is necessary to effectively allocate fiscal revenue rights and fiscal expenditure rights, reasonably stipulate taxation rights, charging rights, pricing rights, and fully protect the rights of various entities such as taxpayers, workers, and consumers; We must effectively use all kinds of macro-economic control power and market regulation power to make the various rights and interests structures of economic law subjects more reasonable in order to effectively reduce social costs and reduce the burden of various subjects. To this end, it is necessary to further clarify the specific path of economic law to alleviate the "double pressure".

---

[44]Zhang 2012, The right to economic development: from the perspective of economic law, *Modern Law Science*, Issue 2.

[45]China's fiscal expenditure on education in 2012 reached 4% of GDP for the first time. This statutory ratio has made education expenditure more rigid. Similar social security expenditures are also considered to be more typical rigid expenditures.

4.2.5 *Specific Ways to Use Economic Law to Mitigate the "Double Pressure"*

"Double pressure" is a major issue concerning the overall economy and society, and its solution requires the comprehensive use of various legal systems. Among them, the adjustment of economic law is particularly helpful to alleviate the "double pressure", protect basic human rights, and protect national interests, social public welfare and private interests. To this end, we should focus on understanding the specifics of mitigating the "double pressure" from the perspective of economic law path.

Based on the "separation of two powers" framework of state fiscal rights and national property rights at the "economic constitution" level, a country must pay attention to national planning and people's livelihood, protect national fiscal rights and national property rights according to law, and achieve balanced protection of "two powers" only to better alleviate the "double pressure". If the exercise or realization of the above-mentioned "two powers" is hindered or restricted, it will increase financial or people's livelihood pressure. Because of this, fiscal law and the entire economic law must promote the balanced protection of "two powers", which is an important goal of economic law adjustment.

From the specific path of economic law adjustment, according to the different situations of "double pressure", economic law will have different arrangements for the structure of right and meaning, which will help to directly or indirectly affect various types through the distribution of right and meaning. The specific rights and interests of the entity have relieved and released all kinds of pressure.

In terms of easing fiscal pressure, how to obtain fiscal revenue, how to make fiscal revenue and expenditure more balanced, prevent the emergence of sovereign debt crisis, how to prevent fiscal risk and resolve fiscal crisis are important issues that must be considered when determining the specific adjustment path of economic law. Because a country's fiscal revenue is based on economic development, and economic development requires the promotion and protection of economic law, the various sector laws of economic law actually directly or indirectly affect the country's public economy and affect the country Fiscal revenue, thereby helping to alleviate fiscal pressure.

Specifically, the adjustment of the power structure of economic law has a direct role in alleviating fiscal pressures, and is especially important for the distribution of fiscal revenue rights. It is through the establishment and implementation of the tax-sharing fiscal system since 1994, the tilted allocation of tax revenue rights, and the territorialization of "non-tax revenue" such as land revenue rights that has led to the continuous increase in government revenue at all levels. This has alleviated fiscal pressures to a certain extent. However, with the slowdown of economic growth in recent years, the sharp decline in land revenue, the increase in people's livelihood investment, and the expansion of tax reduction areas, fiscal pressure has further increased. In this regard, it is not only necessary to make appropriate adjustments to the structure of rights and interests in economic law, to rationally allocate income distribution rights, to take care of local fiscal revenue capabilities, and to increase the strength of transfer payments, but also financial law, industrial law, price law and competition law. At the same time, it is also necessary to further transform government functions, make further progress in the areas of constitution, administrative law, reduce fiscal expenditures in an all-round way, and achieve what Guan Zhong described as "use with a limit",[46] which is very important to alleviate fiscal pressure.

In terms of alleviating the pressure on people's livelihood, the laws of various sectors of the economic law, including economic law, have important functions in protecting national property rights, competition rights, income rights, and the right to survival and development. For example, the adjustment of financial law directly affects the stability of currency value and price levels, as well as financial order and financial security, which will affect the national income distribution rights or the protection of national property rights; the adjustment of the competition law will help to ensure the fairness and legitimacy of competition and maintain market order, efficiency, fairness, and security. National employment, income, distribution, and even people's livelihood as a whole, have a direct and important impact. In short, various specific adjustments to economic law directly affect the formation and mitigation of people's livelihood pressures.

Based on the internal relation between the two types of pressure, when focusing on the specific path of "decompression", we must also pay attention to and emphasize coordination at the macro level to strive for a win-win situation. In fact, the relief of people's livelihood pressure will help to better solve financial problems; if only the increase of fiscal revenue is considered, but the burden of the people is not taken into account, the "double pressure" will eventually be further increased, just like the principle revealed by the famous "Laffer curve". Therefore, we should truly implement the economic clauses in the Constitution from the height of the "economic constitution", promote the comprehensive adjustment of various economic law norms, comprehensively alleviate the "double pressure", and promote the healthy operation and coordinated development of the economy and society.

In order to realize the comprehensive adjustment of economic law, we must also pay attention to the specific sectoral laws of economic law, each of which should have its own emphasis, and should take into account the specific implementation path. For example, fiscal law and tax law are important to alleviate fiscal pressures and people's livelihood pressures. Therefore, we must emphasize "consideration" and "parallelism" instead of only considering the relief of fiscal pressures. The adjustment of the financial law involves the stability of the currency value and the determination of interest rates and exchange rates, which directly affects the property rights of citizens, and should focus on the relief of people's livelihood pressure; similarly, the adjustment of competition law helps to regulate monopoly and unfair competition behaviors, protects the rights and interests of consumers, and can effectively alleviate

[46]Guan Zhong warned that "the rulers shall collect wealth from the people within a limit, then a nation, though it is small, will be safe and sound; if they are always insatiable, then a nation, no matter how large it is, will be in danger".

the pressure on people's livelihood. As mentioned earlier, "double pressure" constitutes an important driving force for the continuous improvement and development of economic law. At the same time, in the process of continuously alleviating and releasing the "double pressure", and in the process of comprehensive adjustment and consideration, economic law itself has also been effective development.

4.2.6 Conclusion

This section proposes that "dual pressure" is a major practical issue that should be paid attention to in the field of distribution. It discusses the objective existence of "dual pressure" and its internal relationship with the adjustment of economic law. And the economic law path to mitigate it, emphasizing the important value of comprehensive adjustment of the specific system of economic law for mitigating the "dual pressure". On this basis, we should further refine and extend attention to the following issues.

Aiming at the "double pressure" objectively and its legal path of slow release, further research should be carried out from the perspective of system analysis. In fact, as an important part of a country's economic system, the public and private economic systems face the pressures of fiscal pressure and livelihood pressure, respectively. Both of the above two systems are closely related to the legal system. Moreover, the legal system, as an external environment in which the economic system persists, is an important input factor affecting the economic system, and is especially helpful for solving the problems and pressures of the economic system. Among them, the economic law system has a more direct and important role in mitigating the "dual pressure" of the economic system.

"Double pressure" directly affects economic growth, social development, and political stability. How to use legal means to mitigate "double pressure" is an important task for modern countries ruled by law. The "double pressure" inherently associated with the adjustment of economic law not only promotes the emergence and development of economic law, but is also a major problem to be solved in the adjustment of economic law. From the perspective of the right structure of economic law, it helps to better analyze the cause of "double pressure". At the same time, the effective allocation of various specific powers and rights of the subject and related obligations in economic law is exactly what economic law can reduce. In addition, paying attention to the comprehensive adjustment of various laws of economic law at a macro level will help to find the internal connection between various specific paths to mitigate the "dual pressure", thereby helping to better utilize the economic law system and the overall effectiveness of law system.

The thinking of "double pressure" is related to the study of the theory of value and genesis of economic law, and involves the foundation of the economic law and the mechanism of its dynamics. It is not difficult to find that "double pressure" is an important driving force for the production and development of economic law, which is a concrete embodiment of the principle of "pressure changing power" and helps to reveal the problem of the dynamic mechanism of the economic law system operation; At the same time, to how to ease the major practical issue of "double pressure", the institutional construction of economic law must respond positively. This is both an important reflection of the "responsiveness" of economic law and an important reflection of the function or output of the economic law.

In the case of "double pressure", the governance of the country or the adjustment of economic law must pay special attention to the tension and interaction between the two types of pressure. In particular, the "two types of distribution" under the "separation of two powers" framework That is, the distribution of national finance and the distribution of individual interests, which really improve the earning capacity and level of income of the two types of entities, thereby providing economic support for the relief of "double pressure". At the same time, the level of rule of law in economic law should be further improved, so as to build a long-term rule framework for the sustainable development of the country and the people, and strive to promote the formation of a benign "reward relation" between the country and the people, so as to comprehensively "double pressure" and sustained relief and release.

4.3 Economic Law Regulation of Distribution Structure

4.3.1 Background and Issues

Since ancient times, distribution has always been related to national economy and people's livelihood. It runs through many fields such as economy, society and even politics and law. It affects not only political stability, economic growth, social development and cultural prosperity, but also national wealth accumulation and basic human rights protection. Throughout Chinese and foreign history, many disputes, institutional changes, and even regime changes often arise from "distribution problems" such as improper or imbalanced distribution.[47] Therefore, it is necessary to pay close attention to and effectively resolve distribution problems.

Since China's reform and opening-up, with the rapid economic growth, the economic aggregate and social wealth have expanded rapidly, but problems such as excessive distribution gaps, unfair distribution, and imbalances in distribution caused by many factors have also become increasingly prominent, which has affected

---

[47] Confucius once sadi "those who have kingdoms and possessions should not be concerned that they have not enough possessions, but should be concerned that possessions are not equally distributed; they should not be concerned that they are poor, but should be concerned that the people are not contented. For with equal distribution there will be no poverty; with mutual good will, there will be no want; and with contentment among the people, there can be no downfall and is solution. Although people have a variety of understandings of Confucius' distribution thoughts, they still have practical significance. Throughout history, the emergence of many "rules of chaos" is probably related to the imbalance in distribution caused by uneven, unfair and improper distribution. Therefore, we must remain vigilant about the distribution risks and distribution crises that may arise from imbalances in distribution.

economic development and society. Unity and social harmony[48] require a response and adaptation of the economic foundation and superstructure. In fact, the actual need to solve the problem of income distribution was originally the direct cause of China's reform and opening up; and continuously solving the problem of distribution was the whole mission of reform and opening-up.

The formation of the above distribution problem is directly related to the unreasonable distribution structure. In different types of distribution systems in different countries, the distribution structure is always the most important factor affecting the realization of the distribution function. Therefore, to solve all kinds of distribution problems, it is necessary to trace the source, optimize and adjust the distribution structure, effectively prevent distribution imbalances, and achieve Guotai civil security by effectively "determining division and ending disputes".

From the perspectives of development economics, development sociology, and development politics, China's economic and social development has now reached a critical stage-with the acceleration of industrialization, urbanization, marketization, and internationalization, various types problems of "binary structure" have come up endlessly, the distribution imbalance is very serious, and the distribution problem is quite prominent. To bypass the so-called "middle-income trap"[49] that many countries have failed to avoid, alleviate various social contradictions, resolve social disputes, and maintain stable economic growth while ensuring social stability and political stability, it is necessary to effectively adjust the distribution structure to regulate distribution activities in accordance with the law and ensure the distribution order; at the same time, it is necessary to strengthen the study of "development law" in view of various distribution problems in development.[50]

The formation and adjustment of the distribution structure are subject to a specific distribution system. The advantages and disadvantages of the distribution system directly affect the fairness of distribution, involve distribution justice, and are related to the rule of distribution. Regardless of the constitution or other laws, as long as it includes a distribution system, the powers and rights of distribution should be

---

[48]The idea of "social solidarity" put forward by Durkheim is also important for studying the issue of distribution. Durkheim, Qu Dong (trans.), Social Division of Labor, 2000, Beijing: SDX Joint Publishing Company.

[49]The concept of "middle-income trap" was proposed by the World Bank in the East Asian Economic Development Report (2006), emphasizing that when a country breaks out of the "poverty trap" and its economic growth reaches around USD3,000 per capita GDP, due to internal and external reasons such as the mode of economic development, it is easy for it to fall into the stagnation in economic growth, serious polarization between the rich and the poor, corruption and democratic chaos, and various contradictions to stand out, leading to its inability to compete with low- and high-income countries, and difficult to enter the list of high-income countries for a long time, thus falling into the so-called "middle-income trap". So China must adjust the distribution structure in a timely manner, solve the distribution problem, and work hard to circumvent this trap.

[50]Distribution issues are important issues that need to be addressed in terms of national economic, social development, and the construction of the rule of law. "Development law", which aims to study prominent legal issues in the development process, should take them as important research objects. Zhang Shouwen, 2005, "Science of development law" and development of legal science—on the development concept in economic law theory, Law Science, Issue 3.

effectively defined among relevant distribution subjects, and the distribution structure should be effectively adjusted to ensure its rationality and legitimacy, and to maximize the solution to all kinds of distribution problems arising in the process of economic and social development.

According to the framework and philosophy of "development law", the adjustment of the distribution structure is inseparable from the adjustment of the law. Whether it is the distribution of wealth or income, or the distribution of related resources, power or benefits, it is inseparable from the effective adjustment of laws. Among them, economic law, as a typical "distribution law", is particularly important for its adjustment function, and the public has high expectations. It can be said that to optimize the distribution structure, it is necessary to strengthen the adjustment of economic law, and to continuously improve the level of legalization of adjustment.

Strengthening the adjustment of economic laws and other related laws to promote the optimization of the distribution structure is also closely related to the macro background of the country's transformation of economic development methods. At present, China has shifted its focus from "economic growth" to "economic development".[51] It not only emphasizes the quality and efficiency of economic development, but also reaffirms the importance of social distribution and social equity. Changing the economic development mode requires the adjustment of various structures, including industrial structure, investment structure, consumption structure and distribution structure,[52] which has been discussed in the economics community a lot, but the research in the legal field is still very lacking, so for the macro distribution system. It is very necessary to explore how to promote the optimization of the distribution structure through the adjustment of the law from the perspective of law.

This section argues that the large number of distribution problems in reality has brought complex economic, social, and even political issues; Improper, uneven and unfair distribution, resulting from imbalances in the distribution structure. To achieve a relatively balanced distribution, the distribution structure must be adjusted. The distribution structure itself is also an important part of the economic structure and social structure. According to the theory of system theory and structural functionalism, "structure determines function", "a good structure produces positive functions". Only by constantly optimizing the distribution structure can we make it is more balanced and reasonable.

---

[51]In formulating the "Ninth Five-Year Plan", China proposed to "advance the transformation of the mode of economic growth" and "realize the transformation of the mode of economic growth from extensive to intensive", but the above goals were not effectively achieved. As the total economic volume continues to rise, the worship of GDP has also been continuously strengthened, and the problems of the quality and efficiency of economic development and ecological protection have become increasingly prominent. To this end, China's *Outline of the Twelfth Five-Year Plan for National Economic and Social Development* (hereinafter referred to as the "Twelfth Five-Year Plan") emphasizes that the main line of accelerating the transformation of economic development methods must run through the entire process of economic and social development and various fields.

[52]In the process of adjusting various structures, China has a prominent problem of "emphasizing policies and neglecting laws". The level of rule of law in structural adjustment needs to be improved. Zhang Shouwen, 2011, Thinking about the "Double Adjustment" from the perspective of economic law, *Law Science*, Issue 1.

In addition, the optimization of the distribution structure is inseparable from the adjustment of relevant laws, especially the effective adjustment of economic laws that directly affect distribution. Based on the positioning of the problem and the important impact of the distribution structure on the distribution problem, this section will first discuss the relationship between the distribution structure, the distribution system, and the right to the distribution of income from a legal perspective, so as to illustrate the internal relationship between the distribution structure and the adjustment of economic law The necessity and possibility of adjusting the distribution structure using legal means such as economic law; On this basis, this section will further explore the institutional causes of the distribution structure and its problems, explaining the function and speciality of economic law and other legal systems to solve the distribution problem, and the impact of rights or power allocation on the distribution structure; Based on the above discussion, this section will also refine the distribution theory of economic law, especially the theory of distribution structure adjustment, and combine the three types of distribution problems: imbalanced distribution structure, excessive distribution gap, and unfair distribution. Institutions and measures to strengthen economic law adjustments, in order to better protect the distribution rights of various subjects, maintain distribution order, and achieve distribution justice.[53]

It should be noted that observing the internal relationship between the distribution structure and the adjustment of economic law in the macro distribution system and the legal system, and the impact of the allocation of rights on economic law on different types of distribution structure, will be more helpful to discover the adjustment of economic law Positioning, limitations, and links with other relevant legal adjustments, thereby helping to reveal the complexity of distribution structure adjustments and the need for economic law adjustments, and how to optimize the distribution structure through adjustments to specific systems of economic law.

4.3.2 Allocation Structure, Institution and Distribution Power

To study the economic law adjustment of the distribution structure, we first need to analyze the internal relationship between the distribution structure and the adjustment of the economic law. To this end, in a general sense, it is necessary to explore the close relationship between the distribution structure and the distribution system, and

[53]Many scholars from ancient times to modern times have conducted in-depth discussions on distribution justice. For example, Aristotle included justice in the "four virtues" and specifically addressed the issue of distributive justice; Rawls, in his *Theory of Justice*, puts forward the principle of justice, i.e., the principle of freedom and equality, as well as the principle of equality of opportunity and the principle of difference, and emphasized that in order to realize the above principles, the government needs to regulate and interfere; but Hayek opposed the concepts of social justice and distribution justice, and Nozick also opposed government intervention in distribution. Nevertheless, more and more scholars believe that it is valuable to emphasize distribution justice, and the state should fulfill its responsibility to maintain fairness and justice in the field of distribution.

to reveal the impact of the distribution system on the distribution structure; at the same time, it is necessary to further clarify the direct distribution of income distribution rights in the distribution system to the distribution structure Influence, find the key to the adjustment of distribution structure. These two aspects are discussed below.

4.3.2.1 Internal Relation Between Distribution Structure and Distribution System

In a country's distribution system, the distribution structure directly determines the distribution function. To achieve the "positive function" of distribution, it is necessary to adjust the various distribution structures to form an effective distribution mechanism to achieve "distribution normal" and distribution equilibrium.

In recent years, China's macro distribution structure has attracted much attention. For example, since the reform and opening up, in terms of the main structure of distribution, the proportion of government, enterprises and individuals' income in the entire distribution system has shown a clear trend of change: Generally, from 1978 to 1995, with the implementation of policies and systems such as "decentralization and profit sharing", the proportion of national fiscal revenue in the entire income distribution system decreased year by year, and the proportion of residents' individual income increased year by year; However, since 1996, the proportion of government and corporate income has increased year by year, and the proportion of personal income of residents has decreased year by year. Therefore, the trajectory of the change in the proportion of national fiscal revenue has shown a "U-shaped curve", and the proportion of the individual income. The trajectory appears as an "inverted U curve".[54] The above two types of curves reflecting the characteristics of China's macro distribution structure are worthy of attention. Aiming at the problem of imbalance in the distribution structure of the state's fiscal income and corporate profits and the slow growth of residents' personal income, the adjustment of the legal system must be adopted to change the unreasonable distribution structure and continuously increase the proportion of residents' personal income in the total national income. Strengthen the distribution and consumption capacity of residents.

In fact, not only the above-mentioned main structure, but also the urban-rural structure, industry structure, and regional structure in the distribution structure are also related to specific legal systems. It is precisely the arrangement of various specific legal systems that directly affects the formation of various specific structures in the distribution structure. It should be said that the impact of the legal system on various specific distribution structures is the basis and prerequisite for studying economic law and other legal adjustment issues. Clarifying the direct impact of the legal system

[54]The reform of the tax-sharing fiscal system in China and the large-scale tax law reform in 1994 are important reasons for this change. Zhang Shouwen, 2009, The meridian penetrating the development of China's economic law: from the perspective of distribution, *Tribune of Political Science and Law*, Issue 6.

on the distribution structure is particularly helpful in analyzing the necessity and feasibility of various legal system adjustments such as economic law.

Generally speaking, various types of legal systems involving the distribution of assets (including personal income distribution, corporate profit distribution, and national financial distribution) constitute a variety of distribution systems regarding the distribution of private and public goods, affect the formation of various distribution structures. At the same time, based on the constraints of the "matters and ideology" and "limited resources" and the widespread reality of "interest subjects", distribution is an important issue that runs through many fields such as economy and society.[55] Distribution is regarded as a very basic economic or social relationship. It will inevitably have an important impact on superstructures such as laws, and it will also affect the formation of various specific distribution systems. And how to "determinate points" and thus "stop disputes" is precisely the very important function of law.

Examining various legal regulations, it is not difficult to find that the distribution system usually focuses on the subject, the object, the time and space of the distribution, and the rights, methods, and methods of distribution. There are various structures such as space-time structure and rights structure, and it is precisely the above-mentioned various distribution structures that directly affect the results of distribution, and are related to whether the distribution is improper, unbalanced, and whether it will cause various distribution problems.

For example, from the perspective of the main structure of distribution, in the distribution structure composed of "workers" and "owners of elements such as capital",[56] the relative decline in the ability of workers to distribute income and the improvement of the distribution capabilities of owners of factors such as capital, widening the distribution gap of the distribution subject. In the distribution structure composed of rural residents and urban residents, especially in the distribution structure composed of farmers and citizens, the relative decline in the income of rural residents or farmers will directly lead to an excessively large urban-rural gap. The differences in the distribution capabilities of the above-mentioned various types of

---

55 Many scholars have discussed the importance of distribution. For example, Ricardo argued in Principles of Political Economy and Taxation that "determining the rules that regulate distribution is a basic issue of political economy. In Clark's *The Distribution of Wealth*, he argues that "a crucial economic issue is the distribution of wealth among different claimants". In this regard, Martin Bronfenbrenner summarized that when emphasizing the importance of distribution, "some people regard the distribution of income, wealth, and rights as an economic issue that is far more important than 'scarcity' or 'efficiency'". Martin Bronfenbrenner, Fang Min et al. (trans.), 2009, Income Distribution Theory, Beijing: Huaxia Publishing House, pp. 1–2.

56 From the perspective of the elements involved in distribution, the theoretical community generally agrees that the most important factors are five categories, namely labor, land, capital, management, and technology. Early economists such as Durgo focused on labor, land, and capital, and the corresponding three types of income: wages, rent, and profits (including dividends and interest). However, the labor factors are particularly important, so they are often listed separately, thus forming two types of distribution subjects: "laborers" and "owners of capital and other elements". Durgo, Tang Risong (trans.) 2007, *A Survey of the Formation and Distribution of Wealth*, Beijing: Huaxia Publishing House.

entities directly bring about the problems of excessive distribution gaps and distribution imbalances, which need to be solved through adjustments to the distribution system.

In addition, the main structure of the above distribution is also closely related to the spatial structure. The spatial distribution of subjects with different distribution capabilities is very uneven, which will lead to regional distribution gaps. Such as the international gap between North and South, the gap between China's eastern and central and western regions, and so on. At the same time, from the perspective of the object of distribution,[57] the "unbalanced" distribution of wealth, income, and resources in different industries and different fields has also formed a gap between industries or fields. In the final analysis, the above-mentioned gaps are caused by the distribution system.

In short, there is an internal relation between the distribution structure and the distribution system: On the one hand, the distribution system determines the formation of the distribution structure; on the other hand, the distribution structure is also a realistic embodiment of the distribution system. Economic law, as an important type of distribution system, has an important influence on the formation of various types of distribution structures. Therefore, the adjustment of the distribution structure cannot be separated from the adjustment of economic law, and the adjustment of economic law has an important position.

4.3.2.2 The Key to Adjust the Distribution Structure Is to Change the Allocation of Income Distribution Power

The various types of distribution problems that need to be resolved due to the irrational distribution structure constitute the practical needs of the distribution structure adjustment; and the legal reasons for the various distribution problems are mainly reflected in the irrational allocation of income distribution rights. Therefore, the key to the adjustment of the distribution structure is to change the allocation of income distribution rights.

The right of income distribution, often referred to as the right of income or distribution, is the right of the relevant entity to obtain income based on certain rights or powers. The right to income distribution, as a right that directly affects the survival and development of the subject, is related to the basic human rights of the individual. For the enterprise, it is related to the continuous operation of the enterprise. For the third sector, it is related to the survival of the organization in a non-profit state. For the state, it is related to the normal operation of the state machinery and the effective supply of public goods. Therefore, in the entire distribution system, different entities must enjoy the right to income distribution, and the allocation of the income

[57]The object of distribution is broader in a broad sense, mainly including income, wealth, resources, rights, and power. From the perspective of distribution structure, it is mainly the distribution structure of income or wealth. Wealth is directly related to income, so the two are sometimes used universally; resources affect income and wealth, especially natural resources such as land and mineral resources; rights and powers affect income, wealth, and resource ownership from a legal perspective.

distribution right directly affects the rationality of the distribution structure, affecting the fairness of the starting point of distribution, fairness of process, and fairness of results.

In real life, citizens enjoy the right to income distribution according to law based on their labor property rights and various rights such as equity, debt, and intellectual property rights, while the state enjoys various rights and rights such as taxation rights, charging rights, and ownership rights according to law The right of income distribution forms the "binary structure" of the state and national income distribution rights. However, whether it is between the state and its citizens, or between them, the right to the distribution of income is not homogeneous and cannot be viewed in equal amounts. The imbalance in the allocation of income distribution rights of various entities directly leads to differences in their distribution capabilities and distribution results, which in fact has caused many problems such as excessive distribution gaps, unfair distribution, and imbalanced distribution structures. To solve the above-mentioned distribution problem, it is necessary to optimize the distribution structure, legally change the allocation of income distribution rights of relevant subjects, and make the income distribution rights system more reasonable.

For example, from the perspective of the distribution gap, in a market economy, to emphasize competition and pursue efficiency, it is necessary to acknowledge a reasonable distribution gap, which is the proper meaning of a market economy. But at the same time, the distribution gap must also be moderate and reasonable. Otherwise, if the distribution gap is too large, it will seriously affect economic development and social stability. Due to the generally low income of farmers and industrial workers in China, the income distribution gap between different groups is too large, the Gini coefficient continues to rise,[58] and the lack of domestic demand is very prominent. Although the government has used various means to try to stimulate domestic demand for many years, the problem of domestic demand is still outstanding and far from root cause. For this reason, after the 2008 economic crisis, in the face of sudden declines in external demand and poor exports, China's parallel huge investments, structural tax reductions, and home appliances to the countryside have attempted to expand the domestic market, especially the rural market; meanwhile, In order to reduce the income distribution gap and improve the consumption power of residents, a reform framework for income distribution systems that "reduces, expands, and limits" has been established, emphasizing legal changes to the current allocation of income distribution rights, and increasing the number of low- and middle-income groups. Income and truly achieve common prosperity.

For another example, from the perspective of fair distribution, the problem of unfair distribution needs to be solved by changing the allocation of income distribution rights. In any country, respect for labor, fair distribution, and getting what you want are extremely important directions. If monopoly, resource endowment, and

[58]As for China's Gini coefficient, different conclusions are drawn due to different statistics and calibers. However, both official and non-governmental statistics believe that China's Gini coefficient has exceeded the internationally recognized warning line of 0.4 in 2000, and in recent years, it has been considered that it has exceeded 0.47, or hovered around 0.5.

other non-market factors exist, the gap in distribution between different industries and regions will be formed, and this gap is due to the hard work of individuals. There is no direct correlation between hard work and hard work, which will lead to serious unfair distribution. Therefore, the income distribution rights of relevant entities in related industries and regions must be fairly allocated. Because the initial distribution is carried out in accordance with the general market principles and market principles, the fair value is not reflected sufficiently, and it is easy to form unfair distribution. Therefore, the state emphasizes that fairness must also be reflected in the initial distribution.[59]

For another example, from the perspective of the distribution system, if the "rich country, rich people" or "people rich country strong" is the ideal scale,[60] the overall structure of the current distribution system has serious structural imbalances: the growth rate of government fiscal revenue has continued to be too fast for many years, while the growth rate of residents' income has continued to be too slow for many years. At the same time, the proportion of residents' labor remuneration in the initial distribution continued to decline. The aforementioned imbalance in the distribution structure not only does not help the development of the private economy, but also affects the sustainability of the public economy. Therefore, special imbalances in the distribution structure must be adjusted to form a more reasonable system of income distribution rights.

In short, whether the above-mentioned problem of excessive distribution gap or unfair distribution, or the adjustment of an imbalanced distribution structure, requires changes to the existing allocation of income distribution rights, and comprehensive coordination of relevant systems is required. These types of problems and the adjustment of economic law can play a prominent role. It can affect the "weight" changes of different types of income distribution rights and adjust the income distribution results of different subjects.[61]

In addition, studying the adjustment of economic law in the distribution structure not only needs to reveal the above-mentioned connection between the distribution structure and the economic law, but also needs to grasp the impact of various types of legal adjustments on the distribution structure in a wider legal system, which helps to find The relationship between the adjustment of economic law and other laws, and the particularity of the adjustment of economic law, illustrates the need for coordination and complementation of economic law and other laws, and the need for comprehensive adjustment.

---

[59]Our government has recognized that "a reasonable income distribution system is an important reflection of social equity". Therefore, in October 2007, it was proposed that "the initial distribution and redistribution must deal with the relationship between efficiency and fairness, and redistribution must pay more attention to fairness", and emphasized that "protection of legitimate income, regulation of excessively high income, and suppression of illegal income".

[60]Wang (2000).

[61]In the past, the economics community paid attention to the "weight" of various income distribution rights from the perspective of value and contribution, but the research in the legal field was generally lacking. The mapping of such rights to benefits and their quantification are worthy of further study.

4.3.3 *Diversified Legal Adjustment of Distribution Structure*

As mentioned earlier, the internal relationship between the distribution structure and the distribution system requires that the adjustment of the distribution structure must change the corresponding distribution system, and it is the key to change the allocation of the right to the distribution of income in law. This type of distribution system explores the multiple legal adjustments to the distribution structure and the particularities of economic law adjustments.

Considering that there are various divisions of the distribution structure, and usually people pay great attention to the first distribution and redistribution (sometimes also pay attention to the "tertiary distribution"), the following focuses on the distribution structure formed by combining two distributions. Explain the important effects of traditional laws such as the Constitution and civil and commercial law on primary distribution, and the important functions of modern laws such as economic law and social law on redistribution. Based on this, the space and speciality of the adjustment of economic law are discussed.

4.3.3.1 Traditional Adjustment of Initial Distribution and Distribution Structure

In view of the extremely important distribution system, Article 6 of the Constitution of our country specifically stipulates that the basic distribution principle and distribution system are "implement the principle of doing everything in its power and distribute according to work", "adhere to the distribution according to work as the main body and coexist multiple distribution methods; corresponding to this, it also stipulates that "the basic economic system in which public ownership is the mainstay and multiple ownership economies develop together". Because the form of ownership and the way in which products are distributed are important contents of production relations, the two had relatively strong correspondence and consistency in a certain period (especially after the "1982 Constitution" was promulgated). However, with the deepening of reform and opening up and the development of the market economy, the correspondence between the "subject status of public ownership" and the "subject status of distribution according to work" is gradually weakening, and the proportion of "distribution according to factors" in various distribution methods The gradual improvement makes the "main distribution as the main body" more importantly reflected in the number of people participating in the distribution, but not necessarily the amount of distribution, and has brought about a continuous distribution gap when multiple ownership economies and multiple distribution methods coexist.

According to the above-mentioned provisions of the Constitution on distribution methods in China, an important distribution structure of "combining distribution according to work and distribution according to factors" has been formed in the field of primary distribution.[62] Among them, people still have differences on whether "labor" in "distribution according to labor" refers to labor, labor volume, labor results, or labor property rights.[63] As for the various elements in "allocation by elements", people usually pay more attention to capital, resources, technology, management, etc. These elements are very important in production and operation activities. From the perspective of economics, the above-mentioned factors have different contributions in production and operation, and their market values or "weights" of obtaining income are different, thus forming a gap in income distribution. In recent years, it is precisely the emphasis on "allocation according to factors" and the improvement of capital and other factor owners' ability to obtain income, which has led to differences in distribution, widened the distribution gap, and exacerbated inequalities in distribution.[64] To comprehensively study the weight or proportion of the distribution of the value of factors such as labor, not only economic analysis, but also legal research.

From a legal point of view, the above-mentioned distribution according to work directly involves labor rights or labor property rights, while distribution according to factors involves a series of rights such as equity, debt, and intellectual property rights of related entities, and then investment rights. The above-mentioned various types of rights imply the income distribution right of the subject, or in other words, the income distribution right is an important "power" of the relevant property rights of various subjects. All types of income, whether it is salary income or labor service compensation, whether it is business income or dividends, interest, dividends, royalties, etc., must be based on income distribution rights.

These rights are of great significance in the initial distribution. No matter between power and rights, or between various kinds of specific rights, the "power" and "benefit" are not balanced, and the "power" and "benefit" are not the same. Different types of rights have different returns due to their nature, which will greatly affect the distribution gap and distribution equity. It can be seen that the differences in the power distribution capabilities of various rights need to be highly valued and studied in depth.

The above is mainly based on the constitution, a brief legal analysis of the important "combination of distribution according to work and distribution according to factors", it is not difficult to find out that this distribution structure corresponds to a series of important rights, and formed from it Important rights structure. Due to

---

[62]Since October 2007, China has reiterated that "it is necessary to adhere to and improve the distribution system with distribution according to work as the main body and multiple distribution methods coexisting", and emphasized "a sound system for participating in the distribution of production factors such as labor, capital, technology, management and other contributions". This makes the distribution structure of "allocation according to work" and "allocation according to factors" clearer.

[63]The economics community has many different views on this. In recent years, some scholars believe that it should refer to the property rights of labor forces, and think that it is more helpful to protect the interests of workers. Yao Xianguo, Guo Jiqiang, 1996, On the property right of labor force, *Academic Monthly*, Issue 6.

[64]Subject differences, spatial differences, and time differences are important factors affecting the formation of distribution differences. Distribution differences and unfair distribution will bring structural risks and require effective regulation of fiscal and tax laws. Zhang Shouwen, 2011, Differential distribution and its financial and tax regulations, Taxation Research, Issue 2.

the different nature of the rights of different subjects and their ability to earn, certain tensions will form between labor and capital factors, and between labor and investment, and may lead to "labor-capital" conflicts that affect income distribution and distribution gaps This requires special research.

The rights of income distribution of various subjects established in the Constitution are directly related to the protection of basic human rights. Research on human rights theory and the rule of law should be strengthened. At the same time, the concrete realization of the income distribution right is related to the specific property rights owned by various subjects. In view of the differences between labor property rights and the property rights of capital, land, knowledge and other elements, and are protected by different laws, the conflict and coordination between these rights are also directly related to the coordination between various laws.

Generally, laws such as labor law, property law, contract law, intellectual property law, company law, banking law, securities law, insurance law, and bankruptcy law (they are mostly traditional civil and commercial law norms) will make specific provisions for the above types of rights and became an important source of the first distribution system. Strengthening the coordination of the above-mentioned laws on the right of income distribution is extremely important for solving the problem of distribution.

In short, from a legal perspective, the distribution structure is a rights structure composed of the distribution rights of income enjoyed by various entities. These distribution rights are based on the property rights of labor and capital, and are embodied in the constitution and related specific distribution systems. In general, the various types of property rights and related income distribution rights involved in the initial distribution are mainly established and protected by traditional laws such as the *Constitution* and the *Civil and Commercial Law*.

4.3.3.2 Redistribution and Adjustment of Distribution Structure by Modern Law

The initial distribution focused on the contribution of various factors to the market, paid more attention to efficiency, and did not give enough emphasis to equity, making it difficult to solve problems such as large income gaps. In order to make the distribution between members of the whole society more reasonable, while recognizing a moderate gap, the state must pay attention to prevent polarization and implement a secondary regulation distribution system, which is the redistribution system.

The primary distribution is the distribution among market entities. The redistribution is based on the primary distribution. The state-led secondary distribution[65] is a structural adjustment of the primary distribution. In order to slow down or prevent the

65 Regarding the specific types of redistribution, there are scholars divided into four categories, namely aid redistribution, compensatory redistribution, insurance redistribution and fair redistribution. Hu Angang, Wang Shaoguang, 2003, *The Second Transformation: National Institutional Construction*, Tsinghua University Press, pp. 275–311.

serious problems of uneven distribution, unfairness and imbalance that may exist in the initial distribution. In the process of redistribution, it involves not only the distribution structure between enterprises or residents, but also the distribution structure between the state and citizens. For effective adjustment of these structures, modern laws such as economic law and social law need to play a more important role. Among them, financial means such as transfer payments, tax incentives such as tax reduction and exemption, and social security means can all become important means of redistribution[66]; correspondingly, a series of important rights and powers are also involved, such as the state's financial rights, taxes rights, and social security rights of individual members of society, taxpayer rights; etc. how to allocate the above powers and rights directly affects whether the distribution problems such as excessive income disparity can be effectively resolved.

From the perspective of history and reality, in the process of modernization, the problems of excessive distribution and unfair distribution have occurred or are happening. In 1971, Kuznets, the Nobel Laureate in Economics, raised the issue of the relationship between per capita wealth growth (efficiency) and per capita wealth distribution (fairness) from the perspective of development economics. At the beginning of development, the growth of per capita wealth will lead to an increase in income gap, but at a certain stage, with the further growth of per capita wealth, the income gap will gradually narrow, thereby forming an "inverted U curve"[67] that changes the income distribution status with economic development. Although some people have different views on the "Kuznets Hypothesis", at least from the situation since China's reform and opening up and the development reality of some other countries, this hypothesis is still worthy of attention, and more and more people It is recognized that preventing the widening of the distribution gap requires the state to solve it through effective distribution system arrangements. Among them, the effective adjustment of economic law, especially economic law, is more important.

Positioning the adjustment of economic law in modern law is of particular significance. Originally, the original function of finance and taxation was to participate in distribution and obtain income, but with the development of the public economy, finance and taxation must not only be used as a means for the country to obtain income, but also become an important means of macroeconomic regulation and control aimed at solving market failures. In line with this, the adjustment of modern economic law must not only ensure that the state participates in the distribution of social products, but also play a role of redistribution through macro-control to ensure economic and social equity, thereby achieving its adjustment goals.

---

[66]China's Twelfth Five-Year Plan outline specifically stipulates that "acceleration and improvement of the redistribution and adjustment mechanism based on taxation, social security, and transfer payments as the main means. According to this, the main legal system involved in redistribution is the fiscal and tax law and social security law.

[67]Simon Smith Kuznets is known as "the father of GNP in the United States". In the paper *Economic Growth and Income Inequality* in 1955, he put forward the "inverted U curve" hypothesis. Kuznets hypothesis is also used in environmental and legal research to illustrate the impact of excessive economic development and income distribution on the environment and social order.

As mentioned earlier, in the legal system of a country, many laws involve the distribution of income, wealth, resources, rights and other aspects, such as inheritance distribution in inheritance law, bankruptcy property distribution in bankruptcy law, and corporate law. Profit distribution, labor income distribution in labor law, etc., so that various laws include distribution specifications to varying degrees, but these distribution specifications are relatively scattered, and are mainly used to solve the problem of initial distribution. Relatively speaking, in the field of economic law, economic law is a more typical "distribution law", which mainly solves the problems related to the country's participation in national income distribution and redistribution, as well as the problem of resource allocation and social wealth distribution in the public economy. It is very broad and has connections with various subjects. Therefore, when studying the issue of distribution, economic law and specific economic laws are always insurmountable, and their role in redistribution is huge, and it is especially helpful to solve problems such as excessive distribution gaps, unfair distribution, and imbalanced distribution structures. At the same time, since the adjustment of economic law will have an important impact on the various elements involved in the initial distribution, its function of ensuring the fairness of the initial distribution should not be ignored. These are the particularities of the adjustment of economic law. Based on the extensive and important function of economic law in distribution, it is generally necessary for countries to use economic law as the main and direct means of adjustment when adjusting the distribution structure.

In fact, the disparity in distribution is too large, which can easily be transformed into unfair distribution due to improper distribution and discomfort. Whether the disparity is too large or unfair, it is reflected as an imbalance in distribution structure at the macro-level. Economic law, which aims to solve market failures such as distribution imbalances, has a direct and important impact on the interests of various subjects, so it can become an important part of adjusting the distribution structure, achieving redistribution goals, ensuring fair and appropriate distribution, and preventing improper and imbalanced distribution tool.

In short, through the multiple legal adjustments of the distribution structure, it is not difficult to find that the distribution structure is not only an economic structure, but also a legal structure, especially a rights structure. Whether it is initial distribution or redistribution, whether it is the distribution between market entities or between the state and the national, it corresponds to a series of rights, which is directly reflected in the allocation of related rights. Therefore, the adjustment and optimization of the distribution structure need to be gradually realized through the adjustment and improvement of related laws such as economic law. At the same time, the distribution theory in the theory of economic law is also required to guide.

4.3.4 *Refining Economic Law Theory from Distribution Structure Adjustment*

The economic law adjustment of the distribution structure needs theoretical guidance and support, and it needs to reflect the corresponding concepts and value pursuits to ensure the systematic, scientific, and internal consistency of the adjustment of the distribution structure and the construction of the economic law system. For this reason, economic law theory should have an important component, i.e., the "theory of distribution",[68] and more specifically the theory of adjustment of distribution structure. In general, however, previous economic law studies lacked systematic attention to this. Therefore, it is necessary to combine the previous discussions and the institutional practice of economic law to further refine the distribution theory in the field of economic law and more specific adjustments to the distribution structure theory. In fact, in the distribution theory of economic law, the theory of distribution structure adjustment is the core, because the institutional arrangement or adjustment of the entire economic law revolves around the adjustment of the distribution structure in a certain sense. The theory and system of law are investigated and analyzed.

Combining the previous theoretical discussions with realistic institutional practices, the distribution theory in economic law theory can be refined as the theoretical basis of economic law in the adjustment of distribution structure, which specifically includes relevance theory, utility theory, goal theory, moderation theory, system theory and category theory. A brief analysis is as follows:

(1) The relevance theory emphasizes that the relationship between distribution and the system, and the relationship between the distribution structure and the adjustment of economic law, are important foundations for adjusting the distribution structure using economic law; without the above-mentioned connection, the adjustment of economic law cannot affect the distribution structure. As mentioned earlier, the large-scale distribution system stipulated by economic law has an important impact on the formation and reform of the distribution structure. At the same time, the allocation of income distribution rights by various economic entities will directly determine the rationality of the distribution structure. In order to optimize the distribution structure, it is necessary to allocate the income distribution right reasonably in economic law. Relevance theory focuses on solving the necessity and feasibility of "adjusting the distribution of economic structure by economic law", emphasizing the need to continuously optimize the allocation of income distribution rights in economic law.

(2) Utility theory emphasizes that economic law has a special function for adjusting the distribution structure. The previous discussion shows that for the adjustment of the distribution structure, the functions of different types of laws are different: The traditional law's adjustment function for initial distribution is often greater; while the modern law's adjustment function for redistribution is more prominent. From the

[68] Since "a variety of distribution theories cannot be summed up into a whole that can be universally used, generally accepted, or generally verified", the overall and macro distribution theory has been "dissatisfied". Martin Bronfenbrenner, Fang Min et al. (trans.), 2009, Income Distribution Theory, Beijing: Huaxia Publishing House, p. 371.

perspective of macro-control, the function of economic law to solve the problem of redistribution is even more striking. In addition, since the adjustment of economic law will also affect the relevant elements of primary distribution, its function for primary distribution cannot be ignored. In the adjustment of the distribution structure, the function of economic law is more special, and the scope of its role is wider.

(3) The goal theory emphasizes that economic law, as a typical distribution method, aims to achieve the benefits of macro-control and resource allocation by regulating distribution behaviors and guaranteeing distribution rights, ensuring economic fairness and social fairness, thereby promoting economic and social Benign operation and coordinated development. The adjustment of the distribution structure should also help improve the effectiveness of macro-economic control and resource allocation, guarantee and promote fairness and justice, and promote stable economic growth and social harmony and stability. It can be seen that the adjustment of the distribution structure should be consistent with the adjustment goal of economic law.

The objective of economic law is directly related to its aforementioned functions and is inseparable from the specific value of economic law. Values such as fairness, efficiency, order, and justice are also very important for adjusting the distribution structure. Through the effective adjustment of economic law and the optimization of the distribution structure, it should be more conducive to improving the fairness of distribution, improving the efficiency of distribution, ensuring the order of distribution, and thereby realizing distribution justice.

(4) The moderation theory emphasizes that distribution must be modest and "proportional".[69] The adjustment of the distribution structure is directly related to the theory of rule of law, human rights, and macro-economic control theory. Whether it is based on considerations of restricting government power, guaranteeing basic human rights, or based on the effectiveness of regulation and control, the distribution of wealth or income must be appropriate, especially for nationals. To cause undue harm, efforts should be made to minimize the impact on the people.

The moderation theory also contains some important ideas to guide the adjustment of the distribution structure. For example, based on the government's positioning in providing public goods, the government cannot compete with the people for profit, and its income can meet the provision of public goods, without having to account for an excessively high proportion of national income. In addition, in terms of the state's collection ratio, to achieve the goal of "rich country and rich people" or "people rich and strong country", we must truly "rich people" and realize "people's wealth". According to the well-known "Laffer Curve", a country's taxation must be moderate, the tax rate must not be too high, and it must not enter the taxation restricted area. The tax burden must be reasonable to foster more Tax source. From the perspective

[69] When talking about the justice of distribution, Aristotle believed that "fairness must be moderate and equal", emphasizing that "the justice of distribution lies in proportion, and the injustice lies in violation of proportion". *Aristotle,* Liao Shenbai (trans.), 2003, *Nicomachean Ethics*, Beijing: The Commercial Press, p. 134, 136.

of system practice, the Taxation Reform Act of 1986[70] in the United States, which embodies this important idea, provides important ideas for tax law reform worldwide. China has a lot of opinions on "wide tax base and low tax rate", but it is actually a reflection of modest thinking. Similarly, the "half-principle"[71] formed by the German Federal Constitutional Court in trial practice emphasizes that private property should be used primarily for private use, and the tax burden should not exceed the "half" of its due or tangible benefits in order to better protect private property rights. In this process, it is very important to establish a benign "take-grant relation",[72] which is the premise and basis of a benign interaction between the state and the people, and also an important basis for the continuous improvement of the level of legalization of the government.

The moderation theory is also closely related to the above-mentioned goal theory.It emphasizes that in terms of the means to achieve the goal, whether it is the adjustment of the distribution structure or the adjustment of economic law, moderation must be emphasized; only by modest distribution can fairness, justice and goodness be formed. Order of distribution, all kinds of subjects and their behavior can be sustainable.

(5) The system theory emphasizes that the distribution problem is very complicated. Whether it is to adjust the distribution structure or to solve the distribution problem through economic law, it needs to be considered systematically as a whole. In fact, economic law requires the support of various systems within the economic law to solve the problem of distribution. At the same time, to fully solve the problem of adjusting the distribution structure, economic law still has great limitations. It is necessary to continuously improve its own legal structure to achieve the distribution structure "double adjustment" with the structure of economic law itself, and strengthen coordination with other relevant legal systems to better regulate distribution relationships and form a good distribution order.

In addition, system theory also emphasizes that the allocation of income distribution rights in economic law directly affects the relevant distribution structure and the adjustment function of economic law. Therefore, we must pay attention to the rationality of the structure of income distribution rights and dynamically adjust the corresponding right structure In order to better realize the function of the economic law system.

(6) The category theory emphasizes that a large number of systems in economic law all specify the subject of distribution, the behavior of distribution, the distribution of rights, the distribution of obligations, and the distribution of responsibilities,

---

[70]The basic idea of the Taxation Reform Act of 1986 in the United States is "cancel the preferential treatment, promote fairness, expand the tax base, reduce tax rates, simplify management, and promote economic growth". This idea still has important significance today.

[71]Influenced by Judge Paul Kirchhof, the German Federal Constitutional Court developed the theory of optimal property right taxation from 1993 to 1995, emphasizing that the tax liability of the taxpayers' property as a whole should be applied to the "half principle" to prevent the state from overtaxing, thereby Strengthen legal protection of private property rights. Ge Kechang, 2005, Basic Issues of Tax Law-Fiscal Constitution, Taipei: Yuanzhao Publishing Company, pp. 230–238.

[72]Zhang (2005).

and solve the distribution problem through the arrangements of these distribution systems, preventing distribution imbalances and ensuring distribution order, realizing distribution fairness and distribution justice, thus forming a series of important "distribution" categories. These categories are very important for constructing a more systematic distribution theory of economic law. At the same time, by constructing a distribution category system, we can re-examine the entire economic law and economic jurisprudence, thereby helping to better understand why "economic law is a distribution law" and why "distribution is an important clue throughout the entire economic law".

The above is only a brief analysis of several important distribution theories that have a greater impact on the adjustment of the distribution structure. In fact, the content of the above theories is very rich, not only important for the adjustment of the distribution structure, but also for improving the current economic law system and promoting distribution Structural optimization is also of great value. For this reason, it is necessary to combine the above theories to discuss the adjustment of economic law for various types of realistic distribution problems.

4.3.5 Economic Law Adjustment to Real Distribution Problems

Adjusting the distribution structure and optimizing it continuously should focus on solving the imbalance of the distribution structure at the macro level, and the distribution problems such as excessive distribution gaps and unfair distribution. For this reason, we need to adjust the internal structure of economic law, change the unreasonable allocation of rights, comprehensively promote the improvement of the specific system of economic law, and achieve effective adjustment of economic law.

4.3.5.1 Economic Law Adjustment to the Imbalance of Distribution Structure

The imbalance of the distribution structure is a major problem that should be resolved in the adjustment of economic law. The system of economic law is perfect, especially for important and special distribution structures. For example, the "ternary structure" constituted by the three main bodies of government, enterprise, and individual has always been highly valued; at the same time, the "ternary structure" composed of high-income, middle-income, and low-income people has also drawn attention from all walks of life. Aiming at these two types of "ternary structure", economic law should reasonably define the income distribution rights of various types of subjects and provide fair protection in the design of the system.

As mentioned earlier, in recent years, the proportion of residents' income in national income and the proportion of labor remuneration in the initial distribution have been relatively low. These low "two proportions" are important as imbalances in the distribution structure. The manifestation has attracted great attention from the country and all walks of life.[73] For a long time to come, how to increase the "two proportions" is both an important mission for the adjustment of the distribution structure and an important goal for the adjustment of economic law.

(1) Economic law adjustment to low proportion of residents' income

In response to the problem of the low proportion of residents' income in national income, many important arrangements should be made in the adjustment of economic law. Through various legal means that affect redistribution, the amount of residents' income has been continuously increased, and the proportion of the income of residents in national income has been continuously.

In terms of increasing the income of residents, there are many economic law instruments available. For example, by implementing the transfer payment system and increasing the amount of financial subsidies and social security, residents' income can be improved and truly "used for the people"; through adjustments to various tax law systems, residents' taxes can be appropriately reduced negative levels, truly "get more and less", thereby substantially expanding the disposable income of residents.

While increasing the amount of residents' income, it is still necessary to pass economic law adjustments to increase the proportion of residents' income as a whole. Since the beginning of the 21st century, China's fiscal revenue has been significantly higher than the growth rate of GDP in successive years, and its proportion in the overall national income has been increasing year by year, and has been criticized by many people. How to form a reasonable income distribution structure between the state and the national through the improvement of the economic law system is necessary to ensure the income distribution order and solve the problem of "excessive extraction" of the current economic law system.

There have been various economic and legal reasons for the above-mentioned phenomena that fiscal revenues have increased sharply in successive years. Among them, various types of "double taxation" are the more important legal reasons. Regardless of the taxation of double taxation, or the legal or economic double taxation, it will seriously damage national rights and interests, and affect the effective development of relevant subjects.[74] At present, the unreasonable taxation of double taxation caused by the uncoordinated economic and legal system, and the excessive tax burden caused by it, have directly affected the increase of the income level of

[73]In October 2007, China proposed to "increasing the proportion of residents' income in the distribution of national income and increasing the proportion of labor remuneration in the initial distribution". In recent years, it has become a common consensus to rationally adjust the relationship of income distribution, strive to increase the two proportions, and reverse the trend of widening income gap as soon as possible, and it has been included in the *Twelfth Five-Year Plan*.

[74]In recent years, global inflation has continued to rise, and China's domestic inflation problem is also very prominent. Faced with the rising CPI, people are surprised to find that the problem of repeated taxation has become an important inducement that causes prices to rise too fast. Therefore, for tax system double taxation, the overall optimization of the tax system must be considered, and coordination and integration of tax legislation must be strengthened.

residents and the overall proportion. It should be a focus of improving the current economic law, especially the economic law system.

The above-mentioned attempts to promote fair distribution in the field of direct taxes are certainly important, but the impact of the commodity tax system on distribution should not be ignored for a long time. After all, the real main tax in our country is the commodity tax, and the tax burden of the residents mainly comes from the commodity tax. In view of the fact that individual residents are both consumers and the ultimate bearers of the commodity tax burden, how to reduce certain commodity tax burdens and thereby increase the disposable income of residents is an important issue that is worthy of in-depth research, but is masked.

In fact, even with the "dominant" issues that the public pays more attention to, there are still many perceptions that need to be changed. For example, the adjustment of the personal income tax law is directly related to whether personal income can really increase. From the perspective of income distribution, the tax law that needs to be improved is not just the deduction standards and tax rate grades for salaries earned by the National People's Congress. The entire law needs to be comprehensively and systematically revised, including adjustments to tax items and tax rates such as labor compensation, various types of investment income, capital gains tax items, adjustment of tax rates, and fair treatment of individuals of different nationalities. If no comprehensive consideration is made, and only an article is made on wage income, the role of the law in regulating income distribution will be greatly reduced. For another example, in order to improve the real estate tax system, we must consider the most fundamental "property tax" attribute of real estate tax, and we cannot use it as the supreme magic weapon for regulating house prices. At the same time, we must comprehensively complete the real estate system and take into account the state. The idea of "increasing the property income of citizens" is put forward; otherwise, conflicts and contradictions in legislative thinking may be formed.

The above aspects mainly focus on the adjustment and improvement of the tax law system. In fact, the adjustment and improvement of the narrow fiscal law system should also be paid close attention to. For example, excessive government fund income and excessive fees will directly affect the amount and proportion of residents' income; the questionable "land finance" issue will also affect residents' income, and it is necessary to improve the tax sharing system and regulate the distribution order 2. Adjust the angle of distribution structure to solve it. At the same time, cracking the historical "Huang Zongxi's Law" problem[75] to prevent the residents from continuously increasing the burden, so that a reasonable distribution system can be effectively implemented for a long time, especially the continuous improvement of economic law system. Because distribution, adjustment of distribution structure, and legal adjustment of distribution relationship are all "complexity issues", the

[75]Prof. Qin Hui summarized the thought of Huang Zongxi as "Huang Zongxi's Law", emphasizing that the historical tax and fee system reform increased the burden on the people due to the increase of various "miscellaneous fees" after the reform. Therefore, preventing the "rebound" of miscellaneous fees is of particular significance for today's tax and fee reform. Qin Hui, Nov 03, 2000, Tax merge reform and "Huang Zongxi's Law", *China Economic Times*.

corresponding system improvement countermeasures need more multidimensional considerations and comprehensive design.

(2) Economic law adjustment in which labor compensation accounts for a low proportion in primary distribution

The low proportion of labor remuneration in the initial distribution process will directly affect the formation process of the "olive" income distribution pattern, which is related to the foundation of social stability and national governance. Increasing the proportion of labor remuneration in primary distribution also requires corresponding improvements and adjustments in the economic law system.

In related statistical analysis, the personal income of residents usually includes four types, namely wage income, transfer income, property income and operating income. For many years, the proportion of wage income in the personal income of Chinese residents has always reached about 80%.[76] Under such a high situation, it is necessary to fully reflect the principle of distribution according to work and improve the weight of the labor income distribution right, to increase the proportion of labor compensation, we need to achieve it through the adjustment and improvement of various economic law systems.

For example, in the domain of commodity tax, sales income and business income, which are the basis of taxation, are directly related to labor compensation, so that various types of commodity tax systems such as VAT, consumption tax, and business tax will also have an important impact on labor compensation. In addition, the levy rate for small-scale taxpayers, as well as the requirements for thresholds in the VAT and business tax systems, will affect the final level of labor compensation of relevant entities.

For another example, in the field of personal income tax law, labor remuneration is directly related to the types of income such as wages, salaries, labor remuneration, and manuscript remuneration stipulated in the tax law; at the same time, it is also related to the income from production and operation of individual industrial and commercial households, and income from contracted and leased operations closely related. Institutional adjustments in these areas, especially in terms of tax items, tax rates, and tax incentives, will have a direct impact on residents' labor income. Even in the field of corporate income tax law, labor remuneration is an important content to consider when determining the deduction items-whether to deduct, how to deduct (limit deduction or actual deduction), is not only related to the wage system, but also linked to the corporate income tax system. It can be seen that the income tax system has a greater impact on labor compensation.

The above-mentioned adjustments to various types of tax laws, including the cancellation of the agricultural tax in 2006, all focused on how to increase the amount

[76]Zhang Dongsheng (edit), 2013, *Annual Report on Income Distribution of Chinese Residents*, Beijing: Economic Science Press, pp. 5–7.In addition, according to the National Bureau of Statistics, in 2013, China's total annual urban residents' per capita income was 29,547 yuan, of which wage income increased by 9.2% in nominal terms from the previous year; the annual net per capita rural income of rural residents was 8,896 yuan, of which wage Income increased by 16.8% in nominal terms over the previous year.

of labor compensation. At the same time, how to increase the proportion of labor compensation on a macro level also involves the relationship between labor income and capital income, as well as institutional arrangements in various aspects. From the perspective of tax law only, how to tax the two types of income involves the adjustment of the income distribution structure of different types of residents. According to the division of "industrial income" and "non-industrial income", the tax burden of hard-working income such as labor remuneration should be relatively low. Such an institutional arrangement is conducive to protecting the interests of most low- and middle-income earners.

In order to protect the interests of low- and middle-income earners and increase their labor remuneration income, the "weight" of the property rights of labor force must be solved. To this end, the wage system and other related systems should be further improved and matched. In the process of improvement, fairness and efficiency must also be taken into account, otherwise, unilateral emphasis on fairness regardless of overall efficiency may ultimately be detrimental to the improvement of residents' income levels.

4.3.5.2 Adjustment of Economic Law for Excessive Distribution Gap and Unfair Distribution

The above-mentioned imbalances in the distribution structure will lead to prominent problems such as excessive distribution gaps and unfair distribution. At the same time, these distribution problems will further exacerbate the imbalance in the distribution structure. In light of the above-mentioned closely related distribution issues, economic law adjustments must be targeted.

Generally, people pay more attention to the problem of excessive income distribution gap between residents, and the emergence and persistence of this problem are also related to the large distribution gap between other subjects. For example, a large distribution gap between different levels of government will directly affect the income distribution of individual residents. Often local governments with tighter financial resources pay more attention to the collection of various types of fiscal revenue, making the taxes and fees in their areas higher than those in other places, which has an important impact on residents' income distribution capacity and consumption capacity. For this reason, the fiscal distribution gap between the central and local governments, as well as between local governments, should be solved mainly by improving the tax sharing system, especially through the transfer payment system. For another example, for the overall distribution gap between the state and the national, it is necessary to consider that the income growth of residents must not only be synchronized with economic growth, but also be slightly faster than development of economic growth.

Aiming at the problem of too large a distribution gap between residents, it is necessary to improve the fiscal subsidies and various taxation systems to achieve "subsidizing the poor" and "raising taxes on the rich". At the same time, because the causes of the large distribution gap are very complex and involve many systems, it is necessary to improve related supporting systems. For example, in view of the excessively high income of employees in monopoly enterprises (especially some large SOEs), it is necessary to strengthen legal regulations on the payment of dividends, cost accounting, and wage payment standards to make their income distribution more reasonable.

In addition, the income distribution gap between residents is also related to regional disparities and industry disparities. Many research results in these areas have been made. Judging from the adjustment of economic law, regional disparities are related to the settlement of horizontal fiscal imbalances in the transfer payment system. In terms of reducing industry disparities, the related commodity tax and income tax systems and the state capital operating budget system can play a role.

As mentioned earlier, under the conditions of a market economy that emphasizes competition and differences, income distribution gaps are inevitable. However, if the income distribution gap is too large, and equal and equal quality labor cannot get the same remuneration, the problem of unfair distribution will arise, which needs to be solved by strengthening the adjustment of economic law.

For example, the wage income of different industries is very different. The average wage of the securities industry is 9 times[77] the average wage of the livestock industry. Such a large gap, in many cases, has no direct and inevitable connection with the labor and efforts of employees in various industries, mainly due to the particularity or monopoly of the industry, which is undoubtedly unfair. It can be seen that there is a considerable correlation between the distribution gap and unfair distribution.[78]

It should be noted that the solution of various distribution problems requires the cooperation of various systems of economic law. For example, the cooperation of fiscal law and tax law is very important, because tax law mainly solves the problem of income, and fiscal law can solve the problem of expenditure. The cooperation of the two can better solve the problem of distribution equity. In addition, unfair distribution can have multiple manifestations. For example, if a country's tax laws are not highly compliant, tax collection and management is ineffective, and tax evasion is flooded, it will constitute a substantial unfair distribution for law-abiding persons. If the system is unreasonable, or the law enforcement is not strict, and tax deductions are arbitrarily made, it will also constitute a kind of unfair distribution for the subjects who have not received tax benefits. As for non-tax income too much, the distribution order is chaotic, and it will even make people feel that the distribution is unfair. All these need to be gradually resolved through the continuous improvement of the economic law system.

---

[77]Zhang Dongsheng (edit), 2013, Annual Report on Income Distribution of Chinese Residents, Beijing: Economic Science Press, p. 91.

[78]This unfair distribution reflects the irrationality of distribution. Li Yining argues that it is difficult to make clear the issue of unfair distribution, he suggests that the expression of "rational distribution" is more appropriate than "fair distribution". Li Yining, 1994, Rationality and coordination of income distribution, *Social Science Front*, Issue 6.

4.3.6 Conclusion

China's economy and society have developed into an important historical stage. Contradictions in various aspects have become increasingly prominent, and the problem of distribution is particularly prominent. In the process of transforming the mode of economic development, the adjustment of the distribution structure has become increasingly important. Distribution is related to survival and development, stability and security, solidarity and harmony. Therefore, we must attach great importance to and practically solve the problem of distribution.

The existence of the distribution problem stems from the unreasonable distribution structure. To adjust and optimize the distribution structure, it is necessary to adjust the distribution system, because the distribution system is closely related to the distribution structure, and the distribution system determines the distribution structure, and the distribution structure reflects the distribution system. The key to adjusting the distribution structure is to change the allocation of income distribution rights in the distribution system, and to clarify the "weight" and attributions of various income distribution rights, so as to better protect the distribution rights of relevant entities, maintain the distribution order, and achieve distribution justice.

The distribution system is usually prescribed in many different types of laws, each of which has a different function in adjusting the distribution structure. Among them, the traditional laws such as the *Constitution* and the *Civil and Commercial Law* have a more prominent role in solving the primary distribution, while the modern laws such as the economic law and the social law have played a greater role in solving the problems of redistribution. Compared with the adjustment of other laws, the adjustment of economic law has its special characteristics: it not only helps to solve many distribution problems in the field of redistribution, but also has a certain impact on various elements involved in the initial distribution, which helps to solve the problems related to the initial allocation. Therefore, in the adjustment of the distribution structure, the scope of application of economic law is wider and its role is more prominent.

The adjustment of the economic law of the distribution structure requires corresponding theoretical guidance, and it is necessary to refine the distribution theory in the economic law theory. Economic law, as a typical "distribution method", itself contains distribution theory, which includes relevance theory, utility theory, goal theory, moderation theory, system theory, category theory, and so on. These theories can not only provide theoretical guidance for the adjustment of distribution structure, but also provide theoretical support for the adjustment and improvement of specific systems of economic law.

With regard to the improvement of the economic law system, in view of the major practical problems such as imbalances in distribution structures, excessive distribution gaps, and unfair distribution in China, the internal structure of economic law needs to be adjusted to change its unreasonable power allocation and decentralization model. We should also continue to improve the specific institutional design of economic law in combination with the distribution theory in economic law theory.

In combination with the above discussions, it is necessary to further emphasize and reaffirm: the state must adjust the distribution structure in a timely manner in response to the actual distribution problem; the distribution structure is an important factor leading to the distribution problem, and it is also a reflection of the legal structure and rule of law of a country, reflecting the legalization of the country Ability and level. Therefore, the distribution structure is of global concern and cannot be underestimated. It must be optimized.

In addition, the distribution structure is a kind of rights structure, and the rationality of the allocation of income distribution rights is the key. Therefore, we must not only study the economic structure of distribution, but also the legal structure of distribution, and continuously solve the distribution problem through the adjustment of the distribution structure and the structure of the law's own rights. This helps to promote the adjustment of economic law in the distribution structure and the improvement of the economic law system.

From the analysis framework of "development law", as a major issue in economic and social development, distribution is an important research object of "development law". The adjustment of the distribution structure and related consumption structure, investment structure, industrial structure, and regional structure to promote balanced, coordinated, sustainable, and healthy development of the economy and society is an important adjustment goal of economic law and social law, and an important task in the development of law. The refinement of the distribution theory of economic law will help to enrich the content of "development law".

Many distribution categories involved in the distribution theory of economic law, such as distribution function, distribution subject, distribution behavior, distribution power, distribution right, distribution capacity, distribution imbalance, distribution fairness, distribution efficiency, distribution order, distribution justice, distribution performance, distribution structure, rule of law, etc., are closely related to many disciplines such as philosophy, political science, economics, sociology, etc., all need to be studied in depth. If the distribution category system can be effectively constructed, the overall theoretical study of economic law will be greatly promoted.

The distribution problem is a typical "complexity problem", and the adjustment of the distribution structure is extremely complicated. Although the adjustment of economic law is very important, it still has its limitations. To effectively adjust the distribution structure and better solve the distribution problem, we must systematically consider the coordination of various legal systems and policies and measures, and comprehensively improve the scientificity and rule of law of the distribution structure adjustment, so as to form a good distribution order and promote The healthy operation and coordinated development of the economy and society.

4.4 Differential Distribution and Its Economic Law Regulation

4.4.1 Presenting Problems

"It was the best of times, it was the worst of times",[79] quoted from Charles Dickens. A judgment of the times is made on basis of multiple dimensions such as politics, economy, society and law, while economic development and social equity are the fundamental measures. Economic efficiency and social equity are usually taken into account at the same time, i.e., rapid economic growth and coordinated development of society cannot be biased. To balance the two dimensions and prevent bias, we shall pay great attention to distribution—an important bond between economy and society. Economic distribution or social distribution, or the more essential social wealth distribution, any of them is an important yardstick for judging the times.

Social wealth distribution is an important theme of all times. The "order-chaos cycles" and social changes in history are usually under direct impact of wealth distribution. The thought of "even distribution of wealth" and the cultural perception of "not worry about poverty, but rather about the uneven distribution of wealth"[80] reflect Chinese people's concern about the wealth distribution and their livelihood, as well as their anticipation for an "even" and "equal" treatment. However, the ubiquitous differences in real life directly lead to differences in distribution, thereby making the "uneven" distribution a normal state. How to correctly look the differences in distribution? How to adjust these differences? The answers to these questions may affect the choice for development paths of the economy and society.[81]

With a view to the development path of China in the contemporary era, the adjustment of distribution has been a main line running through the entire process of the reform and opening-up. In recent years, the issue of distribution, especially unfair

[79]This famous saying of Dickens is applicable to many domains despite of diverse perspectives of observation and judgment. The economic boom in previous years has made the nationals of many countries thank for the good times; however, the endless social and environmental problems brought about by rapid growth have led many people to complain about the bad times.

[80]Confucius (551–479 BC), Chinese philosopher, proposed the thought of "even distribution of wealth" in his *The Analects* (Chapter 16 Chief of the Ji Clan), saying that "those who have kingdoms and possessions should not be concerned that they have not enough possessions, but should be concerned that possessions are not equally distributed; they should not be concerned that they are poor, but should be concerned that the people are not contented. For with equal distribution there will be no poverty; with mutual good will, there will be no want; and with contentment among the people, there can be no downfall". This thinking has a profound impact on the distribution pattern in China.

[81]In the past, many countries under the planned economy system attached great importance to narrowing the distribution gap, opposing the differences in individual distribution, and advocating egalitarianism. The Chinese thought of "even distribution of wealth", which is also against the differences in distribution, shows that people care more about fair distribution in ancient times. In contrast, the slogan of "let some people get rich first", which was put forward by Chinese leaders in the 1980 s, demonstrates people's recognition of the distribution differences in a given period.

distribution, has drawn great attention from all walks of life. China is now aware of the importance that efficiency and equity must be balanced, instead of laying particular stress on efficiency. To this end, China shall face up to the differences in distribution and control them within reasonable limits through system arrangements such as promulgation of policies and enforcement of laws.

The differences in distribution are ubiquitous due to many factors, and thereby forming differential distribution—an important type of distribution. We need to objectively analyze the positive role of differential distribution, and delve into its negative impact, especially the resulting risks, and the risk prevention and control through legal means. In order to highlight the key points, this section mainly analyzes the important factors that affect the differences in distribution, dissect the structural risks that may be brought by differential distribution, reveal the internal relation between differential distribution and economic law regulation, and the necessity of economic law regulation, and then introduce the definition and protection of distribution rights in the realm of economic law in combination with the unfair distribution caused by differential distribution.

4.4.2 Important Factors Affecting Distribution Differences and Dimensions of Analysis

Distribution differences are ubiquitous in real economic and social life, and in the overall distribution pattern. Generally, the formation of distribution differences is mainly influenced by three factors, i.e., subject differences, spatial differences and time differences. Correspondingly, there are three important dimensions for studying the distribution differences, i.e., subject dimension, space dimension and time dimension.

(1) From the subject dimension, all subjects participating in distribution, whether it is the state, enterprises, individuals or others, have distinctively different abilities, rights or powers, and information in distribution. For example, each country has its unique fiscal strength and proportion of fiscal revenue in its GDP; an enterprise differs from others in profitability and distribution ability; individuals earn different level of income and have different ability in distribution. Based on these differences, a special income distribution in a given period comes into being. For this reason, it is necessary to analyze these differences and their rationality, which is particularly important for studying the issue of social distribution.

At present, the individual income distribution has become China's most noticeable problem. The distribution differences are prominently reflected by an excessively high Gini coefficient at 0.47[82] which is a conservative estimate based on government

[82]Some scholars argue that China's Gini coefficient reached 0.47 in 2004; such figure back in 1993 was 0.407, which exceeded the internationally accepted alarm level at 0.4. Liu Yongjun et al., 2009, *Research on the income distribution gap among Chinese residents*, Beijing: Economic Science Press, p. 2.

statistics, showing that the unfair distribution is quite conspicuous, i.e., the rich, who have a small proportion of the total population, occupy a large proportion of wealth, while the poor, who have a large proportion of the population, only possess a small proportion of wealth. There are huge differences in the distribution between urban and rural areas, between different industries, and between enterprises of different ownership.

For the measurement of distribution differences, the Gini coefficient is an important indicator, which is able to intuitively describe the fairness or unfairness of individual income distribution, but this is not enough, we still need to refer to other coefficients such as the proportion of government fiscal revenue and corporate income in the entire social wealth, because the income distribution of other important subjects directly affects the adjustment of individual income distribution.

(1) From the spatial dimension, regional differences are also worthy of attention. Looking around the world, it is not difficult to find that the North-South differences are a prominent manifestation of the distribution differences. After all, the level of economic development determines the average level of income distribution, and the overall income level in developed countries or regions is always higher. In China, the differences between east and west are an important manifestation of the distribution differences. We shall pay special attention to this kind of geographical differences when analyzing income differences. In fact, in China and many other countries, the urban-rural dual structure, which is based on W. A. Lewis' dual structure theory, is an important manifestation of both distribution differences and regional differences. In the eastern, central or western part of China, urban-rural differences exist on the whole; and the income of urban residents is usually higher than that of rural residents. Although it is important to pay attention to the living and other costs in different regions, we should also take account of the "purchasing power parity" and people's actual income level in different regions.

Since all subjects exist in a certain space, the spatial dimension is an extension and limitation of the subject dimension; and it also demonstrates the important relation between the two dimensions. We can have a real-life experience when studying the distribution differences from the spatial dimension or from the perspective of regional differences.

(3) We also need to pay attention to the time dimension. The time differences of distribution have different impacts on the relevant subjects, and concern the time value of money. In the same distribution pattern in the past, at present and in the future, the level of actual income is not the same if considering factors such as inflation. In different periods of time, the same amount of money has different actual effects on subjects. Given this, in social security and other domains that need a large time span (such as the deferred taxation in the realm of tax law), we shall pay special attention to the specific system arrangements.

From a more macroscopic perspective, different regions are at different stages of development, which is in essence a time difference. And different development stages and development levels have different manifestations in distribution.[83] In the regions that are at the advanced stage of development, the local distribution level is usually higher. Owing to the differences in the time or stage of development, China has made differential system arrangements such as transfer payments and export tax rebates.[84]

The above three dimensions of subject differences, spatial differences and time differences have directly led to distribution differences. The three dimensions are closely related. Among them, all subjects exist in a certain time and space; therefore, when examining the distribution subjects, we shall refer to the spatial and time dimensions, so that the subject differences will appear more concrete. For example, in the cities of the same rank in China's eastern and western regions, the civil servants holding the same position find their income level varies greatly at present, and will remain so in the future. The similar distribution differences are seen everywhere, and must be taken into account for system design.

4.4.3 Differential Distribution and Its Structural Risks

The above-mentioned distribution differences have given rise to an important form of distribution, i.e., differential distribution. Such distribution is directly related to the differences in time, space, abilities, rights and duties of the subjects taking part in distribution, and refleced in different distribution opportunities and different distribution results.

Differential distribution is different from "even distribution" or "non-differential distribution". The important assumption of even distribution is that there was no difference between subjects, so that the distribution would be uniform and equal. Such kind of distribution appears to be equal, but it may sacrifice efficiency and do harm to the genuine equity. In contrast, differential distribution care more about efficiency; it is not absolutely unfair, but more capable of ensuring substantial equity. In short, while discussing the different types of distribution, the issues about efficiency and equity are hard to bypass, and the public is usually more interested in the core value of equity.

Regardless of the types of distribution, equity is the top concern in the realm of law. Generally, moderate differences in distribution are of rationality; but excessive

[83]In 1960, the American economist W.W. Rostow put forward the "theory of stage of economic growth" in his works *The Stages of Economic Growth*, in which he divides the economic development process of a country into six stages: traditional societies, pre-conditions for take-off, take-off, drive to maturity, age of high-mass consumption, and beyond consumption. At different stages there are varied requirements for distribution and consumption. Likewise, R.A. Musgrave argues that the proportion of the fiscal distribution will change at different stages of economic development.

[84]In determining the focus of transfer payments, China usually leans towards the less-developed regions. In arranging the counterpart support, China insists that the developed provinces and cities shall support the underdeveloped areas. When the central government launches any new policy, it will not subsidize the developed regions but let them raise the funds on their own.

differences may result in unequal distribution, then such rationality will no longer exist, but cause public suspicion and dissatisfaction with distribution, affect social stability and economic development, and even endanger the stability of the regime, thus forming "distribution risks" which may evolve into "distribution crises". The uprisings and revolutions in many countries in history were more or less associated with the distribution crises caused by mounting distribution risks.

From the ancient times to date, the individual income distribution always occupies an important position in the entire distribution system. The gap in individual income should be kept within reasonable limits to ensure the long-term social security and national peace. The fair distribution of individual income is an important means to address the "order-chaos cycles", with the core objectives of reducing unreasonable differences, narrowing unreasonable gaps in distribution, respecting and protecting the basic human rights such as the right to existence and the right to development. The realization of the above goals is directly related to the legitimacy, regulatory power and coercive power of the government.

Differential distribution is prone to bring about unfairness, result in imbalanced distribution structure, and thus giving rise to multiple types of "structural risks". All of these risks exist in a certain distribution system, they need to be prevented and resolved according to specific conditions.

For example, the structure of various subjects and their distribution ratios are important issues in the entire distribution system; they not only have economic and social significance, but also have political and legal significance. In any country "the people will never welcome the government that monopolizes social wealth but support the one that shares wealth with them".[85] If the state occupies a higher proportion of social wealth and leaves a smaller proportion of wealth to its nationals, it will shaken the foundation of the market economy, affect the survival and development of the nationals, and constitute structural risks in the distribution pattern. It is necessary to reduce the proportion of fiscal revenue in the total GDP or in the overall social wealth, alleviate the national tax burden[86] and various non-tax burdens, only by this way will the nationals lead a better life and have more development opportunities.

For another example, in the individual distribution system, the amount of wealth occupied by different groups is also an important issue in distribution structure. If wealth is held in the hands of a few people, while a majority of people earn a low income, the Gini coefficient of the entire society will be over-high, which will affect the survival and development of so many individuals, and then affect the overall economic and social development. In order to prevent structural risks in the individual distribution system, it is necessary to implement the policy of "raising the income of low-income group, expanding the size of middle-income group, and readjusting the income of high-income group through fiscal and tax policies" in light of the different situations of different groups, so as to transform the "pyramid-shaped" individual distribution pattern into the "olive-shaped" one.

---

[85]Quoted from Chapter 14 of the Great Learning in the *Analects of Confucius*.

[86]Whether it is the Tax Misery Index or the global tax rate ranking, China ranks high with a relatively higher tax rate. Of course, some scholars are against the relevant calculation methods.

Besides, in the system of distribution factors, the respective proportions of the distribution according to performance and other factors are also an issue of distribution structure. From the perspective of equity, the distribution according to one's performance shall keep playing a dominant role. If the majority of workers cannot obtain an appropriate proportion of income based on their performance, and if a society cannot implement the "distribution according to one's performance", the people's recognition of honest labor will be battered, and the distribution risks will become increasingly apparent. For this reason, the relevant laws shall motivate people to work hard and honestly, refrain from making money for nothing, trading power for money, earning improper gains or profiting from corruption, for the purpose of mitigating the distribution risks, ensuring distribution equity and reducing social grievances. In this regard, the famous economist Jean-Baptiste Say had long ago proposed that a country's tax law shall benefit morality cultivation and encourage people to work hard, and then made it an important principle. In short, how to encourage honest labor, promote genuine creation, and fairly distribute the social wealth created by labor? They are the issues to be taken seriously in the realm of law.

It needs to be emphasized that among all kinds of structural risks, the allocation risks in the dual structure of the state and the nationals need to be paid special attention. Because if the income of the two types of subjects in the overall wealth is unreasonable, it will be too heavy, and there will be a huge distribution risk-either the people will not talk, or the country will not be a country.

In short, the difference in distribution is directly related to the difference in the structure of the relevant subject, and the risk brought by the differential distribution is also related to a certain structure and is reflected as structural risk. At the same time, the continuous accumulation of distribution risks is likely to lead to a distribution crisis. Attention must be paid to timely prevention and resolution of distribution risks.[87] Since the reform and opening up in China, the current distribution structure has been formed by continuously adjusting the interest structure, but the current imbalance in the distribution structure has affected the stable growth of the economy and the coordinated development of society to a certain extent. To this end, it is important to reaffirm the important value of fair distribution, to overcome difficulties, to comprehensively and systematically resolve the structural risks in various distribution systems, and to solve the problems caused by differential distribution. The effective adjustment of laws requires especially effective regulation of economic laws.

[87]The risk perspective is an important dimension for analyzing economic law issues, and the study of fiscal and tax law issues is also applicable. Zhang Shouwen, 2010, Observing the risk dimensions of economic law, Wu Zhipan (edit), 2010, *Economic Jurist*, Beijing: Peking University Press.

4.4.4 The Need for Differential Distribution and Economic Regulation

Economic law can use specific legalized economic means to moderately regulate and control distribution differences. And this kind of regulation of economic law is particularly important for solving the problem of differential distribution. On the whole, differential distribution requires economic regulation; solving the problem of differential distribution in China requires economic regulation.

4.4.4.1 Differential Distribution Requires Economic Regulation

Distribution activities involve a wide range of issues, and it is inseparable from the adjustment of various legal systems to solve the problem of differential distribution. For example, differential distribution between different regions will lead to fiscal imbalances and affect the provision of basic public goods, and a transfer payment system is required; differential distribution between enterprises will affect the basic living standards of employees and require a minimum wage; Differential distribution among individuals, especially in the case of loss or inadequacy of individual labor capacity, the decline in their income level will affect their basic lives and the need for a social security system; etc. In addition, there are many systems in the tax law field that involve differential distribution, such as non-taxation system, tax exemption system, tax reduction system, deduction system, etc.

Although differential distribution requires the adjustment of various types of legal systems, in the field of economic law, the adjustment of economic law is the most prominent. It is the most important system for regulating distribution differences and controlling distribution risks. Because economic law's regulation and control of distribution differences and risks are particularly important today, economic law is used as an example to illustrate.

According to the theory of economic law, income distribution is the original and basic function of the economy. Guaranteeing and regulating distribution is the basic function of economic law. The entire economic law is all about solving the problem of distribution. For example, in many specific economic law systems, such as the personal income tax system and the property tax system, a large number of specific distribution issues are involved.

From the perspective of distribution, "the entire economic law is an important distribution method". The institutional design of various economic laws, including the establishment of various institutional elements, are directly related to distribution, and are all solving the problem of social wealth distribution. For example, in various types of economic law systems, the subject elements, object elements, and means elements involved in distribution are included, and which subjects are allocated (who is allocated to, and what, how much, and how) problem. The above-mentioned elements can be summarized as the physical and procedural elements of the distribution. Among them, the physical elements are embodied in the subjects participating in the distribution, the objects and types of distribution, the method of distribution (calculation method, and distribution method in special cases), The procedural elements include the time and place allocated. In addition, the distribution process involves many important powers and rights such as priority, immunity, deduction, return, jurisdiction, storage, and supervision, which need to be studied not only from the perspective of the original micro system, it needs to be studied from the perspective of "distribution right".

Distribution right is the basic category in distribution law. Although there is no "distribution law" in actual legislation, as an important type of distribution law, the core issue of economic law is the "distribution" of distribution rights. In this sense, financial power, tax power, and so on in economic law are the concrete manifestations of distribution rights; and the above-mentioned various rights or rights such as priority, deduction rights, storage rights, etc. Specifically, more microscopic manifestations require economic law to make specific allocations.

In addition, distribution is related to consumption power, and is ultimately reflected in the ownership of wealth or the size of consumption power. In order to reduce the negative impact of differential distribution, protect people's livelihood,[88] guide consumption, and promote social equity, in the VAT system, there must be a low tax rate system to help people's livelihood; in the consumption tax system, luxury consumption must be reversed, excessive consumption.[89] In the business tax, there are many tax exemptions for social undertakings, including education, medical care, culture, and child care. Similar systems abound in the field of tax law. In the domain of direct taxes such as income tax and property tax, it is very important for the economic regulation of differential distribution.

4.4.4.2 China's Differential Distribution Requires Economic Regulation

As mentioned earlier, economic law as a distribution law, its important function is to regulate the state-to-state, state-to-national, or state-to-enterprise, individual, and other entities by providing institutional arrangements for distribution, and mutual wealth distribution activities among market subjects. In view of the differences in the distribution of various types of subjects in China, there is still a lot of room for adjustment in economic law, and in particular, it is necessary to better play its regulatory role.

For example, the current state fiscal revenues are relatively high, which is itself a question of economic law. From the perspective of the tax law in economic law,

---

[88]China's current VAT system stipulates a low tax rate of 11%, which involves grain, oil, water, coal, gas, agriculture and other fields, and mainly solves the problems of people's livelihood. By extension, the regulations on VAT exemption are a further reflection of the spirit of the low tax rate system.

[89]Consumption tax is now levied on precious ornaments, jewelry and jade, high-end watches, and yachts, but on the whole, there is still a lot of room for giving full play to the role of consumption tax.

how to solve the problem of repeated taxation under the compound tax system, how to reduce the excessive tax burden, and coordinate the comprehensive adjustment between various tax laws or types of taxes are the overall system construction of tax law Important issues to consider. Various non-tax revenues directly related to national fiscal revenues have also been increasing in recent years, which is directly related to the incomplete or non-compliant legal system of the entire fiscal law field.

Another example is that the Gini coefficient in the field of individual distribution is too high, largely due to the relatively weak role of economic law in the initial distribution stage. For example, there are some loopholes in China's personal income tax system, especially in areas such as the capital market where funds are gathered quickly, the role of tax regulation is often too slight, and even non-taxation or exemption in some areas has brought related problems. In fact, no matter whether it is primary distribution, redistribution, or the so-called third distribution, the effective regulation of economic law is indispensable. At present, China's outstanding problems in the field of distribution are largely related to the lack of economic regulations.

In addition, in China, economic regulation of differential distribution is emphasized, and the main goal is to keep the distribution gap within a reasonable range, rather than completely eliminate the gap. For example, tax incentives and other systems in the tax law reflect differences. It is an exception to formal equal taxation, which aims to achieve substantial fairness. Therefore, the design of the preferential tax system must be reasonable, so that the gap can be narrowed substantially, otherwise the distribution gap will increase. For example, concessions for the young, young, and poor areas, and tax benefits for the disadvantaged, are intended to reduce the distribution gap. As for the transfer payment system in the fiscal law, from the perspective of distribution, it is also reducing the distribution difference in order to achieve fiscal balance and equalization in the provision of public goods to ensure fair distribution.

4.4.5 Unfair Distribution and Effective Regulation of Economic Law

Unfair distribution is a prominent problem that may arise from differential distribution. Generally, the distribution of wealth includes both the division and allocation of wealth. At present, people pay particular attention to two aspects of unfair distribution, one is the unfair distribution of wealth (segmentation and ownership), and the other is unfair distribution of wealth.

From the perspective of unfair distribution, there may be some unfair problems about which should belong to the state, which should belong to enterprises or other organizations, and which should belong to individuals, no matter in the overall proportion of the distribution or the specific distribution of wealth. Therefore, the economic law, as the distribution law, should better ensure the fair division of wealth, make the attribution clear, and truly achieve "dividing and ending disputes".

From the perspective of unfair allocation, what should be allocated to the people's livelihood in the wealth belonging to the country (represented by the state fiscal revenue) to solve the basic human rights protection issues; the public will have their own judgment as to what should be used for infrastructure construction or other public goods. For example, if fiscal expenditures are rarely used in public welfare or social undertakings such as education, medical care, social security, etc., and are used to increase public employee salaries or welfare benefits of state-owned enterprises, or build large buildings, or consume large amounts of public funds, then The taxpayer will think that the taxpayers' money is misused, and the public will think that the wealth allocation is unfair. This is actually an important manifestation of unfair distribution. In fact, many unfair distributions are not reflected in the division or ownership of wealth, but may often be reflected in the allocation of wealth. For example, in a certain period of time, under the condition of fair opportunity, a certain entity obtains a lot of income according to law. People generally do not think that the distribution is unfair, but if the wealth belonging to the above-mentioned entity is improperly allocated, it is used for showing off consumption rather than for donations, people also feel unfairly distributed.

To solve the problem of various types of unfair distribution, various economic law systems must play a role. Generally speaking, to effectively solve the problem of differential distribution and the possible unfair distribution, the following problems need to be solved in a country at least in terms of economic and legal construction:

(1) Between the state and its citizens, the right to wealth distribution must be clearly defined. The wealth distribution rights of citizens must be protected jointly by the Constitution, economic law, and civil and commercial laws. Attention must be paid to distribution according to law, so that the state and its citizens can have their own advantages, and the state's share in the entire wealth of society should not be too high. For this reason, in various fields involving government revenue, such as tax law and charging law, the government must stipulate the government's authority to distribute, emphasizing that the government must "appropriately" and collect it according to law.

(2) Between nationals, whether among enterprises, individuals, or other entities, their respective distribution rights must also be clarified. Ensure horizontal and vertical fairness in the collection of various taxes and fees. Especially in the area of personal wealth distribution, we need to solve the problem of wealth division, attribution, and allocation in the process of initial distribution, redistribution, and three distribution through multiple channels, and continuously promote the balance of wealth distribution.

(3) It is necessary to guarantee the wealth distribution rights of individual citizens by various legal systems. For example, labor law, social security law, civil and commercial law, all must protect the individual's wealth distribution rights. In addition, if only from the perspective of economic law, the tax payment systems such as transfer payment law in fiscal expenditure, consumption tax in the field of tax law, business tax, personal income tax, real estate tax, vehicle tax, deed tax, must also play

an important role effect. In addition, the system of fees, and other systems affecting personal income, must also pay attention to protecting the rights of individuals' wealth distribution.

4.4.6 Conclusion

Affected by differences in subjects, space, and time, differences in distribution are widespread, and an important type of distribution-differential distribution-has formed. Different from equal distribution, differential distribution is based on many inequality and will further exacerbate inequality. Therefore, how to face up to the positive and negative effects of differential distribution, how to limit distribution differences to a moderate range, prevent and resolve distribution risks, and work hard to avoid distribution crises are particularly noteworthy issues. In fact, it is necessary to strengthen economic regulations for differential distribution and the structural risks it may bring, especially the negative effects caused by it. For the problem of differential distribution and the unfair distribution in China, it is particularly important to strengthen economic regulations to achieve effective definition and protection of wealth distribution rights.

The economic regulation of differential distribution further reflects the principle of difference in the entire economic law.[90] As a matter of fact, there is no need for economic regulations to regulate the market without problems such as distributional differences, unfair distributional problems such as unfair distribution, and economic imbalances and social imbalances.

The economic regulation of differential distribution involves the establishment and improvement of many specific systems, some of which have little impact on the actual distribution differences. This is an affirmation of the actual differences, especially the differences in the initial distribution; but there are still a large number of regulation and control systems be reversed, which helps to maintain a moderate distribution difference. There are many systems involved in distribution regulation in economic law. They run through multiple areas of economic law, and each of these areas requires more in-depth research. At the same time, the systems in each area must be coordinated.

In the field of economic law, more research should be conducted on the distribution of social wealth, not just on the distribution of income of individuals, so that the problem of differential distribution can be solved in a broader field, and the problem of imbalanced distribution structure can be better solved Only in this way can we promote the stable growth of the economy and the healthy operation of the society.

In the long-term economic structural adjustment process, through effective adjustment of the distribution structure, it is necessary to reduce the difference in distribution, reduce the negative impact or risk of differential distribution, play the positive role of differential distribution, and in the theory and system construction of economic

---

[90]Zhang (2013).

law, reflect the prevention and control of differential distribution risks, in order to better achieve distribution justice,[91] and promote fair distribution and social stability.

References

He, Fan. 1998a. *Including the market economy into the Constitution: fiscal issues in contemporary China*, p34–39. Beijing: China Today Press.

He, Fan. 1998b. *Including the market economy into the Constitution: fiscal issues in contemporary China*, p39–45. Beijing: China Today Press.

Wang, Dingyu. 2000. *The Thought of "Enriching the People" in the Book of Shang*, 4. Issue: Social Science Research.

Wang, Shaoguang, Hu Angang. *China National Capability Report*, Shenyang: Liaoning People's Press, pp. 6–10.

Zhang, Dongsheng. 2013. *Annual Report on Income Distribution of Chinese Residents*, p91. Beijing: Economic Science Press.

Zhang, Shouwen. 2002. The periodic variation of macro-economic control law. *Peking University Law Journal, Issue* 5: pp. 695–705.

Zhang, Shouwen. 2012. *The right to economic development: from the perspective of economic law*, 2. Issue: Modern Law Science.

Zhang, Shouwen. 2013. *Principles of economic law*, p8–10. Beijing: Peking University Press.

Zhang, Shouwen. 2011, Exploration of Economic Law Theory in the Post-Crisis Era, *Journal of Chongqing University (Social Science Edition)*, Issue 3.

Zhang Shouwen, 2005, *Discussion on Finance and Tax Law*, Beijing: Peking University Press, p. 189, 224.

[91]From Confucius to Aristotle to Rawls, sages and scholars of all ages have paid great attention to the issue of distribution justice, which is also an important issue that needs to be paid attention to in the study of economic law and the construction of economic legal system.

Chapter 5
Risk Theory and Crisis Response

Modern society is a risk society where the accumulation of risks may escalate into a crisis. Therefore, a state and society shall pay attention to prevention and control of risks and promptly resolve crises, so as to maintain the benign operation and coordinated development of economy and society, thereby achieving the goals of economic law regulation. In fact, the emergence and development of economic law is connected with the prevention and control of risks, which is a main line running through the various systems of economic law. The implementation of a large number of economic law systems is for the purpose of risk prevention and control and crisis response. In this sense, "economic law is a law for risk prevention and control" and "economic law is a law for crisis response" are regarded as important propositions and basic theoretical consensuses in the realm of economic law. In view of this, it is necessary to extract a risk theory based on international commonality and local particularity, and also extract a crisis theory and corresponding response strategies.

Considering the practical need for economic law regulation in a modern risk society, this chapter will extract a risk theory in the realm of economic law. On this basis, it will interpret the financial crisis arising from accumulated risks from the economic law perspective; discuss the ways to extend the theoretical study of economic law, improve the economic law system, and strengthen the economic rule of law construction in combination of the crisis response strategies, for the purpose of deepening the economic law theory. Besides, the crisis theory and specific crisis response strategies involved in this process are also important research topics in the realm of economic law.

S. Zhang, *The New Horizon of China's Economic Law Theory*, Understanding China,
https://doi.org/10.1007/978-981-15-8824-2_5

5.1 Risk Society and Risk Theory in the Realm of Economic Law

5.1.1 Presenting Problems

The contemporary society is a risk society where people are exposed to the risks in all dimensions. Take market subjects for example, when engaged in business activities, they are concurrently exposed to market risks, policy risks and legal risks, etc. For this reason, in order to maintain stable and benign development, a state or a society shall keep preventing risks and averting risk accumulation which may evolve into a crisis.

The global financial crisis that broke out in 2008 was the outcome of accumulated financial risks. In order to revitalize the economy and strengthen the rule of law in the post-crisis period, both economic law scholars and jurists have brought forth ideas and doctrines that are largely identical, which are quite important for the theoretical development and system reconstruction of economic law. Owing to the breakout of the economic crisis and the response strategies based on economic law, the economic operation risks and their legal precautions have drawn increasing attention, and the dimension of risks has become more prominent in the realm of economic law. Similar to the dimension of distribution, the dimension of risks is also an important "meridian" that runs through the theoretical study and system construction of economic law.[1]

Based on the dimension of risks (especially for the reason that economic risks are a trigger for the economic crisis) and the need to prevent and resolve economic crises, the academic community shall care about the risk issues in the realm of economic law, identify the special types of risks, evaluate the risk prevention and control system, and examine the inherent relations among risks, crises and security, so as to refine the "risk theory" in the realm of economic law.

5.1.2 Introduction to Risk Issues

Although there are varied definitions of risk, it is acknowledged that a risk refers to an uncertainty or possibility for any damage arising from such uncertainty; risk is closely associated with uncertainty, possibility and damage. The constituents of a risk include risk factors, risk accidents and risk damage. Risks exist everywhere and people have an instinct to seek benefit and avoid harm, thus making risks an important issue in many disciplines. There have been in-depth studies on risks in

[1]As mentioned earlier, economic law is an important "distribution law", and the dimension of distribution is a "meridian" running through the entire realm of economic law. Likewise, economic law is also a law for risk prevention and control, the dimension of risks enables all-sided observation of the theoretical study and system construction of economic law.

the realms of economics and sociology,[2] which will enlighten the similar studies in the realm of legal science. From the perspective of system economics, one of the important functions of a system is to solve the risks brought by uncertainties. With regard to the legal system, its main functions and goals are revolving round risks, i.e., addressing the risk issues in multiple domains, preventing risks, and resolving all kinds of crises triggered by risk accumulation.

Learning from history and keeping abreast with the time, we can find that the risk issues exist in all legal systems, e.g., there are trade risks in civil and commercial law, administrative risks in administrative law, litigation and trial risks in procedural law. The existence of these issues has stimulated the establishment and improvement of so many important systems. For example, the criminal law is put into force to guard against and mitigate the risks of crime; the modern countries employ economic law and social law to deal with the mounting risks in economic and social development. Since a large number of "complexities" and "uncertainties" exist in economic operation, the important function and goal of economic law is to prevent "risks" and "danger", and turn danger into safety.

In all sectors of economic law, there are various risks that need to be addressed, such as the fiscal risks in fiscal law, financial risks in financial law, industrial risks in industrial law, price risks in price law, competition risks in competition law, consumption risks in consumer protection law. These risks are so important that they are directly related to the state interest and public good, and of great significance on the overall economic operation and economic order, as well as the legitimate rights and interests of relevant subjects.

The academic community has paid attention to the above risks, although to varying degrees. For example, the fiscal risks in fiscal law are directly attributed to excessive budget expenditure, over-high debt burden, overweight tax or tax shortfall. How to resolve the problems of excessive deficit and serious debt dependence?[3] How to resolve the problems of unfair taxation and unsustainable taxation? These problems are already discussed in the studies on budget law, national debt law and tax law. Now we shall pay more attention to the taxation risks due to overcharging and the arising resistance risks.

In the realm of economic law, most of the studies on the risk issue revolve round the financial risks, including the credit risk and liquidity risk under the regulatory scope of banking law, and the risks under the regulatory scope of securities law

[2]The research on risk economics and risk sociology has achieved rich results, and they have inspired the studies on the risk issues in the realm of economic law, even if quite a number of scholars still hold different views on risks. Frank H. Knight, 2006, *Risk, uncertainty and profit*, Beijing: The Commercial Press; Ulrich Beck, 2004, Risk society, Nanjing: Yilin Press.

[3]These problems are prevalent in countries such as Iceland and Greece, and they have resulted in so many economic, social and political problems, which is of great concern to the international community after the economic crisis. According to A. Smith, the process of accumulating huge debts is almost the same in the European powers, forcing their nationals to be oppressed by the debts; and these countries may go bankrupt as time passes. A. Smith, 1974, *An inquiry into the nature and causes of the wealth of nations* (Vol. 2), Guo Dali & Wang Yanan (trans.), Beijing: The Commercial Press, p. 474.

and insurance law. A large amount of research results in this regard are valuable references for the study of risk theory in the entire realm economic law.

In short, the risk issue is an important content in all sectoral laws, so that the risk dimension has become an intersection of various sectoral laws and of various legal systems. In a broad sense, all legal systems have the function of risk prevention and control; but in a narrow sense, there are special systems for solving specific types of risks. For this reason, we shall firstly identify the types of risks, and explore the commonality and specificity of the systems for risk prevention and control, so as to pave the way for extracting a risk theory in the realm of economic law.

5.1.3 Two Types of Risks

From the perspective of general risk theory, risks are divided into several types based on different standards, like natural and social risks, political and economic risks, moral and legal risks, property and personal risks. Such classification is of certain value to the study of risk issues, but we still need to take account of the particularities of economic law to further explore the types of risks in the realm of economic law.

Risks are prevalent and divided into diverse types according to different classification standards. From the perspective of risk bearers, there are risks of regulation receptors and risks of regulation subjects based on the binary structure of economic law subjects. For example, the risks of commercial banks, securities companies, insurance firms and other enterprises are all risks of regulation receptors. Strengthening the risk prevention and control of regulation receptors (especially the market subjects that concern the national economy and people's livelihood) helps to prevent greater market risks and safeguard the overall economic security.

In addition, we shall also care about the risks of regulation subjects. As the main body of the public economy, the state is obliged to prevent fiscal risks and crises; to this end, it shall ensure of balance of payments, and pay special attention to controlling the scale of transfer payment and government procurement, and the scale of taxation and bond issuance. In the meantime, the state shall prevent the risks of the "tax state", sustain the tax revenue and satisfy the public needs through optimization of the tax system design.[4] Moreover, in order to prevent financial risks, the central bank shall maintain a moderate scale of currency issuance and strengthen financial supervision. Most importantly, the regulation subjects shall employ economic law to prevent and control a large number of risks in macro-economic control and market regulation.

[4]Joseph Alois Schumpeter is known for his studies on the "tax state", while Wang Shaoguang and other scholars have made explorations into the "budget state". In terms of the public debt scale, developing countries have a public debt about 30% of their GDP, while such proportion in developed countries is above 90% of their GDP, that's why the developed countries are labeled as "debtor state". Thomas Piketty, 2014, *Capital in the twenty-first century*, Ba Shusong et al. (trans), Beijing: CITIC Press, p. 557.

The risks of regulation receptors and subjects are so important in the realm of economic law that they either imply or correspond to the following "binary risks"[5] worthy of attention: macro risks and micro risks, holistic risks and individual risks, public risks and personal risks. The regulation subjects usually pay attention to the macro risks, holistic risks and public risks, while the regulation receptors primarily care about the micro risks, individual risks and private risks. These "binary risks" are focus in both theoretical research and system construction of economic law. In fact, the endorsement of holism in the realm of economic law is consistent with the important status of the macro, holistic and public risks. Moreover, when the micro, individual and private risks reach a certain degree, they may evolve into the macro, overall and public risks. As such, the specific economic law systems shall deal with all types of risks; and the supervision pursuant to the specific market regulation laws shall be intensified in the domains concerning the national economy and people's livelihood.

Relevant to the above types of risks and from a behavioral perspective, the risks in regulatory behaviors of the regulation subjects are defined as regulatory risks, which are systematic risks. The risks in responding behaviors of the regulation receptors are responding risks, which are non-systematic risks but possible to turn into the systematic ones. Both the regulatory and responding risks fall into the regulatory scope of economic law and need to be dealt with by the risk prevention and control system.

5.1.4 Risk Prevention and Control System

As the above types of risks may damage the macro-level, holistic or public interests, or interrupt the benign operation of economy and society, there are important systems for risk prevention and control in all sectors of economic law, so as to avoid risk accumulation, control occurrence and spread of any economic crisis, and safeguard economic security.

Many important laws in China are enacted for the purpose of risk prevention and control. For example, Article 2 of the *Law of the People's Republic of China on the People's Bank of China* prescribes that "the People's Bank of China, under the leadership of the State Council, formulates and implements monetary policies to prevent and resolve financial risks and maintain financial stability". Article 1 of the *Law of the People's Republic of China on Regulation of and Supervision over the Banking Industry* states that this law is enacted to "strengthen the regulation of and supervision over the banking industry, standardize the regulatory and supervisory behaviors, prevent and resolve banking risks, protect the legitimate rights and interests of depositors and other customers, and promote the healthy development of the banking industry".

[5]There is internal correlation between these "binary risks" and the "binary structure" hypothesis in the realm of economic law.

Besides, Article 34 of the *Law on the People's Bank of China* prescribes that "when a financial institution in banking industry encounters any payment difficulty that may lead to financial risks, the People's Republic of China, with the approval of the State Council, is entitled to carrying out inspection of and supervision over the concerned financial institution, for the sake maintaining financial stability". The *Law on Regulation of and Supervision over the Banking Industry* sets out the specific systems respectively for the supervision, early warning and disposal of the risks in financial institutions, as well as the systems for strengthening risk management and internal control.[6] Similarly, the *Law on Commercial Banks* requires the banks to follow the operating principles of safety, liquidity and efficiency, bear risks on its own, establish and improve their own risk management and internal control system. The *Securities Law* and the *Insurance Law*, in particular, set out more risk prevention and control systems.

In addition to the above-mentioned direct and specific risk prevention and control systems,[7] the similar systems, which are of substantial significance, exist in all types of economic law legislations, such as the budget reserve system in the *Budget Law*, deposit reserve system in the *Law on the People's Bank of China*, and essential commodities reserve system, price monitoring system and price intervention system in the *Price Law*.[8] The important consideration for the state to establish these risk prevention and control systems is to "plan ahead", and "think of danger in times of peace; to think so can lead to preparation and preparation averts calamities".

The above examples show that the risk prevention and control systems are a major content of almost all economic law legislations. These systems play an important role in mitigating risks in various domains, preventing and resolving crises resulting from the accumulated risks, and ensuring economic security. They also imply the internal relations among risks, crises and security that are in need of further exploration.

5.1.5 Risks, Crises and Security

The diverse and complicated game among various types of subjects is filled with uncertainties, which have greatly increased the risks in front of all subjects. Market failures and social imbalances are not only a manifestation of risks, but capable of exacerbating them. In a high-risk society, efforts shall be made to mitigate risks, prevent them from escalating into crises, and safeguard economic and social security, which are important goals of economic law regulation.

From the perspectives of risks, crises and security, as well as their correlation, the system arrangements for macro-economic control and market regulation in the realm of economic law are made for prevention and control of various risks in the economic operation. Moreover, whenever an economic crisis breaks out owing to risk

[6] See the provisions in articles 13, 21, 23–24, 27–29 and 38 of this law.

[7] See the provisions in articles 4, 59 and 64 of the *Law of on Commercial Banks*.

[8] See the provisions in articles 27–32 of the *Price Law*.

accumulation, the crisis resolution strategy that is implicit in economic law systems will help to resolve the crisis. Since economic law is able to prevent and control risks, resolve crises, and safeguard economic and social security, it is also named risk prevention and control law, crisis response law, or security law[9]; these titles reflect the correlation among risk, crises and security.

Economic law is a new legal branch in modern times, with functions of risk prevention and control and crisis resolution directly related to its regulatory goals. In fact, the proper meaning of the legislative purpose of economic law is to pursue stable economic growth, thereby safeguarding economic security, and then promoting the benign operation and coordinated development of the economy and society. In their discussions about the purpose of economic law, the academic community has brought forth so many important goals to be achieved through economic law regulation, but they failed to make further interpretation from the dimensions of risks, crises and security. Thinking deeply from the risk dimension is definitely helpful for a comprehensive understanding of the purpose and value of economic law.

The 2008 global economic crisis not only provided a good opportunity for a comprehensive understanding of the nature, functions, purpose and value of economic law, but reminded people to analyze the specific systems in various domains from the dimensions of risks, crises and security, as well as their correlation.

The following important issues are to be solved by specific economic law systems: the fiscal risks, crises and security in the realm of fiscal law; the tax risks, crises and security in the realm of tax law; the financial risks, crises and security in the realm of financial law; the industrial risks, crises and security in the realm of industrial law; the competition risks, crises and security in the realm of competition law. All of these risks, either at the macro-level or micro-level, either holistic or individual, may accumulate and evolve into a crisis and then affect the overall security.[10] Some economic law systems are better at dealing with the above-mentioned risk, crisis and security issues, while the systems that are incapable of doing so need to be further improved.

Based on the above dimensions of risks, crises and security, in the realm of fiscal law, it is still necessary to strengthen the budget balance and budget adjustment, control the scale of deficit and debt, so as to make the budget compilation, review and implementation, as well as the national debt issuance and recovery more standardized. In the realm of tax law, the strict taxation and the fair tax burden are related to the risks in the state tax revenue, and the risks arising from citizens' non-compliance with the tax law, so it is necessary to further enhance the rationality and legitimacy of the tax law system. In the realm of competition law, the competition risks of enterprises, especially the risks of illegal competition (e.g., the risks of unfair competition and the risks of monopoly) emerge one after another, there is still a need to refine the various

---

[9]The crisis response law was proposed a long time ago, but the risk prevention and control law and security law from the crisis-related perspective remain absent, they are in need of in-depth study in the future.

[10]For example, deficits and debts have implications in both economic and political domains. B. Guy Peters, 2008, *The politics of taxation: a comparative perspective*, Guo Weigui et al. (trans.), Nanjing: Jiangsu People's Publishing House, pp. 128–133.

regulatory systems for regulating market order. In addition, although there are a large number of financial risk prevention and control systems in the realm of financial law, the occurrence of financial crisis shows that there are still many deficiencies in the existing system and its collaboration with other systems, and there is still a long way to go to improve the financial risk prevention and control system.

In the specific risk prevention and control systems, there exist the following common problems: how to define the powers and responsibilities of relevant subjects in risk prevention and control, how to specify their obligations in assistance or cooperation, how to establish an effective accountability system, how to create the mechanisms for risk early warning, monitoring, control and mitigation? And how to strengthen the cooperation between systems, such as strengthening the cooperation between the fiscal system and the financial system to avoid the financial crisis that is to be covered by the fiscal spending,[11] and truly reduce systematic risks? These problems also point out the important directions for improving these systems. In combination with the system practices, we shall continuously summarize the principles of risk prevention and control, and refine the risk theory in the realm of economic law.

5.1.6 Risk Theory in Economic Law

The risk theory in economic law is a general theory about the existence of risk and its solution through economic law. Based on the understanding of the risk issues, types of risks, specific measures for risk prevention and control, as well as the underlying correlation among risks, crises and security, it is not only necessary but also possible to refine the risk theory in the realm of economic law.

The risk theory is important for both sectoral laws (e.g., the financial law) and the overall economic law. It not only helps to explain the problems about the emergence, purpose, value and means of economic law from the perspective of risks, but also helps to reveal the specific system structure of economic law, explains why economic law is also a law on risk prevention and control, crisis response and safety guarantee, and expands the understanding of the crisis response law.[12]

As mentioned earlier, the financial or economic crisis stimulates people to think more about the issues related to risks, crises and security. If we can refine the risk theory in the realm of economic law and employ it to guide the construction of specific risk prevention and control systems, avoid the risk points or the pathways for risk occurrence and expansion during the system design, and effectively utilize

[11] Liu (2006).

[12] The crisis response law was proposed by the academic community a long time ago, but its explanations are relatively narrow. If combined with the dimensions of risks and security, the understanding of the crisis response law will be expanded. In fact, being related to risk prevention and control, the crisis response strategy has all along been contained in the economic law system.

the means of protection and control provided by the system, then all kinds of risks in economic law could be solved to a certain extent.

On the whole, risks are an objective existence, which is manifested in various types of risk issues and able to evolve into different types of crises. The risks concerning the economic law subjects and their behaviors, whether macroscopic, holistic and public or microscopic, individual and private, are able to cause or exacerbate market failures, or cause government failures, affect the stability and benign operation of the economy, and even form systematic crises that bring huge negative effects. For this reason, in the realm of economic law, it is necessary to build the risk prevention and control systems, so as to guard against all types of risks, and resolve possible economic crises arising from risk accumulation, ensure economic security, and achieve the overall regulatory goals of economic law.

The risk theory in the realm of economic law shall have rich content. The narrowly sensed risk theory shall at least involve the risk types, so as to present the special risk types in the realm of economic law in addition to the general risk types, which will lay the foundation for the specific system construction; meanwhile, it shall also include the risk prevention and control mechanisms, so as to reveal the particularity of such mechanisms in the realm of economic law; in addition, it also includes the norms for risk prevention and control, i.e., the institutional norms for subjects and their behaviors, right-duty structure and legal liability. The risk theory in a broad sense concerns the emergence, property, purpose, function and value of both risks and economic law.

In addition, risk theory and information theory are internally correlated. Today's information society is also a risk society. In order to solve the risks caused by the uncertainty of information, it is necessary to establish lots of information disclosure systems in economic law, in order to protect the right to know of all subjects, including taxpayers, investors and consumers, and the right to know of regulation subjects. Strengthening information disclosure is of great importance in preventing and mitigating risks. It is also an important reason why the information disclosure system has become a universal system and runs through various economic law systems. Therefore, while studying the risk theory in economic law, we shall pay attention to studying the information theory in economic law.[13]

5.1.7 Conclusion

Whether it is the system construction or legal study in the realm of economic law, it can be observed and analyzed from the risk dimension. Since risks directly concern the interests of subjects, the risk dimension is a kind of basic dimension. Presenting

[13]The information dimension is an important dimension for observing economic law, and some studies in this regard have yielded rich results. Ying Feihu, Tu Yongqian, 2010, Information tools in public regulation, *Social Sciences in China*, Issue 5; Xie Guichun, Feng Guo, 2015, Energy empowerment, information risk prevention and information regulation: the path of financial law reform from the perspective of information, *Northern Legal Science*, Issue 6.

the risk issues and special types of risks in economic law, examining the degree of risk prevention and control, and exploring the internal relation among risks, crises and security at the system level, it is of basic significance for refining the risk theory in the realm of economic law.

Like the main line of distribution, risks are also an important main line running through the theory and system of economic law. In the realm of economic law, a large number of systems are related to the prevention and control of risks. We shall prevent and control risks regularly to avoid the crises arising from risk accumulation, and cope with the crisis more effectively in case of any. Since risk prevention and control is a core issue in various types of macro-economic control and market regulation, we shall make it as the focus when dealing with the system construction for macro-economic control and market regulation. On this basis, the academic community shall combine the system construction practice in the realm of economic law to further refine the risk theory, which is especially important for preventing and resolving economic crises.

5.2 Interpretation of Financial Crises from the Economic Law Perspective

The global financial crisis that broke out in 2008, which is described as disaster "once in a hundred years", was the outcome of accumulated financial risks. Owing to its profound and widespread impact, this financial crisis soon became focus of the entire international community.[14] With regard to financial crises – target of public criticism, an interpretation of their occurrence, extension and resolution from the perspective of economic law is an important task in the realm of economic law. In fact, financial crises involve the problems of various sectoral laws in the realm of economic law, such as financial law, economic law and competition law; all of them are important perspectives for studying financial crises. Many scholars are now dedicated to interpreting financial crises from the perspective of economic law theory, but they have yet brought forth rich results. Therefore, this section attempts to analyze the emergence, extension and solution of financial crises from the perspective of economic law theory, so as to demonstrate the important value of economic law and economic law theory for solving financial crises.

[14]Some people describe the 2008 financial crisis as "once in a hundred years", which seems more disastrous than the 1929 Great Depression which was "once in eighty years". The serious and widespread impact of this financial crisis is partly due to the overlapping of the bottom of several economic cycles, although there are people not believing its severity. Yi Gang, Zhang Fan, 2009, Do not be too pessimistic about the future, *Journal of Finance*, Issue 228.

5.2.1 *Breakout of Financial Crises*

Why there are financial crises? What are the reasons for their occurrence? What economic and legal measures should a country take to prevent a financial crisis? What kind of value should be manifested in these measures? There have been so many different answers to these questions. Now an interpretation from the perspective of economic law theory is provided as follows:

5.2.1.1 Root Cause: "Two Failures"

The "two failures", i.e., market failure and government failure, are the important reasons for the emergence, survival and development of economic law. Therefore, the "two failures" are taken as an important analytical framework for studying economic law theory, and this analytical framework or hypothesis is based on the induction of realistic problems. The "two failures" contain the basic problems to be solved by economic law.[15]

The breakout of a financial crisis is primarily a manifestation of market failure. All financial institutions and ordinary market subjects pursue maximal interests. Their numerous innovative financial products and transactions (esp. the transactions of financial derivatives) are driven by profitability, they do not care about social costs or systematic risks, but rush into unchecked construction and expansion under the "veil of ignorance"; their "financial empire" is doomed to collapse in the end. In many countries, people are in fact aware of the blind and harmful behaviors of market subjects, but they are prone to believe that the market is able to solve problems and efficient in resource allocation, so they prefer deregulation and indulge the financial magnates to make waves. As a result, the market failure caused by information bias and external effects, together with the government failure caused by absent supervision, has led to the occurrence of a financial crisis.[16]

It can be seen that the financial crisis stems from "two failures". To solve the problems of "two failures", we must pay attention to the contradiction between individual profitability and public benefit that prevails in the market economy. Such contradiction, as a basic contradiction in the realm of economic law, is prominent amid the financial crisis. In the financial domain or the entire economic domain, if we only stress individual profitability or the role of market mechanism, market failure is bound to occur, and financial risks are sure to accumulate until evolve into a financial crisis. For this reason, we shall take account of public benefit from the perspective

---

[15]Zhang (2008), p. 7.

[16]It is generally believed that a financial crisis is caused by excessive expansion of financial institutions, lack of self-regulation of financial institutions and rating agencies, inappropriate macroeconomic policies, and mismatch between financial supervision ability and financial innovation. Among them, the first two causes are categorized as market failure, while the latter two as government failure.

of public goods provision, and take account of financial issues from the perspectives of social costs, financial security and stability, economic security and stability.

5.2.1.2 Financial Crises Highlight the Importance of Economic Law Regulation

The occurrence of a financial crisis demonstrates the importance of economic law regulation. The important goal of economic law regulation is to resolve market failure and government failure by constantly coordinating the contradiction between individual profitability and public benefit. Therefore, the economic law regulation will, to a great extent, prevent the breakout of a financial crisis. Since the implementation of the market economy system, China has been paying great attention to the economic law regulation, kept introducing important laws and regulations in the realm of financial law, and strengthened the enforcement of financial supervision laws,[17] which played a significant role in keeping China from being seriously hit by the 1997 Asian financial crisis, and in mitigating the negative impact of the global financial crises on China's financial system. In addition to preventing financial crises, the economic law regulation also helps a country to resolve a financial crisis if it is unavoidable. In the realm of economic law, the regulation based on financial control law and financial supervision law will help to solve so many problems arising from the financial crises, so will the regulation based economic control law, industrial policy law, price adjustment law and investment planning law.

In short, no matter it is for prevention for resolution of crises, we need to strengthen economic law regulation, and rely on the regulatory subjects in economic law to carry out regulatory behaviors pursuant to economic law. The breakout of global financial crises reawakened people to notice the importance the state or government in responding to crises,[18] and retaught people in different countries of the important goals and functions of economic law regulation, which will benefit the system construction and theoretical study in the realm of economic law.

From the perspective of economic law regulation, no matter it is for prevention of financial crises or for resolving the problems brought by the crises, macro-economic control and market regulation need to be implemented according to law: on the one hand, we shall implement financial control and all types of macro-economic control (including economic control, industrial control and price control); on the other hand,

[17] China established the market economy system in autumn of 1992, and started the constitutional amendment in the spring of 1993 to provide for strengthening economic legislation and improve macro-economic control. In order to promote the development of the market economy, China launched a great reform of the fiscal and tax legal systems in 1994, and then intensified the efforts in financial legislation in 1995 for building a systematic legal system for both central bank and commercial bank.

[18] The United States and lots of the EU member states adopted large-scale bailout measures, e.g., directly injecting capital into or buying shares of certain financial institutions, which were suspected to be somewhat nationalization. Given this, some people argue that we have entered the "big government era".

we shall strengthen market regulation (especially the regulation of special markets) and financial supervision, and coordinate the relation between financial innovation and financial supervision.[19] As required by the principle of moderation, we shall achieve moderate innovation and moderate supervision, which involves the values of economic law.

5.2.1.3 Financial Crises Underscore the Value of Economic Law

The values of economic law include the internal function value and the external evaluation value. The occurrence of financial crises highlights the important values of economic law from the following aspects:

(1) The occurrence of a financial crisis shows that some countries have failed to give full play to the internal function value of economic law, i.e., the functions of macro-economic control and market regulation of economic law are not effectively performed. In fact, the countries that are gravely hit by a financial crisis are those with poor financial control and supervision. They worship the power of the market, but debase or despise the power of the government; they fail to combine the forces of the market and the government properly and moderately, but advocate deregulation or non-intervention in terms of financial competition and financial order.[20] Upon the breakout of a financial crisis, people will come to realize that all countries have substantive economic laws, even if they lack of formal economic laws. All countries shall pay attention to these substantive economic laws, and manifest the values of economic law in maintaining the economic order on the whole and in stabilizing the economic growth.

(2) The occurrence of financial crises has made people learn more about the limitations of the traditional sectoral laws, and realize that in order to ensure the healthy and coordinated economic development of a country, traditional law shall closely cooperate with economic law. Such cooperation not only helps to prevent financial crises, but facilitates the economic recovery in the post-crisis period. From the perspective of economics, people are reflecting how to reconstruct the theory of economics (esp. that of macro-economics) after a crisis. From the perspective of legal science, our reflection is far from enough. In fact, we should reconstruct the original incomplete legal theory, because the general legal theory mainly covers the traditional sectoral laws, but fails to absorb the emerging economic law theory, which

---

[19]To properly handle the relation between financial innovation and financial supervision, which is the same to properly handle the relation between the market and the government; this relation reflects the binary subject structure in economic law. Related to this, in order to prevent and resolve financial crises, we shall handle the relations between savings and consumption, and between virtual economy and real economy, which requires comprehensive regulation based on economic law.

[20]The deregulation of financial affairs had been a trend of financial reform worldwide. It intertwines and interacts with financial innovation and technological progress, and closely links with public interests, private interests and political process. K. Dowd et al. (ed.), *The Economics of Money, Banking, and Financial Markets*, Chen Yvlu (trans.), 2000, Beijing China Tax Publishing House, p153–156.

makes it difficult for legal theory to effectively guide the development of sectoral laws and legal practice. We have to confirm and underscore the important value of economic law in the contemporary legal system, only by this way can we better advance the construction of the legal system and improve the level of the rule of law.

(3) The occurrence of financial crises has made people more aware of the external assessment value of economic law. Generally, the external assessment value of a law refers to the goals that people are pursuing through legal regulation, such as fairness, efficiency, security, order and justice. They are also the goals of economic law regulation, and become prominent in financial crises. If the economic law regulation can properly resolve the contradiction between individual profitability and public benefit, and balance both efficiency and fairness, then the problem of market failure will be largely addressed, and the probability of a financial crisis will therefore be greatly reduced. If the economic law regulation can guarantee market order and economic security, especially financial order and security, it will help to prevent and resolve financial crises.[21]

Economic law regulation is of great value either for preventing or resolving financial crises. It helps to safeguard the overall social interests while protecting the interests of financial institutions and other market subjects, balance the relation between efficiency and fairness, and coordinate individual profitability and public benefit, thus helping to form an order of economic law to ensure a country's financial security and overall economic safety, which will facilitate the achievement of the goal of economic law to stabilize economic and social development. Therefore, in the realm of economic law, when dealing with the issues related to financial crises, we shall take into account of the values of fairness, efficiency, order and security. A financial crisis highlights the values of economic law, showing that economic law plays an important role in preventing crises. But at the same time, the resolution of financial crises also reflects the values of economic law, particularly the value of order and the value of security.

The financial order in different countries is exposed to various problems. Due to excessive innovation and competition in the financial domain, and relatively loose financial supervision, the order in the financial domain is problematic, which has led to higher financial risks, and then evolve into a financial crisis. Therefore, speaking of the values of economic law, the value of order and the value of security should be underscored. Take China for example, it shall learn from the lessons of the Asian financial crisis and the global financial crisis, standardize the financial order, and in

[21] In order to maintain financial order and security, the Supreme People's Court of China issued the *Opinions on Providing Judicial Guarantee and Legal Services for Maintaining China's Financial Security and Sustaining Its Comprehensive Economic Development* on December 3, 2008, stressing to safeguard the state-owned financial claim according to law, vigorously crack down on financial violations, rectify and standardize financial and economic order, guarantee the development of enterprises pursuant to law, make every effort to maintain social harmony and stability, and promote comprehensive, coordinated and sustainable economic development. However, the specific practices of some judicial organs have deviated from the requirements for "rule of law" and "equal protection". In view of this, amid an economic crisis, how to correctly position the judicial organs? How to make sure they can perform their statutory functions properly? Ji Weidong, Jan 19, 2009, Judicial responsibilities in an economic crisis, *Journal of Finance*, Issue 229.

particular, properly resolve the problems such as illegal adjustment of interest rates, illegal fundraising, and high interest rate deposits. At the same time, China shall standardize the transaction behaviors in housing market, land market and securities market, and build a standardized market order. Besides, China shall address the problems concerning financial derivatives and asset securitization, so as to better protect the financial order and reduce financial risks and social costs, safeguard the country's financial security and overall economic safety. Under the conditions of an open economy, there have been increasingly close economic ties between all countries around the world, the more important financial order and financial security, and the more difficult it is to maintain financial order and security.

5.2.2 *Expansion of Financial Crises from the Perspective of Economic Law*

The expansion of financial crises is mainly interpreted from two aspects: on the one hand, it is a kind of geographical expansion, i.e., spreading from one country or region to other countries or regions; on the other hand, it is an expansion of economic type or industrial form, i.e., the crisis extends from virtual economy to real economy, from financial industry to other industries. The expansion of financial crises can be analyzed with the binary-structure theory in the realm of economic law.

5.2.2.1 Examining the Expansion of Financial Crises from a "Binary Structure" Theory

According to the binary-structure theory in the realm of economic law, based on objective differences,[22] there are a large number of binary structures at the economic level, which will directly result in the binary structures at the institutional level; in this regard, an integrated solution at the institutional level is suggested. From an economic perspective, there are multiple levels of binary structures, including domestic economy and foreign economy, internal economy and external economy, real economy and virtual economy. The expansion of financial crises is directly related to the binary structure at the economic level.

For example, in terms of the binary structure of domestic economy and foreign economy, a financial crisis spreads from one country to other countries, showing the

[22]The principle of difference is an important principle in the realm of economic law, and also an important basis of the binary-structure theory. It is the differences that give rise to binary structures, which make it possible to extract a binary-structure theory and establish the basic analytical framework of the economic law theory. Zhang Shouwen, 2013, Principles of economic law, Beijing: Peking University Press, pp. 8 ~ 10.

close relation between domestic economy and foreign economy against the background of economic globalization, i.e., the domestic economy of a country is impossible to develop without an external environment, especially in the financial domain, any external financial turbulence will quickly affect a country's domestic economy. For this reason, in order to prevent and resolve relevant risks or crises through the economic law regulation, a country must take account of the relation between domestic economy and foreign economy, integrate with the prominent problems brought about by economic globalization, and employ the legalized tools of macroeconomic control and market regulation. It can be seen that the two sets of economic systems that originally corresponded to domestic economy and foreign economy must be comprehensively considered to solve the global financial crisis in an integrated manner. In fact, the system integration in this regard involves both domestic economic law and international (or foreign) economic law.

For another example, in terms of the binary structure of real economy and virtual economy, a financial crisis is spreading from virtual economy to real economy, which will have an important impact on the Chinese economy in particular. In fact, China's economic law has been highly valued after the implementation of the market economy system. The financial control legal system and financial supervisory legal system have become increasingly perfect and extensively applicable. Therefore, China's financial system on the whole was free from being seriously stricken. Compared with the traumatic financial systems of many developed countries, the financial system of China was "safe and sound". However, China saw its real economy dramatically affected by the international financial crisis, and the impact has been gradually deepening, which is directly related to the excessive proportion of China's outward-oriented economy and over-high dependence on foreign markets. Based on this situation, in order to prevent further expansion of the financial crisis, China shall place focus on its real economy, i.e., on the basis of ensuring financial order and security, China shall work hard to resolve the problems in real economy through the regulation based on economic laws and other relevant laws, including industrial restructuring and optimizing economic structure, so as to address the problems of unemployment, bankruptcy, price fluctuations, currency instability, and imbalance of international payments. It can be seen that holding onto the main contradiction in a binary structure is important for solving all the problems arising from an expanding financial crisis; moreover, it is necessary to integrate the systems for solving the problems in both real economy and virtual economy, so as to prevent the wrongdoings as "catching one and losing another" and system inconsistencies.

In addition to the above two types of binary structures, the binary structure of internal economy and external economy is also worthy of attention. Generally, people are more interested in the external economy formed by the transactions between independent market subjects, but fail to pay enough attention to the internal economy constituted by a large number of affiliated companies. In fact, a large quantity of internal economy, such as the one formed by multi-national corporations or enterprise groups, has become a remarkable economic force, and exerts both positive and negative impacts on the stable development of economy. The occurrence and expansion of financial crises are usually directly related to the internal economy. For example, when a problem occurs in the core part of an affiliated company, it will affect other affiliates in the economic chain and produce a chain reaction, which is exactly illustrated by the bankruptcies of several major investment banks in the United States and the resulting linkage effects.[23] It can be seen that the problems in the internal economy formed by affiliated companies shall be properly solved through the economic law systems; and a special economic law system is needed for dealing with the internal economy formed by financial institutions. As such, the economic law system for the external economy shall be integrated with such system for the internal economy, so as to better solve the problems such as the occurrence and expansion of financial crises, as well as the derivational problems of massive unemployment, rising prices, and imbalance of international payments.

5.2.2.2 Reflecting on the Expansion of Financial Crises

The expansion of financial crises shows the complexity and solidarity of the economic system. By observing the expansion path of financial crises, it is not difficult to find that if a country or region enjoys more economic freedom, and if it is more open up to the outside world and more dependent on foreign trade, then will be more likely to be impacted by a financial crisis and the crisis will expand at a faster pace. Therefore, from the perspective of economic law, how to deal with freedom and control, how to open up moderately, how to make good use of the two markets (domestic and international), and how to solve the complex problems caused by the binary dual structures? They are important questions to be answered and guaranteed through effective institutional arrangements.[24] Otherwise, if the regulation based on economic law and other relevant sectoral laws fails to pay its role, the financial crisis will expand rapidly, which may not only lead to the declining market value of enterprises, economic downturn, widespread bankruptcy and unemployment, social unrest and other problems, but may trigger political and legal crises.

From a philosophical or theoretical perspective, the occurrence and spread of financial crises is under the direct influence of the laissez-faire philosophy and the theory neo-liberalism economics, and at the same time directly associated with the practices of deregulation and over-emphasis on market mechanism in many countries since they follow a laissez-faire thought. It can be roughly verified by the countries where the financial crisis originated and by the victimized countries. From the perspective of economic law, we'd better take a "dialectical approach" to regulate economic operation and the behaviors of market subjects, so we do not agree with the neo-liberal proposition that emphasizes too much on the important role of the market. The "regulative feature", one of the key features of economic law regulation, stresses to combine positive promotion with negative restriction, combine the state macro-economic control and market regulation with market-based resource allocation, sticks to the "two hands" approach, and requires to properly solve the problems

[23] Wang (2008), Issue 20.

[24] Zhou (2011), Issue 1.

of "two failures",[25] which shows that the economic law theory contains deep understanding of market failure. It is an outcome of economic law after coping with crises. Therefore, in order to avoid the occurrence of major financial risks or crises, there shall be central bank law and commercial bank law that set out provisions in this regard, as well as securities law that provides for special financial supervision.

In terms of "evidence-based medicine", the economic law into the Taoism and Confucianism in China, it is pay attention to grasp the two aspects of contradiction, stressed or dialectically look at the problem in two, and emphasizes the distinguish primary and the secondary contradictions, the main aspects and the secondary aspects, on the basis of to the doctrine of the mean, reasonably and effectively implement governance. In the process of governance, the state should emphasize "benevolence" in the provision of public goods, and emphasize "governing a big country as if it were cooking a small fish" in the adoption of macro-economic control and market regulation measures. It can be seen that the study of the financial crisis is also conducive to further enhancing people's understanding of the philosophy of economic law.[26]

5.2.3 *Resolution of Financial Crises*

How to solve the global financial crisis, which has occurred and is expanding, is the most important practical problem for all countries in the world. From the perspective of economic law, in addition to the economic law countermeasures that people pay more attention to solve the crisis, it is especially necessary to clearly solve the basic principles that should be followed in the financial crisis and the assumption of legal responsibility, especially the government's assumption of responsibility.

5.2.3.1 Basic Principles to Be Followed for Resolving Financial Crises

The basic principles of economic law, i.e., the principle of statury, the principle of moderation and the principle of performance,[27] are also applicable to the solution of financial crises, i.e., the three basic principles of economic law must be followed for resolving financial crises.

[25]Since the government, owned by all social members, has coercive power, taxation power, restraining power and punishment power, it is especially advantageous in correcting market failure. J. E. Stiglitz, Zheng bingwen (trans.), 1998, *The Economic Role of the State*, Beijing: China Fortune Press, pp. 74–77.

[26]Due to the relatively recent development of economic law, the study of economic law philosophy is obviously insufficient. With the deepening of the understanding of the various branches of economic law, the study of the philosophy of economic law will also be valued, and it will be able to better guide the study of the various branches of economic law.

[27]Zhang (2008), pp. 63–65.

(1) We must act in accordance with the law to solve all kinds of problems related to financial crises. For example, after the crisis, despite the urgent situation, countries with relatively developed rule of law are very careful to act in accordance with the law. A simple example showing the emphasis on the statutory principle is that the United States $700 billion financial rescue package, which was the result of repeated congressional deliberations, instead of through the budget spending decision directly made by the Us Government. In addition, the statuary principle requires not only statutory rights and interests, duties and obligations of relevant subjects, but also emphasizes the need for "statutory procedures". This is particularly important in the process of macro-economic control and market regulation in response to financial crises.

Similar to the statutory entity, the statutory procedures is also the due meaning of the statutory principle. In accordance with the principle of statutory procedures, the resolution of all crisis matters, even if they are urgent, shall be handled in accordance with legal emergency procedures; at the same time, the non-emergency matters should be handled in accordance with the general procedures of the law. Only when all kinds of matters are handled in accordance with statutory procedures can crisis management have a basic legal basis and avoid any crisis the legal system in addition to the financial crisis.

Similarly, considering the statutory principle, China should ensure the legitimacy of all kinds of market rescue plans. For example, when China decided to use 4 trillion yuan to rescue the market, did the plan for spending the fiscal funds need to be examined and approved by the NPC or its Standing Committee? There were doubts at the start.[28] In addition, with respect to the transition of VAT and the adjustment of consumption tax (especially the adjustment of the tax system for refined oil products), is it necessary to hold hearings, solicit public opinions, and subject to the institutional adjustments made by the NPC rather than the State Council? These issues need to be studied carefully.[29] In fact, every regulatory measure related to financial crises involves the public interest, and all of them need for the implementation of the statutory principle.

(2) The resolution of financial crises should follow the principle of moderation, which is very important for the effective resolution of the crises. The introduction of any regulatory measures, the introduction or adjustment of any kind of legal system, will involve the interests of different subjects, exert an important impact on the choices of market subjects, and affect the resolution of various problems in the crises. In addition, a financial crisis is not only a "crisis", but an "opportunity", the

[28]Strictly speaking, expanding expenditures and implementing a proactive fiscal policy are the measures to respond to crises; but legally speaking, it involves budget adjustment due to changing circumstances, and the budget adjustment need to be approved by the legislature, rather than by the executive meeting of the State Council.

[29]The VAT to be transited from production-based to consumption-based, and the tax on refined oil also needs to be adjusted, which will somewhat help to cope with the financial crisis. These adjustments are not only a solution to the crisis, but also related to changes in the tax law system, which needs to strictly abide by the statutory taxation principle and the legal preservation principle. Zhang Shouwen, 1996, On the statutory taxation principle, *Chinese Journal of Law*, Issue 5.

adoption of various regulatory measures should not be overcorrected, appropriateness is very important to prevent excessive behaviors.

We should follow the principle of moderation, pay particular attention to identifying problems, following rules, and avoiding imposing additional burdens on all types of subjects. In particular, the intensity, orientation and intensity of regulatory measures should be moderate. The amount of tax cuts, the determination of various preferential policies, the issuance of national debt, and the adjustment of import and export scale should be appropriate. Moreover, the adjustment of export tax rebate rate, the adjustment of interest rate, exchange rate, and deposit reserve ratio shall also remain moderate.[30]

In addition, even when solving the crisis, environmental issues should be taken into account, as well as sustainable economic and social development. We should never neglect all the other things when dealing with a crisis, and we should also pay attention to the benign economic operation, instead of thinking too highly of the GDP. We should highlight the quality and efficiency of economic development when resolving a crisis, and make efforts to optimize and adjust the structure to conquer the difficult problems.

(3) In addition to the above statutory principle and the principle of moderation, the resolution of financial crises should also focus on the principle of performance. In fact, performance considerations are actually contained in the above two principles. Control and regulation based on the statutory principle is an important guarantee for performance. The control and regulation based on the principle of moderation, while emphasizes the balanced protection of rights and interests of various subjects, also implies the guarantee of performance. In this sense, the three principles are closely linked.

According to the principle of performance, solving financial crises depends on the actual performance and effect of various types of control and regulation. A financial crisis is firstly an economic problem, but it also involves other domains. Therefore, the adoption of various control or regulatory measures in economic law should not only pay attention to economic performance and effect, but also to social and even political performance, especially the effectiveness of law. Only in this way can we effectively solve financial crises.

According to the principle of performance, we should not only pay attention to the immediate performance, but also to the long-term performance; including both economic performance and social performance. It is neither wise nor in line with the spirit of scientific development to focus only on immediate performance and the resolution of immediate crises, while ignoring long-term performance. However, from the realistic perspective, in a crisis or other critical situation, it is easy for

[30]After the financial crisis, China had repeatedly adjusted the export tax rebate rate. At the same time, it also repeatedly adjusted interest rates and deposit reserve ratios in order to deal with the issue of the balance of imports and exports, reduce financial risks, and stimulate domestic demand. Such frequent adjustments of taxes are relatively rare in China. There are different perceptions as to whether these practices are appropriate. Bai Chong'en et al., 2011, Empirical analysis of the impact of adjusting the export tax rebate policy on China's exports, *The Quarterly Journal of Economics*, Issue 3.

people to focus only on the present and may not consider enough about the long-term performance. Therefore, it is necessary to make a comprehensive judgment on the overall interests. In addition, attention should be paid not only to economic performance, but also to performance in other domains (such as social benefits and environmental benefits) which are often closely related to long-term performance.

5.2.3.2 Responsibilities in Addressing Financial Crises

The resolution of financial crises involves both positive and negative aspects. Speaking of the positive side, the problem of development should be well addressed, so that the crisis could be defused with negative effects mitigated in the process of development. Speaking of the negative side, we should solve the problem of responsibility. By clarifying the obligations and responsibilities of relevant subjects, as well as their specific responsibilities, it will help to play the role of punishment and compensation, and thus preventing or reducing the negative effects brought by the financial crisis. In fact, the positive and negative aspects mentioned above exactly reflect the characteristics of economic law that can combine positive motivation and promotion with negative restriction and prohibition. Therefore, both aspects should be noted when solving the crisis.

From the legal perspective, people tend to pay more attention to the accountability of negative aspects. Therefore, attention should be paid to the attribution of responsibility. Among all possible forms of responsibility, some are economic responsibility and some are non-economic responsibility; some are the responsibility of the government, some are the responsibility of market subjects. All of these responsibilities need to be clarified.

For example, in the process of solving the financial crisis, it is very important to distinguish the economic responsibility of relevant subjects. Some financial institutions and other relevant market subjects may assume corresponding economic responsibilities; no matter they are punitive or compensatory, they will play a certain role in safeguarding the rights and interests of relevant subjects and ensuring the normal financial order.

In the process of resolving financial crises, some forms of responsibility are very important. Such as credit deduction and eligibility deduction in economic law. Many problematic financial institutions had higher credit ratings before the crisis, which had a negative impact on the crisis. Therefore, the issue of credit rating has been questioned a lot.[31] For those financial institutions that have problems, credit reduction must be performed, which is also a way to for them to undertake legal responsibility. At the same time, eligibility reduction is also important. The exemption of relevant

[31] The lack of self-regulation by financial institutions and rating agencies has distorted risk information and asset pricing. This is an important cause of financial crises. Therefore, some people have raised questions about credit ratings, and even about their legal liability. Ni Shoubin, et al., 2009, Probing into the legal liability of credit rating agencies in the context of financial crises, Social Science, Issue 8.

entities' financial qualifications is undoubtedly a heavy legal responsibility for some market subjects. Therefore, these forms of responsibility are of great concern.

In addition to a large number of punitive responsibilities, in the process of resolving the financial crisis, many compensatory responsibilities are bound to be involved. However, due to the crisis, the compensability of many market subjects will be relatively reduced. Therefore, in many cases, compensation cannot be made in the same amount, but only in small amount according to certain rules. In this case, there will also be issues such as the right of priority, and the consideration or sequencing of multiple interests, especially national interests, public benefit and private interests.

The responsibility involved in resolving the financial crisis includes not only the responsibility of private subjects, but also the responsibility of the state. In fact, the financial crisis is a prominent manifestation of market failure. The financial crisis cannot be resolved by the market mechanism. It requires government assistance, and the government needs to use various means to solve it. For this reason, the very basic issue of the relation between the government and the market needs to be solved. At the same time, this is also a question of governing the country according to the constitution. It is important to pay attention to the fact that the financial crisis will bring fiscal burdens. Financial crises are often covered by the fiscal expenditure. The prominent public hazards of the financial crisis have a large negative impact on the public interest, making the government unable to stand still, and do its utmost save the marke. The above-mentioned role of the government makes the financial crisis not only greatly increase fiscal risks, but also may trigger fiscal crises. The national bankruptcy of Iceland due to the financial crisis is an important manifestation of its government's fiscal crisis.[32] This is indeed a question worth pondering. The government's financial assistance to save the market needs the money from the taxes paid by taxpayers, and whether the majority of taxpayers should be paid for the misconduct or even illegal acts of individual market subjects. At the same time, it may also involve the state regulatory responsibility or the issues such as regulatory responsibility. All of these factors have made the accountability more complicated.

5.2.3.3 Financial Crisis and Comprehensive Adjustment of Economic Law

From the perspective of the economic law system theory, the coordination and comprehensive adjustment of the various sectoral laws of economic law will help to better perform the functions of the system. To fundamentally resolve the financial crisis, it is also necessary to emphasize the comprehensive adjustment of various sectoral laws of economic law to promote the coordinated development of economy and society. In fact, each sectoral law addresses many issues of macro-economic

[32] In the national bankruptcy crisis of Iceland, the IMF played an important rescuing role. But there are different views on the causes. Some people believe that the crisis was caused by the confrontation between the US dollar and the euro. If so, international financial competition and legal coordination are of great concern.

control and market regulation from different angles. The solution of these issues helps to prevent and resolve the financial crisis.

The problems brought about by the financial crisis are multifaceted, including sharp declines in external demand, overcapacity, difficult business operations, and sharp increase in unemployment. To resolve these problems, multiple measures need to be taken, and the implementation of these measures is inseparable from relevant laws, especially economic law. For example, in the process of resolving the financial crisis, industrial law is required to adjust the industrial structure according to law; to regulate the behavior of investment plans in accordance with law, the planning law is needed; to regulate all kinds of pricing behaviors in accordance with law, the price law is needed; to increase budget input and make budget adjustments in accordance with law, the fiscal law is required; to implement tax incentives in accordance with law, the tax law is required; to regulate monopolies in accordance with regulations, the anti-monopoly law is required; to effectively prevent unfair competition in accordance with law, anti-unfair competition law is required; to strengthen consumer protection in accordance with law and resolve consumer protection issues caused by the bankruptcy of financial institutions, the consumer protection law needs to be further improved. The above-mentioned adjustments to the industrial structure, the specifications for investment behavior, pricing behavior, budgeting behavior, taxation behavior and competition behavior are all realistic requirements for solving the financial crisis. To meet these realistic requirements, comprehensive adjustment of the various sectoral laws of economic law is required.

In fact, the financial crisis is a major issue that involves multiple aspects, and the adjustment of a sectoral law is inadequate. Even in the realm of economic law, a single sectoral law like financial law is far from enough, what is needed is comprehensive adjustment of various sectoral laws. In this way, we can standardize and protect the various measures adopted to resolve the financial crisis, and at the same time, we can better promote the coordinated development of economy and society, and thereby fundamentally resolve the financial crisis.

Of course, in many sectoral laws of economic law, the adjustment of financial law is still very important in terms of resolving the financial crisis. From the perspective of economic law, financial law includes financial regulation law and financial supervision law, including in specific central bank law, commercial banking law, bank supervision law, securities law, insurance law, trust law, guarantee law and other laws. The regulatory and regulatory laws involved have a direct and important role in resolving the financial crisis.[33] In addition, the international coordination in the financial field, the important role of relevant international organizations and international treaties should not be underestimated. These are the domino effects for better

[33]In fact, the role of relevant financial regulation and regulatory laws and regulations should not be ignored. For example, in response to the Great Depression of 1929–1933, and the chaos of the financial order, especially the investment order, the US Congress passed the Grass-Steagall Act, the Banking Act of 1933, in 1933, emphasizing Restrictions on the bank's business formed a pattern of strict division of banking, securities and insurance. However, on November 12, 1999, the United States passed the Financial Services Modernization Law and repealed the Glass-Steagall Law. Chen Xiaomin, et al., 2000, *The Bank of America Act*, Beijing, Law Press, pp. 54–56.

solving the expansion of the financial crisis, and for better fundamentally solving International financial issues are of great significance.

The above-mentioned requirements for the comprehensive adjustment of economic law at the domestic and international levels need legislative support, which is also the basic requirement of the aforementioned statutory principles and other related principles. In fact, the prevention and resolution of the financial crisis requires the effective allocation of rights and interests in economic law, strengthens regulation and supervision accordingly, and determines the division and termination of disputes in accordance with legal rights and obligations arrangements. In addition, as mentioned earlier, to fundamentally resolve the financial crisis, especially stable economic growth, including price stability and international balance of payments, etc., and to promote stable economic growth in accordance with the law, a substantial or Formal economic growth law, etc. Similarly, strengthening legislation in the areas of industrial law and investment law, and improving legislation in the areas of price law and competition law are important to prevent and resolve financial crises.

The above legislation needs to be strengthened to make it truly a legislative system. At the same time, only through comprehensive adjustments in economic law can we support each other, coordinate with each other, and jointly achieve the overall goal of legislation. This is important not only for the prevention and resolution of the financial crisis, but also for other related issues. Only in this way can we achieve true comprehensive adjustment, so that we can not only recognize the problems and contradictions reflected in the financial crisis, but also find appropriate countermeasures to these basic problems and contradictions, and better align the system and mechanisms in economic law. Good allocation of rights and interests, better separation of responsibilities, better promotion of direct coordination of various laws, and the healthy operation and coordinated development of the economy and society.

5.2.4 Conclusion

The problems brought about by the financial crisis are multifaceted and need to be studied from different angles. It is necessary to analyze the economic law theory. This section focuses on combing and analyzing the problems of the occurrence, expansion, and resolution of the financial crisis from the perspective of economic law theory. It is not difficult to find out: The occurrence of the financial crisis stems from "two failures". Through the occurrence of the financial crisis, we can see the importance of economic law adjustment and the important value of economic law; The expansion of the financial crisis can be analyzed through the dual binary structure of domestic and foreign economies, the real economy and the virtual economy, the internal economy and the external economy, and the importance of using dialectical governance in economic law is further emphasized; with regard to the resolution of the financial crisis, the basic principles of statutory principles, moderation principles, and performance principles in economic law should also be followed. Pay attention to the determination and sharing of responsibilities after the crisis, and emphasize the comprehensive adjustment of various sectoral laws that pass economic law. Fundamentally solve the problem of coordinated development of the economy and society, so as to fundamentally prevent and resolve the financial crisis.

In the process of discussing the above issues, we have always emphasized the perspective of economic law theory, from which we can see the explanatory power of economic law theory in explaining major practical issues, and at the same time, it also reflects the guiding power of theory. Due to space limitations, many important contents in the theory of economic law have not yet been unfolded. If we can make further in-depth discussions from the perspective of economic law theory, while taking into account law and other theories of other related disciplines, it is necessary to prevent the occurrence and expansion of the financial crisis and effectively solve many problems brought about by the financial crisis. It will be of great help to effectively resolve many aspects of the financial crisis.

5.3 Economic Crisis and Theoretical Exploration

As the haze of the economic crisis gradually dissipated, the economies of various countries began to enter a "post-crisis era" with gentle development and full of uncertainty. In view of the causes of the crisis and the various problems it brings, countries around the world who are suffering from it are pondering deeply. At the same time, in the post-crisis era, how to prevent and resolve new economic crises, how to promote economic recovery, how to launch effective competition between countries on the new starting line, how to strengthen the relevant economic and legal construction, more serious discussion. The above-mentioned various important issues are directly related to the adjustment of economic law, so it is necessary to conduct research from the perspective of economic law theory.[34]

In fact, in the post-crisis era, the field involved in the adjustment of economic law is very broad, and it is necessary to expand and deepen the theory of economic law in multiple dimensions. Among them, there are many theories that need to be expanded, such as risk theory (for related discussions, see the discussion of risk theory in this book), national competition theory, public economic crisis theory, situation change theory, etc. At the same time, it is necessary to dig deep into the existing ontology, occurrence theory and value theory of economic law. The above-mentioned expansion and digging are very helpful to the enrichment and development of economic law theory.

Based on the above considerations, this section first explores several types of theories that need to be expanded. Based on this, and combined with the characteristics of the post-crisis era, it proposes economic law theories that should be further

[34]There are relatively many studies on the economic law system related to the economic crisis, but the reflection on the economic law theory in the post-crisis era is inadequate. The latter is very important to enrich and develop the theory of economic law.

explored. It is believed that if the academic circles can carry out an in-depth discussion on these theories, it will not only be beneficial to the economic law theory and system construction in the post-crisis era, but also important to the long-term development of economic law and economic legal system.

5.3.1 Expansion of "National Competition Theory"

The "analytical framework of game behavior" in economic law theory emphasizes that theoretical research in economic law must pay attention to analyzing a large number of complex games that exist between various types of subjects.[35] For the game between countries, between countries and nationals, and between countries and nationals, the former economic law theory pays more attention to the latter two categories, and has formed a more developed theory of competition law, but for the game between countries, not enough attention.

In fact, in the era of economic globalization, games between nations are mostly realized through domestic law. Therefore, international games are not only the object of international law, but also important issues to be considered in the study of economic law theory. In view of the fact that many games between countries are inseparable from the institutional arrangement of domestic economic law, in the field of economic law, we should not only pay attention to the competition between enterprises and the corresponding competition law, but also pay attention to the competition between countries and introduce the theory of "state competition".[36]

In the post-crisis era, in order to solve the many problems brought about by the crisis and drive economic recovery as soon as possible, competition among countries is fierce. Originally, national competition was a more concerned issue in the field of international law, but because national competition in the post-crisis era relies heavily on the adjustment of domestic law, especially without the institutional support of economic law, it is in the context of economic globalization. Next, the study of economic law should pay attention to the issue of national competition and strengthen the economic regulation of national competition.

In order to get out of the crisis and revitalize the economy as soon as possible, all countries have taken various measures to actively promote economic recovery. The role of the state has become increasingly prominent, and competition between countries has also intensified. Among them, fiscal competition, tax competition, financial competition, and industrial competition are fierce. The main means used by countries in the competition process is precisely the legalized economic means.

For example, in terms of fiscal competition, in order to cope with the economic crisis, countries have expanded fiscal expenditure, issued a large number of national

---

[35]Zhang (2004), pp. 154–162; Zhang (2009), pp. 10–11.

[36]As for "national competition theory", no systematic research has been carried out in the realm of economic law. In fact, national competition is not only an important issue for international economic law scholars to study, but also an important research object of economic law.

debt, increased the quantity of government procurement, and increased the scale of transfer payments, in order to improve consumption capacity, stimulate domestic demand, stimulate economic growth, and solve the problem of insufficient demand in the international market. Accordingly, expansionary fiscal policy (or "active fiscal policy") and the related system formed by it have become the common means adopted by countries in financial competition in crisis and post-crisis era. Of course, with the gradual recovery of the economy, the negative impact of fiscal competition has also been shown, which requires comprehensive study and prudent regulation.

In terms of tax competition, countries often implement large-scale "tax cuts", at least the so-called "structural tax reduction", in order to activate and recover the economy. In fact, tax competition has always been an important means often adopted by national competition. Especially in terms of introducing foreign capital, a large number of tax incentives and the method of reducing tax rates are common practices of national competition, and sometimes they have some effect. However, once vicious tax competition is formed, it will have a negative impact on all aspects, especially national interests.[37] Therefore, tax competition needs to be coordinated to prevent countries from dumping public goods by reducing the price of public goods in order to achieve certain short-term goals. Fundamentally speaking, the dumping of public goods may damage the interests of taxpayers as well as the interests of the state, and seriously affect the competition order between countries.

In terms of financial competition, various types of financial competition, including exchange rate competition (multiple nations depreciating their currencies), and dominant currency competition (against the dollar-dominated currency position and competition for currency dominance), are very noticeable in the post-crisis era. At the same time, various countries have reflected on the deficiencies in financial regulation and financial supervision, strengthened the regulation of interest rates and deposit reserve ratios, and tried to make the money supply more appropriate. As financial competition and related financial regulation and financial supervision directly affect the development level and quality of the real economy, it is related to whether a country can escape from the mud of the crisis, so people often pay attention to financial competition, especially to the "currency war". Moreover, it shows the important impact of financial competition on economic development.

In terms of industrial competition, in order to speed up economic recovery, countries have stepped up industrial structure adjustments[38] in order to achieve overall economic competition goals. In fact, after the crisis, it is often an important period

---

[37]The issue of International Tax Competition has long attracted widespread attention from the international community. In order to avoid vicious tax competition, the EU and OECD adopted reports on vicious tax competition as early as 1997 and 1998, emphasizing the development of vicious tax competition. Judgment standards and elimination measures for tax competition in order to minimize its adverse effects.

[38]Industrial restructuring is just a very important aspect of economic restructuring. In fact, in the post-crisis era, China attaches great importance to the adjustment of the overall economic structure, especially the adjustment of industrial structure, investment structure, distribution structure, consumption structure, regional structure and many other structures to maintain the competitive advantage of the country.

for the formation and development of emerging industries. As long as a country adjusts its industrial structure in time, it may occupy an active position in the process of industrial development. Therefore, in terms of structural adjustment, especially in terms of industrial layout, competition among countries is always very fierce,[39] and in the corresponding legislative or institutional design, legal methods such as finance, finance, and planning are often used in coordination and use.

These kinds of competition will bring many problems. For example, fiscal competition with the main characteristics of expanding budget expenditures may generate a large number of deficits; and the increase in deficits will not only cause prominent problems in the public economy, but also lead to income contraction for related groups, leading to protests and strikes, declining government enforcement capabilities and a crisis of legitimacy[40] have further exacerbated economic, social and political crises.

In terms of national competition, there are many issues worth studying. For example, national competition is directly related to national capacity or national competitiveness. How does a country translate its will into reality, which competitions between countries are fair competitions, and which are unfair competitions? Can a country's lower exchange rate constitute a disguised subsidy, and how is it related to exports? Is it complementary to the adjustment of the economic structure? In addition, the order of national competition is important. How to form rules among countries, how to abide by relevant rules together, how to prevent conflicts and even wars, etc. are all important issues worthy of study.

One of the important goals of national competition is to promote or achieve stable growth of the national economy, which is consistent with the adjustment goals of a country's economic law. How to maintain stability involves many issues such as employment, population, environment, resources, energy, social security, and so on. The coordination of economic and social goals in economic law requires in-depth research from the perspective of economic law.

In short, in the theory of economic law, the "national competition theory" needs to be expanded. Considering that each country has many interests such as political and economic interests, it is also regarded as a rational "economic man" to a certain extent. Therefore, certain theories and principles of corporate competition can also be applied to the study of national competition theory. In the "National Competition Theory", we must not only study basic issues such as the type and means of competition, but also study the objectives, means, order, responsibilities, rights, and other issues of national competition from the perspective of economic law. Fairness issues (for

---

[39] According to Porter's famous theory of national competitive advantage, a country's values, culture, economic structure, and history have all become sources of competitive advantage. Therefore, the adjustment of the industrial structure, which plays an important role in the economic structure, after all, plays an important role in improving the country's overall competitiveness. Michael E. Porter, *The Competitive Advantage of Nations*, 2002, Beijing: Huaxia Publishing House.

[40] Similar problems have occurred in many European countries. In order to fulfill the international law obligations of controlling deficits stipulated in the *Stability and Growth Pact*, many countries have encountered many problems affecting economic stability and social harmony, especially Greece and other countries.

example, is it fair to ask that the RMB appreciation is unilateral), etc. In the course of studying these issues, we can use the economic law system as the basis, and besides various fields, we can also use economic law theory as a guide to explore the problems at each specific stage.

5.3.2 Expansion of the "Public Economic Crisis" Theory

The economy can be divided into private economy and public economy, so the economic crisis actually includes two aspects: one is the "private economic crisis" and the other is the "public economic crisis". In the past, people often paid more attention to the "private economic crisis", and the economic crisis usually started from the private economy. The same is true of the economic crisis triggered by the financial crisis in 2008. However, in the process of resolving the "private economic crisis", it may also trigger the "public economic crisis", which may affect the further resolution of the "private economic crisis" or cause the emergence of a new "private economic crisis".

For example, since the economic crisis in 2008, countries have adjusted their public economic policies and adopted public economic means to resolve the private economic crisis. Whether it is the expansion of budget expenditures, the issuance of national debt, the reduction or exemption of taxes, the expansion of transfer payments, or the increase in social security expenditures, all belong to the use of public economic means. But at the same time, the fiscal deficit has also increased significantly, which is the most direct cause of the "public economic crisis".

Increasing deficits, or the various debt crises that arise, are issues that all countries must face seriously.[41] In order to reduce the deficit and prevent the "public economic crisis", EU member states tried to strictly abide by the Stability and Growth Pact and tighten government spending, which also affected investment in the private economy, leading to weak economic growth in Greece, Spain and other countries. Dissatisfaction with various groups, such as marches, continued. Debt crises in many European countries have caused widespread concern in countries around the world.[42]

In fact, not only Europe, but also the United States has been plagued by a severe debt crisis, and many cities have been on the verge of bankruptcy. With the emergence and intensification of the "public economic crisis" in the post-crisis era, all countries are facing prominent issues such as whether to increase taxes, issue additional currencies, and whether they can effectively respond to inflation. These issues will

---

[41] After the economic crisis in China, the scale of deficits in 2009 and 2010 increased sharply compared with previous years, and even exceeded one trillion yuan. In recent years, the fiscal deficit has continued to increase. The fiscal deficit in 2016 was 2.18 trillion yuan, accounting for 3% of GDP, a record high, and the total government debt has increased further.

[42] Some scholars believe that the root cause of the debt crisis is too cheap funds and excessive debt. Therefore, it is necessary to pay attention to and watch out for the excessive debt of the government and the risks caused by it. Daniel Stelter, Hu Kun (trans.), 2015, *21st Century Debts*, Beijing: Beijing Times Chinese Document Bureau, pp. 55–56.

affect the security of the public economy. From the perspective of law, it is necessary to extract the corresponding "public economic crisis" theory from the perspective of economic law.

In the past, the economic law scholars paid more attention to the impact of the private economy on the public economy, and emphasized the fundamental status of the private economy or the dependence of the public economy on the private economy. In fact, the public economy will also have an important impact on the private economy. Today, the scale of the public economy is huge enough, and it has become an important force that cannot be ignored to affect the private economy.

Based on the important impact of the public economy on the private economy, legal regulation in the field of public economy is very necessary. Among them, it is particularly important to strengthen legal control over government budget expenditures, especially to strengthen legal regulations[43] on state investment, government procurement expenditures, and local government borrowing rights. In addition, no matter in terms of substantive law or procedural law, the legal provisions must be clear and enforceable, so as to better ensure the effective allocation of rights and powers and achieve comprehensive protection of the legal benefits of various subjects.

5.3.3 Expansion of "Situation Change Theory"

The occurrence of the economic crisis will have an important impact on the economic activities of private subjects and on the economic arrangements of the country or government. Generally, for the economic expectations or economic arrangements of various entities, the occurrence of an economic crisis is difficult to predict, so it is a relatively major change in the situation.

Based on the impact of the change of situation on the economic activities of private subjects, the principle or system of change of situation has been established in the field of private law such as contract law; similarly, since the change of situation will have an important impact on the economic arrangements of the state or government, it also needs to be made in the field of public law rule arrangements. In view of the close relationship between the government's economic arrangements and the adjustment of economic law, it is necessary to conduct extensive research on the principle or system of change of situation in the field of economic law.

For example, in the field of economic law, the occurrence of an economic crisis as an important situation change may bring many legal issues, including budget adjustments, changes in budget priorities, changes in the taxation system, the issuance of special government bonds, and so on. In order to cope with the economic crisis, countries mainly use economic means to rescue the market, and extensively expand budget

[43] As early as 1919, Alfred Manners emphasized that debt should be studied from an economic and legal perspective, and in his book *State Bankruptcy: Economic and Legal Reflections*, in the long run, the history of national debts can be called the history of a country's bankruptcy. Baker & Perez, Yuan Long (trans.), 2013, Why the State Goes Bankrupt, Beijing: China Electric Power Press, p. 1.

expenditure, tax cuts and other means, so that the deficit surge, and produced many destabilizing factors affecting the sustained economic growth, therefore, around the situation changes caused by many legal issues, very worthy of study.

The occurrence of the economic crisis, as a change of situation, has the most direct effect of making the original form of a budget with a balanced budget become unbalanced. According to relevant legal principles, the situation change should take place after the budget approval has taken effect and before the implementation is completed. If it has occurred during the budget review, it should be taken into account during the review process, and should not be adjusted afterwards; meanwhile, the situation change should be significant Changes that involve central-level budget adjustments usually involve a relatively large economic crisis across the country.

The change of situation makes the various budget entities to implement the original budget or it is unfair or difficult to implement. On the one hand, the economic crisis has prevented the obligations of the budget collection subject from being effectively fulfilled; on the other hand, due to disasters or crises, the difficulties of the relevant payment subject have greatly increased, and the basis for completing its tax or payment tasks has changed. When the economic downturn affects the tax base, which directly affects the completion of the budget collection task, it is undoubtedly necessary to adjust the size and structure of the budget and reorganize the budget. This reflects the spirit of "substance over form", that is, the essence of economic life is higher than the form of the original budget balance.[44]

In short, as long as economic activities are involved, the problem of changing circumstances may exist. Economic activity, as an important public economic activity, will also be affected by changing circumstances. Whether it is the performance of a private contract or the completion of a national budget plan, consideration should be given to changing circumstances. Therefore, it is necessary to carry out the extended research on "theory of situational change" beyond private law, pay more attention to the broad application of general legal principles of situational change, and the impact of situational change on regulatory behavior.

In the field of economic law, to expand the research on "theory of change of situation", we need to analyze the jurisprudence of change of situation and explore whether the principle of change of situation can be universally applied to the relevant fields of economic law and the particularity of application. The development of theories, and the improvement of specific legislation in economic law.

---

[44] Allen Schick believes that budget change is a mix of politics, policy, and procedures (processes), which makes sense. Related to this, changes in the situation of budget adjustment are political, economic and legal. Alan Hick, Gou Yannan (trans.) 2011, *Federal Budget: Politics, Policy, Process* (3rd Edition), Beijing: China Finance and Economic Press, p. 1.

5.3.4 Exploration Into Existing Economic Law Theories

The cycle of the economic cycle has become the normal state of economic operation. The study of common problems in the post-crisis era by the economic law scholars is also of universal significance. It is undoubtedly helpful to promote the improvement and development of economic law theories in combination with the problems of the post-crisis era.

The existing theories of economic law include ontology, generative theory, value theory, normative theory, and operational theory. The foregoing types of theories that need to be expanded are closely related to normative theory and operational theory of economic law. The theory of operation is further deepened. Therefore, only the ontology, occurrence theory and value theory in economic law theory are taken as examples to briefly explore the in-depth digging of the existing economic law theory.

(1) From the perspective of the ontology of economic law, the occurrence and spread of this crisis makes people more clearly recognize the limitations of market regulation and the necessity of government regulation. At the same time, in the process of solving the crisis, people also see the limited role of the government. It is based on the recognition of market failure and government failure, as well as the important role of law in solving the "two failures", that people realize the importance of economic law as an independent legal department.

From the perspective of the economic crisis, market failures will cause economic risks, lead to economic imbalances, and may cause economic crises. Therefore, in order to solve economic imbalances and prevent economic crises, macroeconomic regulation and market regulation must be carried out. Judging from the regulation and regulation of countries in crisis response and post-crisis era, modulation according to law is very important. As macroeconomic control and market regulation deviate from the legal trajectory and the spirit of the rule of law, more legal issues will inevitably arise. Therefore, regulating regulation and regulation is an important task and mission of economic law. In this sense, economic law is not only a law that regulates the relevant competition behavior of market subjects, but also a law that regulates various types of modulation behaviors implemented by the state.

Judging from the characteristics of economic law, the adjustment methods of economic law have outstanding economic and regulatory characteristics, and the adjustment methods with such characteristics are exactly helpful to the resolution of the economic crisis. Moreover, no matter in the post-crisis era or other stages of economic development, it is necessary to effectively promote economic development, and it is necessary to add a large number of norms with encouragement and promotion functions in economic law, and form a large number of "promoting economic laws".[45]

In connection with the above characteristics of economic law, in practice, many people often easily understand macro regulation and control as austerity and repression, especially in the real estate market and the capital market. The intensity of austerity is actually incomplete. In fact, not to mention whether the regulation of an industry and field belongs to the "macro regulation" in the original sense. Only

[45]Zhang (2009), Issue 6.

in terms of the two dimensions of regulation itself, the regulation of each market must reflect the regulatory nature. Should be treated differently, which is especially important in the post-crisis era. At the same time, this is a more comprehensive understanding of the adjustment of economic law.

(2) Judging from the genesis theory of economic law, the true comprehensive and complete establishment of economic law as an independent sector law came after the economic crisis of the 1930s, which led to the emergence of a macro-economic control law of modern significance. In the time of responding to major crises, the macro-control law exists as a crisis response law. However, because the economic cycle is unavoidable, and even frequently occurs, it is only the magnitude of the fluctuations. Therefore, the macro-economic control law is no longer just a crisis response method in a very period of time, but has become an important guarantee law for stable economic operation under normal conditions.

At the same time, the important prerequisites and foundations for the emergence and development of economic law. It has also been identified as a modern market economy by many scholars. In fact, if the economic risks in a market economy do not cause economic imbalances, and the spontaneous role of the market mechanism can solve major problems of economic operation on its own, then economic law is not necessary and there is no possibility of development; it is precisely the complicated economic life under the conditions of modern market economy and the periodic economic crisis (including the solution of many problems in the post-crisis era) that requires a higher level of macro-control and market regulation, and an economic law different from the traditional departmental law.

In addition, economic and social risks are often closely linked. Economic law aims to solve many problems brought about by economic risks and economic crisis. While the economic law comes into being and develops comprehensively, the social law aiming at solving various problems brought about by social risks and social crisis has also been comprehensively developed. The study of the occurrence of economic crisis and many problems in the post-crisis era is helpful to better understand why the foundation of economic law and social law have internal consistency, and why the emergence and development of the two are closely related.

(3) From the perspective of the value theory of economic law, the current economic crisis has further highlighted the importance of the purpose of economic law. The purpose of economic law, as a concentrated expression of the value of economic law, emphasizes the goal of promoting stable economic growth, which is inherently consistent with the function of economic law in preventing and resolving economic crises. Based on the inherent unification of economic law adjustment goals and the function of the system, in the post-crisis era, more attention should be paid to the design and effective implementation of the economic law system, to play its role in preventing and defusing economic risks, and strive to resolve various types of economic imbalances that may arise Try to prevent the frequent occurrence of severe economic crises.

In addition, whether it is a crisis response or a solution to many problems in the post-crisis era, we must strictly implement the three principles that specifically embody the value of economic law, namely the legal principle, the moderation principle, and the performance principle. Judging from the statutory principles, in the process of crisis response in our country, cases of violations of the statutory principles have occurred.[46] In the post-crisis era, important regulations and regulations involving many fields should be strictly implemented. From the principle of moderation, both macro-control and market regulation must be moderate, especially the relationship between the government and the market, respect for economic laws, and emphasis on legality; if the principle of moderation is violated, it may cause a new economic crisis or affect the future Solutions to many problems in times of crisis. From the perspective of performance principles, the economic crisis has caused the economic operation to be very "non-economic." It may destroy the accumulated economic growth results for many years, and the important goals and functions of economic law adjustment are precisely to solve the various problems that occur during the economic operation. This kind of "non-economic" problem will increase the overall efficiency and effectiveness. Therefore, whether it is a crisis response or a solution to many problems in the post-crisis era, we must adhere to the principle of performance, use many adjustment methods of economic law, adjust the economic structure according to law, promote scientific planning and development, and achieve overall economic efficiency and benefits.

In the post-crisis era, in order to enhance the effectiveness of regulation and regulation, and to solve concrete problems in reality, sometimes the statutory principles cannot be understood rigidly. It is necessary to make a comprehensive and dynamic understanding of them in order to comprehensively reflect the requirements of the three principles. In addition, the determination and maintenance of statutory procedures related to regulation and control, and the grasp of the "degree" in the principle of moderation, all need to be further explored in the study of the value theory of economic law.

5.3.5 Conclusion

In the post-crisis era, every country attaches great importance to strengthening the adjustment of economic law, and adopts a variety of adjustment methods of economic law. At the same time, the development of practice also requires extensive research and deep exploration of economic law theory. This expansion and digging is of

[46] If the 4 trillion yuan investment involves budget adjustment, it should be approved by the Standing Committee of the National People's Congress in accordance with the "Budget Law", but this huge investment has never passed the statutory approval process, and people from all walks of life have criticized it. In addition, some scholars believe that the 4 trillion investment plan is an expedient move to the rapid recovery of the world economy, which will help stabilize the economy and society in the short term, but sacrifices the optimization of China's economic growth mode, which may lead to marketization. The retrogression of reform ideas. Wang Xi, Lu Rong, 2009, The short-term role and long-term impact of the four trillion investment plan under the crisis, *Journal of Sun Yatsen University (Social Science Edition)*, Issue 4.

great value to the enrichment and development of economic law theory, and to the improvement of the economic law system.

From the perspective of expanded research, this section briefly discusses several important theories that should be paid attention to in economic law research, including the theory of national competition, the theory of public economic crisis, and the theory of change of situation. Because the theory of risk is very important, this book has been listed separately. Section), the extended research on these theories is very helpful to deepen the theory of economic law (especially the normative theory and operational theory of economic law. In addition, in combination with the existing economic law theory, this section briefly discusses some issues that need to be explored in terms of the ontology, genesis, and value theory of economic law. Whether it is the above-mentioned extended research or in-depth digging, it will play an important role in enriching and improving the theory of economic law, and it will also make the theory of economic law more comprehensive and more instructive.

From the perspective of the development of the global economy, economic risks, economic imbalances, and economic cycles have become common phenomena and common problems in the process of economic operation. Related theoretical research on crisis or post-crisis must also become an important part of theoretical research on economic law. In part, and based on the purpose and principles of economic law itself, the theoretical expansion and deepening of the post-crisis era will continue to rise in the entire economic law theoretical system. To this end, the academic community should further explore the theory of economic law and strive to discover the principles and laws in order to better promote the deepening of economic law theory, especially the crisis response theory, and promote the development of economic law system construction and the rule of economic law. Level up.[47]

5.4 Crisis Response and Effective Development of Economic Law

5.4.1 Presenting Problems

Development is the most important theme in contemporary countries. The development of a country must follow the laws, focus on the coordination and sustainability of development as a whole, and constantly prevent and resolve various crises in order to achieve the healthy operation and effective development of the economy and society. At the same time, the development of a country requires the supply of a large number of public goods, and therefore cannot be separated from the country's macroeconomic control and market regulation. The level of legalization of regulation and regulation is directly related to the comprehensive and coordinated development of the economy and society, affecting the realization of people's well-being and human

[47]Zhang (2006), Issue 2.

rights. Therefore, we should not only focus on the coordination and effectiveness of a country's development, but also its relevance to the economic rule of law and people's well-being.

From the perspective of the coordination and effectiveness of development, how to prevent and resolve economic crises and social crises is undoubtedly an important issue of continuity. The international financial crisis or economic crisis since 2008, as a concentrated outbreak of many problems accumulated in the course of economic operation, not only seriously affects the effective development of the economy, but may also trigger crises in many fields such as politics, society, and law. In the face of crisis, only when we are in dire straits, move by the camera, and dialectical treatment, can we turn the danger and turn the crisis into security.

To cope with the economic crisis, various countries have adopted a variety of economic policies. For example, the large-scale use of fiscal policy tools, such as large-scale budget expenditures, tax reductions, additional issuance of national debt, and government procurement, played an important role in the response to the crisis. The implementation of the above-mentioned various economic means cannot be separated from the effective guarantee of economic law. As a result, there is an inherent connection between crisis response, economic rule of law, and the well-being of the people.

In fact, based on statutory principles, in many areas such as budgeting, taxation, and national debt, it is necessary to act strictly according to law, even in times of crisis. Because of this, in the process of countries' response to crises, the adjustment of economic law has received much attention, and economic legislation has been further improved and improved. However, at the same time, due to many factors such as the emergency response to the crisis, various problems that depart from the spirit of the rule of law may also occur, which may cause hidden concerns in the construction of the economic and legal system. If not adjusted in time, a crisis in the development of economic law may be formed, affecting effective development of economic law.

In view of this, this section will focus on the analysis of various economic methods used in China's response to the crisis, explore the legal issues existing therein, and raise the issue of the effective development of economic law, emphasizing that in crisis response, we must not only focus on the effectiveness of the economy. For development, we should also pay attention to the rationality and legitimacy of various institutional arrangements to resolve the crisis, especially economic policies and related legislation that are important means of responding to the crisis, and should be in line with the spirit of the rule of law, so that the purpose of economic law can be better achieved. In addition, this section also emphasizes that the response to the crisis and the effective development of economic law will help deepen the study of economic law; at the same time, the further study of economic law will help promote the effective development of economic law and also help the crisis prevention and resolution. For this reason, this section also puts forward some economic law theories that should be paid more attention to in order to deepen the study of economic law.

5.4.2 *Analysis of the Main Economic Measures to Deal with the Crisis*

In the process of responding to the financial crisis, fiscal crisis, and the overall economic crisis, various countries have widely used economic means, especially economic means such as budget expenditure and tax relief. Judging from China's situation, the main economic instruments used in response to the crisis include budgetary instruments, tax instruments, national debt instruments, government procurement instruments, and transfer payment instruments. For these means, we can make further concrete analysis.

(1) Budget means. After the crisis, China restarted its proactive fiscal policy, expanded budgetary expenditures, and solved the problem of insufficient effective demand through government public funding. The country's plan to invest 4 trillion yuan in two years has attracted widespread attention at home and abroad. It is a direct and important means to respond to the crisis, just like the US$700 billion economic stimulus plan proposed by the United States.

(2) Taxation means. The taxation measures implemented by our country in response to the crisis are very rich. The options are as follows: (i) In terms of tax rate adjustment, in order to promote the development of the capital market, the state reduced the stamp duty rate on securities transactions to 0.1%[48]; in order to increase tax revenue and achieve the goal of guiding consumption, the consumption tax rate for liquor and cigarettes was increased, and so on. In addition, the state has adjusted a series of "quasi-tax rates". For example, in the field of VAT, the levy rate for small-scale taxpayers has been reduced to 3%. At the same time, the export tax rebate rate has been increased to encourage exports.[49] (ii) In terms of tax base adjustments, such as the implementation of consumer-type VAT, adjustments to the deduction items or scope of corporate income taxes, and at the same time, "fax to tax" for refined oil products, etc. (iii) In terms of tax incentives, a large number of tax reductions and exemptions have been implemented, such as exemption of interest on savings deposits in personal income tax.[50]

---

[48]On Sep 18, 2008, the MOF and the SAT announced that starting from the following day, they would adjust the method of collecting stamp duty on securities (stock) transactions, and will change the current A-share and B-share equity issued to the purchase, sale, inheritance and gift The transfer document levies a stamp duty on securities (stock) transactions to both parties at a tax rate of one-thousandth, which is adjusted to a unilateral tax, and the transferee is no longer taxed.

[49]On Oct 21, 2008, the MOF and the SAT jointly issued the *Notice on Increasing the Export Tax Rebate Rate of Certain Commodities* to appropriately increase the export tax rebate rate for 3,486 items of textiles, clothing, toys, etc. 25.8% of the total number of products.

[50]On Dec 5, 2008, the NDRC, the MOF, the MOT and the SAT jointly issued the *Refined Oil Price Tax Reform Plan (draft)*. The plan clearly states that the six tolls, including the original road maintenance fee, were levied instead of a refined oil consumption tax. The reform of refined oil prices, taxes and fees has been implemented since January 1, 2009.

(3) National debt means. The national debt method has already become an important measure to deal with economic fluctuations.[51] In 2007, China decided to issue 1.55 trillion special government bonds in installments. In addition, a considerable part of the 4 trillion yuan investment plan implemented in China came from the issuance of government bonds. In the process of responding to the economic crisis, whether it is to make up for the deficit or to stimulate domestic demand,[52] the means of national debt has an important role.

(4) Means of purchase. The government's public procurement directly affects the interests of the majority of market players, as well as the overall prosperity and recovery of the market. The use of procurement methods is not only related to the interests of micro-subjects, but also to national interests and the development of the national economy. It can play a macro-economic control role to a certain extent. Whether it is possible to purchase domestic products with priority,[53] and the scale, proportion, and quantity of purchases, etc., are not only important issues in domestic law, but even international economic and legal coordination.[54]

(5) Means of transition. Although government procurement and transfer payments are both important forms of budgetary expenditure, their nature and areas are different after all. In terms of crisis response, there must be not only government procurement that directly affects the production and operation of market entities, but also transfer payments that ultimately have an important impact on the survival and consumption of the general population. Therefore, the state's transfer payments in social security and related subsidies are an important measure to deal with the crisis and boost consumption. Our government has invested a lot in social security. In terms of medical security alone, the state has proposed plans to invest 850 billion yuan. In addition, the improvement of the overall level of endowment insurance and the further expansion of protection coverage require a large amount of national input.

The above-mentioned types of instruments are very important economic instruments, and they are directly or indirectly related to many other economic policy tools. For example, in response to the crisis, China has proposed adjustment and revitalization plans for the top ten industries. The introduction of these plans may seem like industrial policies or planning tools, but they cannot be separated from the

---

[51]Especially in 1998, due to the financial crisis and floods, the deficit increased greatly, China began to issue a large number of national debts in response to economic fluctuations and stimulate domestic demand.

[52]Due to many factors such as the economic crisis, China's deficit in fiscal year 2009 reached an unprecedented 950 billion yuan, of which the central fiscal deficit was 750 billion yuan. Such a huge scale of deficits constitutes huge pressure on the issue of national debts. At the same time, issues such as the reasonable size of national debts and the issuance of local debts have attracted widespread attention from all walks of life.

[53]In response to the crisis, the United States has proposed giving priority to the purchase of domestic goods, which has aroused widespread concern in the international community.

[54]Government procurement involves many industries and fields, so the government procurement law is closely related to many industry laws, and involves coordination with many laws such as the Railway Law, Highway Law, Construction Law, and National Defense Law. At the same time, in the context of economic globalization, international coordination of government procurement among WTO members is also very important.

support of economic measures. Even monetary policy needs to be coordinated with fiscal instruments. It can be seen that the coordination and cooperation of various economic instruments is indeed very important to respond to the crisis.

From the various methods listed briefly above, China's economic measures adopted in response to the crisis are rich and colorful, including not only economic measures such as budget and taxation, but also related measures such as finance, industry and planning. Therefore, it is necessary to comprehensively and objectively analyze and evaluate the specific use of various economic instruments and their important role in resolving the crisis.

Under the principle of statutory principles, the adoption of the above-mentioned various economic instruments cannot be separated from the legal confirmation and guarantee; the application process of the above-mentioned various instruments is also the process of the implementation of economic law. Therefore, studying the implementation of the above-mentioned various measures will help to find out the problems existing in the construction of the economic and legal system through the response to the crisis, and thus help to explore the path to its future improvement.

5.4.3 Problems Existing in China's Economic Rule-of-Law Construction from the Perspective of Crisis Response

Examining the various economic measures adopted in response to the crisis, we can find outstanding problems in China's economic and legal construction. Although people have paid attention to this, the academic and practical circles still need to further sort out and deepen it. Among the many problems in China's economic and legal system construction, the following issues deserve special attention.

5.4.3.1 Issues of Legislative Institution

The economic legislative system is an old issue that people have been discussing for many years, but it is also an important topic that has been for a long time. Its core is the allocation of economic legislative power. According to strict statutory principles, and in accordance with the requirements of "legal preservation" and "parliamentary reservations", economic legislative power should be mainly exercised by the legislature. The government can only exercise some legislative power through the authorization of the law or the legislature, and should not become an economy. The most important holder of legislative power. Even when considering the actual regulatory needs and the response to crises, and thus promoting the "dynamic" statutory principle, it is necessary to pay attention to the limitation of the government's economic legislative power and make the "dynamic" easier to be in a subsidiary position. Statutory principles can not only maintain their reasonable core, but also keep pace with the times; it can not only solve the urgent problems in economic life, but also meet the basic requirements of the rule of law.

Judging from the various measures adopted in crisis response, the strong position of the government in economic legislative power is very prominent, which is related to the excessive government legislative power in history and the urgent need to deal with the crisis in reality. Regardless of the arrangement of tax reduction or exemption, or adjustment of the tax base and tax rate, etc., changes in various tax elements should have been implemented with "legal preservation". Departments operate directly. In the long run, the effective development of economic law will be affected.

Therefore, although the economic measures adopted in response to the crisis have certain economic rationality, some measures do not conform to the spirit of the rule of law and legal requirements and cannot be long-term and fixed. Only by fundamentally solving the problems of the legislative system, clearly defining and configuring the legislative power of relevant subjects, and ensuring that they are exercised in accordance with the law, can the economic law itself develop better.

5.4.3.2 Exercise of Power

The various economic measures adopted in the response to the crisis involve the exercise of multiple powers, among which the more important are the right to budget expenditures, the right to adjust budgets, the right to adjust tax base rates, the right to determine tax preferences, the right to issue national debt, and procurement. Control rights, transfer payment rights, financial control rights, etc. The allocation of the above powers has been stipulated in the legislation, but in the specific exercise, there may be excessive power, abuse of power and other problems, leading to the exercise of some subjects of power is not sufficient, incomplete, not timely, and thus has many negative effects.

For example, in the above-mentioned 4 trillion investment plan, the central government has to increase expenditure by 1.18 trillion, which has caused the budget to be more balanced in its original balance of payments, which has led to a large increase in the central budget deficit, which has involved huge budget adjustments. Since the 4 trillion yuan investment plan is so huge and involves a total budget adjustment of 1.18 trillion yuan over two years, both the major investment plan and the budget adjustment should be examined and approved by the Standing Committee of the NPC according to its power to review and approve the budget adjustment. However, the actual situation is the introduction of the investment plan and the adjustment of the budget. The decision was made only by the executive meeting of the State Council and was not approved by the Standing Committee of the NPC. The issue of power exercise is obvious. This is also an important reason why the 4 trillion investment plan was widely criticized shortly after its launch. In fact, if the Standing Committee of the NPC can fully and timely exercise the power to approve and approve budget adjustments, such an important crisis response measure can be formally legitimacy and be better complied with.

The 4 trillion investment plan is also closely related to the exercise of the right to issue national debt. In the case of a large increase in deficit due to the expansion of budget expenditures, national debt will inevitably become the most important means to make up for the deficit. As mentioned earlier, as China decided to issue 1.55 trillion special government bonds in 2007. Due to the large scale of the issue and spanning several years, the Standing Committee of the NPC had specially approved it,[55] so that it was at least formally in line with the authority to approve government bonds Exercise requirements. Usually, according to the statutory principle of national debt, in order to better reflect the supervision, all national debt issuance, no matter whether used to deal with the crisis, should be exercised by the national legislature national debt issuance approval power, government departments can not exceed their powers to approve, otherwise it is against the basic spirit of the rule of law.

The 4 trillion investment plan is also closely related to procurement control rights. The state's huge investment plan is designed to stimulate domestic demand, adjust the structure, and restore the economy. An important form of investment plan implementation is government procurement. Because government procurement is tilted in which areas, and whether domestic goods have the right of first refusal, etc., it will affect the product sales and economic recovery of different industries, different regions, and different countries. Therefore, the procurement control right is also very important.

The 4 trillion investment plan is only a means for China to deal with the crisis. The many economic law issues involved, especially the exercise of power, deserve deep reflection. For example, with regard to the above-mentioned budget adjustment and approval powers, China's Constitution and Budget Law provide very clear provisions, but there are problems such as the failure of power subjects or incomplete power. For another example, the right to approve the issuance of government bonds should also be exercised by the legislature, and it has been exercised by it in history, but it seems that it has not exercised its power when responding to the crisis. As for the procurement control right mentioned above, it has not yet been completely treated as a relatively independent power in general, and therefore lacks a macro or overall exercise mechanism. These deficiencies will eventually have a negative impact on the overall crisis response and the effective economic development.

In addition, China has adopted many tax measures to deal with the crisis, including the so-called structural tax reduction, the transformation of value-added tax, the adjustment of consumption tax, the industrial adjustment and revitalization plan, etc., which involve the decision-making power of tax preferences, the right to determine the tax base, the right to adjust tax items and tax rates and other important powers in economic law. As for the exercise of the above powers, there are basic provisions in the law, but there are still some problems in the specific exercise. At present, as mentioned above, these powers are mainly exercised by the state council and

[55]According to the Resolution of the Standing Committee of the NPC on Approving the Issuance of Special Treasury Bonds by the Ministry of Finance to Purchase Foreign Exchange and Adjusting the Limit of the Balance of Treasury Bonds at the End of 2007, the Ministry of Finance issued 1.55 trillion yuan of special treasury bonds. A special government bond is mainly used to cope with the problems of excess liquidity in the financial sector.

its functional departments. Although it is convenient to deal with problems in the economic field in a timely manner, it falls far short of the requirements of the rule of law. In addition, due to the economic crisis tax reduction factors increase, and the need to increase tax revenue, so the problem of legal collection and management will become increasingly prominent, the exercise of tax collection and management power must make due restrictions.

The above-mentioned various types of economic law powers are statutory powers, and all kinds of authorized subjects must actively exercise them, and they must neither give up nor exceed or abuse them. Only by carrying out their duties and following their own tracks, with both supervision and coordination and exercising power in accordance with the law, can the basic goals of economic law be achieved.

5.4.3.3 Issues of Transparency

Transparency directly affects the right of information of relevant subjects. The transparency of the rule of law in economic law is directly related to the rights of citizens and taxpayers. The transparency of economic law legislation and law enforcement has always attracted much attention because it is directly related to the basic rights of relevant subjects. Regardless of the normal state or the time of the crisis, basic transparency in the economic sphere must be maintained.[56]

From the actual situation, the transparency of China's economic law legislation urgently needs to be further improved. The legislation of economic law involves the basic property rights of citizens, and it directly affects national interests, social public welfare and private interests, so it must not be careless. In a certain sense, the legislation of economic law should reflect the coordination and balance of interests between the state and the nationals. If economic law legislation is regarded as an "agreement" between the state and the nationals in a broad sense, the "agreement" has far-reaching impact, so it must be transparent. In particular, the public should know why a certain legislation is introduced and what its background is. At the same time, the basic content of the legislation must be widely solicited, and the interests of all parties must be fully coordinated. Only in this way can economic law legislation better reflect the will of the people and the will of the country, and it will be more enforceable and operable.

In the course of responding to the crisis, China has also paid attention to the legislative transparency of economic law. For example, in the process of "fee-to-tax" reform of refined oil, opinions from all walks of life have been widely sought, at least in the form of transparency, but the time for soliciting opinions was so short that some people considered it too "formal". But similar "formalist" legislative participation

[56]OECD countries and IMF and other international organizations pay great attention to fiscal transparency and pay attention to regulating it in various legislative forms. IMF, 2001, Fiscal Transparency, Beijing: People's Publishing House.

is not common. For example, the amendments to the three very important temporary regulations on VAT, consumption tax, and business tax have not been widely consulted. "Mysticism" in other areas of tax legislation is also common.

The afore-mentioned problems of weaker economic law legislation transparency will greatly affect the basis and effectiveness of law enforcement. For example, the opaqueness in the implementation of the amount, direction, and performance of transfer payments, and the problem of levying "overtaxes" in the field of tax collection and management due to the crisis have attracted people's attention. As for the "old problems" such as insufficient transparency of budget expenditures at all levels, they have not yet been completely resolved.[57] If the enforcement of economic law can be strengthened and supervision in various areas can be strengthened, many problems in law enforcement will be better solved.

The *Regulations on the Disclosure of Government Information* currently in effect in China has promoted the transparency of legislation and law enforcement. According to the "Regulations", a lot of information about the construction of the economic legal system should be made public according to law, which will undoubtedly help to further improve the construction of the economic legal system.

5.4.3.4 Procedural Issues

Regardless of legislative decentralization or exercise of power, neither the improvement of the transparency of the rule of law nor the expansion of public participation are inseparable from procedural guarantees. The importance and modernity of economic law require that the norms of substantive law and the norms of procedural law be "melted into one furnace". Therefore, a large number of procedural law norms are involved in economic law legislation. Nevertheless, the issue of procedural safeguards is still quite prominent.

For example, in an emergency such as a financial crisis, there should be emergency procedures for the government to conduct macro-control. For example, in terms of economic regulation, it should be clear under what circumstances, which subject initiates the emergency procedures, which subject proposes the emergency budget expenditure plan, which subject examines and approves, which subject executes, and which subject supervises. How specific emergency committees are formed, how they are discussed, how decisions are made, and so on, all need procedures to ensure that. The introduction of the aforementioned 4 trillion investment plan also involves procedural safeguards.[58] If the 4 trillion investment process is unclear, or there are procedures that are not followed, it will lead to an intensification of the "money advancement", which will seriously affect the use of funds.

---

[57] Starting from the central government's first disclosure of departmental budgets to the community in 2010, by 2016, the number of departments with open departmental budgets has increased from 75 to 102, and the scope of disclosure has expanded from general budgets to government fund budgets and state capital operating budgets. In addition, It also separately disclosed the "three public" budget.

[58] China has been preparing the *Regulations on Government Investment*, and investment decision-making procedures are very important.

In addition, the exercise of the macro-control power of various subjects also requires procedural guarantees. Whether it is the regulation of the issuance of currency and national debt, or the adjustment of the tax base and tax rate; whether it is the determination of tax incentives or the implementation of transfer payments, etc., it is necessary to ensure procedures. However, from the perspective of actual practice, the implementation of the above-mentioned macro-control actions still lacks open and detailed procedural arrangements, so it is impossible to achieve comprehensive control according to law, which is still a certain distance from the requirements of economic rule of law.

The above-mentioned procedural guarantees directly affect the legislation and enforcement of economic law, the exercise of various types of macro-economic control power and market regulation power, and then the transparency of the rule of law in economic law. If all aspects of the legal construction of economic law can be carried out in accordance with open and detailed procedures, it will not only help improve the transparency of the rule of law, but also better protect the public's important constitutional rights such as the right to information, participation and supervision right.

It can be seen that procedural guarantees are important for better economic law legislation and enforcement, for various entities to effectively exercise various types of macro-economic control rights and market regulation rights, to improve the transparency of the rule of law, and to protect the various rights of the public. Only by effectively improving the level of procedural guarantees can we effectively promote the effective development of economic law itself.

5.4.3.5 Legal Consciousness and Legal Concept

With the improvement of the country's legal system, the public awareness of law and the concept of the rule of law continue to improve and strengthen, which is undoubtedly an important progress. But at the same time, we must also examine the existing deficiencies in legal consciousness and the concept of the rule of law in the light of the problems existing in the response to the crisis.

For example, the exercise of various types of macro-economic control power and market regulation power not only requires the public to have a strong legal awareness, but also requires the leaders and staff of the state organs that exercise the power to control power to have a strong legal awareness. Correct legal awareness is very important to form the concept of the rule of law. Whether we can truly act in accordance with the law and whether we can bring all regulatory actions into the orbit of the rule of law is undoubtedly very important for achieving the regulatory goals. The overall effect of the adjustment of economic law will be better if it is possible to unify sectoral and regional interests with the overall interests of the country as a whole, and if we can pay attention to protecting the rights and interests of various entities in a balanced manner when exercising various macro-economic control rights and market regulatory rights.

In short, many of the above-mentioned problems in the construction of the economic and legal system also existed when there was no crisis, but some problems were more prominent in the crisis response process. As long as the causes of the above problems are continuously improved, the economic legislative system is continuously improved, the allocation and exercise of various macro-control powers and market regulatory powers are properly solved, the transparency of the rule of law in the economy is continuously enhanced, and the protection of procedures is strengthened, legal awareness and the concept of rule of law are enhanced It will greatly help solve the problems in the development of economic law and avoid legal crises. By strengthening the legal construction of economic law, it can promote the effective development of economic law.[59]

5.4.4 Promote the Effective Development of Economic Law

The "effective development" of economic law is an important proposition worthy of attention.[60] Economic law, as an important legal department in a country's legal system, how to develop and how to effectively develop it is of great significance to the overall legal system construction and academic research in related fields. For this reason, the specific issues affecting the effective development of economic law have been discussed in combination with the economic measures adopted in response to the crisis. Next, it is necessary to further refine the "effective development" in conjunction with the aforementioned issues and to clarify the inherent requirements of "effective development"And important values, so as to better promote the effective development of economic law.

In terms of "effective development", the so-called "effective", on the one hand, emphasizes that economic law must conform to the laws, public opinion, and the spirit of the rule of law in order to make it legal and effective; on the other hand, it is also emphasized that the development of economic law must focus on the whole of economic law, consider the internal coordination of the economic law system, and attach importance to the sustainability of economic law itself, so as to make its development more efficient and effective.

In terms of "effective development", the so-called "development" emphasizes not only the increase in quantity but also the improvement in quality. Therefore, the legislation of economic law is not as much as possible, but should focus on solving the aforementioned problems, including: First, the legislative system must

[59]Some scholars believe that the essential requirement for the implementation of the economic rule of law strategy is to restrict the power of the government with the rule of law, standardize the government's economic management behavior, and ensure that the market fully plays the role of allocating resources. Gu Gongyun, 2014, On the Strategy of Economic Rule of Law in the Context of Resuming Reform, *Law Science*, Issue 3.

[60]The related issue of the effective development of "economic theory" is also worthy of attention. Zhang Shouwen, 2005, On "Effective Development" of Economic Law Theory, Studies in Law and Business, Issue 1.

be coordinated. The distribution of legislative power should be coordinated, and legislative bodies at all levels and types exercise their respective legislative powers according to law, which is conducive to the inherent harmony and unification of the economic law system. Second, all kinds of power allocation must be harmonious and appropriate. Only when all kinds of powers, especially all kinds of macro-control powers and market regulation powers, are properly allocated and the relevant subjects exercise their powers fully, timely and completely, can the objectives of economic law be effectively achieved. Third, we must increase the transparency of economic law. Transparency reflects the communication between relevant subjects. Only when the economic legal system can effectively output and feedback, and strengthen the system's input, can it operate continuously. Fourth, we must strengthen procedural guarantees. Without procedural guarantees, the formulation and implementation of economic law will be out of order and norms. At the same time, with procedural guarantees, the operation of economic law will be more efficient and effective. Fifth, we must raise legal awareness and strengthen the concept of the rule of law. Legal consciousness and the concept of the rule of law are very important to the solution of the above-mentioned various problems, which directly affect the effective development of economic law.

According to the above-mentioned inherent requirements of "effective development", the gains and losses in many aspects of economic law system construction can be analyzed. For example, in recent years, the State Council and its functional departments have formulated a large number of economic laws and regulations. At the same time, other laws also imply a large number of economic laws and regulations. The overall number of economic legislation is not small. However, the mere amount of legislation does not necessarily mean the development of economic law, let alone the "effective" development of economic law. Because the systematization of these legislations is not enough, there are still many deficiencies in the economic law system in its due structure, hierarchy, function, coordination, etc. There are not many high-level legislations, and some important legislations are still not as good as they are; The coordination between different levels and the same level of legislation is not enough. Legislative crossovers, overlaps, conflicts, conflicts, etc. still occur from time to time, and there is still a lot of room for the overall function of the economic law system. The existence of the above problems indicates that the effective development of economic law needs to be further promoted.

The effective development of economic law has important value in various fields such as economy and law. On the one hand, the effective development of economic law helps promote the effective development of the economy, especially the introduction of a large number of economic control measures in accordance with the law. The effective exercise of various types of economic regulation and control power can help prevent and resolve economic crises, and in the process of responding to economic crises (especially financial crises and fiscal crises), economic law itself can be further developed. On the other hand, the effective development of economic law itself has promoted the improvement and improvement of the economic legal system, making the operation of economic law more in line with the basic spirit of the rule of law, thereby helping to solve various types of outstanding problems that may arise in the development of economic law and resolve them. The types of crises that may arise, and thus the improvement of the overall legal system, are also of great value for the effective realization of the rule of law.

In order to promote the effective development of economic law, the relationship between quantity and quality, form and god should be solved. In terms of the relationship between quantity and quality, we cannot simply attach importance to the quantity of legislation, and we must especially pay attention to improving the quality of legislation; In terms of the relationship between form and god, not only must many economic legislations have a general legal appearance, but also they should in particular embody the spirit of the rule of law in order to ensure that economic law is legal and effective. Because the number of evil laws that violate the spirit of the rule of law, the greater the number, the greater the harm.

To promote the effective development of economic law and continuously improve the quality of law and enforcement of economic law, attention should also be paid to "comprehensive, coordinated, and sustainable",[61] and its development should be considered from the perspective of the overall economic law. Only based on the whole of the economic law system can we better consider the issue of coordination, complete the main laws, various types of legislative facilities, complement each other without conflict, and form an overall synergy. At the same time, only by embodying the spirit of the rule of law, reflecting the demands of the people, and reflecting the laws of the economy, can the development of economic law be sustainable and effective.

5.4.5 *Effective Development of Economic Law and Deepening of Economic Law Research*

As mentioned earlier, only by constantly preventing and resolving economic crises can we better promote the coordinated and effective development of the economy and society, and the various economic measures taken in the course of responding to economic crises require the protection of economic law. In fact, the effective development of economic law and the improvement of the level of economic rule of law are very helpful for preventing and resolving economic crises, and for further deepening the study of economic law. At the same time, the deepening of economic law research will further promote the effective development of economic law and better prevent and resolve the economic crisis.

Many of the aforementioned problems in the construction of the economic legal system in the course of responding to the crisis need to be further explored. This is

---

[61] Effective development and scientific development are inherently consistent, and both are the requirements inevitably raised by the use of systematic analysis methods. Economic law, as an important part of the legal system, "all its operations are always operations in society", of course, it must also follow the basic requirements of a healthy system operation. Luhmann, Zheng Yiqian (trans.), The Law of Society, Beijing: People's Publishing House, 2009, pp. 14–15.

very important for the deepening of economic law research. The following types of economic law theories are involved, and in particular, further research is needed.

5.4.5.1 Risk Prevention and Control Theory

As mentioned earlier, from the perspective of risk prevention and control, economic law is an important risk prevention and control method. The reason why economic law can prevent and control the risks in the operation of economic society is because economic law has a specific function. Economic law can ensure the economic and social equity by ensuring the effective distribution of income, so that various entities such as the state, enterprises, and individuals can have their own advantages; by ensuring the effective allocation of resources and effective macro-control, it can promote the healthy operation of the economy and society; By taking into account fairness and efficiency, protecting basic human rights, and promoting the development of various entities such as enterprises, to promote the coordinated and stable development of the economy and society, so as to prevent and resolve many risks such as economic and social risks to a certain extent. Therefore, economic law is an important risk prevention and control law.

Not only the economic law as a whole has the function of preventing and controlling related risks in the process of economic operation, but also the specific economic law system can prevent and control specific economic risks. Generally, economic risks include fiscal risks and financial risks, and fiscal risks include budget risks, tax risks, national debt risks, procurement risks, and repayment risks. All these risks need to be prevented through specific systems in economic law control.

In fact, just like the private economic subject, the state, as the subject of the public economy, also needs to guard against risks and crises. For example, in the field of economic law, fiscal risk in fiscal law is directly related to excessive budget expenditure, excessive debt burden, excessive tax burden, or insufficient tax revenue. It is very important to effectively solve the problems of unfair tax burden and unsustainable levy. In terms of system construction, particular attention should be paid to the balance of revenues and expenditures, especially the scale of transfer payments and government procurement, and the scale of taxation and debt issuance, so as to form a benign "take-grant relation".

Based on the above theoretical understanding and practical needs, in the future economic legislation, combined with the formulation of the revised Budget Law and National Debt Law, and the introduction of multiple tax laws, the budget balance and budget adjustment, deficit and Debt scale control and other systems make the institutional arrangements for the compilation and review of budgets, and the issuance and collection of government bonds more standardized. In addition, since taxation efforts and the fairness of tax burden affect the collection of the state and the compliance of the people and the tax risks caused by it, further attention must be paid to the rationality and legality of the tax law system and the taxability theory in tax law.

5.4.5.2 Information Disclosure Theory

As we all know, today's risk society is largely related to insufficient and uncertain information. In order to solve the risks caused by the uncertainty of information, information disclosure systems need to be established in many areas of economic law to protect the right to know of various subjects, such as the right to know of taxpayers, the right of investors, and consumers' right to know, and the manager's right to know, etc. Strengthening information disclosure will play an important role in preventing and resolving various risks and crises. Therefore, whether it is to study the response to the crisis or to study the development of economic law, we should pay attention to the theory of information disclosure.[62]

The disclosure of information in economic law includes the disclosure of information from the state to the national, and also the information report of the national to the state. The core is the question of the right of the state or the citizen to know. Generally, people pay more attention to the right of citizens to know. For example, the issue of the right to know the budget in the field of budget law has always been compelling, and has been mentioned before. In addition, in terms of taxpayer rights, the taxpayers' right to know is often regarded as an important right.[63] As for the issuance and use of government bonds, as well as the right to know in terms of transfer payments, government procurement, and government fees, it is also very worthy of attention.

In addition to the citizens' right to know, in order to strengthen management, the state also needs to obtain relevant information. Therefore, in many systems, there are also a lot of regulations on the state's right to know. In particular, enterprises, individuals and other subjects should be required to monitor their economic activities and income. And other relevant situations to report and report, so that the state can make judgments in terms of taxation, fees, debt issuance, etc., and can also make arrangements in terms of fiscal expenditure.

It should be noted that the right to know of citizens is generally prescribed from the perspective of rights, and the right to know of the state is often prescribed from the perspective of national information obligations. For example, the taxpayer's right to know in China's current tax law is mainly the right to understand the provisions of national tax laws, administrative regulations and situations related to tax procedures, including the time, methods, steps and documents required to handle tax matters, the legal basis, factual basis and calculation method of tax payable assessment and other tax administrative decisions, legal remedies and conditions to be met in case of disputes, etc.

---

[62] In this sense, the information dimension is also an important dimension for the study of economic law. Zhang Shouwen, 1996, Consumers; Right to Access to Information and Its Legal Protection, *Peking University Law Journal*, Issue 1; Ying Feifu, 2001, Basic Functions of Economic Law from the Perspective of Information, *Modern Law Science*, Issue 6.

[63] Whether it is China or some other countries, the taxpayer's right to know is more valued, which is an important basis for taxpayers to exercise their related rights. For this reason, in the *Announcement on Taxpayer Rights and Obligations* issued by the SAT on November 6, 2009, the taxpayers' right to know was also clarified as the first important right.

Corresponding to the above right to know, the current tax law system also stipulates the taxpayers' information obligations, including the obligation to provide information in a timely manner, that is, in addition to providing tax-related information through tax registration and tax declaration, taxpayers should also provide other information in a timely manner Special information such as changes in business conditions and various disasters. In addition, taxpayers have the obligation to report other tax-related information, including the reporting obligation of transfer pricing information with affiliated companies, the obligation to explain the tax arrears of mortgagees and pledgees, and the reporting obligation of business mergers and divisions. Reporting obligations for all accounts, reporting obligations for disposing of large amounts of property, etc.

Regardless of the type of subject, the right to know needs to be realized through adequate information disclosure. To this end, it is necessary to strengthen the research on the entity and procedure system of information disclosure in economic law, and to extract a more systematic theory of information disclosure.[64]

5.4.5.3 Situational Change Theory

As for the theory of situational change, it has been discussed previously. The financial crisis or economic crisis has brought about major changes in the situation. It not only seriously affects the performance of private contracts, but also causes the original form of the budget to break even, which affects the implementation of the national budget. Therefore, we must not only pay attention to the application of legal principles of situation change in the field of private law, but also consider its application in economic law and other public law fields, and refine the theory of situation change in the field of economic law.

The economic law problems brought about by the change of situation are various, such as the problem of budget adjustment, the change of priority of budget expenditure, the problem of fine-tuning the tax system, the issue of special government bonds, the improvement of the economic procedure law, and so on. These issues involve many important areas of economic law and are an important part of the construction of economic law systems, requiring in-depth research.

To study the theory and system of situation change in the field of economic law, we must consider many factors such as the significance of the situation, the unpredictability of the change, and the breadth of the overall situation change, and are closely related to the substantive and procedural law of the economic law. Self-sufficiency, put forward the constituent elements of the situation change, analyze the changes in economic matters, the adjustment of rights and interests, and the sharing of responsibilities to further enrich the theory of economic law.

---

[64]For the issue of information disclosure, cross-research is needed from the perspective of economic law and information law. Zhang Shouwen, Zhou Qingshan, 1995, Information Law, Beijing: Law Press·China, p. 63.

5.4.5.4 Control and Regulation Theory

In the development of crisis response and economic law, macro-control and market regulation are undoubtedly very important issues. But on the whole, the research on theories and systems of macro-control and market regulation is not enough. It is necessary to promote related research based on the perspective of modern laws such as economic law and social law. No matter from the system practice of each country or from the perspective of economic law theory's expansion, it is necessary to further strengthen the research of regulation and regulation theory.

5.4.6 Conclusion

This section focuses on the analysis of various economic measures used in the crisis response process, and proposes five types of important issues that China should pay attention to in terms of economic and legal construction. The solution will affect the effective development of economic law, and even cause a crisis of economic law. Therefore, we must attach great importance to it and work hard to resolve it.

It should be acknowledged that in the process of crisis response, economic means do have a particularly important role, but its role cannot be achieved without the strong guarantee of economic law. Only by solving the problems of the legislative system, the exercise of power, transparency, procedural guarantees, and legal awareness and the concept of the rule of law, and continuously improving the rationality and legitimacy of the economic law system, can the effective development of economic law be promoted, and the Relevant issues in the fields of society, politics, law, etc., to prevent and resolve various crises that may or have already occurred. The above understanding is especially helpful for refining crisis theory in economic law and specific crisis response theory.

There is a close link between crisis response and effective development of economic law: On the one hand, crisis response provides an important opportunity for the effective development of economic law, and helps people to further clarify what is effective development, why it is effective, and how to develop effectively; On the other hand, the effective development of economic law objectively provides important legal guarantees for the effective development of economic, social and other fields, and helps prevent and resolve various crises such as economic and social crises. Problems, and possible legal crises, are particularly direct and important.

Both the crisis response and the effective development of economic law will help promote the deepening of economic law theory. At the same time, the in-depth development of theoretical research on economic law will further promote the level of rule of law in economic law, promote the effective development of economic law, and further promote the healthy operation and coordinated development of economy and society, thereby helping to prevent and resolve risks and crises. From the perspective of crisis response, the effective development of economic law, and its relationship with economic law theoretical research, in economic law theoretical research, the research on risk prevention and control theory, information disclosure theory, situation change theory, regulation and regulation theory should be further strengthened. This is of great significance to the overall development of economic law theory.

References

Liu, Shangxi, et al. 2006. *Macro financial risks and government fiscal responsibility*, 11. Beijing: China Financial Publishing House.

Wang, Zili. 2008. *Moral hazards and lack of regulation: the underlying causes of the US financial crisis*, 20. Issue: China Finance.

Zhang, Shouwen. 2004. *Reconstruction of economic law theory*, 154–62. Beijing: People's Publishing House.

Zhang, Shouwen. 2008a. *Science of Economic Law*, 7th ed, 7. Beijing: China Renmin University Press.

Zhang, Shouwen. 2008b. *Science of Economic Law*, 63–65. Beijing: China Renmin University Press.

Zhang, Shouwen. 2009. *Pandect of economic law*, 10–11. Beijing: China Renmin University Press.

Zhang, Shouwen. 2009, On the promoted economic law, *Journal of Chongqing University (Social Science Edition)*, Issue 6.

Zhang, Wenxian. 2005, The Rule of Law in China in the Age of Globalization, *Journal of Jilin University (Social Science Edition)*, Issue 2.

Zhou, Xiaochuan. 2011, Financial policies and response to financial crises: the formation background, internal logic and main contents of a macro-prudential policy framework, *Journal of Financial Research*, Issue 1.

Chapter 6
Economic Legislation and Rule-of-Law Theory

The content discussed in the previous chapters—proper handling of the "tripartite relations" and relevant regime issues; implementation of the idea of coordinated development and promotion of development by economic law; settlement of distribution problems, risk prevention and control, and crisis response; deepening of development and distribution theories, and refinement of risk and crisis theories—is in the final analysis directly associated with the specific systems of economic law, relevant legislations or the rule of law construction. Therefore, it is particularly important to strengthen the economic law legislation, continuously improve the quality of legislation, elevate the level of economic rule of law, and refine the corresponding theories of economic rule of law.

In the realm of economic law legislation, many issues need to be resolved. For example, the pilot legislative work may lead to scattered legislation, but the legislative integration will somewhat help to solve this problem. As such, it is an important issue to balance the unity and decentralization of legislation, and constantly improve the level of economic rule of law. In order to resolve the above problems, it is necessary to adhere to the statutory principle and ensure the rights of relevant subjects within the framework of the rule of law. For example, while pressing ahead with the "structural tax reduction", China shall implement the statutory taxation principle, and balance the rights of taxpayers and the state taxation power, it is an issue worthy of discussion. In addition, how to improve the state governance ability through the path of economic law is another important issue for strengthening the economic rule of law. In the process of discussing the above-mentioned issues, we need to abide by the rule-of-law principle and refine the rule-of-law theory.

For the above considerations, this chapter firstly discusses the legislative integration and pilot legislation of economic law from the perspectives of centralized and decentralized legislation; and then demonstrates the importance in following the statutory principle and strengthening the economic rule of law by taking the tax reduction right in the "structural tax reduction" as an example; and finally explores the path of economic law for building up the state governance ability, highlights the

S. Zhang, *The New Horizon of China's Economic Law Theory*, Understanding China,
https://doi.org/10.1007/978-981-15-8824-2_6

value of economic law regulation to the overall economic rule of law in China, and examines the possibility of advancing the economic rule of law construction.

6.1 Legislative Integration of Economic Law

6.1.1 Background and Issues

Against the background of comprehensive deepening of reform and advancement of the rule-of-law construction, China is now dedicated to the unification and integration of the systems in many domains. Since all kinds of reforms shall be "based on the law" and in line with the rule-of-law spirit, China has given top priority to improving legislation while continuing the rule-of-law construction, which has caused a new upsurge in legislation.[1]

Since economic law is closely associated with civil law and administrative law, and of special value to the overall rule-of-law construction, a comparative study of the three laws' legislative path[2] will help to reveal their commonality and regularity at the legislative level. Looking back on the development course of the three laws, we can find that although they are affected by the thinking of "constructivist legislation", they have different degrees of legislative integration: in the realm of civil law, China enacted the *General Principles of Civil Law* before starting decentralized legislation, and it did not resume the compilation of a civil code until recent years. In the realm of administrative law, a unified and integrated legislation remains absent, and quite a number of laws came out through decentralized legislation. Similar to administrative law, the backbone legislations in the realm of economic law are also decentralized; not as systematic as the administrative legislation or comparable to the civil legislation. Nonetheless, before China starts the comprehensive rule-of-law construction, all of the three major sectoral laws have been subject to "decentralized legislation", which shows their commonality or consistency in the legislative model.

The reason why the "decentralized legislation" became a common path of separate sectoral laws is due to the difficulties in legislation, varied degree of consensus, and different stage of development. At present, all major sectors of economic law have their own representative laws,[3] and these laws will be increasingly perfected

---

[1]Back in the 1990s when China just established the market economic system, it soon embarked on the relevant legislative work on a large scale. In recent years, especially after the introduction of the 2013 Reform Decision and the 2014 Rule-of-law Decision, China accelerated the stipulation, revision, abolition and interpretation of national laws, and thereby creating a new wave of legislation, which encompasses many economic law consensuses. Zhang (2014a), Issue 2.

[2]In the realm of economic law, many scholars tend to compare economic law with civil and commercial law and administrative law in their study. For these three sectoral laws, are they consistent in terms of codification? Or to what extent are they consistent? Whether the development path of other sectoral laws has reference significance to economic law? Such topics are worthy of studying.

[3]The macro-economic control laws include the *Budget Law* and the *Government Procurement Law* in the fiscal sector; the *Law on Enterprise Income Tax* and the *Law on the Administration of Tax*

along with the continuous improvement of the economic rule of law. Based on the achievements in "decentralized legislation" and in the new period where China is advancing the rule-of-law construction in an all-round manner, in order to achieve higher-level "legislative integration", is it necessary to promote the legislative unification, consolidation or synthesization in the realm of economic law? How about the level and scope of the legislation? These important questions are of great concern during in the economic rule-of-law construction and in the legal studies. Meanwhile, with the gradual completion of separate legislation in civil law and administrative law, the call for developing a civil code and an administrative code has been growing,[4] which will further stimulate the academic community to think about promoting the legislative integration of economic law.

Although the researches and discussions on the legislative integration of economic law have never stopped,[5] lots of the important problems in this regard still need in-depth study in combination with the rule-of-law development and theoretical progress in the new period. For example, is the legislative integration of economic law really necessary? How to define the form, scope and level of the legislative integration? Which kind of legislative integration is feasible? For the legislative integration that is both necessary and feasible, are there any problems in theoretical support and system construction ought to be addressed?

While discussing the above issues, there is no way to bypass the disputes between constructivism and evolutionism, holism and individualism, rationalism and empiricism, systematic thinking and practical thinking.[6] From the perspectives of constructivism, holism, rationalism and systematic thinking, it is no doubt necessary to promote the legislative integration; but from the perspectives of evolutionism, individualism, empiricism and practical thinking, more attention shall be paid to decentralized legislation in certain periods or stages. Each of these doctrines or ways of thinking has its own rationality, so we cannot take a one-sided view, but take account of the rule-of-law situation in different countries and different periods to decide whether and to what extent the legislative integration should be promoted. In fact, integration and decentralization are relative concepts; an either-or choice shall

---

Collection in the tax sector; the *Law on the People's Bank of China*, the *Law on Regulation of and Supervision over the Banking Industry*, the *Securities Law* and the *Insurance Law* in the financial sector. The market regulation laws include the *Anti-monopoly Law*, the *Anti-unfair Competition Law*, the *Law on Protection of Consumer Rights and Interests*, and the *Law on Product Quality*.

[4]The opinions on the compilation of a civil code are in abundance, and there are also discussions about the formulation of a unified administrative code. Jiang (2012), Issue 5.

[5]In the 1960s, some Soviet-East European countries once attempted to integrate the legislations in the realm of economic law. China drew up the *General Principles of Economic Law* in the mid-1980s, and organized extensive researches and discussions on these principles in the late 1990s; moreover, there are also intermittent discussions on the *Economy Basic Law* and the *Economic Code*, which have provided an important basis for today's legislative improvement.

[6]There had been an argument on whether the *British Common Law* should be codified, some scholars like Bacon and Bentham were advocates, while Blackstone and Maine were against it. The debate between Thibaut and Savigny on whether Germany should have a unified civil code was more famous, which reflected the collision and confrontation between these opposite theories. Wang (2003), Issue 2.

be made to improve the quality of legislation and guarantee the implementation of laws, rather than seek legislative integration for its own sake.

Based on the above considerations, this section will discuss the legislative integration of economic law that is concerned by the academic community from the dimensions of need and possibility; this process of discussion may involve the thinking about the economic law legislative theory. Although some scholars have long ago suggested that the focus of legal research shall be shifted from legislative theory to interpretive theory, they failed to probe into the differences between each sectoral law—as far as economic law is concerned, so the legislative theory still needs in-depth study, which will at the same time enrich the operating theory of economic law.

6.1.2 Multi-dimensional Need for Legislative Integration

As mentioned earlier, while China is advancing the rule-of-law construction in an all-round manner, the development of economic law has entered into a new stage. In this new period, whether we should promote the legislative integration of economic law and whether it is necessary to do so are the questions that need to be answered at the first place. As such, the following paragraphs will unfold analysis from the interconnected dimensions of legal system changes, function realization and academic accumulation, in an aim to discover and reveal the internal need for promoting the legislative integration.

6.1.2.1 The Dimension of Legal System Changes

China has paid great attention to the system construction of economic law since it launched the reform and opening-up. From the perspective of legal system changes, before the market economy system was established in 1992, the legislative system of economic law in China was still in its infancy. Since 1993 when the "socialist market economy was included in the Constitution", the provisions in the economic constitution—groundwork for the economic law legislation—have become increasingly complete, the legislation in all sectors of economic law has developed rapidly, and gradually adapted to the requirements of the market economy system. China specially spent three years in building a basic framework of the economic law system, which includes the market regulation legislation in 1993,[7] the economic

[7]The most representative legislations include the *Anti-unfair Competition Law* (which contains some content of the anti-monopoly law), the *Law on Protection of Consumer Rights and Interests*, and the *Law on Product Quality*, which constitute the basic structure of the present market regulation laws.

legislation in 1994,[8] and the financial legislation in 1995.[9] Through two decades of development, in the face of mounting problems in economic and social development, the state began to highlight the comprehensive deepening of reform under the rule-of-law framework, and clarify the functions of the two major resource allocation systems (the market and the government),[10] thus ushering the legislation of economic law into a new stage. Owing to the stipulation, revision, abolition and interpretation of many economic law norms, the necessity for the legislative integration and the "higher law" attribute of economic law have become increasingly prominent.

Through a review of the changes on China's economic law system since the reform and opening-up, it is easy to find that this is a process where the modern economic law sprung up from nothing, from less to more, from low level to high level, from decentralized to integrated, and all sectors of economic law have developed to varying degrees.

For example, the realm of economic law has been and is now undergoing frequent legislative integration. The two sets of tax systems, respectively for domestic-funded and foreign-related enterprises, are finally unified and integrated, which is remarkable achievement. Moreover, the respective legislative integration of the *Law on Enterprise Income Tax*, the *Law on Individual Income Tax*, and the *Law on Vehicle and Vessel Tax* not only ended the state of legislative decentralization for domestic-funded and foreign-related enterprises, but raised the level of legislation.[11] In addition, "replacing business tax with VAT" and the reform of real estate tax system are part of the process where legislation decentralization moves towards integration.[12] The revision of the *Budget Law* and the formulation of the *Government Procurement Law* are also important manifestations of legislative integration.[13]

---

[8]The most representative legislations include the *Budget Law*, the *Decision of the State Council on Implementing the Tax Sharing Fiscal Administration System*, and more than a dozen tax laws and temporary tax regulations, which constitute the basic structure of the present fiscal and tax laws.

[9]The most representative legislations include the *Law on the People's Bank of China*, the *Law on Commercial Banks*, and the *Insurance Law*, which constitute the basic structure of the present financial laws.

[10]Zhang (2014b), Issue 5.

[11]The *Law on Enterprise Income Tax* unifies the two income tax systems respectively for domestic-funded and foreign-related enterprises. The *Law on Individual Income Tax* unifies the original individual income tax, individual business income tax, and individual income adjustment tax. The *Law on Vehicle and Vessel Tax* unifies the vehicle and vessel use tax and the vehicle and vessel license plate tax. Moreover, the above-mentioned legislative integration is finally established in the form of laws.

[12]"Replacing business tax with VAT" is to "absorb and merge" the business tax system into the VAT system, which represents a milestone in the legislative integration of the domestic commodity tax. The reform of real estate tax system, which involves the housing property tax and the urban real estate tax and unifies the housing property tax system and the land holding tax system, is recognized as a kind of legislative integration.

[13]Despite of some problems, the revised *Budget Law* integrates the four relevant budget systems into one law, which has promoted the legislative integration to some extent. Before the *Government Procurement Law* was promulgated, the similar local regulations had been prevailing in many parts of China. During the legislative process of the *Government Procurement Law*, the content of local regulations was integrated accordingly.

The above-mentioned legislative integration is limited to a certain sector of economic law. According to the general law of legal system changes, the development of all sectoral laws is a process from low level to high level, and from decentralization to integration, which is an internal demand for the modernization of the rule of law. As for the levels of legislative integration of economic law, should it be the "sub-sectoral law level", or the "regulatory group level" of macro-economic control law and market regulation law, or even the "system-wide level"? A detailed analysis is required in this regard. For example, the enactment of a macro-economic control law which was promoted by the academic community is the legislative integration at the "regulatory group level"; in the future, the compilation of an economic code will represent the legislative integration at the "system-wide level".

Based on the general traditions of civil law countries, the systematization or codification of legislation is more valued in these countries. Even in common law countries, the substantial increase in statute law is a trend that cannot be ignored, and the influence of constructivism and rationalism on economic legislation is relatively greater.[14] From the dimension of dynamic legal system changes, strengthening legislative integration is an internal demand for systematization of the legal system. The course of economic law legislation in all countries from decentralization to integration shows that "moderate" legislative integration is necessary, and it is in line with the basic direction of legal system changes or rule-of-law modernization.

6.1.2.2 The Dimension of Function Realization

The important impetus for the above-mentioned system changes is attributed to the realistic demand for performing the functions of legal system amid the economic and social development. In the new era of comprehensively deepening reform and advancing the rule-of-law construction, China has presented higher requirements for ensuring fair competition, promoting the formation of a unified market and a unified rule-of-law system, while the corresponding top-level design and legislative integration directly affects the realization of the functions and goals of the economic law system.

Among the various legal sources of economic law, there are a large number of laws, administrative regulations and sectoral rules; they have a direct and significant effect on the construction of the rule-of-law system. However, these legal sources came out in a decentralized manner, sometimes they cannot fully reflect the overall value, purpose or principles of economic law for various reasons, which will affect the overall coordination of the economic law system, and go against the performance of the functions of economic law as rules of conduct and rules of adjudication. Therefore, we need to better ensure the effective operation of market mechanism and government agencies; to this end, it is necessary to promote the legislative integration

[14] According to Savigny, legislators may be affected by strong national rationality when they are about to change the existing laws. It is even more prominent in the legislation of economic law. Savigny (2001c), p. 14.

based on the refined theories, principles and rules of economic law. Consequently, in front of the complicated economic and social issues, we can employ the unified rules of economic law to carry out comprehensive regulation or miscellaneous adjustment that is more in line with the rule-of-law spirit, so as to make up for the deficiencies in the adjustment of the laws, regulations and rules that were stipulated in a decentralized manner, and to realize the functions of economic law system in a better way.

Economic law not only has guarantee function and normalization function like general laws, but also has special control function and regulation function. We have to organically integrate the relevant economic law systems and make the statutory regulatory approaches more coordinated, only by this way can we effectively prevent conflicts in regulation, solve the "complexity matters" that "spring up" in the complicated economic and social systems, and reduce the problems of less complementarity and coordination caused by the implementation of single laws and regulations. In short, strengthening legislative integration is an internal requirement for realizing the economic law function, and also a practical demand for solving the complicated economic and social problems.

In addition, in the process of legislative integration, should we pay more attention to judicial trials than to government regulation? Relatively speaking, civil and commercial law usually provides adjudication rules for judicial trials, while the economic law not only provides adjudication rules, but also regulation rules for the government to perform economic functions. Especially for those economic systems and mechanisms with commonality, we shall strengthen their legislative coordination and integration to better realize the overall function of economic law. In this regard, there is some similarity between administrative law and economic law.[15]

6.1.2.3 The Dimension of Academic Accumulation

Since China implemented the market economy system, the theoretical consensus on economic law study has increased notably.[16] There have been discussions about the basic theories such as the goals and objects of regulation, basic principles, forms of subjects, behavioral models, right-duty structure, and types of liabilities in the realm of economic law. These discussions have provided important theoretical support for the legislative integration of economic law, and made it more possible than ever to refine and consolidate the economic law systems.

Advancing the legislative integration of economic law not only helps to test the achievements that have been achieved, but also consolidate the theoretical knowledge recognized by the academic community, thereby increasing academic accumulation, avoiding low-level repetitive research work, further discovering the underlying

[15]The government is an important subject in the implementation of economic law and administrative law. The theories and principles of the two laws are applicable to some common domains; moreover, the two laws have common demand in the realization of system functions.

[16]Qiu (2013), Issue 4.

issues in economic law theory, which will promote theoretical progress and academic development, and achieve higher-level academic accumulation.

Historically, the legislative integration in various realms was actually a "big review" of academic research, which had promoted academic accumulation. For example, in the process of compiling the civil code, many issues concerning the theories and practices of civil law were discussed, which was undoubtedly helpful for the continuous development of civil law theory.[17] Similarly, advancing the legislative integration of economic law is at least of great significance for reviewing the academic achievements, examining the existing problems, clarifying the development direction in the future, and increasing academic accumulation.

In short, the researches and practices on the legislative integration not only test the existing theoretical consensus, but push the academic accumulation to a higher level, and tighten the connection between theoretical study and the practical system construction, so that the economic law theory will have stronger explanatory power and guidance ability, and then lay a solid foundation for further legislative integration. Therefore, from the perspectives of testing and developing the economic law theory and increasing academic accumulation, it is necessary to promote the legislative integration of economic law.

6.1.2.4 Integration of Three Dimensions

Although there are other dimensions for discussing the necessity of legislative integration of economic law, the above three dimensions at least bring us a fundamental understanding of the reasons for doing so. From the perspective of the legal system changes, the continuously improved systematization of the legal system is a general trend of the rule-of-law development, and the legislative integration of economic law is an internal need for the rule-of-law construction. From the perspective of function realization, the realistic economic and social development presses for the legislative integration to solve the problems of restricted or impaired functions caused by system inconsistency or discordance, or irrational structures, so as to effectively fulfill the regulatory goals of economic law. From the perspective of academic accumulation, advancing the legislative integration will help to increase the academic accumulation of economic law, build up the explanatory power and guiding power of economic law theory. All in all, from past to present, from macro-level to micro-level, from structures to functions, from system construction to academic research, it is necessary to promote the legislative integration of economic law.

In addition, we shall be aware of the close correlation among the three dimensions: The legal system changes reveal the trend and direction of the legislative integration of various sectoral laws from a historical and dynamic perspective, and highlight that the development of economic law shall follow the general laws of legal system changes.

---

[17] For example, in the process of compiling the civil code, the scholars started re-examining the most fundamental issues, such as the regulated objects and basic principles of civil law. These efforts are useful for deepening the economic law theory. Cai (2015), Issue 2.

The reason why the legal system changes in this way is that the economic and social development demands for realizing the functions of the legal system. Given this, we shall keep advancing the legislative integration and enhancing the coordination of the legal system, so that we can better perform its functions and solve practical problems. In the meantime, the realization of the system functions relies on theoretical reflection and foresight, especially the corresponding theoretical consensus as the basis of top-level design, and further academic accumulation in the process. The recognition of the "integration" of the three closely correlated dimensions helps to explain the reason for advancing the legislative integration of economic law.

6.1.3 Realistic Possibility of Legislative Integration

The legislative integration of economic law requires not only sufficient theoretical preparation, but also system practices as the foundation or reference; both the theoretical consensuses and system practices shall be organically combined. Through years' research, the Chinese academic community has reached so many consensuses on the basic theories of economic law, which can provide important theoretical support for the legislative integration. At the same time, from the perspective of the legal system, the rich legislative experiences in the realm of economic law make it possible for advancing the legislative integration. All of the above factors have greatly increased the feasibility of legislative integration.

The legislative integration needs to be implemented from multiple dimensions such as the legislative model, legislative form, legislative content and legislative timing, which will give rise to multiple options for legislative integration, while the underlying practical possibilities are in need of further examination and discussion.

6.1.3.1 Compatibility of Legislative Models

Economic law legislation is usually divided into two models: decentralized and comprehensive (or integrated). Many countries mainly practice the decentralized legislation, but a trend towards the comprehensive model has appeared, despite of varied realms and degrees, which is not only related to their special situation in different historical periods, but also to the imbalanced development of different legal realms. Take the realm of anti-monopoly law for example, the US *Antitrust Act* is in the form of a single comprehensive code, it is a set of acts developed through vertical decentralized legislation in a chronological order, but they are interconnected, coordinated and gradually integrated into one; in the civil law countries such as Germany, Japan and Russia, their anti-monopoly legislation is relatively comprehensive. Take the realm of tax law for example, since the statutory taxation principle is highly valued, the tax laws in many countries boast a higher degree of codification: the *US Internal Revenue Code* is subject to the comprehensive legislation; the *German General Tax Law* and the *South Korean National Tax Basic Act* are also classified as a form of comprehensive legislation, regardless of their title as "general law" or "basic law". In addition, the *Economic Code* of Czechoslovak is an economic law "code"[18] known for its higher level and stronger comprehensiveness. In a word, the comprehensive legislation, regardless of its level, helps to make up for the gaps arising from decentralized legislation and pave way for more effective legal adjustment.

In terms of the advantages and disadvantages of different legislative models, the decentralized legislation is usually more flexible, which facilitates a single law to come out as long as it matures, and it is ready to be amended separately, but sometimes there may be problems of lack of integrity and coordination, and the resulting omissions in legal adjustment will affect the realization of fairness and efficiency. The comprehensive legislation is just the opposite of the decentralized legislation. Therefore, we'd better integrate the two types of legislative models in combination with the differences, particularities and complexities of the problems that need to be solved by economic law. We shall firstly practice the decentralized legislation and wait for its development to reach a certain stage, and then explore the common rules at a higher level to properly integrate the relevant decentralized legislation, so as to make up for the absence or deficiency of the original legislation.

Promoting the legislative integration of economic law is not to deny the existing decentralized legislation, but to achieve the goal of separate legislative integration according to different situations. For example, on the one hand, we can "rebuild or extend" the original legislation,[19] i.e., retain a reasonable part of the existing legislative achievements, make supplement or correction to them in case of any missing, defective or biased provisions, and at the same time consolidate and extend the relevant norms to form general terms or common specifications; on the other hand, we can pursue a "newbuild", i.e., while retaining the original legislation, we can introduce the superordinate "general legislation" or "basic legislation", so that the original decentralized legislation and the subsequent integrated legislation could be integrated to better cope with the complicated economic life and resolve the deficiencies in economic law adjustment.

It can be seen that even if the decentralized legislation is widespread, the comprehensive legislation remains in existence. The two types of legislative models are compatible with each other and moving ahead in parallel, making it completely feasible for the legislative integration. It should be noted that after the decentralized legislation of economic law has reached a certain scale and accumulated some experiences, it will be more realistic to promote the legislative integration.

6.1.3.2 Choice of Legislative Form

Based on the above feasible models for comprehensive legislation, we also need to choose the forms of legislation. In this regard, the academic community has proposed

---

[18] Jiang (1981).

[19] The content of a code is twofold, i.e., one part of it is composed of existing laws, while the other part contains new legal provisions. Savigny (2001a), p. 15.

some specific forms of legislation, e.g., the *Outline of Economic Law* (or the *General Rules of Economic Law*), the *Economy Basic Law* (or the *Basic Economic Law*), the *Economic Code*, and the *General Principles of Economic Law*. Since different legislative forms will lead to differences in the specific content of legislation, we should pay attention to the relation between "legislative genre" and "legislative theme" to choose the appropriate forms of legislation.

Regarding the legislative form of the *Outline of Economic Law*, scholars at home and abroad have presented their viewpoints and started relevant studies long time ago.[20] As early as 1985, some well-known Chinese economic jurists suggested to formulate the *Outline of the Economic Law of the People's Republic of China*, and brought forth a draft outline for comment before 1986 when the *General Principles of the Civil Law* was introduced.[21] From 1997 to 1999, many Chinese scholars were discussing the drafting of the *Outline of Economic Law* at the annual meeting of National Economic Law for three consecutive years.[22] The relevant studies have since then never stopped.[23] It should be said that the *Outline of Economic Law*, as an important form of legislative integration of economic law, has remained focus of attention for a long time.

In addition to the *Outline of Economic Law*, some scholars advocated the legislative form of the *Basic Economic Law*.[24] With a view to the legislative practices in some countries or regions, the legislation in the form of "basic law" is usually the constitution or constitutional law, like the *Basic Law of the Federal Republic of Germany* and the *Basic Law of the Hong Kong Special Administrative Region*. In the 1990s, China drafted the *Basic Tax Law* which has yet come out despite of several times of revision, one of the important reasons is that there have been doubts about whether the tax law could be in the legislative form of the "basic law". Later, some scholars suggested an alternative of the *General Principles of Tax Law*. By the same token, if the form of the "basic law" applies to the legislative integration of economic law, the same controversies about the *Basic Tax Law* will come into being. Therefore, when the conditions for the "basic law" are yet mature, an alternative of the "general rules" may be more realistic and feasible.

Another form closely related to the above *Basic Economic Law* is the *Economic Code*. The *Economic Code of the Czechoslovak Socialist Republic (1964)*[25] had been taken as a model by some scholars. In fact, the scholars of the Soviet Union and China had worked out the drafts for the *Economic Code*, but they had not gone through the

---

[20] Hell et al. (1981), pp. 1–81.

[21] From February 25 to March 3, 1986, initiated by the Research Centre for Economic Legislation under the State Council, nearly 20 Chinese economic jurists, including Yang Zixuan, Liu Wenhua, Xu Jie and Li Changqi came together to work out a draft economic law outline for comment, which contains 54 articles in a total of 10 chapters.

[22] The Seven-person Research Group (2000), pp. 6–21.

[23] Yang (2000), Vol. 2; Lu and Li (2000), Issue 1.

[24] Li (1991), Issue 4; Yuan and Zhu (2014), Issue 3.

[25] Jiang (1981).

process of legislation.[26] After all, the "code" is the top-level legislative integration that requires higher conditions in all aspects. Therefore, whether the *Economic Code* could be formulated at the current stage requires a comprehensive assessment.[27]

Savigny has divided the process of legal development into three stages: the first stage of "customary law" or "natural law" that exists in the common sense of a nation; the second stage of "academic law" that exists in the mind of jurists; and the third stage of "codification" that combines natural law with academic law. Savigny believed that Germany at that time was in the second stage. Is China's economic law also at the "academic law" stage at present? Will the scholars integrate their understanding of economic law with the basic consensus and social needs of the public? They are important issues that need to be studied for the formulation of the *Economic Code*.

Since 1954, the *Civil Code of China* has undergone five times of drafting, the controversy was even more serious in the recent two rounds of drafting. In the realm of civil law, which features a long history and relatively mature theories and legislation, it is hard to promote high-level legislative integration. As such, we shall be prepared to deal with the difficulties in the codification of economic law. In addition, we shall care about the compilation of the *Administrative Code*, since the administrative law scholars may encounter the similar problems that are more related to economic law.[28]

In short, all of the above legislative forms are possible choices at present, which need to be further clarified according to the level and scope of legislative integration and the consensus in various aspects. Considering the consistent attitude of the national legislature, the time to formulate the *Basic Economic Law* is not mature enough currently; without the promulgation of the *Civil Code*, it is unlikely to include the *Economic Code* into the legislative planning in the foreseeable future. Therefore, the three legislative forms of the *Outline of Economic Law*, the *General Rules of Economic Law*, and the *General Principles of Economic Law* may be more feasible.

However, with a view to the existing legislation, the "outline" is generally chosen for adopting any planning or planning-like legislation, such as the "outline" for the five-year plans (a national development plan of China for every five years from 1991 to 2020) adopted at the National People's Congress, and the *Outline for Comprehensively Promoting Administrative Implementation by Law* (Guofa [2004] No. 10) and the *Outline of the National Intellectual Property Strategy* (Guofa [2008] No. 18), both were released by the State Council. Since the basic laws enacted in the past were not yet in the form of the "outline", which may have certain adverse effect on the formulation of the *Outline of Economic Law*.

---

[26]In 1969, the Academy of Sciences of the USSR organized some economic law scholars to work out a draft for the *Soviet Economic Code*; in 1985, the commission headed by Laptev completed the drafting work, but failed to submit it to the legislative body for review. In March 1963, some Chinese scholars drafted the *Economic Law of the People's Republic of China*, which also failed to go through the legislative procedure. He (2002), pp. 584–593.

[27]No. 2 Research Group on the Compilation of the Economic Code (2015), Issue 1.

[28]In the realm of administrative law, some scholars equate the *Administrative Procedure Law* with the *General Principles of Administrative Law* or the *Administrative Code*. Jiang (2004), Issue 5.

Relatively speaking, the form of the *General Rules of Economic Law* is affirmed by many scholars, and the *General Principles of Economic Law* is also recognized as an important alternative, because it is able to refine the common systems of various decentralized legislation without breaking the original legislative structure, which is undoubtedly important for improving the systematic level of economic law. In fact, the current work in compilation of the *Civil Code* is starting from the drafting of the *General Principles of Civil Law*; likewise, the administrative law community also suggests formulating the *General Principles of Administrative Law*[29] at the first place. Compared with the other forms of legislation, the formulation of the *General Principles of Economic Law* may be a technically feasible option at present for its lower cost, smaller resistance and higher efficiency.

Considering the choice of the legislative forms in the past, the *Macro-economic Control Law* or the *Basic Law on Macro-economic Control* are likely to be put into the legislative procedure,[30] and the relevant research is still underway. Besides, some deputies to the NPC once delivered the legislative proposal on the *Economic Law of the People's Republic of China*, but no substantial progress has been made so far.[31] All of the above-mentioned attempts have implications for the choice of legislative forms in the future.

6.1.3.3 Choice of Legislative Content

After clarifying the legislative model and legislative form, we need to choose the legislative content in the process of legislative integration. Generally, the form of legislation, and the level and scope of integration will affect the content of legislative integration, but no matter which legislative form is adopted, it is sure to contain some of the most basic content. For the purpose of the legislative integration, we need to identify and extract the greatest common divisor (GCD), it is necessary to choose the most basic content of legislation, which will affect the basic structure or style of legislation.

(1) No matter it is the *General Principles of Economic Law*, the *General Rules of Economic Law*, the *Outline of Economic Law* or the *Economic Code*, it shall firstly set out the "general provisions" for its legislative purposes, objects or scope

[29] In the past, most of the administrative law scholars were arguing that it was difficult to codify the administrative law. However, after the adoption and implementation of the *General Principles of Administrative Law* in the Netherlands, people have been increasingly aware of the possibility of codifying the administrative law, some scholars have begun to re-examine this issue, believing that it is possible for China to codify its administrative code, and advising China to start with the formulation of the *General Principles of Administrative Law*.

[30] In 2001, on behalf of their delegations to the NPC, Yang Zixuan, Zhao Xueqing, Wang Jian and Li Hao, respectively delivered the proposal on the formulation of the *Macro-economic Control Law of the People's Republic of China*.

[31] In 2012, Huang He and other 29 deputies to the NPC put forward the proposal on the formulation the *Economic Law of the People's Republic of China*, in an attempt to enact a basic economic law of China.

of regulation, and basic principles. The specific provisions for the above content depend on the understanding of many theoretical issues about economic law, e.g., the regulatory goals or purposes, regulated objects, basic principles and value.

(2) Economic law is the embodiment of the economic constitution,[32] the system arrangements or power distribution related to the economic constitution are of fundamental significance for the system construction of economic law; therefore, the norms of the system law or organizational law are indispensable content in various types of economic law. For this reason, the legislative integration of economic law, regardless of the legislative form, shall define the relevant basic systems, so as to delimit the boundary between the government and the market, and clarify the relation between relevant state organs.

(3) Regardless of the level of legislative integration, the substantive law system of economic law remains the core content. For this reason, various types of legislative integration need to clearly define the basic subjects and the subject structure of economic law, specify their types of behavior (including the noncompliance behaviors), and on this basis, define the duties and responsibilities, rights and obligations of relevant subjects of relevant subjects, as well as their corresponding legal liabilities. The above-mentioned legislative integration is especially helpful to promote the development and improvement of the normative theory of economic law.

(4) Corresponding to the above-mentioned substantive law system, the procedural law system of economic law may not be ignored. No matter it is the procedure for control or regulation, it is especially important for regulating the behaviors subject to control and regulation, and protecting the relevant rights of the regulation receptors. Moreover, the relevant accountability procedure or right relief procedures are also indispensable.

The above aspects are the most basic content to be included into all kinds of high-level economic law legislative integration. Of course, in conjunction with the above-mentioned various systems, and from the perspective of legislative technique, some other relevant content can also be specified in the high-level legislative integration, such as the "system coordination rules" (the right to interpret relevant laws, effective dates, and conflicts of jurisdiction), the time, place, temporal or spatial effect of relevant behaviors, and the relation between economic law and international treaties.

6.1.3.4 The Timing of Legislation

The timing of legislation concerns the implementation of the legislative model, legislative form and legislative content. Generally, in order to grasp the timing for certain legislative integration, we shall take account of the following important conditions for reference: whether it caters to the economic and social development, whether the legislators and the public have sufficient consensus on the legislation, and whether the legal theories are adequately prepared. The satisfaction of the above conditions directly affects the realization of the goals of economic law legislation integration.

[32]Zhang (2013a), Issue 4.

Considering the pressing need for economic and social development, in order to comprehensively deepen the reform and advance the construction of a unified rule-of-law system, we need to strengthen the legislative integration in various realms. Take the realm of economic law for example, the relevant fiscal system, financial system, investment system and competition system are undergoing reforms, these system changes present the demand for legislative integration. Moreover, some special domains under comprehensive reform, such as the establishment of free trade zones and the public-private partnership (PPP) system, are involved with a large scale of system integration of economic law.[33] No matter it is for confirming the reform achievements, or for responding to the pressing need to comprehensively deepen the reform, we shall consolidate the latest developments in the economic law systems, so as to better improve the coordination of the systems, improve their efficiency, fairness and predictability, and manifest the internal requirements of economic rule of law.

In response to the pressing need of economic and social development, legislators used to pay more attention to "prior to carry and try" in the relevant domains, thus making "decentralized legislation" fairly prevalent.[34] Nowadays, along with the comprehensive promotion of law-based governance of the state, legislators and the public have reached more consensuses on the need to strengthen the top-level legislative design and unify the legal system. On this basis, it is more possible to get to grips with the common problems in the previous legislation, make up for the gaps in regulation, and promote effective legislative integration. In addition, the long-term academic research on the economic law legislation also provides important theoretical preparations for the legislative integration. On the whole, the timing to promote the legislative integration of economic law is more mature than before.

How to grasp the legislative timing has always been a complex issue. Savigny has argued that as long as the laws of a nation are undergoing positive evolution, there is no need to formulate a code, even if there is the most suitable condition for codification.[35] In the case of the laws of China, especially economic law, are they still going through positive evolution? Can we promote the legislative integration of the currently evolving laws? These important questions about the timing of legislation need to be further examined by the academic community.

---

[33]China has introduced a large number of normative documents that concern the economic law systems for fiscal, tax, finance, industry, investment and competition. Therefore, the above-mentioned comprehensive reforms actually involve the integration of a large scale of economic law systems.

[34]China has formed a pilot model in the realm of tax legislation and even in the entire realm of economic legislation. Zhang (2013b), Issue 4.

[35]Zhang (1993), p. 210.

6.1.4 Conclusion

The legislative integration of economic law is a process. With a view to the direction of legal system changes, the realization of system functions and effective academic accumulation, there are both need and necessity to promote the legislative integration of economic law. In terms of legislative model, legislative form, legislative content and legislative timing, there are multiple possibilities or options for legislative integration. In response to the above needs, how to make effective choices amid various possibilities is a great test for both legislators and researchers. Owing to the above needs and possibilities, various factors shall be taken into account in the legislative integration, and the reasonable factors contained in different "-isms" or "dimensions" shall be integrated, so as to make the legislative integration more comprehensive and integrated. To this end, legislators and researchers need to have historical attainments and systematic vision.[36]

Legislative integration can be divided into different levels and realms, and not all of the legislative integration is high-level "codification". Therefore, we have to study different types of legislative integration to satisfy the need of different domains, so that the legislative integration of economic law not only meets the national conditions, but also keeps improving the quality and level of legislation, thereby providing more guarantee for law enforcement and justice.

In this sense, continuously promoting high-quality legislative integration remains "the contemporary mission of legislation and legal science".[37] It is self-evident that legislative integration is the contemporary mission of legislation. Why is it also an important mission of legal science, especially science of economic law? It is at least because the process of legislative integration is involved with many important economic law theories, such as system theory, origin theory, purpose theory, object theory, principle theory, subject theory, behavioral theory, right-duty theory, responsibility theory, procedure theory and legislative theory. Economic law is ought to provide important theoretical support for legislative integration, and its theoretical consensus is fairly important for achieving the goal of legislative integration. Therefore, solving many theoretical problems of legislative integration is itself an important task or mission of economic law study.

In addition, since the legislative integration are examined in the dimensions of legal system changes and function realization, the afore-mentioned "historical attainments" and "systematic vision" need to be manifested in research methods. Among them, it is natural for the historical analysis method, the systematic analysis method (esp. the structural function analysis method) and the comparative analysis method to become the important methods for the legislative integration. According to this, the comparative analysis and the comprehensive consideration of ancient and modern

---

[36] According to Savigny, jurists shall possess two indispensable qualities, i.e., historical attainments and systematic vision. They are particularly important for both the jurists and the legislative integration of economic law. Savigny (2001b), p. 37.

[37] The English title of Savigny's book *Vom Beruf unserer Zeit für Gesetzgebung und Rechtswissenschaft.*

times and in China and foreign countries shall run through the process of economic law legislation integration.

Legislative integration is indispensable in any great era. There are the *French Civil Code* in the times of free competition and the *German Civil Code* in the period transiting from free competition to monopoly, both of them are important models of legislative integration. In the modern times featuring poor government functions, the civil code had been the focus of legislative integration. However, along with the establishment and development of a modern market economy system, the state economic functions have become increasingly prominent, it is more necessary to strengthen the legislative integration of economic law, and introduce the *Economic Code* in the future when the conditions are mature enough, which is able to manifest the great progress in the system civilization of human society.

6.2 The "Pilot Model" of Economic Legislation

Since the reform and opening-up, China has increased attention to economic legislation, and achieved notable progress despite of some remaining gaps and omissions. In economic legislation, tax legislation is extremely important and highly representative.[38] In the foreign-related domain, the income tax legislation, which is the earliest economic legislation after the reform and opening-up, has laid an important foundation for China's taxation rule of law and the overall economic rule of law.[39] Moreover, the large-scale economic legislation in each development cycle is led by the tax legislation. Although China has already built a basic framework for tax legislation, the current tax law system is not rational and perfect enough.[40] Therefore, we still need to probe into the issues of tax legislation, which will greatly promote the overall economic legislation.

With a view to China's legislative process since the reform and opening-up, we can find that the country has been attaching great importance to the "pilot" of legislation, which is an important feature of China's tax legislation. For example, in the early days of the reform and opening-up, the State Council introduced several tax regulations

[38] China's reform and opening-up and economic legislation were unfolded almost at the same time, and they have maintained positive interaction since then. The tax legislation, as the earliest economic legislation since the reform and opening-up, is highly valued for its significant role. Whenever the reform is deepened or the macro-economic control is implemented, it directly has something to do with tax legislation.

[39] After the reform and opening-up, China enacted the *Individual Income Tax Law* (1980) and the *Income Tax Law for Foreign Enterprise* (1981) which are the earliest laws in economic legislation. Moreover, these two tax law, which were passed by the national legislature, are superordinate to the later temporary tax regulations.

[40] Although the National People's Congress already announced that China has formed its legal system, there is only a basic framework for tax legislation, since lots of important laws are not introduced, and the legislative structure is still being improved.

(drafts) for "trial".[41] With the deepening of the reform and opening-up, many tax regulations are no longer in "trial", but they are still "provisional".[42] In recent years, China carried out the "pilot tax reform" in the realms of VAT, real estate tax and resource tax, in this process any adjustment of tax elements or the reform of tax collection and management shall go through the legislative procedure. Therefore, the above-mentioned "pilot tax reform" is essentially "legislative pilot". The long-term, large-scale and frequent legislative pilots, as a common and important phenomenon in the realm of tax legislation in China, are worthy of attention and research.

In fact, "pilot goes first" or "prior to carry and try", as a mindset of Chinese legislators, has been widely applied in many legislative realms and formed a "pilot model". The legislature has many considerations when making the "pilot" decisions, for example, the legislative experiences from the "pilot" in some areas help to identify the design defects in the existing system, which will guide the system improvement and reduce the implementation cost. Such considerations are somewhat reasonable, and thought to be "scientific" since they are similar with the famous scientific philosopher Karl Popper's "trial-and-error approach". Therefore, "pilot before promotion" has become an important path for China to build and improve its systems.

In order to carry out the legislative "pilot", we shall firstly identify which domains are ought to or able to be "piloted", and whether the "pilot" can solve the above issues concerned by lawmakers, thereby truly improving the defective system and reducing the rule-of-law cost. If a legislative "pilot" does not help to improve the system, but increase cost and cause new confusions, it is no doubt undesirable.

More than that, the "pilot" shall take account of the basis, feasibility, necessity and rationality, and pay attention to the value goals of equity and efficiency. If the "pilot" does not have sufficient legal basis, or it may affect the equity between the relevant subjects and the efficiency of the system operation, then it should not be carried out. Accordingly, the specific tax legislation "pilot" shall conform to the statutory principle, fairness principle and efficiency principle, which are important criteria for testing its legitimacy, rationality and necessity. Besides, these principles or criteria are also an important dimension for studying the "pilot model" in tax legislation.

As the primary tax in China, VAT has important and typical significance. The following subsection will, with the VAT legislation pilot as an example, discuss the legitimacy and rationality of the "pilot model" in tax legislation, and reveal its

---

[41]On September 18, 1984, the State Council approved the Ministry of Finance's *Provisional Measures for the Second Step in Replacing the Profit Delivery of State-owned Enterprises by Taxes*, and issued relevant tax regulations (drafts) according to the authorized legislative decision of the NPC Standing Committee made in 1984. These regulations (drafts) were made up of the *Product Tax Regulations (Draft)*, *Value Added Tax Regulations (Draft)*, *Business Tax Regulations (Draft)*, *Salt Tax Regulations (Draft)*, *Resource Tax Regulations (Draft)*, and *State-owned Enterprise Income Tax Regulations (Draft)*.

[42]In accordance with the NPC's authorized legislative decision in 1985, the State Council formulated and implemented a series of provisional tax regulations, thus ending the trial of tax "regulations (drafts)". Currently, most of China's tax laws are actually the "provisional regulations" on taxation formulated by the State Council.

pros and cons, so as to promote the improvement of the overall tax legislation and economic legislation.

6.2.1 "Pilot" VAT System

As the foremost tax, VAT is levied in a wide range, not only covering the sales of goods, the provision of taxable labor services, the imports and exports, but "extending its scope" through legislative "pilot". Since VAT income has been accounting for more than one-third of China's entire tax revenue, it has a huge impact on the taxation and wealth distribution of the state and the national, so the rationality and stability of VAT legislation is of great importance, but China's VAT system has remained in "pilot". The following content examines the legal issues in the pilot process of VAT legislation, in an aim to reveal the common problems existing in the "pilot model" of tax legislation through this typical example.

In view of the development course of the VAT system in China, the product economy remained strong in the early days of the reform and opening-up. The industrial and commercial tax or product tax occupied a prominent position. As a substitute tax for product tax in the future, the VAT just sprouted at that time. In order to solve the problem of double taxation resulting from the collection of product tax, the then economic departments carried out a "pilot program" of VAT in certain industries.[43] Considering that the State Council did not have tax legislative power, the Standing Committee of the NPC made a decision on September 18, 1984 to authorize the State Council to "draft relevant tax regulations in the process of replacing the profit delivery of state-owned enterprises by taxes and reforming the industrial and commercial tax system, issue the draft regulations for trial implementation, and then revise them based on the trial experience, and submit them to the Standing Committee of the NPC for deliberation".[44] Accordingly, the State Council promulgated the *Regulations on Value-added Tax (Draft)*[45] on the day of obtaining the authorization, and put them into "trial" for ten years until the State Council

[43]In Mar 1980, the SAT and the MOF investigated the VAT calculation in Liuzhou City and then started the VAT system design, and later carried out the VAT pilot programs the machinery industries in Liuzhou and Shanghai. From 1981 to 1982, the MOF successively selected two industries (machinery and agricultural equipment) and three products (sewing machine, bicycles and electric fans) to implement the VAT pilot program, and issued the *Provisional Measures on Value-added Tax*. China Taxation News, *The establishment and development of China's VAT system*, Dec 25, 2012.

[44]The *Decision of the Standing Committee of the NPC on Authorizing the State Council to Reform the Industrial and Commercial Tax System and Issuing the Draft Tax Regulations for Trial*, which was adopted on Sep 18, 1984.

[45]According to the regulations (draft), the VAT taxpayers include the units and individuals that produce and import taxable products within the territory of China; the tax items are divided into two categories as "A" and "B", there are 12 tax items, including machinery, automobiles, agricultural equipment, steel, bicycles, sewing machine and electric fans, with the tax rates ranging from 6 to 16%. In the later trial process, the MOF successively issued a series of documents on expanding

introduced the *Provisional Regulations* on *Value-added Tax* in 1993. Although the *Provisional Regulations* were no longer in "trial" as a draft, the VAT system has kept changing—a large number of normative documents developed by the Ministry of Finance (MOF) and the State Administration of Taxation (SAT), which were for the purpose of making up for the omissions, have made the *Provisional Regulations* out of recognition and exist in name only. By the start of the 21st century, the VAT system had become relatively mature and stable, but the "transitional pilot" aimed at transforming the "production-oriented" VAT to the "consumption-based" VAT was implemented in the northeastern China in 2004 and gradually spread to the central region, and finally promoted all over the country in 2009 under the pressure of the financial crisis. By that time, the call to upgrade the *Provisional Regulations* on *Value-added Tax* to a "law" was increasingly louder. However, before the VAT legislation was upgraded to a higher level, some new pilot programs were put in place: since 2012 China implemented a pilot program of replacing business tax to VAT in Shanghai, and then introduced the pilot program in Beijing and other provinces and cities (also known as the "expanding pilot"), this pilot has become the focus of entire tax system reform during the "12th Five-Year Plan" period (2011–2015).

Through a brief review of the "pilot" VAT legislation, we can find that the VAT system has remained in "trial" and gone through constant changes. There are many objective reasons for this situation, such as the diversified and complicated of socio-economic relations, and the continuous changes in the economic system (from a planned economy to a planned commodity economy, and finally to a market economy), which force the tax law system to be adjusted to adapt to the economic system changes. Moreover, there are also many subjective reasons, e.g., legislators fail to thoroughly understand the VAT principles and the corresponding system, they are not fully aware of the trend and speed of the national economic and social development, and their legislative skills and capabilities need to be greatly improved. Nevertheless, from an ought-to-be perspective, VAT features an "integrated chain", which means that the VAT system is ought to be universally applicable throughout the country, so the "pilot" VAT system must be stabilized and applied across the country to directly affect the overall economic development.

The changes on the VAT system have never stopped, which will affect the ought-to-be legal stability and universality of tax laws.[46] How to achieve a proper balance and coordination between stability and variability is especially important for the rule-of-law taxation.

In recent years, China has carried out pilot system reform in the domains such as real estate tax and resource tax.[47] In China, "pilot before promotion" is a common

the scope of VAT taxation, and gradually increased a total of 31 tax items such as chemical fiber, textiles and clothing, with tax rates ranging from 8 to 45%.

[46]Chinese legislators and scholars have been discussing the stability or universality of various tax laws, including the VAT system. Zhang (2001), Issue 5.

[47]In recent years, China has been relying on the "pilot model" in promoting tax legislation. In addition to the "expanding pilots" of VAT in Beijing and Shanghai, there are also pilot real estate tax in Shanghai and Chongqing, pilot resource tax in Xinjiang, and pilot environmental tax in Hubei.

practice for carrying out any economic reform and economic legislation. The rationality of this "pilot model" is due to the limitation of human reasoning, especially because the government is inexperienced in economic management, and legislators are not fully aware of the principles, techniques and effects of economic legislation. At the beginning of the reform, due to lack of experience in economic transition, institutional change and top-level design, and relatively inadequate economic theory and rule-of-law theory, it is necessary to adopt the "pilot first" approach. However, after considerable progress is made in the market economy and legal system construction, there are available experiences from developed market economies and emerging market economies, as well as abundant domestic experiences, should we continue implementing the "pilot model"? Should the "pilot program" remain in a large scale? Is the "pilot model" legitimate? How about its impact on efficiency and equity? These issues are worth studying. The following content will take the "pilot" VAT legislation as an example to unfold the discussion.

6.2.2 Legitimacy of the "Pilot" Legislation

No matter which kind of legislation is "piloted", it must be "legally based", which directly concerns the legitimacy and validity of the legislation; the legitimacy and validity of the behavior of authorization when there is need for legislative authorization; as well as the stability and variability of legislation.[48]

As mentioned earlier, China's VAT legislation has been in a "trial" state. At the beginning of the reform and opening-up, the national economic departments came to notice the drawbacks of repeated taxation of industrial and commercial tax, so they thought about introducing the French VAT system and carrying out some VAT pilot programs in certain industries in a few cities. In order to ensure the legitimacy of the reform of the industrial and commercial tax system led by the State Council, the Standing Committee of the NPC passed an "authorization decision" on September 18, 1984 to ratify the State Council's reform plan; on this basis, the State Council issued six "regulations (drafts)" for trial, including the *Regulations on Value-added Tax* (draft), thereby making the VAT legislation legitimate, at least in a legitimate form.

While the *Regulations on Value-added Tax* (draft) were in trail, the State Council gradually expanded the scope of VAT collection from the original 12 tax items to 31. Regarding such "expansion", the State Council neither followed the 1984 Authorization Decision to revise the *Regulations* nor followed the 1985 Authorization Decision to formulate the "provisional regulations", thus making the legitimacy of such "expansion" questionable.

As replacement, improvement and supplement to the *Regulations on Value-added Tax* (draft), the *Provisional Regulations on Value-added Tax* formulated by the State

[48]Owing to its multiple functions, such as income distribution and macro-economic control, the variability of tax law is worthy of attention. Zhang (2002), Issue 6.

Council came into effect in 1994, and its legislative basis is generally considered to be the 1985 Authorization Decision, the core content of which is that the NPC "authorizes the State Council to work out the provisional rules or regulations on the issues related to the economic system reform and opening up to the outside world when necessary and according to the Constitution, provided that these rules or regulations do not conflict with the relevant laws and the basic principles of the relevant decisions of the National People's Congress and its Standing Committee"[49]; only on this basis can its legitimacy could be ensured to a certain extent.

However, if the 1985 Authorization Decision is used as the legislative basis for the *Provisional Regulations on Value-added Tax*, then the regulations shall comply with the restrictions set by the NPC on the legislative scope, necessity and legitimacy; otherwise, the legislative basis or legitimacy of the regulations remains questionable. Some doubts need to be clarified to respond to the above restrictions: Is the VAT legislation a matter of economic reform and opening up? Is it necessary for the State Council to dominate the VAT legislation? Does the State Council's VAT legislation and laws conflict with the basic principles of the relevant decisions of the national legislature?

If the "economic system reform and opening up" is broadly interpreted, it will be understandable to include the tax reform and related tax legislation into the State Council's legislative domain according to the "authorization decision", which explains why people have not delved into the legitimacy of the State Council's tax regulations. But strictly speaking, the NPC's "authorization decision" should be explicit, specific and time-bound, rather than vague, overly broad and indefinite; otherwise it may seem like "blank authorization". In fact, in the NPC's "authorization decision", the terms or expressions as "the issues related to the economic system reform and opening up" and "if necessary" are relatively broad and vague,[50] thus giving the State Council a great legislative space, and leading to a large number of "provisional regulations" in all domains. Although the legal system construction of China was speeding up in the short term, it is worth pondering whether the "authorization decision" itself is appropriate.

In addition, the "authorization decision" requires to "abiding by the Constitution" and not conflicting with the laws, but pays little attention to the issue whether the State Council's tax legislation violates the laws and their basic principles. According to the provisions of Article 8 of the *Legislation Law of China*, pursuant to the statutory

---

[49]On Apr 10, 1985, the *Decision on Authorizing the State Council to Formulate Provisional Rules or Regulations on the Economic System Reform and Opening up to the Outside World* was adopted at the 3rd Session of the Sixth National People's Congress.

[50]Similarly, Article 1 (8) of the *US Constitution* grants the Congress the power to tax, spend, regulate international trade and interstate commerce, and authorizes the Congress "to enact all necessary and appropriate laws to implement these powers"; however, the terms "necessary" and "appropriate" are controversial due to their ambiguity. Through the constant constitutional interpretations of Justice Marshall and others legislators, the power of the federal government has been continuously expanded. It can be seen that there may be problems of vagueness no matter the legislation is authorized by the Constitution or the legislature, but the authorized subjects in China and the US are greatly different. Zhang (2011), pp. 95–103.

taxation principle, all the basic taxation systems or the basic taxation elements should observe the "legal reservation" principle, and all the tax laws are formulated on this basis. With regard to the VAT legislation, it is ought to be upgraded to a higher level upon years' pilot experiences and rich experiences in other countries.

Based on above-mentioned multiple factors, the national legislature shall come up with VAT laws as soon as possible, instead of continuing adhering to the 1985 Authorization Decision in the long run, and no longer relying on the state administrative organs as the subjects of tax legislation. Regardless of the "transitional pilots" or "expanding pilots" of VAT legislation, they should not be a reason to delay the direct legislation of the NPC, which is required by the *Legislation Law* and the statutory taxation principle, and helpful to ensure the legitimacy of VAT legislation.

In accordance with the statutory taxation principle, all taxation elements shall be legally prescribed. Therefore, the adjustment of important taxation elements involved in each "pilot" VAT legislation shall be strictly statutory. In fact, no matter it was the "pilot collection" of VAT in the wake of the reform and opening-up, or the "pilot implementation" of the *Regulations on Value-added Tax (draft)*, and the "pilot expansion" of VAT, all involve the changes in tax items and rates; the "pilot transition" of VAT involves the exercise of taxpayers' deduction right, which directly affects the adjustment of tax base. In short, any change or adjustment of the taxation elements shall strictly follow the statutory taxation principle to ensure the legitimacy of the "pilot programs".

For example, the "pilot expansion" expanded the scope of VAT taxation, which has directly affected the tax structure based on the dual division of "goods and services"; at the same time, as a cross-tax systematic adjustment, the "pilot expansion" not only affects the business tax, but also the surcharges such as urban construction tax, which concerns the implications of VAT and the effectiveness of the VAT system. Therefore, we shall attach great importance to the legitimacy of the "pilot expansion".

Of course, the "pilot transition" of VAT also concerns the adjustment of tax bases and tax rates, which has a significant impact on taxpayers' physical rights and interests. Moreover, the inclusion of some tax items of the business tax into the VAT had alleviated the tax burden, so the "pilot transition" of VAT has been taken as a major move in the "structural tax reduction". However, whether it is the "structural tax reduction" or other tax control measures, its legitimacy is usually overlooked. This is a prominent and long-standing problem in China's tax law realm. Given this, we need to seriously address this situation from the perspective of construction of a law-based government.

In short, from the product economy to the commodity economy to the market economy, China's VAT system has been in "trial", far from the requirements of statutory taxation principle, and seriously affects the stability of the system. Although the changes in economic structure and systems have generated a large number of new transaction behaviors which are becoming increasingly complex, providing an important basis for the collection of VAT, they also have made the VAT system keep changing and show a prominent "variability".[51] As such, it is important to strengthen the balance and coordination between the stability and variability of the tax law system. Even if the tax laws do not have a higher degree of "stability" like some traditional laws, they shall be relatively stable at least. The VAT is the primary tax, its system changes directly concern the operational freedom of enterprises and the property rights of citizens. Therefore, it is necessary to ensure its basic stability and predictability, as well as the more important "certainty" based on stability.[52]

Another problem also deserves attention. According to the 1985 Authorization Decision, "the regulations that are tested by practice during their implement shall be enacted by the National People's Congress or its Standing Committee when conditions are available", i.e., the statutory taxation principle remains to be observed. However, we had been concerning the "authorization" in the past, instead of the ultimate legislative power and ultimate responsibility undertaken by the legislature. Therefore, it is necessary to correct the biased understanding of the "authorization decision". From the perspective of ensuring legitimacy, the NPC and its Standing Committee shall assume the responsibility of "enacting laws" and upgrade the VAT legislative level.

6.2.3 Equity in the "Pilot" Legislation

The "pilot" VAT legislation concerns not only the issue of legitimacy, but also the more perceptible issue of fairness. In fact, most types of "pilot" legislation are system changes targeting at some problems about unfairness. For example, the "transitional pilot" of VAT is to solve the unfair deduction, and the "expanding pilot" is to solve repeated taxation or unfair tax burden[53]; while the pilot reform of the real estate tax is to solve the unfair distribution of income or real estate resources.[54] Since various types of "pilot" legislation are associated with fair value and designed to solve some unfair problems, the "pilot" legislation has gained a certain degree of rationality.

---

[51]For example, after the establishment of the market economy system, although the *Provisional Regulations on Value-added Tax* and its *Rules for Implementation* already set out many specific provisions, the fiscal and taxation departments still had to issue a large number of normative documents to make up for their deficiencies, which is due to the complicated economic activities, and at the same time shows the "variability" of the VAT system.

[52]Nowadays, it is fairly important to increase the certainty of tax laws. According to Hayek, although increasing "certainty" is the purpose of the law, what the law eradicates are only some sources of uncertainty. Hayek (2000), p. 213.

[53]On Nov 16, 2011, the MOF and the SAT issued the *Pilot Program for the Replacement of Business Tax with VAT*, which emphasizes to "regulate the tax system to make tax burden reasonable" and "basically eliminate repeated taxation".

[54]The *Provisional Measures on the Pilot Collection of Real Estate Tax on Certain Personal Housing*, which were implemented by both Shanghai and Chongqing municipalities as of Jan 28, 2011, aim at "adjust income distribution, guide housing consumption, and effectively allocate real estate resources".

The important goal of each country's VAT system is to solve the unfairness caused by repeated taxation. As a typical "neutral" tax, VAT should not bring additional profits or losses to taxpayers. However, due to various reasons, the above-mentioned principles are not fully reflected in the system, which has resulted in system unfairness. In view of this, whether it is a comprehensive revision of the law in one step or progressive "pilot" legislation, we should earnestly implement the principle of fairness. In addition, the unfairness that may be caused by the "pilot" legislation and the limitations in solving the unfairness are prone to be overlooked. As such, particular attention should be paid to the following issues in the pilot VAT legislation:

(1) "Pilot" legislation may lead to new problems of unfairness. Each type of "pilot" legislation is "tested" on a local "point', which may contradict the "universal" principle. Due to the particularity of applicable laws, the "pilot" in certain regions or industries sometimes forms the so-called "depression effect", which directly affects the interests of different subjects in different regions and industries, and also affects the realization of value of fairness. For example, from the perspective of substantive fairness, the "transitional pilot" of VAT in northeastern China in 2004 was necessary, though it did not involve many industries or a large amount of tax revenue, it caused differences from other regions and industries, and made them feel a bit "unfair", that's one of the important reasons why China extended the pilot program to the central region and even the whole country. In addition, a more "universal" VAT system is more helpful to resolve repeated taxation and more helpful to safeguard fairness, while the "pilot" VAT system in certain industries or regions will not solve the repeated taxation, but may trigger the new problems of unfairness. For example, in the process of "expanding" the scope of VAT, the discontinuous taxation chain in some industries has caused unfair tax burden to taxpayers, such problems deserve our special attention.

(2) "Pilot" legislation cannot solve the problem of unfair tax burdens upon different types of taxpayers. The scope of VAT is huge, and taxpayers are in wide variety. As an "impersonal tax", VAT does not care about the differences and fairness between subjects like the "personal tax". Therefore, no matter how the "pilot" legislation is implemented, it cannot resolve the differences caused by the diversified subjects and the unfairness in the design and implementation of the VAT system.[55] For example, with regard to the special VAT invoices, specific deduction criteria and actual tax burdens, general taxpayers and small-scale taxpayers are treated differently. Despite of the "Pareto improvement" in legislation, the treatment and status of taxpayers in tax laws are yet unified. No matter it is the "transitional pilot" or the "expanding pilot", the VAT system cannot resolve the unfair tax burden of taxpayers caused by their different status. Although the VAT is "neutral" or "undifferentiated", the differences between taxpayers themselves and the system design will result in differences in the rights and tax burdens of taxpayers, and lead to vertical unfairness.

[55] In the pilot process of "business tax-to-VAT", a common phenomenon is that the taxpayers, with organic composition of capital relatively low, may find their tax burden increasing. The increasing tax burden of logistics enterprises is an example in this regard.

(3) "Pilot" legislation is difficult to solve the unfair distribution of tax revenue. On the one hand, as a commodity tax, VAT is closely related to the place where the goods are sold,[56] i.e., territorial jurisdiction is highlighted, and is therefore directly related to local tax revenue. On the other hand, VAT is a typical shared tax, it concerns the central tax revenue, so the fair distribution of tax revenue is of great significance. As a matter of fact, the idea of "business tax-to-VAT" was brought forth a long time ago, but put aside for a long time only because it affects local core interests. Therefore, the state specially emphasizes not to affect the local tax revenue when "expanding the scope of VAT collection".[57] As long as there is interest disparity between the central and local governments, there will be "permanent differences" in the interests represented by the two levels of taxation organs.

The "pilot" VAT legislation involves many fairness issues, and sometimes brings about new unfairness issues. Among them, the unfairness between pilot and non-pilot regions or industries deviates from the "unification of the rule of law" and "unification of the tax system" required by the market economy, and affects the fair competition between enterprises. We must spare no effort to solve this problem.

6.2.4 *Efficiency of the "Pilot" Legislation*

In addition to the issues of legitimacy and fairness, various types of "pilot" tax legislation also involve efficiency issues. For example, the "pilot" real estate tax legislation in Shanghai and Chongqing municipalities is designed to promote the healthy development of the real estate market, and prevent the economic overheating and the bubble bursts from affecting the overall economic efficiency; the "pilot" offshore duty-free policy in Hainan Province tries to stimulate domestic demand[58] to raise economic efficiency. From the dimension of efficiency, all types of "pilot" legislation shall abide by the principles of economic efficiency and administrative efficiency.

According to the principle of economic efficiency, the "pilot" VAT legislation is ought to promote economic development. In fact, no matter it is an "expanding pilot" to prevent or reduce repeated taxation, or a "transitional pilot" to expand the scope

---

[56]Fikentscher argues that whether a certain tax can be levied depends on the connection point in tax law. The place of sale is an important connection point for exercising tax jurisdiction over VAT and other types of sales taxes. Fikentscher (2010), p. 32.

[57]According to the *Pilot Program for the Replacement of Business Tax with an VAT*, the existing fiscal system shall maintain basically stable during the pilot period; the VAT that replaces the former business tax will remain ascribed to the pilot region, and all types of VAT revenue will be stored separately; any reduction of tax revenue arising from pilot VAT is borne by the central and local governments in accordance with the current fiscal system. In this way, there will be no additional impact on local tax revenue.

[58]Refer to the *Announcement of the Ministry of Finance on Piloting the Offshore Duty-free Shopping Policy in Hainan Province* ([2011] No. 14) released in March 2011, and the *Announcement of the Ministry of Finance on Adjusting the Offshore Duty-free Shopping Policy in Hainan Province* ([2012] No. 73) released in October 2012.

of tax deduction, the main goal is to stimulate the vitality of enterprises, raise the efficiency of economic operations, and promote the economic development. In this sense, both the above two types of "pilot" are in line with the principle of economic efficiency.

In addition, the "expanding pilot" of VAT, as a typical indirect tax, reduces the tax burden of some subjects that were used to paying business tax; it will exert a certain impact on prices and on the subjects that ultimately bear the tax burden, alleviate the pressure on enterprises and residents on the whole, and promote the economic development, thereby demonstrating its compliance with the principle of economic efficiency.

As required by the principle of administrative efficiency, the "pilot" legislation should reduce the tax collection cost of taxation authorities or the compliance cost of taxpayers as much as possible, since these costs are ultimately borne by taxpayers. Any increase in taxation cost not only reflects the low administrative efficiency of taxation authorities, but increases the burden on taxpayers and then affects economic efficiency. In addition, we shall also pay attention to the taxation cost of the entire tax system, especially the coordination cost between taxation authorities.[59]

For example, the "expanding pilot" directly involves the coordination between two levels of taxation authorities (Shanghai is the only area in China that has one level of taxation authority). In this regard, by following the principle of efficiency and from the cost-benefit perspective, we shall take full account of the coordination or restructuring cost, especially the rationality of the two levels of taxation authorities (both national and local). As we all know, without the two levels of taxation authorities, all the relevant costs will be reduced accordingly, including the tax collection cost of taxation authorities, the compliance cost of taxpayers, as well as the coordination or restructuring cost. If the two levels of authorities are combined into one, as long as there are reasonable institutional arrangements and explicit provisions for tax power, tax category and tax revenue, the revenue distribution between the central and local governments can be properly handled. In other words, with the two levels of taxation authorities, stable institutional arrangements are still indispensable to ensure the reasonable tax revenue distribution between the central and local governments. If the tax revenue obtained by local governments is not enough to support its performance of powers or functions, it will undoubtedly increase the local fiscal pressure, and generate the intractable problems of "land finance", "charging finance" or other "non-tax revenue finance". Therefore, the key solution is that the tax revenue distribution shall be reasonable and the government functions shall be genuinely transformed. The establishment of tax authorities cannot address all problems; we have to optimize the allocation of tax power, which is the permanent cure to straighten out the relations between various "systems".

[59] Kasper and Streit (2000), p. 152–56.

6.2.5 Further Thinking on the "Pilot Model" of Legislation

Legitimacy, fairness and efficiency involved in the "pilot" VAT legislation are common issues in all types of tax legislation and even in the entire economic legislation. To properly deal with these issues, we shall adhere to the three basic principles of statutory, fairness and efficiency. Since the "pilot" VAT legislation is fairly typical, the issues involved are of reference value for studying the "pilot" economic legislation as a whole. Based on the previous analysis, in the process of implementing the "pilot" economic legislation in China, we need further speculation on the following issues:

(1) The "pilot" legislation shall pay attention to legitimacy at multiple levels.

Legitimacy shall be maintained for either conventional economic legislation or "pilot" legislation as a reform exploration. The previous discussions on the legitimacy of the "pilot" VAT legislation have shown the common problems in tax legislation and the entire economic legislation. China has been in the process of reform and transition for quite a long time. If the 1985 Authorization Decision remains effective, then the "approval of the State Council", either substantive or formal, will be easier to lead to "pilot" legislation or "amendments to laws" on most categories of tax. Such practice has been criticized for lack of legitimacy. Consequently, the legitimacy of the 1985 Authorization Decision as a basis for "pilot" legislation is questioned. The above problems have a far-reaching impact on the seriousness and compliance of economic legislation and the development of economic rule of law.

The *Legislation Law of China* essentially specifies the powers and levels of economic legislation. Whether the "authorization decision" made at the beginning of the reform and opening-up should be abolished, and whether a deadline should be set for ending the transitional "authorized legislation", these issues are worth exploring. Considering the overall development trend, ambiguous and excessively broad authorization, or the need for strengthening the statutory principle or the "legal preservation" principle, we should think about abolishing the old-time "authorization decision" in due time.[60]

The "pilot" legislation covering multiple categories of tax aims at reforming the existing system, but it may sometimes overly concern about tax regulation and tax collection, while ignoring the operational freedom and protection of property rights. How to balance the relation between the two aspects has always been an important task of China in the construction of economic rule of law. Since the statutory principle of taxation elements fails to be strictly observed in practice, which is has been a common occurrence, we must emphasize the full compliance with the statutory taxation principle so as to better achieve the goal of economic rule of law.

[60]In recent years, many scholars have been making appeals to strengthen the legislative power of the NPC, and they are discussing the issues about authorized legislation and the violation of the statutory taxation principle. Zhang (1996), Issue 6.

While placing the emphasis on the legitimacy of the "pilot" economic legislation, we shall comply with the statutory principle for legislative basis and system adjustment, and in the meantime reiterate that the "pilot" legislation shall conform to the constitutional principles and protect the fundamental interests of citizens. To make sure of the higher-level legitimacy, the "pilot" economic legislation may neither harm the overall interests nor the long-term benefits of citizens; otherwise, it will lose its validity or legitimacy. According to this, the pilot reform of real estate tax should not only comply with the basic statutory principle, but do good to the overall and long-term interests of citizens, and also protect the private interests of taxpayers, which is of great significance for ensuring the effectiveness of economic legislation.[61]

(2) The "pilot" legislation shall take account of both fairness and efficiency.

Since the "pilot" economic legislation affects the national property rights and management rights, it may bring additional burdens to taxpayers and affect the fairness of taxation. At the same time, unfair economic legislation has a distortion effect, which will negatively impact efficiency. Therefore, good economic legislation shall pay attention to the close relation between the values of fairness and efficiency, balance their relation in system design, and strictly follow the principles of fairness and efficiency, so as to realize the relevant values of order and justice. In the process of performing the normative function and distribution function through economic legislation, we shall prevent the "pilot" legislation from bringing about new issues of unfairness, and work hard to achieve the "Pareto improvement" in efficiency.

In fact, whether it is fairness or efficiency, it is directly related to the fiscal system, taxation system and financial system in the economic domain. Therefore, the reasonable division of macro-economic control power and market regulation power, the reform and improvement of the economic system, are even more important for the "pilot" economic legislation.

(3) The future direction of the "pilot model".

In addition to the issues of legitimacy, fairness and efficiency in "pilot" legislation, we shall think about the following issues: Should we continue the widespread "pilot" model for economic legislation? How to look at the negative effects brought by the "pilot" programs? Are there any alternatives for replacing the "pilot" model?

As mentioned earlier, it was necessary and reasonable to implement the "pilot" legislation at the beginning of the reform and opening-up. However, China has so far accumulated rich experiences in legislation and in tax collection and administration, and it is able to learn about the relevant practices from other countries, is it still necessary to carry out the "pilot" legislation in such a frequent and extensive manner? This question is worth our reflection. In fact, if our prejudgments on the effects of legislation could be more accurate, then it would be no longer necessary to verify the legislation through any "pilot program"; moreover, an improper "pilot program" may infringe on the overall legislative pattern.

---

[61] Zhang (2012a), Issue 11.

Along with the development of the rule-of-law construction, and when definite principles and systems are available, we shall focus on the establishment of a stable institutional framework, instead of "trying" everything. For example, some people think that the "structural tax reduction" is a temporary measure to cope with the crisis, so it is fine with some "pilot" tax cuts. But from a legal perspective, no matter what the tax reduction is titled, it is a serious legal proposition concerning the basic rights of citizens such as property rights. Therefore, the "pilot program" for the "business tax to VAT"—though it is a major form of "structural tax reduction"—should not be promoted on a regular basis.

6.2.6 Conclusion

Economic legislation involves complex distribution of interests, a wide range of regulation, and greatly differentiated implementation environment. These factors have made the practice of "pilot before promotion" reasonable and widely implemented, thus forming a "pilot model" of economic legislation. Although the "pilot program" is usually carried out to address the problems in the existing system, we must pay attention to the possible lack of legitimacy and the negative impact on equity and efficiency in the "pilot" process. Therefore, it is necessary to admit and study the shortcomings of the pilot program or system design, as well as the defects of the "pilot model".

Considering the importance and typicality of the "pilot" VAT legislation, this section mainly analyzes the problems in this regard, and proposes the common issues that may be involved in various types of tax legislation and even in the "pilot" economic legislation, including the issue of legitimacy, and the issue of rationality in terms of fairness and efficiency. (1) In terms of legitimacy, we should pay special attention to the legitimacy of the "pilot" economic legislation in its legislative basis or specific system design and rights protection. It the realm of economic legislation, authorized legislation is the most prominent issue, the NPC's "authorization decision" should be abolished in due time, and relevant tax legislation should be carried out pursuant to the provisions of the *Legislation Law*. At the same time, the design of various specific systems must strictly follow the statutory principle. On this basis, we shall take account of the public benefit and the long-term interests of citizens, and protect the basic rights of market subjects. (2) In terms of rationality, the rationality of the "pilot" economic legislation shall be reflected in the system improvement through the accumulation of experiences, and also in the integration of important values such as fairness and efficiency. On the basis of meeting the requirements of legitimacy, the "pilot" economic legislation shall try to solve the existing unfairness problems as much as possible, and avoid bringing new unfairness problems; at the same time, economic and administrative efficiency shall be truly improved. For this reason, additional efforts shall be made to address the system issues in the domain of economy.

Based on the necessity and rationality of the "pilot model", we should pay particular attention to its possible shortcomings, and consider the conditions and costs of the "pilot model". Generally speaking, when the economic and social development has made considerable achievements, and when the experiences in both legislation and economic management are constantly increasing, based on the rule-of-law spirit and unless it is particularly necessary, the "pilot" practice should be minimized and efforts should be made to eliminate possible institutional differences, achieve the unification of the basic legal system, and continuously improve the level of economic rule of law.

6.3 "Structural Tax Reduction" and Economic Rule of Law

6.3.1 Background and Issues

As an important means to cope with economic and political crises, the tax-cut measures are frequently and widely used in all countries.[62] After the 2008 financial crisis broke out, China had seen all kinds of costs remain high and people's livelihood under great pressure, the burden on enterprises was even heavier, which had directly affected its development right and competitiveness.[63] In this context, there was an urgent need to adjust the economic structure, reduce the national burden, and stimulate market vitality. Therefore, "moderate tax reduction" has become a consensus.

In order to promote the "moderate tax reduction", in recent years China has advocated "structural tax reduction",[64] i.e., the "tax cut targeting at specific subjects and specific domains to achieve specific purposes", which is different from the large-scale and parallel tax reduction, but differentiated "moderate tax reduction". The above generalization of "structural tax reduction" emphasizes the "specificity" or "peculiarity" of tax cut without paying particular attention to its "structural" characteristics. In fact, all tax reduction is related to the structure, which depends on the current tax law structure and affects the structural changes of the tax law itself. It also affects the macro-level economic structure, fiscal structure, tax structure and distribution

[62]After the financial crisis in 2008, the US, Germany, the UK, Japan, Australia and many other countries started cutting taxes. Among them, the *Emergency Economic Stabilization Act of 2008*, the *Energy Improvement and Extension Act of 2008*, and the *Tax Extenders and Alternative Minimum Tax Relief Act of 2008* introduced in the US involve tax cuts of more than US$100 billion, the impact was particularly huge.

[63]There are discussions on the direct relation between tax reduction and the economic development right of market subjects from the perspective of economic law. Zhang (2012b), Issue 2.

[64]Since the formal introduction of the "structural tax reduction" in 2009, China has taken it as an important means of solving economic and social problems, and has pay increasing attention to this means. Previously, the academic community has already paid attention to the "structural tax reduction", and some scholars argued to make it as a strategic choice. An and Wang (2004), Issue 11.

structure. But the studies on the above-mentioned impacts remain weak. Therefore, there is still a need for in-depth research on many "structural" issues arising from "structural tax reduction".[65]

The problems are much more than that. Most people usually study the "structural tax reduction" from an economic perspective, and focus on its policy, necessity and rationality, but fail to pay enough attention to the legitimacy of tax reduction from the perspective of law and jurisprudence, especially the subjects and power base of tax reduction, the protection of rights involved in tax reduction, and the due process of tax reduction, which have affected the legislation and effective implementation of "structural tax reduction". The important reason for these problems is the serious neglect of the foremost issue of tax reduction right.

In fact, the possession of tax reduction power is an important prerequisite for tax reduction; whether a tax cut is feasible and how to carry out a tax cut, it is constrained by the tax reduction right. The existence, size and strength of tax reduction power have a substantial impact on "structural tax reductions". Considering that the tax reduction power is a key factor affecting the "structural tax reductions", this section mainly analyzes the tax reduction power in the "structural tax reduction", in an attempt to examine the problems existing in China's economic rule of law and explore the ways to improve it.

In recent years, the research results on the basic theory of tax powers have been increasing, but the research on the tax reduction power, as a specific tax power, is still insufficient.[66] The discussion of tax reduction power, in particular, helps answer the questions such as the legitimacy of "structural tax reduction", thereby helping to enrich and develop the theory of tax powers, advancing the development of tax law theory and the taxation rule-of-law construction, deepening the economic law theory and refining the theory of economic rule of law, it is necessary to strengthen the research in this regard.

In view of this, this section analyzes and sorts out the specific path of "structural tax reduction" in combination with China's system practice, raises the issue of tax reduction power contained therein, emphasizes the statutory principle for tax reduction power and its impact on the adjustment of tax reduction elements, and discusses how to properly exercise the tax reduction power according to law, in order to respond to the issues about China's "structural tax reduction", including legitimacy, subjects and power exercise rules. On this basis, this section also contains a more specific analysis in combination with the tax reduction power involved in the reform of the VAT system, in order to reveal the economic rule-of-law issues in this regard.

---

[65] Some scholars have discussed the relation between "structural tax reduction" and the optimization of the tax system structure, showing that the "structural" issues involved in "structural tax reduction" have been recognized. An (2012), Issue 5.

[66] At present, the tax law scholars generally pay more attention to the three basic tax powers: tax legislative power, tax collection and management power, and tax revenue power; and there is no special and systematic research on the specific tax reduction power. In addition, some scholars dedicated to taxation studies have divided tax powers into tax legislative power, tax law enforcement power, and tax judicial power, which is different from the understanding of the tax law scholars. Xu (2003), p. 3.

Through the above analysis, this section attempts to show that "structural tax reduction" is not just a policy issue or an economic issue, but also a legal issue; "structural tax reduction" is inseparable from the adjustment of the tax law structure, it must be based on tax reduction power as provided for in the tax law and seriously solve the problems of illegal or improper exercise of tax reduction power in practice, so that "good governance" can be realized under the framework of economic rule of law.

6.3.2 Discussing Tax Reduction Power from the Perspective of "Structural Tax Reduction"

The academic community has different views on the connotation and origin of "structural tax reduction". Generally, people think that "structural tax reduction" is an important measure to deal with the 2008 financial crisis. However, if the "structural tax reduction" is based on the adjustment and improvement of the fiscal revenue and expenditure structure and the tax law structure, then we can say that after China entered the WTO and solved the problems of the "two declining proportions"[67] in the fiscal domain, it started the "structural tax reduction" since 2004.[68] This judgment is consistent with reality with a view to the changes in China's tax law structure and the "specificity" of "structural tax reduction". Therefore, an examination of the changes and specific path of China's tax law system since the beginning of this century, especially since 2004, will help to better discover the tax reduction power that is involved therein.

After China's accession to the WTO and with the further improvement of the market economy system, the growth rate of GDP, total imports and exports, and total fiscal revenue of China have become a global concern, but various structural problems affecting the macro-economy are becoming increasingly prominent. How to optimize the structure, especially by improving the structure of fiscal revenue and expenditure, and the tax law structure to ease the "pressure on people's livelihood", guarantee and improve people's living standard, enhance corporate competitiveness, and promote equity in social distribution? These problems are so imminent that

[67]China started the comprehensive implementation of the tax-sharing system and the large-scale tax law reform in 1994, an important reason for doing so was the declining proportion of fiscal revenue in GDP and the declining proportion of central fiscal revenue in overall fiscal revenue. The declining "two proportions" will seriously affect the country's macro-economic control ability and effective regulation. After the restructuring, the growth rate of China's tax revenue has been much higher than the GDP growth rate for many years. However, the problem of excessive tax burden on market subjects has caused widespread concern, and the calls for tax reduction have kept rising.

[68]The more clear-cut "structural tax reduction" pilot was mainly carried out in 2004, while some individual explorations may be started earlier. For example, as early as 2000, China suspended the imposition of adjustment tax on the fixed asset investment (the suspension of taxation is also a path of "structural tax reduction", which will be discussed later), but our understanding of "structural tax reduction" was not explicit enough.

directly affect the fulfillment China's objectives.[69] It is against this background, China has been adjusting and optimizing the tax structure, and implementing the substantial "structural tax reduction". There are two specific paths of "structural tax reduction": one is the overall adjustment of tax types, which is embodied in "abolition, suspension and merger" of certain tax types; the other one is the adjustment of the internal taxation elements of a certain tax type, which is embodied in the changes in taxation items, tax bases and tax rates.

6.3.2.1 Viewing Tax Teduction Power from the Perspective Overall Tax Type Adjustment

Based on the classification of tax types or tax categories, China's tax law system has long been composed of three tax types: industrial and commercial tax law, agricultural tax law, and the customs tariff law. It is related to the tax collection and management system in which tax authorities, financial institutions and customs co-exercise the tax powers (esp. the tax collection and management power), as well as multiple division criteria for industry, commerce and agriculture, and for domestic and foreign affairs. However, the multiple division criteria and the tax collection and management system have brought problems such as unclear definition of tax powers and irrational tax law structure, which need to be solved through adjustment of the tax powers of taxation subjects and the implementation of the "structural tax reduction". Since the agricultural tax law is a kind of domestic tax law, and in the broad agricultural tax system, agricultural tax and animal husbandry tax were abolished; at present, the only existing taxation subject for the arable land occupation tax and deed tax) is no longer the fiscal departments, but become the tax authorities,[70] thus making the original agricultural tax law has ceased to exist. Therefore, the tax law system should be under a more rigorous "binary division" into domestic tax law and "foreign-related tax law". In this way, through the "structural tax reduction" and the adjustment of tax collection and management power, China's tax law system and the structure of collection subjects have changed from "ternary" to "binary" (see the table below).

Changes in tax law system brought by "structural tax reduction"

The "ternary structure" of the original tax law system	The "binary structure" of the current tax law system	The "binary structure" of the current taxation subjects
Industrial and commercial tax law	Domestic tax law	Tax authorities
Agricultural tax law		

(continued)

[69]Tax cuts are very important to alleviate the "livelihood pressure". Zhang (2012c), Issue 5.

[70]According to the *Notice of the Ministry of Finance and the State Administration of Taxation on Accelerating the Transfer of the Functions for Collection and Management of Farmland Occupation Tax and Deed Tax from Local Fiscal Departments* (Caishui [2009] No. 37), which was released on Dec 31, 2009, the functions for collection and management of the two taxes will be transferred from local fiscal department to local tax authorities.

(continued)

The "ternary structure" of the original tax law system	The "binary structure" of the current tax law system	The "binary structure" of the current taxation subjects
Customs tariff law	Foreign-related tax law	Customs

In the process of transforming China's tax law system from "ternary structure" to "binary structure", a very important step is the abolition of agricultural tax and other taxes through "structural tax reduction". After the Central Government announced the exemption of agricultural tax in Heilongjiang and Jilin provinces in 2004, other provinces followed suit actively, and in the end, the Standing Committee of the NPC adopted the decision to abolish the regulations on agricultural tax, which was implemented as of January 1, 2006.[71] Whether the tax burden on farmers could be effectively reduced was questionable, it was indeed an important step in "structural tax reduction" and has promoted the adjustment and optimization of the tax law structure in general.[72] As for the power to abolish the agricultural tax, as a tax reduction power, how to properly exercise it or whether it has been properly exercised according to law is worth studying.

Of course, the "abolished" taxes in China are not limited to the agricultural tax, even the slaughter tax and feast tax that had been influential for some time were abolished. After the *Provisional Regulations on Slaughter Tax* was abolished in 2006,[73] the *Provisional Regulations on Feast Tax* was also repealed in early 2008.[74] These adjustments are based on economic and social factors, and also on the considerations of collection efficiency. For the subjects involved in the abolished tax types, the "tax reduction effects" is more prominent.

In addition, with regard to the specific paths of "structural tax reduction", China also "suspended collection" certain tax types, which reflects the spirit of tax reduction in another approach. For example, the adjustment tax for fixed-asset investment

[71]The *Decision of the Standing Committee of the National People's Congress on the Abolition of the Regulations of the People's Republic of China on Agricultural Tax* was adopted by the 19th Meeting of the Standing Committee of the Tenth NPC of China on Dec 29, 2005. The *Regulations of the People's Republic of China on Agricultural Tax*, adopted at the 96th Meeting of the Standing Committee of the First NPC on Jun 3, 1958, were about to be abolished as of Jan 1, 2006.

[72]Objectively speaking, the legislators at that time might not take it as an important step of "structural tax reduction", nor did they realize its significance for optimizing and improving the tax law structure. After all, the optimization or overall design of the tax law system had not received much attention at that time, and it was the most direct thinking at that time to solve the "three rural" issues and reduce the burden on farmers.

[73]According to the State Council Order No. 459, the *Provisional Regulations on Slaughter Tax*, which was issued by the then Government Administration Council (predecessor of the State Council) on Dec 19, 1950, was to be abolished as of Feb 17, 2006.

[74]On Jan 15, 2008, the State Council released the *Decision on the Abolishment of Certain Administrative Regulations*, stating that the *Provisional Regulations on Feast Tax* is to be abolished immediately, because the "the objects of adjustment have vanished and become invalid". But to be exact, such statement as "the objects of adjustment have vanished" is inaccurate.

was "suspended" in 2000.[75] To "suspend the tax collection", although it is abides by the principle of taxation efficiency and takes into account of the economic and social development in a given period, its effect as "administrative regulations" remained questionable, because there were no laws or administrative regulations on "suspended collection", but some documents containing such notes as "with the consent of the State Council" or "decisions of the State Council". After all, there are more stringent legislative requirements for the formulation of administrative regulations.[76] If a document issued by a functional department or a direct agency under the State Council contains the expression as "with the consent of the State Council", and then it becomes applicable across the country like administrative regulations, it not only violates the with existing rules, but largely deviates from the basic rule-of-law requirements. According to the theory of tax power, both the power to collect tax and the power to suspend tax are important tax legislative powers, implying that the exercise of the power to suspend taxation shall be based on tax legislation. At the same time, in accordance with current legal regulations, the suspension of taxation shall also comply with the law despite of any authorization by law, and there shall be relevant provisions in administrative regulations.[77] It can be seen that according to the current legal requirements, the provisions for the power to suspend collection cannot be lower than the level of administrative regulations in any case, and the basis for suspending the adjustment tax for fixed asset investment is flawed.

In addition to the abolition or suspension of certain taxes as mentioned above, China also "merged" some taxes. "Merging" is directly related to "abolition"; it is achieved by abolition of relevant taxes and regulatory documents for certain tax laws. Its main purpose is, mainly based on the principle of national treatment, to solve problems of the "two sets of tax laws" that are "differentiate domestic enterprises from foreign-related enterprises". For example, the existing enterprise income tax is "merged"[78] on basis of two income tax types, i.e., the income tax respectively levied upon domestic enterprises and foreign-related enterprises, similar to the "merger by new establishment". The prevailing property tax, vehicle and vessel tax, which are also formed by the original "domestic and foreign-related tax types" but

---

[75] According to the *Notice on the Suspending the Collection of the Adjustment Tax on the Fixed-assets Investment* issued by the MOF, the SAT and the National Development Planning Commission on Dec 17, 1999, the adjustment tax on the fixed-assets investment would be suspended as of Jan 1, 2000. According to the *Decision of the State Council on Amending and Abolishing Some Administrative Regulations* promulgated on Nov 9, 2012, the *Provisional Regulations of the People's Republic of China on Collection of the Adjustment Tax on the Fixed-assets Investment* was to be abolished as of Jan 1, 2013.

[76] The *Regulations on the Procedures for the Formulation of Administrative Regulations,* which came into effect as of Jan 1, 2002, set out strict provisions on the procedures for formulating administrative regulations.

[77] There are specified provisions in this regard in Article 3 of the *Law of the People's Republic of China on Tax Collection and Administration.*

[78] The two taxes are "enterprise income tax" and "income tax of enterprises with foreign investment and foreign enterprises". The unified *Law of the People's Republic of China on Enterprise Income Tax* was adopted by the 5th Session of the Tenth National People's Congress and put into effect as of Jan 1, 2008.

retain the original tax names and related systems, are more similar to "merger by absorption".[79] These "mergers" also have a direct impact on the tax law structure. Although the tax reduction effect is not as direct and prominent as the tax abolition and suspension, it still has a certain tax-cut effect on relevant subjects. After all, with the original "domestic and foreign-related tax types", the subjects paying taxes at different rates certainly have different tax burdens. By unifying the tax laws and "merging" tax types, it can cut the number of taxes in the tax system, and in the meantime adjust the tax rates according the "principle of the lower the better", so that the tax burden on certain subjects will be alleviated and thereby generating a "tax reduction effect". For example, in terms of enterprise income tax, although the statutory nominal tax rate of domestic-funded enterprises and foreign-related enterprises was 33% in the past, the actual tax burden on domestic enterprises was often higher than that on the foreign-related enterprises. Through unification of tax laws and "merger" of tax types, the nominal tax rate of domestic enterprises can be reduced to 25% at least or even lower, marking a kind of "tax reduction revenue" brought by the "merger" of tax types.

The specific paths for the above three types of tax reduction correspond to different spheres, and different subjects that exercise the tax reduction power. See the details in the table below:

Paths, tax types and exercising subjects of tax reduction

Specific path	Tax reduction sphere	Exercising subjects
Abolition	Agricultural tax (2006) Slaughter tax (2006) Feast tax (2008) Adjustment tax on fixed-assets investment (2013)	Standing Committee of the NPC State Council State Council State Council
Supension	Adjustment tax on fixed-assets investment (2000), then abolished in 2013	MOF, SAT, NDRC
Merger	Enterprise income tax (2008) House property tax (2009) Vehicle and vessel tax (2007)	NPC State Council State Council

The "abolition", "suspension" and "merger" of the above-mentioned tax types, as the specific paths of "structural tax reduction" in China, are in a decreasing order in the effect of tax reduction. Among them, the "abolition of taxes" has the most prominent effect on tax reduction, because it no longer levies taxes in a certain domain; the tax reduction effect of the "suspension of taxes" ranks the second, since it only stops the taxation for a certain period of time without abolishing any tax type; in the case of "merger of taxes", it abolishes a certain tax, but levies a new tax on the

[79]The urban real estate tax, vehicle and vessel license plate tax originally levied on foreign-related companies and foreign individuals were respectively replaced by the house property tax (Jan 1, 2009) and vehicle and vessel use tax (Jan 1, 2007, later renamed vehicle and vessel tax) which are levied on domestic enterprises, thus realizing the unification of house property tax and vehicle and vessel tax.

relevant subjects,[80] so the tax reduction effect depends on the taxation elements of the new tax type, but the tax burden on taxpayers tends to be alleviated along with the declining tax collection on the whole.

In addition, when analyzing the tax reduction effect, we shall not only focus on a specific tax type, but on the overall tax burden. For example, the tax reduction through the above-mentioned paths has alleviated the problem of the "tax system-based repeated taxation". Where there are multiple taxes imposed by the state, it will be more likely for the same subjects to be repeatedly taxed, so that the overall tax burden will also increase under the same conditions. Abolition and merger of relevant taxes and reduction of the number of taxes will help to reduce the "tax system-based repeated taxation", which will then ease the tax burden as a whole. Repeated taxation is an important cause of rising prices in China and increasing the burden on enterprises and residents, so alleviating and solving the problem of repeated taxation will not only have a tax reduction effect, but also help to solve the problem of "stagflation".

It is worth noting that the afore-mentioned "structural tax reduction" have different paths, and the subjects that exercise the tax reduction power are also different. There are three main types of subjects, i.e., the NPC and its Standing Committee, the State Council and its competent ministries and commissions, and the SAT. In terms of "abolition" of taxes (including the "abolition" for "merger"), the tax reduction legislative power is exercised by the NPC and its Standing Committee; In terms of "suspension" of taxes, the tax reduction legislative power is exercised by the State Council and its competent departments. The above arrangements have different degree of impact on the tax law structure. After all, the "abolition" or "merger" of taxes directly affect the system and structure of the tax law, and they have a greater impact on all aspects; while the "suspension of taxes" is under the premise of retaining the concerned taxes, so its impact is relatively small.[81]

Among the above types of exercising subjects, is the State Council exercising too much tax reduction power? Can the ministries and commissions of the State Council exercise the legislative power in tax reduction? These are important issues worthy of attention, and will be further discussed later.

---

[80]For example, the "income tax of enterprises with foreign investment and foreign enterprises" was abolished, but a new "enterprise income tax" was to be collected; the "urban real estate tax" upon foreign-related enterprises was abolished, but a new "house property tax" was to be collected; the "vehicle and vessel license plate tax" upon foreign-related enterprises was abolished, but a new "vehicle and vessel use tax" was to be collected.

[81]If certain taxes or tax items are "suspended", it is sure that they are inconsistent with the economic and social policies of a particular period, so the impact of the suspension is relatively small. In addition to the suspension of the adjustment tax on fixed-assets investment, the temporary exemption of "interest tax" is another example. According to the provisions of the *Law on Individual Income Tax*, the State Council decided to, starting from Oct 9, 2008, suspend the collection of the individual income tax on the savings deposit interest (including RMB and foreign currency savings interest income). Although this "decision" would slightly affect China's overall tax revenue, it was spoken highly by all sectors of society.

6.3.2.2 Viewing Tax Reduction Power from the Adjustment of Taxation Elements

The specific paths of "structural tax reduction" are not only reflected in the overall adjustment of tax types as mentioned above, but also in the adjustment of tax items, tax rates, tax bases, and tax incentives in a specific tax system. Among them, the tax reduction by adjusting preferential taxation measures is a generally concerned and familiar path for market subjects, while the tax reduction by adjusting tax items (e.g., tax items, tax rates, and tax bases) are less concerned, so it should be discussed separately.

In fact, there have been a large number of institutional practices to cut taxes by adjusting tax items. Generally, the adjustment of tax items is often by means of cancellation or change of a certain tax item within the same tax category. For example, in the domain of consumption tax, the "automobile tyre" tax had been levied for a long time in the past, but it would be ceased since 2006 to abide by the spirit of "structural tax reduction". In addition, the adjustment of tax items is sometimes reflected in cross-tax changes. For example, since January 1, 2012, China started a "pilot program" (or "expanding pilot") in Shanghai to replace business tax with VAT.[82] As a typical "structural tax reduction" measure implemented years ago, this "expanding pilot" was to incorporate some business tax items into the scope of VAT, so that the relevant industries (transportation and modern service industries) would no longer bear a heavy business tax burden, solve the problem of increased tax burden caused by repeated taxation in the domain of business tax, so as to achieve the purpose of "substantial tax reduction". The above-mentioned paths for "structural tax reduction" have positive significance for advancing the adjustment of economic structure and improving the tax law structure. However, it is worth studying which subjects are qualified to exercise the tax reduction power, such topic is discussed later in this section.

In the above two types of "tax item adjustments", tax item adjustments within the same tax category will affect the "breadth" of taxation. When the breadth of taxation is restricted, or the originally taxed tax item is cancelled or the tax burden is lightened. When tax items are replaced, there will be a tax reduction effect. For cross-tax adjustments, the tax reduction effect will be reflected under the influence of other tax rates, tax bases and other factors while the breadth of the original tax items remains unchanged.[83] It can be seen that when adjusting tax items, we must also pay attention to changes in factors such as tax rates and tax bases in order to fully examine its "tax reduction effect".

---

[82]In Nov 2011, with the consent of the State Council, the MOF and the SAT jointly issued the *Pilot Program for the Replacement of Business Tax with VAT*. According to this program, Shanghai began the pilot program on Jan 1, 2012; other provinces and cities including Beijing joined in this program since Aug 1, 2012. The same pilot program for transportation industry and some modern service industries was launched nationwide since Aug 1, 2013.

[83]For example, if the taxation items of the transportation industry that originally levied business tax were unchanged, if the value-added tax was changed (based on the new 11% tax rate), the actual tax burden of the relevant taxpayers would decrease.

Generally, the adjustment of tax rate directly affects the "depth" of taxation, and a reduction in tax rate can directly lead to the effect of tax reduction. Therefore, reducing tax rate is often an important tool for "structural tax reduction". For example, the afore-mentioned Enterprise Income Tax Law, which has been implemented in China since 2008, is to reduce the nominal tax rate that was generally applicable to domestic and foreign-funded enterprises from the original 33% to 25%.[84] Not only is the effect of tax reduction very obvious, but it is also in line with the trend in most countries around the world to improve corporate competitiveness by reducing income tax burdens. In addition, China's *Personal Income Tax Law* has been revised several times, and the minimum tax rate applicable to wage income has been reduced from 5 to 3%., Its tax reduction effect is also generally concerned. The above tax rate adjustments in the two major income tax areas involve the collection of direct taxes, and the effect of tax reduction is more direct. It is particularly helpful to protect and improve people's livelihood, promote economic recovery in the "post-crisis era", improve corporate competitiveness, and achieve equity competition. In fact, not only in the income tax field, similar tax rate adjustment measures are widely used in various tax fields. In view of the importance of adjusting the tax reduction right, it is necessary to ensure that it can be exercised properly according to law.

In addition to the above adjustments to tax items and rates, the adjustment of the tax base is also very important for tax reduction. For example, in the area of indirect taxes, in order to cope with the financial crisis, better reflect the "neutral" characteristics of VAT, reduce and prevent double taxation, and promote the transition from a "production-based VAT" to a "consumer-based VAT" Since January 1, 2009, China has expanded the scope of VAT deductions nationwide, lowered the VAT tax base, and comprehensively promoted tax reduction in the field of VAT. For another example, in the field of direct taxation, an important way for China to improve its personal income tax law is to continuously increase the deduction standard for wage income, so as to achieve the goal of tax reduction by reducing the tax base. However, as with the adjustment of the tax items and rates mentioned above, how the tax reduction right to adjust the tax base is exercised according to law is also worth studying.

In short, whether it is the above-mentioned overall tax adjustment, or a partial change in the tax elements of a certain tax, it is an important path for "structural tax reduction". The overall tax adjustments achieved through the "abolition", "suspending", and "merging" taxes, as well as the adjustment of tax elements by changing the tax headings, tax rates, tax bases, etc. of a tax are related to the overall tax law structure and a specific The internal structure of tax law is related. It should be said that the specific tax law structure directly affects the "structural tax reduction", and the promotion of the "structural tax reduction" will have a direct impact on the tax law structure.

[84]For example, according to Article 28 of the Corporate Income Tax Law, the tax rate applicable to small and small profit enterprises is 20%, while the tax rate applicable to high-tech enterprises supported by the state is 15%.

In addition, in the process of combing the specific path of "structural tax reduction", it is not difficult to find that various tax reduction paths are actually related to tax reduction rights. As for the relationship between tax reduction rights and "structural tax reductions", the definition, power source, exercise, and restrictions of tax reduction rights, and the legality of "structural tax reductions", the academic research is still insufficient, so it is necessary to conduct further specific discussions.

6.3.3 *Tax Reduction Power as a Basis for "Structural Tax Reduction"*

6.3.3.1 Multiple Definitions of Tax Reduction Power

The implementation of "structural tax reduction" must be based on statutory tax reduction rights; if there is no tax reduction right, no type of tax reduction is legal. In accordance with the legal principles of taxation and the provisions of relevant laws such as the *Tax Collection Management Law*, no entity shall make a decision to reduce taxes without authorization. Considering the diversity of the path of "structural tax reduction", the basis of power should be "tax reduction power in a broad sense".

The so-called "tax reduction right in the broad sense" refers to the tax reduction right, which includes the power to reduce the tax burden of taxpayers by reducing tax types and items, reducing tax rates and tax bases, suspending tax types and reducing tax amounts. As an important part of tax rights, the "tax reduction right in the broad sense" corresponds to the "tax increase right" or "tax increase right". It differs from the "tax reduction right in the narrow sense" since it is the basis of "tax reduction measures" in special tax measures. Special tax measures are juxtaposed with basic tax elements such as tax items and tax bases, and the "tax reduction measures" they contain are only a way to reduce taxes. The "tax reduction right in the broad sense" that this section focuses on, corresponds to the multiple paths of tax reduction. It may not only involve multiple tax elements, it may even go beyond tax elements, and it will be related to the existence and abolition of tax types and the overall Changes in tax law structure have been linked.

Based on the above-mentioned broad understanding of tax reduction rights, the tax reduction rights discussed in this section include the legislative and law enforcement powers for tax reduction, so they cannot be equated with the "tax reduction approval power" of taxation authorities at the level of law enforcement. In accordance with the legal principles of taxation, tax reduction legislative power is the basis for exercising tax reduction enforcement powers and more specific tax reduction approval powers. In the process of implementing "structural tax reduction", the objectives of exercising tax reduction rights may be multiple, such as fair distribution, macro-economic control, improving people's livelihood, ensuring stability. These goals need to be reflected in relevant tax laws and regulations through the exercise of tax reduction legislative powers and implemented through tax reduction enforcement activities.

From the perspective of the overall tax right theory, the country's tax right (or taxation right) includes both the right to increase taxes and the right to reduce taxes.[85] But in the past, people often easily understood the taxation right as a tax increase right and ignored the tax reduction right. In fact, whether the tax is increased or reduced, it is the normal state for the state to exercise its tax power. The realization of "positive encouragement and promotion" and "negative restrictions and prohibitions" through the adjustment of tax burden is an important manifestation of the function of tax law.

In addition, in the sense of the Constitution, the above tax reduction right is actually the state's "tax reduction decision power", and related to this is the national "tax reduction right". Based on the national's right to claim a tax reduction, the state should consider whether to decide whether to implement a tax reduction. Of course, the exercise of the right to claim tax reductions of a country's nationals must be related to the country's decision to reduce taxes through legislative activities of the people's congress or parliament. Although the nature and level of the right to claim tax reduction and the right to decide on tax reduction are different, they are closely related under the framework of the rule of law and are also important factors affecting the rule of law system.

At the constitutional level, based on the "subjective dual structure" of the state and the people, and based on the ideal and reality of "all power belongs to the people", the right to claim a tax reduction is more basic. The reality of social development concerns the legitimacy of government taxation. In this sense, the state's right to make tax reduction decisions must be restricted and restricted. In addition, if the "contractual assumption" between the state and the national is agreed, the tax reduction right of the national also corresponds to the taxation right of the country. The exercise of the two types of claim is reflected in the game of public goods pricing. Regardless of which theory you agree with, you should pay attention to the right of citizens to claim tax reductions. At the same time, the state's tax reduction rights should be limited according to law, that is, the emphasis on "statutory tax reduction rights".

6.3.3.2 Tax Reduction Right and Its Problems

The basis of "structural tax reduction" is the statutory tax reduction right. In accordance with the legal principle of taxation, all powers and rights related to taxation must be statutory, and the right to tax reduction is no exception. Based on the protection of national property rights, people usually emphasize that the "exercise of tax

---

[85]As mentioned earlier, tax law scholars mainly divide tax rights into three categories: tax legislative power, tax collection and management rights, and tax revenue rights. Of course, some scholars refer to tax collection and management rights as tax administrative powers. See Chen (2010), p. 108–09. However, from the perspective of increasing or reducing the tax burden, tax rights can also be divided into tax increase rights and tax reduction rights, which are mainly related to the aforementioned tax legislative powers, and will have a direct impact on tax collection and management rights and tax revenue rights.

increase right" must follow the statutory principle, but there are few mentions of the "exercise of tax reduction right". In fact, whether it is the right to increase or decrease taxes, the exercise of it will affect the interests of the state and the people; all types of tax rights that affect the legitimate rights and interests of various entities must be strictly statutory. Among them, the exercise of the state's tax reduction right is not only related to the protection of national tax or financial interests, but also directly affects the property interests of relevant nationals, and may lead to unfair tax burden among taxpayers. The exercise of tax reduction rights is directly related to the adjustment of related taxes, tax items, tax rates, tax bases, and tax incentives.The introduction and suspension of taxation and changes in taxation elements must strictly implement the principle of taxation. The exercise must also strictly follow the legal principles.

In accordance with strict taxation principles, the exercise of tax reduction rights must strictly abide by the Constitution and laws, so that the legal benefits of various subjects can be effectively guaranteed. Article 56 of China's Constitution specifically stipulates that "citizens have the obligation to pay taxes in accordance with the law". According to this, the basis and basis for citizens to perform their tax obligations can only be laws, and the basis for reducing or exempting tax obligations can only be laws. In addition, the law directly affects the determination of taxpayers' tax obligations through the provision of tax types and tax elements; In connection with this, in order to exercise tax reduction rights through changes in related taxes and taxation elements in order to reduce or reduce taxpayers' tax obligations, they must also comply with legal requirements. In addition, whether the taxation authority can reduce the taxpayers' tax liability can only depend on the provisions of the law. This is not only a requirement and reflection of the legal principle of taxation, but also an important limitation on the exercise of tax reduction rights.

In our country, the spirit of "statutory tax reduction rights" is not only reflected in the constitutional level, but also relevant tax laws have more specific provisions on tax reduction rights. For example, Article 3, paragraph 1, of the "Tax Collection and Management Law" of China stipulates: "the introduction and suspension of taxation, as well as tax reduction, exemption, rebate, and supplementary tax, shall be implemented in accordance with the provisions of the law. Enforcement of formulated administrative regulations, the suspension, reduction, exemption, and refund of taxes involved in the above provisions are directly related to the exercise of "tax reduction rights in a broad sense"; And requiring it to "implement in accordance with the provisions of the law" is the embodiment of the principle of taxation; In addition, this article emphasizes the strict principle of tax law, because it stipulates that: "Only if authorized by law by the State Council", will it "implement in accordance with the provisions of administrative regulations formulated by the State Council".

The above provisions are also the concrete implementation and spiritual embodiment of Article 56 of the aforementioned Constitution. In accordance with the spirit of the Constitution,[86] the principle of statutory taxation must be strictly enforced.

[86]Some countries have already stipulated the principle of legal taxation in the constitution, so it is not just the spirit of the constitution. For example, Article 317 of the Constitution of the Bolivarian

Therefore, Article 3 of the Tax Collection Management Law only stipulates the "tax reduction right in a broad sense" only at the legal level, and administrative regulations where legally authorized Level. The regulations and local regulations issued by the State Council's tax-related functional departments (such as the Ministry of Finance, the State Administration of Taxation, and the General Administration of Customs) are not reflected in this article. Therefore, if strictly based on the provisions of this article, neither departmental regulations nor local regulations can be used as the basis or legal source for the exercise of tax reduction rights; accordingly, ministries and commissions of the State Council cannot be the main body of tax reduction legislation. Of course, the reality is far from the requirements of the above regulations.

In addition, in the Tax Collection Management Law and supporting implementation regulations, Administrative Measures for Tax Reduction and Exemption (Trial) and Administrative Measures for Customs Import and Export Goods Tax Reduction and Exemption[87] and other laws, regulations, and rules, there is also a right to apply for tax reduction Provisions were made. Corresponding to this application right, the national taxation authority enjoys the "tax reduction approval right". The above-mentioned provisions on the right to apply for tax reduction and the right to review and approve tax reduction are mainly limited to the level of "enforcement". Whether the taxpayers' tax reduction application or the tax reduction approval of the taxation authority is based on the existing provisions of the tax law, Changes in the tax elements.

In fact, not only cannot the tax elements be changed during the above-mentioned tax reduction application or tax approval process, but also under the requirement of "statutory tax reduction rights", various types of "tax reduction elements" cannot be adjusted without legal procedures. Only in this way can we ensure the orderly tax reduction and the overall distribution order.

The above-mentioned "elements of tax reduction" refer to various important factors directly related to tax reduction, such as suspension of taxation, adjustment of tax items and tax rates, adjustment of tax base determination methods, adjustment of the scope of tax reductions, etc. To reduce the effects of tax reduction, they are both the factors that affect the tax burden and the specific path of tax reduction. The adjustment of the above-mentioned "deduction elements" has a significant impact on the tax rights, tax behavior and tax benefits[88] of the state and the people, as well

Republic of Venezuela (entered into force on December 30, 1999) specifically provides for the principle of legal taxation, namely "statutory taxation. There is no legal basis, no taxes can be paid, and no donations can be collected. There is no legal requirement to exempt, reduce or use other tax benefits.

[87]See the Administrative Measures on Tax Reduction and Exemption implemented by the State Administration of Taxation on October 1, 2005 (Guo Shui Fa [2005] No. 129), and the Import and Export of Customs of the People's Republic of China implemented by the General Administration of Customs on February 1, 2009 Measures for the Administration of Goods Deduction and Exemption.

[88]Tax rights, tax behavior, and tax benefits are three basic categories in the field of tax law and reflect the core issues in the field of tax law. For related research, please refer to Zhang (2003), Issue 7.

as the fairness of taxation and the distribution of income, so special care must be taken.

Because the above-mentioned "elements of tax reduction" are particularly important, some countries even make restrictions on the levy of certain taxes directly in the constitution. For example, the US Constitution states: "No tonnage tax on ships may be levied without the consent of Congress". The ship tonnage tax is a relatively small tax.[89] Many citizens may not know its existence, but it has an important impact on international and domestic trade or freedom of trade. The tonnage tax on ships in China used to follow the regulations of the 1950s for a long time, and the new regulations were not fully implemented until 2012.[90] However, there is still no legislation at the legal level, which is indeed inconsistent with the strict requirements of taxation principles.

There are no clear rules on which taxes can be levied or suspended in China, because it is still unclear which taxes should be included in a reasonable tax system, and the tax system and tax law system are both changing and developing. But with the development of the market economy and the maturity of the tax law system, China's tax law system should also be relatively stable. The main tax systems that should be included in the tax law system and the basic tax elements of each tax system should be reasonably clear. It helps to make effective legal restrictions on the adjustments of various "reduction elements".

Emphasizing the legal adjustment of tax reduction rights and "factors for tax reduction" according to law is not only of great value to the development of tax law theory or public law theory, but also of great significance to system practice. The perspective of the tax reduction system practice will help to further reveal the problems in the legal aspects of tax reduction rights, so as to clarify why the tax reduction rights should be exercised properly according to law.

6.3.4 Proper Exercise of the Tax Reduction Power

Based on the previous discussions on the basic paths of the "structural tax reduction", the definition of the tax reduction power as the basis of the "structural tax reduction", and also based on the understanding of the importance of the "statutory tax reduction power", a review of the institutional practices in the "structural tax reduction" shows that there are many legal problems in the subjects, scope and procedures of exercising

[89]Article 1, paragraph 10 of the United States Constitution states: "No state shall levy any tonnage tax on ships without the consent of Congress". This is very important for reducing the burden on enterprises and promoting domestic free trade and fair competition.

[90]In the past, China has long applied the Interim Measures of the People's Republic of China Customs Vessel Tonnage Tax approved by the Finance and Economic Committee of the Government Affairs Office on September 16, 1952, and issued by the General Administration of Customs on September 29, 1952, to levy vessel tonnage tax until January 2012. The new Interim Regulations on Ship Tonnage Tax of the People's Republic of China came into effect on the 1st, and the above-mentioned Interim Measures were explicitly abolished.

the tax reduction power. Only in the framework of economic rule of law can we ensure that the tax reduction power is properly exercised according to law, and better solve the above problems.

From the perspective of legislation, the structure of a country's tax law will directly affect "structural tax reduction". In the tax law system, which types of taxes should be abolished, suspended or merged all cannot be decided arbitrarily, and various factors must be fully considered to properly exercise the tax reduction power in accordance with the law. For this reason, particular attention should be paid to the subjects, scope, procedures and principles of exercising the tax reduction power.

(1) In terms of the power-exercising subjects, the source of the tax reduction power and the legitimate power-exercising subjects shall be clearly defined according to the provisions of the Constitution and relevant laws. China has repeatedly emphasized that the tax legislative powers (including tax reduction legislative power) must be highly centralized, while local governments only exercise the tax reduction power only within the scope authorized by the law. At the same time, even at the central level, it is necessary to clarify the tax reduction power of various subjects, especially to prevent relevant subjects from exceeding their powers. Based on the provisions of the *Legislation Law of China,*[91] the taxation legislation involving the basic taxation system must implement the "legal preservation" principle. On this basis, the NPC and its Standing Committee should become the subjects in exercising the power for tax reduction legislation. It is of practical significance to clearly define the subjects of the tax reduction legislative power. For example, the afore-mentioned *Regulations on Agricultural Tax* was passed by the Standing Committee of the NPC, and it abolition should also be decided by the Standing Committee of the NPC. Even if it is indeed necessary to abolish it, the legislative procedures must be followed, and the implementation of this law should not be ceased by the local governments themselves while the law is still valid. It should be said that it is important to clarify the power-exercising subjects in preventing the unauthorized exercise of tax reduction legislative powers and in ensuring the proper exercise of tax reduction power in accordance with the law.

Throughout the course of China's "structural tax reduction", we can find an important feature: in most cases, the tax legislative power is mainly exercised by the State Council, and accordingly, the State Council becomes an important subject in exercising the tax reduction legislative power. The formation of this feature is directly due to the decisions made by the Standing Committee of the NPC and the NPC in 1984 and 1985 to authorize the State Council to take charge of the legislation. Before the major changes in the tax law in 1994, the above-mentioned authorized legislation had played a positive role in the construction of the basic framework of China's tax law. However, after China established a market economy system, it continued to utilize the "authorization decision" to improve the modern tax law system, which has generated considerable problems. The Standing Committee of the NPC was aware of

[91] According to Article 8 (6) of the *Legislation Law of China*, the matters concerning the basic tax system can only be enacted by law.

this situation and specifically abolished the 1984 Authorization Decision in 2009,[92] but the 1985 Authorization Decision is still valid, and its unlimited authorization in both deadline and scope has brought many problems, it needs to be abolished in due time.[93] Since tax reduction is related to the basic property rights and other related rights of various subjects, it is the NPC and its Standing Committee that exercise the tax reduction power, which not only reflects the requirements of statutory taxation principle, but also is more in line with the provisions of current laws. The subjects exercising the tax reduction legislative power has gradually changed from the State Council to the NPC and its Standing Committee.

(2) In terms of the power-exercising scope, corresponding to the specific path of the "structural tax reduction", the scope of exercising tax reduction power involves both the storage, abolition, merger and transfer of tax types, and also the adjustment of important "tax reduction elements", particularly tax items, tax rates, tax bases and tax incentives. At present, the first priority in terms of power-exercising scope is to fully implement the statutory principle. For this reason, more attention should be given to granting tax reduction power to relevant subjects through legislative authorization, which helps to better solve the problem of insufficient legal basis, and thus helps to protect the legitimate exercise of tax reduction power. For example, in 2007, China specifically revised Article 12 of the *Law on Individual Income Tax* to provide that "the levy, reduction, and suspension of individual income tax on interest income from savings deposits and their specific measures shall be prescribed by the State Council". According to the above-mentioned legislative authorization, the State Council has a legal basis for exercising the tax reduction power over the interest on savings deposits.

In view of the complexity of the tax law and the social relations to be adjusted by the tax law, the combination of policy and statutory, the unity of stability and variability should be emphasized in the scope of exercising the tax reduction power, so as to better reflect the spirit of "differential treatment", and realize the system function of tax law. Generally, in the domains involving the protection of individual property rights, people often have higher requirements for the legitimacy of tax deduction, and the public pays more attention to the exercise of tax deduction power according to law or the changes in tax deduction paths.

(3) In terms of power-exercising procedures, we must pay attention to procedural issues regardless of the exercise of tax reduction legislative powers or tax reduction enforcement power. However, in the practice of "structural tax reduction", some procedures are still not transparent enough. For example, the adjustment of consumption tax related to fuel tax reform, adjustment of individual income tax deduction for salaries, and the controversial "Crowing Hen in Midnight"[94] during the adjustment of stamp tax rates for securities transactions, there are problems of opaque

[92]The authorization decision was repealed on June 27, 2009 according to the *Decision of the Standing Committee of the National People's Congress on Abolition of Certain Laws.*

[93]Zhang (1996), Issue 6; Shouwen (2012a), Issue 11.

[94]In late May 2007, the officials of the MOF insisted that the stamp duty on securities transactions would not be raised, but on the midnight of May 30 after four working days, the MOF suddenly announced an increase in the stamp duty, causing the stock market to plummet. The public called

procedures to varying degrees. Regarding the above situation, although the general public does not usually question from the perspective of excessive power or abuse of power, it will at least think that the exercise of power is inappropriate. Therefore, special emphasis should be given to the fact that various tax reduction power must be exercised in strict accordance with legal procedures, and further strengthen the system construction of the tax procedural law to better promote the taxation rule of law.

(4) In terms of the power-exercising principles, the exercise of tax reduction power must not only adhere to the afore-mentioned statutory principle, but also implement the principles of fairness and efficiency. Among them, the principle of fairness is embodied in the principle of moderation or proportionality.[95] It requires that the exercise of tax reduction power must be appropriate, and the scope and intensity of tax reduction must be appropriate. At the same time, the relation between policy and statutory must be coordinated to better achieve the function and goal of "structural tax reduction". According to the principle of moderation, which reflects the spirit of fairness, the exercise of taxation power must be "modest" or "restrained" and the exercise of tax reduction power must reflect the "restraining attribute" of taxation power, so that it can be exercised appropriately, and guarantee the legitimate rights and interests of various subjects, realize the stable development of the economy and society, and the long-term stability of the country. Since the "structural tax reduction" will enable specific subjects in specific domains to obtain tax benefits, if the legislative or law enforcement powers of tax reduction are not exercised properly, it will run counter to the fair value contained in the principle of fairness, so "structural tax reduction" shall pay particular attention to substantive fairness; otherwise, from the perspective of formal fairness alone, it is difficult to explain why the state implements or promotes "structural tax reduction".

In addition to meeting the requirements of the fairness principles, the exercise of tax reduction power must benefit economic development and truly reduce the burden on taxpayers, so as to achieve better taxation efficiency. These aspects are the requirements of the efficiency principle. For example, the unification of China's enterprise income tax system has realized the merger of two types of enterprise income tax, which has reduced the overall enterprise burden, promoted fair competition and economic growth, and such "structural tax reduction" is in line with the principle of efficiency. If a country implements the nominal "structural tax reduction" in a certain period, it abolishes some taxes but adds new ones at the same time, which will increase the taxpayers' overall burden and restrict economic development. The approach certainly does not meet the requirements of the efficiency principle.

To implement the above principles of tax law, we need to pay attention to the "convergence" in exercising the taxation power. From the perspective of "convergence",

---

this sudden adjustment of the tax rate by the MOF as the "Crowing Hen in Midnight", and generally questioned the adjustment procedure of the tax rate and whether the MOF was entitled to do so.

[95]The principle of proportionality is helpful to avoid excessive infringement of state power on national legal benefits. It is more important to emphasize the principle of proportionality in tax reduction. If the relevant tax reduction measures violate the principle of proportionality, it is illegal; if the entire law violates the principle of proportionality, it is unconstitutional. Utz (2006), p. 103.

the taxation is only to satisfy the public demand for public goods, so it should not lead to harsh policies, and it should just minimize the burden on taxpayers and rest with the people.[96] Emphasizing the "convergence" of taxation power will not only help to protect the national interests to the greatest extent, but also help to better promote the development of a market economy, improve the efficiency of resource allocation, and promote the economic operation as a whole. It helps to better protect the country's fiscal revenue and achieve a "win-win" situation between the state fiscal revenue and resident income, so as to build a benign "take-grant relation" between the state and the national.

In the course of exercising the taxation power, "expansiveness" and "convergence" often coexist. The "expansiveness" of taxation power corresponds to the power to increase taxes, and the "convergence" corresponds to the power to cut taxes. The exercise of the two powers is the normal state in which the state exercises its power to tax, which reflects the "regulatory nature" of tax law, i.e., the combination of "active encouragement and promotion" with "negative restrictions and prohibitions". It is only in the exercise of taxation power that there is "excessive expansion but insufficient convergence". Therefore, it is necessary to restrict its "expansiveness" from the perspective of statutory principle, fairness principle and efficiency principle.

In recent years, although China has been carrying out the "structural tax reduction", the tax burden on market subjects remains high, which is related to the failure to properly exercise the tax reduction power and the ineffective implementation of tax law principles, and to lack of systematic thinking and overall design on tax reduction. Strictly speaking, China's "structural tax reduction" was "unconsciously" launched in the process of continuously solving many problems in various tax domains. To this end, it is necessary to strengthen the top-level design, comprehensively optimize the tax law structure, build a scientific and reasonable tax law system, and lay a more solid institutional foundation for the "structural tax reduction". In this way, we can prevent the problems of tax reduction power from coming out constantly as in the reform of the VAT system.

6.3.5 Tax Reduction Power in the Reform of VAT System

In the process of exploring the paths of "structural tax reduction", VAT is mentioned for several times. In fact, China's VAT system has been in the process of reform or "pilot", and the important direction of the reform is to continuously reduce the taxpayers' tax burden by better reflecting the principle of VAT, so it is closely related to "tax reduction". China's implementation of the pilot "business tax-to-VAT" for many years is regarded as the most important measure for "structural tax reduction".

[96] Reducing the burden and resting with the people helps to conserve tax sources, thereby achieving inexhaustible sources of tax. Many thinkers have put forward the idea of tax reduction. For example, the Chinese politician Sima Guang emphasized to "take care of the sources for sustainable use". Sima Guang's thinking is inherently consistent with the idea of tax reduction proposed by Laffer who is a representative of the modern "supply school". Xue (2009), pp. 822–823.

Therefore, it is necessary to carry out more specific and thematic discussions in combination with the practices in reforming the VAT system and the tax reduction power, which will not only help to make the previous discussion more detailed, but also help to further verify the relevant conclusions.

In a review of China's reform of the VAT tax system in recent years, there are both adjustments to the internal tax elements of certain tax types brought by the "VAT tax transition" and overall adjustments between the different tax types brought by the "tax reform". As such, both of the afore-mentioned paths of the "structural tax reduction" are reflected in the realm of VAT, and the two closely related paths involve the issue of tax reduction power, which are to be discussed separately below.

6.3.5.1 Tax Reduction Power in Previous Reforms of the VAT System

As China's primary tax, VAT not only covers a wide range, but once accounted for about half of China's total tax revenue. Even if the adjustments of tax bases and tax rates in recent years have lowered the tax revenue, VAT revenue keeping holding more than one third of the total tax revenue. However, the reform of such an important tax has never stopped, and the issues about its tax reduction power are especially typical and universal.

As mentioned earlier, China embarked on the "structural tax reduction" since 2004. The reform of the VAT system is an important part of this endeavor. At that time, the "VAT transitional" pilot in Northeast China[97] aimed at "expanding the scope of tax deduction" was not only an important sign to restart the tax reform after the 1994 tax reform, but also an important step in the "structural tax reduction".[98] It is conducive to promoting the adjustment of the industrial structure in the Northeast, and also helps to optimize the structure of the tax law itself. Although the new tax system was initially limited to certain industries and regions, it was later promoted

[97]In accordance with the *Opinions on Implementing the Revitalization Strategy for the Old Industrial Bases in Northeast China* (ZhongFa [2003] No. 11), released by the Central Committee of the CPC and the State Council, the MOF and the SAT, with approval of the State Council, worked out the *Provisions on the Certain Issues about Expanding the Scope of VAT-based Deduction in Northeast China* (CaiShui [2004] No. 156). The "provisions" are the direct basis for exercising the tax reduction power in the realm of VAT in the Northeast.

[98]The VAT transitional pilot that began in the Northeast region and the trials of exempting agricultural tax in Heilongjiang and Jilin provinces are important measures of "structural tax reduction. However, at that time, various circles had not paid attention to this point of view, nor did they notice the importance and significance of restarting the reform of tax system.

to the central region[99] because of its tax-reduction effect, and eventually became an important national system in 2009.

The promotion the "VAT transition" across the country was directly attributed to the pressing need for the "structural tax reduction" after the financial crisis. The further expansion of the deduction scope as a result of the system transformation directly reduced the VAT tax base; at the same time, the reduction of the levy rate on small-scale taxpayers further reduced the overall VAT burden. By adjusting the taxation elements within the VAT system, there will be a significant "tax reduction effect".

The "VAT transition" is the second path of the "structural tax reduction", and the tax reduction power involved has not drawn enough attention from the academic community. By examining the direct basis for the "VAT transition" from pilot areas to the whole country, it is not difficult to find that most of them are following the "rules" or "provisional measures" formulated by the MOF and the SAT to expand the scope of VAT deduction. Although these normative documents embody the spirit of the Central Committee of the CPC and the State Council, their level of effectiveness remains still too low. After all, whether it is the expansion of the deduction scope or the adjustment of the levy rate, it involves the substantial provisions on taxation elements. Strictly speaking, such content should be stipulated in the law,[100] but the direct basis of the "VAT transition" obviously does not meet the requirements of the statutory taxation principle.

In addition, in the process of promoting the "VAT transition" pilot, although the provisions on expanding the scope of deduction have a tax reduction effect, they are only in "trial" in certain industries or regions. This is contrary to the inherent requirement that VAT shall be levied uniformly throughout the country[101] and that its chain is kept intact. It deviates from the principles of taxation and tax law, fails to

---

[99] According to the *Opinions of the Central Committee of the CPC on Promoting the Rise of the Central Region* (ZhongFa [2006] No. 10) which express to carry out the VAT reform in the central region, and the *Notice of the State Council on the Six Central Provinces' to Implement the Similar Policies for Revitalizing the Old Industrial Bases in Northeast China and the Development of the Western Region* (GuoBan [2007] No. 2), the MOF and the SAT formulated the *Provisional Measures for Enlarging the Scope of VAT-based Deduction in the Central Region* (CaiShui [2007] No. 75). The "provisional measures" were the direct basis for exercising the tax reduction power in VAT in the central region at that time. It was different from the basis for exercising the tax reduction power in the Northeast region, and it reflects the inconsistency of the basis for exercising the tax reduction power.

[100] The exercise of the tax reduction power should be prescribed by law, and some countries have made strict restrictions on this power in their constitution. For example, Article 219 of the *Constitution of the Republic of Haiti* states that "any exception, increase, reduction or cancellation of taxes can only be prescribed by law". Accordingly, the exercise of the tax reduction power must be strictly subject to the legal preservation principle.

[101] VAT is a typical neutral tax. In order not to distort the sale of goods in a unified market, it should be applied uniformly throughout the country. Not only that, from the perspective of ensuring the free circulation of goods and fair competition, all types of indirect taxes, including VAT, should also be applied uniformly throughout the country. Therefore, although the United States does not have a federal-level VAT, it still emphasizes the uniform application of indirect taxes, and even stipulates this in the constitution. For example, Article 1 (8) of the *United States Constitution* stipulates that

fully embody the rule-of-law spirit, or implement the principles of statutory taxation, fairness and efficiency.

It can be seen that although the "VAT transition" is important and can produce the effect of "structural tax reduction", there are outstanding problems in the basis and method of exercising the tax reduction power. These problems require special attention since they not only existed in the previous practices in "VAT transition", but also in the currently ongoing "business tax-to-VAT" pilot programs.

6.3.5.2 Tax Reduction Power in the Current "Business Tax to VAT"

As the most important step in the "structural tax reduction", the "business tax to VAT" reform plays a dominant role in China's improvement of the overall tax law system. It is of particular concern from the central government to the local governments, since it concerns their relation and the major interests, as well as industrial restructuring, protection of taxpayers' rights and interests, and the future direction of China's tax law.

Such an important reform need to have a strongly designed overall framework and a solid basis. From the perspective of overall design, since the VAT and business tax are levied on the dual objects of goods tax (cargo and services), the sphere covered by "business tax-to-VAT reform" is very broad. With the reform making progress gradually, the original "two taxes" were replaced by only "one tax".[102] Due to the "business tax-to-VAT reform", in the case of a complete tax deduction chain, it can not only avoid repeated taxation in the realm of business tax, but also reduce the tax burden of taxpayers, so the effect of "structural tax reduction" will be very prominent, this will help the development of many industries that originally levied business tax, as well as the realization of China's goal of economic restructuring.

The "business tax-to-VAT" is to achieve the "structural tax reduction" through the adjustment of overall tax types; it is the first path of the "structural tax reduction". As a long-established business tax will be "absorbed and merged" by the VAT, there will be dramatic changes in the VAT system, including the tax collection scope, specific tax bases, determination of tax rates, which will lead to major adjustments of the rights and interests of numerous taxpayers, and directly affect the property rights, operating freedom, and occupation choices of market subjects, so the litigimacy of such reform must be considered.

In the practice of "business-to-VAT reform", the direct basis for exercising the tax reduction power is the "pilot program", "notice" and "measures issued by the MOF

the Congress has the power to "regulate and impose direct taxes, indirect taxes, import taxes, and goods taxes, but all indirect taxes, import taxes, and goods taxes should be unified nationwide".

[102] In light of China's *Twelfth Five-Year Plan* and its specific implementation steps, China's "business tax-to-VAT reform" was divided into three steps and about to be completed by 2015. Of course, some business tax items (e.g., the financial industry) were not fully incorporated into VAT to become a unified tax, showing that there are still difficulties to overcome.

and the SAT,[103] which were "approved by the State Council". The documents are of the same effect as the afore-mentioned regulatory documents on the "VAT transition", and therefore contain the issue of legitimacy. From the perspective of the reform of the VAT system and the practice of other tax law systems, the basis for exercising the tax reduction power lacks legitimacy. It has become a long-standing shortcoming in China that needs to be resolved through the improvement of the taxation rule of law.

In essence, the promotion of "structural tax reduction" through "business tax-to-VAT reform" and enhancement of the competitiveness of enterprises, and then promotion of the structural adjustment and industrial upgrading, are all led by the State Council, and the basis for the State Council to exercise the tax reduction power is presumed to be the "authorized legislative decision" made by the NPC in 1985. As mentioned earlier, this "decision" has been questioned,[104] since not only violates the statutory taxation principle, but also conflicts with the *Law of the People's Republic of China on Tax Collection and Administration*, and other specific laws and regulations, so there are obvious flaws in its legitimacy, and it is "untenable".

The afore-mentioned "VAT transition" only involves the adjustment of a single tax type, while the "business tax-to-VAT" involves the reform of two important tax systems, which has a greater impact on the basic rights of taxpayers. As the "business tax-to-VAT" involves the major adjustments to taxpayers, tax items, tax rates and tax bases, and the relevant tax items (such as the transportation industry) have been applied to the whole country, it will lead to the current *Provisional Regulations on Value-added Tax* and the *Provisional Regulations on Business Tax* completely different and even exist in name. Regarding the adjustments of these basic tax-related matters, which concern the basic rights of taxpayers, it is indeed necessary to strictly implement the "legal preservation" principle according to the provisions of the *Legislation Law* and carry out the relevant legislation by the NPC, so as to promote the level of VAT legislation as soon as possible, and thoroughly solve the long-standing legitimacy problems in the reform of the VAT system.

In recent years, the problems of insufficient legal basis exposed by the reform of the VAT system have become increasingly apparent, and the call for raising the level of VAT legislation has gradually increased. Regarding the legislation for the "business tax-to-VAT reform", if the conditions for the NPC's legislation are temporarily not met, the relevant "decisions" can be made by the Standing Committee of the NPC. A unified VAT law can be introduced until there are matured legislative conditions. It is a more feasible legislative path.

---

[103] Refer to the *Pilot Program for the Replacement of Business Tax with VAT*, the *Notice on Carrying out the Pilot Policy for Business Tax-to-VAT in Transportation Industry and Certain Modern Service Industries*, and the *Implementation Measures for the Pilot Policy for Business Tax-to-VAT in Transportation Industry and Certain Modern Service Industries*, which were released by the MOF and the SAT.

[104] In addition to the academic community, 32 deputies to the meeting of the NPC in 2013 signed the "proposal on terminating the authorization to the State Council to develop provisional provisions or regulations on taxation". At present, whether the NPC can abolish the 1985 Authorization Decision as soon as possible has become a common concern.

In short, for various tax system reforms, including "business tax-to-VAT reform", we must pay attention to the legal basis for exercising the tax reduction power. We should no longer implement the "pilot programs"[105] without restriction based on the NPC's "authorized legislation". We should not only care about the economic gains of economic reform, but neglect the legal basis of the reform. The theories and practices of many countries show that the reform of the tax law system has always been closely related to the "economic constitution". In China, "strengthening economic legislation and improving macro-economic control and maintaining the steady economic growth are not only the basic requirements of the Constitution,[106] but also an important reflection of the state rationality and state functions. Therefore, in order to implement the requirements of the Constitution, it is necessary to strengthen economic legislation in the realm of taxation, which is especially helpful to achieve the goals of "business tax-to-VAT reform" to promote economic structural adjustment and ensure stable economic growth, and further implement the principles of fairness and efficiency of taxation, so that the basic rights of citizens can be better protected.

6.3.6 Conclusion

The "Structural tax reduction" is an important institutional practice that is still underway in China, which has an important impact on economic, political, legal and social development. The "structural tax reduction" did not start in the financial crisis of 2008, but traced back to 2004 when China showed a tendency to make structural adjustments to the tax law system, and the corresponding "structural tax reduction" had manifested in various forms. Because there is almost no difference between the "structural tax reduction" and the tax reduction in a broad sense, this section also discusses the tax reduction in a broad sense, not limited to the "tax reduction" associated with the special measures for "tax exemption".

Discussing the "structural tax reduction" in a broad sense will help to discover the legal issues in a broader spatio-temporal context, especially the most important tax reduction power. In China, "structural tax reduction" is generally regarded as a "policy issue" or "economic issue" rather than a "legal issue" related to economic

[105]Zhang (2013b), Issue 4.

[106]Article 15 of China's Constitution provides that "the state strengthens economic legislation and improves macro-economic control", which is very important to ensure the stable growth of the national economy, and the stable economic growth is directly related to the goal of economic balance. According to Article 109 of Germany's *Act to Promote Economic Stability and Growth (1967)*, the "overall economic balance" is considered to be a core goal of a country. Stober and Xie (2008), p. 333.

restructuring,[107] the legitimacy of "tax reduction" is often overlooked, which has led to many problems in the economic rule of law.

In view of this, this section focuses on the issue of tax reduction power in "structural tax reduction", analyzes the different paths for "structural tax reduction" and the tax reduction power involved in it, and emphasizes the statutory tax reduction power is the basis of "structural tax reduction", i.e., without the tax reduction power, the "structural tax reduction" will have no legitimacy. At the same time, both the legislative power and law enforcement power for tax reduction must be statutory, which is very important for the legal adjustment of various "reduction elements". In addition, the statutory tax reduction power must be properly exercised in accordance with the law. The subjects, scope, procedures and principles of power exercise shall reflect the requirements for legal power exercise, so that the "structural tax reduction" will better reflect the requirements of the basic principles of tax law, such as statutory principle, fairness principle and efficiency principle, as well as the requirements of economic rule of law.

In addition, in recent years, the reform of the VAT system has been the top priority of "structural tax reduction", and the "VAT transition" and "business tax-to-VAT" have reflected the two main paths of "structural tax reduction". Related to this, this section specifically analyzes the tax reduction power involved, further reveals the long-standing lack of legitimacy of the basis for exercising tax reduction power, and proposes that the statutory taxation principle should be strictly followed, the legal preservation principle should be truly implemented, and the legislative level of VAT should be upgraded. The above problems and their countermeasures are equally applicable to the improvement of tax law systems other than the VAT system.

Through the above discussions, it is not difficult to find that "structural tax reduction" is directly related to the adjustment and improvement of the tax law structure. The basis is tax law (the direct basis is the tax reduction power in tax law) instead of "policy". No policy can replace the provisions of the tax law, which is an important issue that requires special clarification. From a legal perspective, "structural tax reduction" is always directly related to the adjustment of the structure of tax law itself; it is a "legal" issue, not just a "policy" issue or an "economic" issue. Therefore, we should consider the problems existing in the dimension of economic rule of law.

"Structural tax reduction" is an important institutional practice in China, it will continue for a long time to come. The above discussions on the issue of tax reduction power show that it is necessary to face up to and effectively solve the problem of the illegal exercise of tax reduction power, emphasize the statutory and restrictions on tax reduction power, and reaffirm the irreplaceability of laws, which is also the important economic rule of law requirement. Although this section focuses on the issue of tax reduction power in "structural tax reduction", these issues are also of particular concern to tax law, economic law, and the entire realm of public law. As

[107]Many issues involved in the process of economic restructuring in China are legal issues, and should not be merely taken as policy issues. This is very important for analyzing the issues of "structural tax reduction. Zhang (2011), Issue 1.

long as the tax reduction power is effectively defined and exercised in accordance with the economic rule of law, and the rights and interests of the relevant subjects are effectively protected, it will definitely help promote the comprehensive development of the taxation rule of tax, improve the theory of tax reduction power, the theory of overall tax power and the theory of tax law, and thereby further promoting the improvement of the economic rule of law theory.

6.4 Enhancement of Governance Ability from the Path of Economic Law

6.4.1 Background and Problems

As the reform deepens comprehensively and the rule of law presses ahead in an overall manner, the issue as how to modernize[108]the national governance systems and governance ability and strengthen construction of the system of rule of law has drawn widespread attention. The enhancement of national governance ability depends on effective construction of the national governance systems, especially the relevant legal systems. Therefore, system construction remains top priority of the national governance.[109]

Economic law is an indispensable part in the modern national governance systems. Being a typical "modern law", economic law concerns adjustment of the "tripartite relations", i.e., the relations between government and market, between the central government and the local governments, and between the state and the citizens,[110] which are of great impact on the national economic governance, even on political and social governance. Thus, economic law is also a typical "law to rule a country". In view of this, it is necessary to explore specific ways to build up national governance ability from the dimension of economic law, which is of great importance to improve the economic rule of law.

The national governance systems are fairly complex whose structure directly affects their functions and improvement of the national governance ability. Therefore, the structure of the national governance systems shall be continuously improved, and the governance systems themselves shall be constantly enriched, so as to improve the

---

[108]Some scholars study the issue of modernizing the national governance ability from the perspective of state power, e.g., Zhang (2014), Issue 3.

[109]With a view to comprehensive deepening of reform and construction of an overall governance system, there are still arduous tasks in front of China to improve its system construction, so it cannot simply say that the focus of legal construction is to shift from legislation to law enforcement, nor the focus of legal study to completely shift from legislation to interpretation.

[110]The dynamic adjustment of the "tripartite relations" is core issue of economic law to be resolved, and involved in all specific systems of economic law, the resulting close correlation between economic constitution is an important aspect why economic law differs from other sectoral laws.

overall governance functions and enhance the governance ability.[111] How to improve the national governance systems from the dimension of economic law and enhance the national governance ability by means of economic law? It is an important issue that each modern country shall treat it seriously and keep trying to solve it.

Being the "law of governing the state" and the "law of promoting development", economic law is highly valued by modern countries. To improve the national economic governance ability, we shall define the economic functions of government, specify its economic functions and powers, and increase institutional supply of the economic law, so as to better regulate macro-control, market regulation and market countermeasures, and achieve the expected objectives of national governance.

Based on the above considerations, this sub-section places focus on "enhancing governance ability by following the path of economic law". Such path seems to have several forks which are interrelated and indispensable, e.g., improving legislation when concerning governance systems, appropriately decentralizing power when improving the systems, for the purpose of building up the subject ability and then enhancing the national governance ability. Hereby, the following part will briefly discuss the path of "legislation-decentralization-capability".

6.4.2 Legislation Path: Improve Governance Systems from the Dimension of Economic Law

The national governance ability or governing ability, which reflects the implementation capability of systems, relies on the establishment of corresponding institutional systems. If there are no institutional systems, or the systems are uncoordinated or seriously unmatched, then the effective implementation of systems will be out of the question. Therefore, from a systematic perspective, the national governance systems shall be improved to build up the national governance ability.

The national governance systems consist of political, economic and social systems. Among them, the economic governance system involves the various systems in the economic field. Based on the real economic life and corresponding to the two major allocation systems as market and government,[112] the economic governance system shall cover all kinds of important economic systems, including economic regimes and mechanisms, and legalized systems as laws and regulations. Among all kinds of economic systems, economic law is undoubtedly important, since it is directly related to legalization of all kinds of important economic regimes, mechanisms or policies. In order to enhance the state economic governance ability, we shall improve the state governance systems from the dimension of economic law.

[111] Improvement of economic governance ability is of great impact on promoting economic development. Zhang and Wang (2013), Issue 3.

[112] Among the overall resource allocation system, market and government are the foremost allocation systems, respectively providing personal and public articles, with different objectives, directions and means, but both of them are subject to legal adjustment. Zhang (2014b), Issue 5.

Although China's national legislature declared in 2011 that "the legal system has taken shape", there is still a lot of room for improvement from the perspective of building the national governance systems, especially the rule of law system. At present, the state has recognized that "good law is the prerequisite of good governance", so it is necessary to strengthen legislation, constantly improve quality of legislation, and enhance the timeliness, systematization, pertinence and effectiveness of legislation.

In the field of economic law, the basic legislation concerning macro-regulation and market regulation shall make greater progress from the perspective of economic governance. For example, according to the Keynesian theory, market mechanism promotes "economic growth", but it cannot guarantee "stable economic growth". Thus, "stable growth" has become one of the top four macro-economic goals set by all countries. Therefore, it is undoubtedly important to introduce the *Law on Promotion of Stable Economic Growth* and establish effective coordination among various important economic systems, so as to prevent drastic economic fluctuations, guard against and resolve economic crises,[113] especially the coordination between the fiscal system and financial system, industrial system, foreign trade system and competition system. From system to mechanism, from entity to procedure, all matters shall be performed within the legal framework so as to reflect regular and systematic governance of complex issues. In case the above-mentioned systems are insufficient, then the national governance systems are hard to take shape, and the national governance ability will be even harder to be improved in an all-round manner.

Among the above systems for ensuring stable economic growth, the fiscal system is fairly important. Like other systems of economic law, the fiscal system is also a crucial means to compensate for market failure and provide public goods. Moreover, it is the foundation and important pillar for national governance, directly related to the state power or governance ability.[114] However, China's fiscal system remains defective despite of being built for years. The *Budget Law of the People's Republic of China*, which came into force since January 1, 1995, finally completed an all-round revision 20 years later, yet it is neither able to solve such basic problems as fiscal decentralization[115]which are widely concerned, nor applicable to all types of budgets. Meanwhile, the principles of taxation law are still suspended, meaning

[113]The *Law for Promoting Stability and Growth*, promulgated in Germany in 1967, is the most reputable law of this kind; it directly links the top four targets of macro-economy (stabilizing commodity prices, adequate employment, economic growth and balance of international payments) with the purpose of legislation and specific systems. The National Development and Reform Commission of China once intended to enact a law of this kind, but failed to add it in the legislation plan of the National People's Congress - top legislative body of China - because of institutional reasons.

[114]As for the issue whether state power is consistent with national governance ability, there are varied understandings. Some articles have introduced the earlier discussions in this regard, saying that such state power as macro-control ability and compulsory execution ability are also the national governance ability, e.g., Wang and Hu (1993), pp. 6–13.

[115]The Budget Law revised in 2014 mainly aims at solving the problems of budget integrity, standardization and openness, yet it fails to effectively solve the problem of fiscal decentralization among all levels of political power.

that the taxation in some areas is not backed up by law, the problem of authorized legislation has not been solved, and a complete modern tax system is yet to be established.[116] The non-legalization of non-tax income has long been criticized. In other fiscal areas, the governments at all levels are unable to systematically resolve such problems as debt, government procurement and transfer payments by relying on the existing laws alone.[117] As for the above problems, whether we are going to improve the specific laws for different fields, or stipulate a higher-level basic fiscal law to avoid such deficiencies as lack of systematization and coordination like individual laws, it is no doubt worth of thinking. And it has become a major issue concerning the overall governance system.

In addition to stipulating new laws to fill the legal gaps, the coordination and systematization of the existing economic law system also needs attention, which is very important for building the modern legal system, because the modern legal system requires a complete legal standard system. In terms of coordination, all fields of economic law involve system problems, and system law holds an important place in economic law. How to achieve coordination among various systems is a fundamental issue that needs to be solved. For example, the basic legislation in the financial field is relatively complete, however, from the perspective of the governance systems, it is an important system problem[118]to strengthen the coordination among "one bank and three commissions"[119]in time of financial regulation and supervision. Moreover, there is an important issue directly affecting the guarantee for fair competition ability, i.e., how to strengthen cooperation among the three major law enforcement agencies for anti-monopoly,[120] in order to ensure the effect of anti-monopoly law enforcement. Similarly, in terms of fiscal system, such issues as how to divide the power for fiscal revenue and expenditure between the central and local governments, or between governments at all levels, how to effectively correspond to administrative power and financial power, are not only related to economic governance, but also affects political and social governance. It can be seen that all kinds of system problems in the field of economic law shall be effectively solved, which is not only required by economic or political restructuring, but necessary for building a modern legal system and a modern governance system and enhancing the national governance ability.

In terms of legislation, the state stresses that "we must coordinate our legislative work with our decisions on reform to make sure that all of our major reforms have a legal basis, and that legislative work is carried out proactively to meet the needs of reform, as well as economic and social development. Any endeavor that

---

[116]Although China plans to build a modern fiscal system, it does not mean that China has already possessed a modern taxation system. Presently, some important taxation systems are still going through significant changes, meaning that they are still defective.

[117]The revised budget law increased the provisions for government debts and transfer payments, but they still seem disperse and unable to systematically resolve the current problems.

[118]Lots of scholars have made researches and assumptions in this regard, e.g., Cao (2009), Issue 4.

[119]Translator's note: "one bank and three commissions" refer to People's Bank of China, China Banking Regulatory Commission, China Securities Regulatory Commission, China Insurance Regulatory Commission.

[120]Wang (2014), Issue 2.

is proven to be effective in practice shall be regularized by legal provisions. Where the practical conditions are not mature enough and in need of pilot programs, the relevant authorization shall be made by following the legal procedures. The laws and regulations that fail to meet the requirements of reform shall be amended and revoked in a timely manner".[121] This instruction is very important for the economic law field. The economic law has all along been closely connected with reform, e.g., the economic law of contemporary China emerged and developed in the process of reform and opening up, and on the other hand vigorously promoted reform and opening up. However, it must be noted that in the process of reform, the legislation for some areas is relatively backward and unable to seamlessly connect with reform decision-making, thus making some major reforms lack legal basis and affecting the legitimacy of reform and compliance of relevant systems. These problems are particularly prominent in the areas carrying out the "pilot" reform programs. For example, Shanghai and Chongqing municipalities in China once conducted the property tax pilot reform, which was believed to lack adequate legal basis. Therefore, all kinds of "pilot" reforms shall be valid and following the spirit of rule of law. Furthermore, those who takes charge of top-level design of the system shall refrain from creating artificial system differences, which may affect application of law.[122] It is just because of these existing problems, the state specially emphasizes to strengthen the legislation of key areas, accelerate the perfection of a legal system that reflects fairness in rights, opportunities and rules, and protects citizens' personal and property rights from infringement. Therefore, in the field of economic law, for the system that concerns fairness in rights, opportunities and rules, and the system protecting people's personal and property rights, the legislation work shall be strengthened, and effective law enforcement shall be maintained, which is fairly important for improving the national governance ability.

6.4.3 Decentralization Path: Differ Economic Functions from Economic Authorities

As mentioned above, in the process of constructing the economic governance system, the core issue is to define the government's economic functions or economic authorities, which directly affects the improvement of relevant systems.

Theoretically, China's 2013 Reform Decision has clearly defined the economic functions of the government as macro-economic control and market regulation. Macro-economic control is for maintaining the stability of the macro-economy, while market regulation is for ensuring fair competition, strengthening oversight

[121] *The Resolution of the CPC Central Committee on Certain Major Issues Concerning Comprehensively Advancing the Law-Based Governance of China*, adopted by the 4th Plenary Session of the 18th Central Committee of the CPC in October 1984.

[122] Such problems are prevalent in China's economic legislation, esp. tax legislation, thus forming the so-called "pilot" practice in tax legislation. Zhang (2013b), Issue 4.

of the market and maintaining market order.[123] These two aspects are the main areas and core issues of economic law. According to the "reform decision", the state shall let the market play a decisive role in resource allocation and in the meantime give full play to the government. In the economic field, it means the government shall do a better job in macro-economic control and market regulation, which is the most important economic function of modern countries.

Corresponding to the two major economic functions of the government, the power of macro-economic control and the power of market regulation (collectively called the power of economic regulation) are the main economic authorities of the government. Some countries have specified economic functions and authorities in their constitutions, and make them as important "components" of their economic constitutions. Some countries have adopted specific economic laws to provide for the economic functions and authorities, and make them as core content of the specific economic system law. No matter what, we shall correctly understand the economic functions and authorities, and prevent from regarding macro-economic control as administrative intervention. Macro-economic control is necessary for market operation. The practice of executing administrative intervention under the guise of macro-economic control must be changed.

At present, the state defines the main tasks of macro-control as maintaining the balance of economic aggregate, promoting the coordination of major economic structures, mitigating the impact of periodic economic fluctuations, guarding against regional and systematic risks, stabilizing market expectations, and sustaining healthy economic development.[124] It should be said that such definition is more consistent with the original intention of macro-economic control and can better reflect the macroscopic and indirect nature of macro-economic, thus helping distinguish it from direct administrative intervention.

The main target of the above macro-control is "healthy development" of economy, i.e., the "benign operation and coordinated development of economy" depicted in the economic theory, which is the high-level goal set for the adjustment of economic law. Therefore, all of the important economic laws have added this target into their legislative purposes. For instance, in terms of the macro-control legislation, the legislative purpose of the *Budget Law of the People's Republic of China* is to "regulate the government's revenue and expenditure behavior, increase budget constraints, strengthen the management and supervision of budget, establish and improve a comprehensive, standardized, open and transparent budget system, and guarantee

[123]The *Decision of the Central Committee of the Communist Party of China on Some Major Issues Concerning Comprehensively Deepening the Reform*, adopted at the 3rd Plenary Session of the 18th Central Committee of the Communist Party of China on November 12, 2013, explicitly states that "the main responsibility and role of the government is to maintain the stability of the macro-economy, strengthen and improve public services, safeguard fair competition, strengthen oversight of the market, maintain market order, promote sustainable development and common prosperity, and intervene in situations where market failure occurs".

[124]The 2013 Reform Decision has made a more clear-cut definition of the targets and tasks of macro-economic control, which is able to better reflect the "macroscopic nature" of macro-economic control. Zhang (2014c), Vol. 15.

the healthy development of economy and society". In terms of the market regulation legislation, the legislative purpose of the *Anti-monopoly Law of the People's Republic of China* is to "prevent and stop monopolistic behavior, protect fair competition in the market, raise the efficiency of economic operation, safeguard the interests of consumers and social public interests, and promote the healthy development of socialist market economy". The legislative purpose of the *Anti-Unfair Competition Law of the People's Republic of China* revised in 2017 is to "promote the healthy development of socialist market economy, encourage and protect fair competition, stop acts of unfair competition, and protect the legitimate rights and interests of operators and consumers". In fact, there are many important economic laws that include the "healthy development" of economy in their legislative purposes, reflecting the common goals of macro-control laws and other types of economic laws.

In order to achieve the goal of macro-control and promote the "healthy development" of economy, the state stresses that the construction of the macro-control system shall take the national development strategy and planning as the guide, utilize fiscal and monetary policies as major instruments, and rely on coordination and cooperation of the fiscal, monetary, industry, price and other policies. As such, the stipulation of economic law, financial law, industry law and price law shall be strengthened. The above aspects correspond to the macro-control law system which is highlighted by the economic law theories, thus reflecting the consensus in the economic law theories, and helping resolve the usual misunderstandings of the economic law theories.[125]

In order to achieve the goal of macro-control and promote the "healthy development" of economy, the state stresses that the construction of the macro-control system shall take the national development strategy and planning as the guide, utilize fiscal and monetary policies as major instruments, and rely on coordination and cooperation of the fiscal, monetary, industry, price and other policies. As such, the stipulation of economic law, financial law, industry law and price law shall be strengthened. The above aspects correspond to the macro-control law system which is highlighted by the economic law theories, thus reflecting the consensus in the economic law theories, and helping resolve the usual misunderstandings of the economic law theories.[126]

Besides, excessive administrative examination and approval and omnipresent administrative intervention are not only far from the connotation and goal of macro-control, but exert negative effect on macro-control, which is proof of insufficient adjustment to administrative law or ineffective law enforcement. The state keeps streamlining administrative examination and approval, yet it does not intend to weaken market regulation or supervision. Administrative examination and approval may not be conflated with market regulation. While taking account of China's prominent issues at present, it is an important path to improve the national economic governance ability by reducing administrative examination and approval, letting the

---

[125]The 2013 Reform Decision has, in several aspects, manifested the consensus on economic law theories in the academic community. Zhang (2014a), Issue 2.

[126]The 2013 "Reform Decision" has, in several aspects, manifested the consensus on economic law theories in the academic community. Zhang (2014a), Issue 2.

government properly perform its administrative functions, and then better perform its economic functions as macro-economic control and market regulation.

The various economic modulation powers, which are important economic authorities and also related to the above-mentioned economic functions, shall be clearly defined and effectively distributed; it will help better define the right of economic freedom of market players. In fact, in addition to the macro-control power and market regulation power explicitly stipulated by law, the government shall "streamline administration and delegate power" to endow market players with more economic freedom.[127] In addition, the exercise of macro-control power and market regulation power will directly affect the rights and interests of relevant market players, so it shall be strictly stipulated and properly exercised according to law, which is fairly important for improvement of the national economic governance ability. Only by constantly strengthening the rule of law in the process of performing the country's economic functions and authorities, and unremittingly improving the modern governance system, can we keep building up our economic governance ability.

Besides, as for the issue about the main body of exercising the macro-control power and market regulation power, the state has further clarified that the central government takes charge of macro-control, while the local governments are mainly responsible for oversight of market, which helps solve the problem of "isomorphic responsibility" of governments at all levels.[128]

6.4.4 Ability Path: Toimprove the Ability of Economic Law Subjects

The aforesaid legislative path and decentralization path are directly related to the construction of the state governance system and improvement of state governance ability, and in the meantime closely related to the ability of specific economic law subjects. The enhancement of the subject ability of various economic laws can further enhance the state overall economic governance ability.

The economic law subjects have two types of ability: the state control and regulation ability and market subjects' game ability. The former is split into macro-economic control ability and market regulation ability, while the latter consists of several specific abilities, like competition ability, participation ability and resistance ability.

---

[127]Zhang (2014b), Issue 5.

[128]In its 2013 "Reform Decision", the State presents to strengthen the responsibility and capability of the central government for macro-control, and strengthen the responsibilities of the local governments for public services, market supervision, social management and environmental protection, which is of positive significance for solving the problem of "isomorphic responsibility". Zhu and Zhang (2005), Issue 1.

In the binary allocation system involving the government and the market, the government-driven resource allocation mainly relies on macro-economic control and market regulation. Along with the development of economic globalization, macro-economic control and market regulation have become more complex, which has put forward higher requirements for the control and regulation ability. For this reason, in its "decision on promoting the rule of law", China stressed to "strengthen and improve macro-economic control and market regulation in accordance with law, oppose monopoly, promote reasonable competition and maintain the order of fair market competition".

The control and regulation ability of regulation subjects depends on the above-mentioned economic functions and economic authorities. Based on their regulation functions, the regulation subjects are entitled to relevant regulation powers according to law, and then possess regulation ability, which reflects the principle of integrating "internal energy" with "external force". In case of inexplicitly defined regulation functions, disordered regulation system, absent or dislocated statutory regulation power, the regulation ability will be affected. In addition, even though there are definite stipulations on regulation function and power, any ineffective enforcement will weaken the regulation ability of the regulation subjects.

Therefore, the important way to enhance the regulation ability of the regulation subjects is to clarify the regulation function and regulation power according to law, and solve the problems about the regulation system. Meanwhile, the regulation subjects shall maintain strict law enforcement, so as to reflect and enhance their regulation ability. With clear understanding of these issues, China put it explicitly in its "decision on promoting the rule of law" to "expedite the construction of a law-based government with scientifically set functions, legally stipulated powers and responsibilities, strict law enforcement, openness and impartiality, honesty and high efficiency, observance of law and integrity", and in the meantime "promote legalization of institutions, functions, authorities, procedures and responsibilities", and "adhere to the principle of resolutely performing the legally prescribed responsibilities, and refraining from any authorized conducts".

Besides, regulation ability can also be enhanced by improving the cognitive ability of the regulation subjects, so as to enable them to assess the situation within the scope of regulation power. Given this, we shall provide information, technology and other guarantees, and establish the legal mechanisms such as information communication mechanism and regulation coordination mechanism for exercising regulation power. We shall provide a legal definition of the regulation system and mechanism, build up the overall regulation ability, and then enhance the state economic governance ability.

In addition to the above-mentioned regulation ability, the game ability of market subjects also affects enhancement of the state governance ability. The market subjects' competition and participation abilities, in particular, are more closely related to the governance ability. In fact, enhanced state governance ability will promote enterprises to engage in fairer and more effective competition, and build up their competitiveness; while stronger competitiveness will then improve the resistance and participation abilities of enterprises. On the one hand, enterprises will be able to reject improper government interference. On the other hand, they can participate in the state economic governance more actively than before, e.g., join in formulating governance rules, which is positive for forming effective and diversified governance.[129] While considering the importance of the participation ability of market subjects, the state has identified public participation as a major legal procedure for making administrative decisions, so to ensure the decision-making system could be scientific, and implemented in an open and proper process based on clearly-defined responsibilities.[130]

In a nutshell, the regulation ability of regulation subjects and the game ability of market subjects have an important impact on the state governance from different aspects. In order to improve the state governance ability, we shall build up the regulation ability and pay equal attention to the game ability.

6.4.5 Conclusion

The state governance ability cannot be enhanced without the efforts in the realm of economic law. As for the paths of economic law, more attention shall be given to the paths of legislation, decentralization and ability, since they directly affect the overall level of economic rule of law.

The enhancement of the state governance ability shall be based on the governance system and with legislation as the prerequisite. Therefore, strengthening the legislation of economic law is of fundamental significance in enhancing the governance ability. Special attention and emphasis shall be given to the legislations need to be strengthened for the governance system, particularly those conducive to the coordination and systematization of legislation, so as to improve the efficiency and effectiveness of the governance and build up the overall governance ability.

The enhancement of governance ability, especially the economic governance ability, requires effective exercise of the powers or rights by the state and the citizens respectively. To this end, the state economic functions and economic authorities shall be explicitly stipulated, the macro-economic control power and market regulation power shall be effectively defined, and there shall be streamlining administration and delegating power to the lower levels, so as to enable market subjects to access

---

[129] There have been various understandings of governance and national governance, some scholars have conducted studies on the specific linguistic evolution, e.g., Li and Ren (2014), Issue 4.

[130] In light of the *Resolution of the CPC Central Committee on Certain Major Issues Concerning Comprehensively Advancing the Law-Based Governance of China*, "public participation, expert argumentation, risk assessment, legality review, and decisions based on collective discussion shall be identified as major legal procedures for administrative decision-making". Public participation, which could better reflect public opinions, has a fundamental position in the legal process for making major decisions, and plays an important role in ensuring institutional compliance of macro-control and market regulation.

to more economic freedom rights or economic development rights[131]; in the meantime, economic law shall be effectively adjusted to regulate the exercise of economic regulation power, and keep promoting the economic rule of law in the process.

The enhancement of state governance ability is directly related to the ability of relevant subjects. Therefore, more attention shall be paid to the government macro-economic control and regulation abilities, and the game abilities of market subjects, especially their competitiveness and participation ability; these abilities will affect the state governance ability from different dimensions.

The above three different paths are interrelated and internally consistent. For instance, the legislative path focuses on enhancing coordination and systematization of legislation through improvement of legislation. The decentralization path pays attention to resolving the relevant system problems through explicit definition and division of economic functions and economic authorities. The distribution of economic functions and authorities during the legislative process have always been a core issue. Therefore, the legislative path is intrinsically related to the decentralization path. Similarly, the above two paths are directly connected with the ability path, since the legislation path is able to clearly define the government economic functions and economic authorities, and then fully endow market subjects with the right to economic freedom, which will improve the economic regulation ability of the government and the game ability of market subjects, and ultimately enhance the state governance ability.

The issue of governance ability could also be analyzed from the dimension of system or the dimension of structure and function. For instance, from the dimension of system, we can analyze the relations between resource allocation system and state governance system, and reveal the necessity and importance of macro-economic control and market regulation from the dimension of government-based resource allocation. From the dimension of structure, we can analyze the structural problems existing in China's economic governance system and the structural problems in other relevant systems. From the dimension of function, we can analyze the obstacles that hinder the economic governance system to perform its functions. The above analyses will help us find out the relevant problems affecting the state governance, and learn to improve the state governance ability and promote the effective development of economic rule of law from the dimension of economic law.

References

An, Tifu. 2012. Several issues on "structural tax reduction". *Taxation Research* (5).

An, Tifu. Haiyong Wang. 2004. Structural tax reduction: tax policy choices under macro-economic constraints. *International Taxation in China* (11).

---

[131]The economic development rights of market subjects are worth of special attention. Zhang Shouwen, The right to economic development: from the perspective of economic law, *Modern Law Science*, Issue 2.

Cao, Fengqi. 2009. Reform and improvement of China's financial supervision system. *Journal of Peking University (Philosophy & Social Sciences)* (4).
Fikentscher. 2010 *Economic Law,* trans. Zhang, Shiming et al., 32. Beijing: China Democracy & Legal System Press.
Cai, Lidong. 2015. Abandonment and retention of the "equity subject relations" doctrine: to choose the provisions for the regulated objects in the Civil Code in the future. *Legal Forum* (2).
Chen, Qingxiu. 2010. *General Tax Law*, 108–109. Taipei: Yuanzhao Publishing Company.
Hayek. 2000. *Law, Legislation and Liberty*, Vols. 2, 3, p. 213. Beijing: Encyclopedia of China Publishing House.
He, Qinhua. 2002. *The Frontiers of Foreign Economic Law Study in the 20th Century*, 584–593. Beijing: Law Press China.
Hell, Rens, Guert Klinger, Outline of Economic Law of the German Democratic Republic, Yu Shutong et al. (trans.), Teaching & Research Office at Beijing College of Politics and Law. 1981. *Selection of Materials on Foreign Economic Law Studies (Economic Law Materials Collection)* 4: 1–81.
Jiang, Bixin. 2012. Towards a unified basic administrative law. *Tsinghua University Law Journal* (5).
Jiang, Ming'an. 2004. Several pairs of relations need to be properly handled in the formulation of administrative procedure law. *Tribune of Political Science and Law* (5).
Jiang, Ping, trans. 1981. *Economic Code of the Czechoslovak Socialist Republic*. Beijing: China Social Sciences Press.
Kasper, Wolfgang, and Manfred E. Streit. 2000. *Institutional Economics: Social Order and Public Policy*, trans. Han, Chaohua, 152–156. Beijing: The Commercial Press.
Li, Long, Ying Ren. 2014. Evolution of the word "governance" - a survey based on semantic analysis and pragmatic analysis. *Law and Social Development* (4).
Li, Changqi. 1991. Several issues concerning the formulation of the Basic Economic Law of the People's Republic of China. *Contemporary Law Review* (4).
Lu, Sanyu, Deqing Li. 2000. On the legislative value of the "economic law outline". *Studies in Law and Business* (1).
Qiu, Ben. 2013, Consensus on economic law. *Modern Law Science* (4).
Research Group on the Compilation of the Economic Code. 2015. Evaluation of the compilation of China's economic code. *Journal of Nanhua University (Social Science Edition)* (1).
Savigny. 2001a. *Vom Beruf unserer Zeit für Gesetzgebung und Rechtswissenschaft*, trans. Xu, Zhangrun, 15. Beijing: China Legal Publishing House.
Savigny. 2001b. *Vom Beruf unserer Zeit für Gesetzgebung und Rechtswissenschaft*, Trans. Xu, Zhangrun, 37. Beijing: China Legal Publishing House.
Savigny. 2001c. *Vom Beruf unserer Zeit für Gesetzgebung und Rechtswissenschaft*, trans. Xu, Zhangrun, 14. Beijing: China Legal Publishing House.
Schliesky, Utz. 2006. *Öffentliches Wirtschaftsrecht*, trans. Yu, Wenguang, 103. Beijing: Law Press· China.
Stober, Rolf, Libin Xie, trans. 2008. *Economic Constitution and Economic Administration Law*, Beijing: The Commercial Press, p 333.
The Seven-person Research Group (Cheng Xinhe, Wang Quanxing, Zhang Shouwen, Shan Feiyue, Chen Naixin, Kong Dezhou, He Wenlong). 2000. Legal Principles and design of the "economic law outline". *Research on Rule of Law*, 6–21. Hangzhou: Zhejiang University Press.
Wang, Jun, ed. 2009. *The Changes of China's Financial System and the Evolution of Thoughts*, Vol. 1, Part 2, 822–823. Beijing: China Financial Publishing House, pp 822–23.
Wang, Shaoguang, Angang Hu. 1993. *Report on China's National Power*, 6–13. Shenyang, Liaoning People's Press.
Wang, Xianlin. 2014. Coordination between supervision of monopolized industries and anti-monopoly law enforcement. *Law Science* (2).
Xu, Shanda. 2003. *Research on China's Tax Rights*, 3. Beijing: China Taxation Publishing House.

Xue, Jun. 2003. The debate between Thibaut and Savigny and its historical heritage: a review of the academic debate on the compilation of a German civil code. *Tsinghua University Law Journal* (2).
Yang, Zixuan. 2000. Establishment and improvement of a legal system adapted to the socialist market economy system and formulation of the "economic law outline". In *Economic Law Review*, Vol. 2, Beijing: Peking University Press.
Yuan, Dasong, Chenglin Zhu. 2014. On the top-level design of the economic rule of law: revisiting the formulation of the "basic economic law". *Sun Yat-sen University Law Review* (3).
Zhang, Changdong. 2014. Study on modernization of national governance ability - from the perspective of state power. *Law Review* (3).
Zhang, Hong, Youqiang Wang. 2013. Periodic evolution of the relations between government governance ability and economic growth: a transnational empirical study based on different stages of income. *Comparative Economic & Social Systems* (3).
Zhang, Naigen. 1993. *Outline of the history of western legal philosophy*, 210. Beijing: China University of Politic Science and Law Press.
Zhang, Qianfan. 2011. *Constitution of the United States*, 95–103. Beijing: Law Press China.
Zhang, Shouwen. 1996. On the statutory taxation principle. *Chinese Journal of Law* (6).
Zhang, Shouwen. 2001. On the universality and limitations of tax law. *Peking University Law Journal* (5).
Zhang, Shouwen. 2002. The periodic variation of macro-economic control law. *Peking University Law Journal* (6).
Zhang, Shouwen. 2003. The Refinement of Tax Behavior and Its Value. *Taxation Research* (7).
Zhang, Shouwen. 2011. Thinking about the "Double Adjustment" from the perspective of economic law. *Law Science* (1).
Zhang, Shouwen. 2012a. Three basic issues on real estate tax legislation. *Taxation Research* (11).
Zhang, Shouwen. 2012b. The right to economic development: from the perspective of economic law. *Modern Law Science* (2).
Zhang, Shouwen. 2012c. The pathway of economic law to alleviate the "double pressure". *Journal of Peking University (Philosophy and Social Sciences)* (5).
Zhang, Shouwen. 2013a. Coordinated development of economic law and the constitution. *Modern Law Science* (4).
Zhang, Shouwen. 2013b. The "pilot model" of China's tax legislation: a case study of the "pilot" VAT legislation. *Law Science* (4).
Zhang, Shouwen. 2014a. "Reform decisions" and economic law consensus. *Law Review* (2).
Zhang, Shouwen. 2014b. The legal adjustment of the relation between the government and the market. *China Legal Science* (5).
Zhang, Shouwen. 2014c. Deepening the economic law theories in the context of deepening the reform, *Economic Law Review*, Vol. 15. Beijing: Peking University Press.
Zhu, Guanglei, Zhihong Zhang. 2005. Criticism of "isomorphic responsibility". *Journal of Peking University (Philosophy & Social Sciences)* (1).

Postscript

The high-speed train is going north at full speed. Reading the manuscript of this book I've just proofread, I'm wondering if I should write a postscript to it. Suddenly I remembered that the outline of this book was finalized on the high-speed rail going south. What a coincidence! Outside the windows there are green earth, ripening crops, densely distributed buildings and power grids—a scene of both the old and the modern time is intertwined and emerging in my sight constantly.

These constantly changing scenes are an epitome of China's reform and development achievements. Nowadays, the development of China is no longer as slow as the old-fashioned "Dongfeng" green trains, but the amazingly high-speed "Fuxing" trains. But no matter how fast they are and how developed the railway network is, they are fixed to their tracks. Likewise, China's economic and social development can never deviate from the orbit of the rule of law, especially the economic rule of law. As such, the economic law theory is in need of further explorations.

Sitting on the fast-running trains, our horizon seems to have extended. While China is vigorously promoting the reform, the rule-of-law construction, and economic development, new problems and new ideas have kept cropping up, and new viewpoints and new theories in the realm of economic law are constantly emerging, which have provided us a new horizon to examine China's economic law theory. In the philosophical sense, different people have different horizons, but it is important that there shall be certain issues in need of our common concern.

For this reason, this book puts forward some important issues about economic law theory in this new era that should draw people's attention, including the important theories that need to be expanded and deepened, such as the "tripartite relations" and system theory, coordination thought and development theory, main line of distribution and distribution theory, crisis response and risk theory, economic legislation and rule-of-law theory. Despite of different understanding among different people, these issues constitute a new horizon of China's economic law theory, and lay an important foundation for the continuous economic law theoretical study and system construction in the future.

This book focuses on the development of theories and practices since the global financial crisis in 2008, especially since China launched the reform, the rule-of-law

S. Zhang, *The New Horizon of China's Economic Law Theory*, Understanding China,
https://doi.org/10.1007/978-981-15-8824-2

construction, and socioeconomic development in an all-round manner. The study of many issues during this period is of great value for improving the theory and system of economic law, and for benefiting the economic rule of law and the entire rule of law. If the Chinese academic community keeps probing into these important issues that are rooted in the soil of China, and earnestly refines relevant theories, they will certainly make important contributions to the development of the world legal study.

Much content of this book has been published as separate papers in Chinese journals. These papers revolve round the same major theme, so they are closely interrelated and containing common theories. For example, in distribution theory there are issues about development theory, in crisis theory or rule-of-law theory there are also issues about development theory. Therefore, the various parts of this book integrate with and support each other, so that this book is able to be more logical and systematical.

I'd like to express my gratitude to the editorial board of this series of book for its organization and coordination. At the same time, my special thanks go to the editors of China Renmin University Press; it is their meticulous work that has brought my book into the view of readers. I will be appreciated for all the comments and suggestions from those who have finished reading this book.

The manufacturer's authorised representative in the EU is Springer Nature Customer Service Centre GmbH, Europaplatz 3, 69115 Heidelberg, Germany. If you have any concerns regarding our products, please contact ProductSafety@springernature.com

Printed and bound by CPI Group (UK) Ltd, Croydon, CR0 4YY
30/09/2026
02225290-0015